GENDER, POLITICS, AND ISLAM

GENDER, POLITICS, AND
ISLAM

EDITED BY

THERESE SALIBA,

CAROLYN ALLEN, AND

JUDITH A. HOWARD

The University of Chicago Press
Chicago and London

The essays in this volume originally appeared in various issues of SIGNS: JOURNAL OF WOMEN IN CULTURE AND SOCIETY. Acknowledgment of the original publication data can be found on the first page of each essay.

The University of Chicago Press, Chicago 60637
The University of Chicago Press, Ltd., London
© 2002 by the University of Chicago
All rights reserved. Published 2002
Printed in the United States of America
06 05 04 03 02   5   4   3   2   1

Library of Congress Cataloging-in-Publication Data

Gender, politics, and Islam / edited by Therese Saliba, Carolyn Allen, and Judith A. Howard.
   p. cm.
   Includes bibliographical references and index.
   ISBN 0-226-73428-5 (cloth : alk. paper) — ISBN 0-226-73429-3 (paper : alk. paper)
   1. Muslim Women — Islamic Countries — Social conditions. 2. Muslim Women — Islamic countries — Political activity. 3. Feminism — Religious aspects — Islam. 4. Women in Islam. I. Saliba, Therese. II. Allen, Carolyn (Carolyn J.) III. Howard, Judith A.

HQ1170 .G43 2002
305.48'6971017671— dc21   2002067318

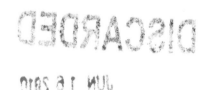

Contents

Introduction
Gender, Politics, and Islam

The image of a veiled woman captioned "The Face of Islam" appears in striking juxtaposition to photos of the crumbling Twin Towers of the World Trade Center. Featured in a *New York Times* photo essay of the year 2001, these oft-repeated media images link the oppression of Muslim women to terrorist violence (December 31, 2001). They also point to the centrality of gender politics in the "war on terrorism" and the ways gender has been manipulated to reinforce the "Clash of Civilizations" thesis of Islam versus the West (Huntington 1993). Harkening back to colonialism, the prevailing discourse implies that "the face of Islam" is to be uncovered by United States military men, whose victory over the Taliban forces is represented by celebratory images of Afghani women removing their *burqas*. Yet this stereotypical "face" of an explicitly gendered Islam covers over a diverse range of women's engagement and activism in contemporary Muslim societies: the Revolutionary Afghani Women's Association's (RAWA) tireless struggle against the Taliban, and their condemnation of the United States' war on Afghanistan as an answer to their plight; Palestinian women suicide bombers' emergence at a perilous impasse of the al-Aqsa Intifada, their actions alternately acclaimed as a new form of "feminist heroism" or descried as an act of despair over their ongoing dispossession by Israeli colonization and destruction of Palestinian society; and Pakistani and Indian women activists joining forces to promote nuclear disarmament, peace, and global justice at a critical juncture in Pakistan-India relations.

In a political environment of increasing hostility toward Islam, this timely collection demonstrates that the face of Islam is not essential or monolithic, nor are Muslim women (veiled or unveiled) mere passive victims of their religion and culture. These previously published *Signs* essays (1997–2002) on women in the Middle East, South Asia, and the Diaspora, from such diverse countries as Bangladesh, Canada, Egypt, Iran, Israel, Pakistan, Yemen, and the Palestinian territories, focus on women's participation in religious, nationalist and cultural movements. These essays demonstrate that the face of Islam is a complex composite—a heterogeneous set of historically and contextually variable practices and beliefs shaped by region, ethnicity, sect, and class, as well as by varying responses to local and transnational cultural and economic processes—all of which have diverse effects on the lives of Muslim women.

From the streets of Cairo to Tehran, the Islamic resurgence of the 1970s led to a revival of Islamic women's movements throughout the Middle East and South Asia that has challenged the secular, liberalizing assumptions of feminism. "Islamic Feminism" and the lively academic debates it inspires are occurring at a time of intensified focus on Islam, even before September 11. With the "Islamic threat" positioned as the new enemy of the post–Cold War era and Arab and Muslim populations on the rise in western metropolitan centers, the attacks, purportedly by a small group of Islamic militants, reinforced long-held anxieties of an Islam bent on destroying the "values" and "lifestyles" of western-style democracy. Moreover, the persistence of Muslim identity and Islamic ideology has posed certain challenges to capitalist modernity and to western cultural, political and economic hegemony, as marked by events of the past three decades. These include the Islamic Revolution in Iran (1979) and recent liberalizing reforms; the Gulf War (1991) and a decade of devastating economic sanctions against the Iraqi people; the Salman Rushdie Affair and its female variant with Bangladeshi writer Taslima Nasrin; the ongoing struggle for Palestinian self-determination and collapse of peace negotiations; the Serbian war against Bosnian Muslims; India and Pakistan's development of nuclear capabilities (the latter characterized by media pundits as the "Islamic bomb") and increasing threat of nuclear conflict as a reverberation of the "war on terrorism"; the victory of Taliban forces in Afghanistan (1996), their imposition of complete veiling and seclusion for women, and their recent defeat at the hands of the United States military and the Northern Alliance (2001); and in the United States, the implementation of discriminatory legislation, from the "Counterterrorism Act" (1996) to the USA Patriot Act (2001), that targets primarily Islamic groups and Muslim and Arab immigrants. Within this hostile context, decontextualized western media images of veiled women serve to depict Islam in general and Islamic fundamentalism in particular as the enemy of Muslim women and cover over complex relations of power that define and delimit Muslim women's agency.

Gender, Politics and Islam counters the "assumption that women who are Middle Eastern, Muslim, and moreover religious fundamentalists are incapable of agency" (Hegland, in this volume, 95). The contributors to this volume are concerned with how women's identities and agency are shaped not only by their religion and gender, but also by nationalism, ethnicity, class, sexuality, and the debates between Islamist and modernist discourses. Although Islam is often defined as the major determinant in these women's lives, only some of the essays focus particularly on Islamic feminism or on the fundamentalist responses to western hegemony and the failures of postcolonial nation-states. Through critique of the prevailing discourses of Orientalism, Islamism, nationalism, modernity, and liberal feminism, these authors examine women's participation in religious, cultural, and nationalist movements and the forms of agency through which they negotiate indigenous identities and attempt to gain political, economic, and legal rights within their societies. Thus the collection's thematic focus on women's agency moves beyond analysis of Middle Eastern and South Asian Muslim women as merely "victims or dependents of governing structures," or as symbols of national or religious identity, and toward understanding these women as agents of their own lives (Alexander and Mohanty 1997, xxviii).

These academic debates about the potentials of an Islamic feminism or feminist nationalism further broaden and complicate emerging transnational feminist theories. In *Scattered Hegemonies,* Inderpal Grewal and Caren Kaplan pointedly question why Muslim fundamentalism appears regularly in today's media as "the primary progenitor of oppressive conditions for women when Christian, Jewish, Hindu, Confucian, and other forms of extreme fundamentalisms exert profound controls over women's lives" (1994, 19). Moreover, much contemporary feminist analysis characterizes religious movements as resulting from the failures of "the postcolonial and advanced capitalist/colonial states" (Alexander and Mohanty 1997, xxv). These analyses effectively point to the western biases against Islam and to the failures of anticolonialist movements and the modern capitalist state to address the material, spiritual, and emotional needs of people in postcolonial societies and in the diaspora (xxv). Yet, despite their persistent critique of applying Eurocentric models to Third World women's lives, these analyses most often assume a secularist model for women's liberation and continue to treat religion in general and fundamentalism in particular as a problematic tool of oppression used against women, rather than as a viable form of feminist agency that produces contradictory effects for women participants. Thus, this critical engagement with the lives of Muslim women expands the boundaries of global feminism by reconceptualizing constructions of feminist agency and suggesting new possibilities for transnational feminist alliances.

As Saba Mahmood has argued in her innovative analysis of the women's mosque movement in Egypt, Muslim women's participation in religious movements should lead us to reconceptualize constructions of human agency as they appear in much feminist discourse (2001, 203). She asserts that existing notions of agency are too limited in understanding the lives of devout Muslim women. Drawing on Judith Butler's paradox of subjectivation (1997), Mahmood redefines agency "not as a synonym for resistance to relations of domination, but as a *capacity for action* that historically specific relations of subordination enable and create" (2001, 203 emphasis added). This redefinition of agency more accurately characterizes women's relationship to national and religious practices and discourses documented by the critics included in this collection. Several authors describe both resistance and complicity, a "paradoxical power" (Hegland) with contradictory ramifications for women. These authors argue that through their participation in religious and nationalist movements, women often achieve some form of political agency, self-realization, or self-representation, as well as a sense of community, even as the patriarchal values and discourses of the movements limit this agency. The contributors' debate over Islamic feminism exposes these complex negotiations: several authors characterize Islamic feminism as part of the "patriarchal bargain" (Kandiyoti 1988) women wager for certain gains; others see it as a viable reformist movement, or even as a potentially new revolutionary paradigm, one that offers a vision of community and social justice that could counter the destructive forces of globalization and Islamic fundamentalism. Moreover, as Mary Elaine Hegland and Anouar Majid assert, Islamic feminism challenges liberal feminism's focus on individualism and individual freedom by emphasizing women's negotiations of selfhood in relation to religious or national communities. In their negotiations for both agency and connectedness to their larger social, religious, ethnic, and national communities, women demonstrate their *capacity for action* in ways that at times confound the emancipatory vision of feminist politics rooted in liberal notions of the self (Mahmood 2001, 208).

Islam, then, is not monolithic in its impact on women's lives. Nor is Islam, as S.M. Shamsul Alam, Elora Shehabuddin, and Majid argue, any more oppressive to women than the workings of the modern secular state. Their essays trace the emergence of nationalist consciousness in South Asia and the Middle East to the influences of European modernity and show the contradictory implications of liberal nationalism for women. These analyses demonstrate the ambivalent effects of nationalism, as well as the failures of corrupt, secular modern states to improve women's lives. They further suggest that it is not Islam per se that oppresses women but, rather, the continuity of patriarchal values within nationalist and religious ideologies that limits women's agency. Nevertheless, women serve as icons and participants in these movements in ways that are both restrictive and potentially liberating. Indeed, the essays in this collection challenge the false dualisms that have often bound Arab and South Asian Muslim women. In particular, the discourse on tradition versus modernity assumes that traditions are static, unchanging, and therefore confining to women, whereas modernity is progressive and necessarily liberating. In this equation, Islamism is usually cast as antimodern and anti-West, when in fact, as Lila Abu-Lughod has pointed out in her introduction to *Remaking Women*, it is rather an "alternative modernity," like third-world nationalism, that is often shaped by the discourses of modernity and westernization it seeks to counter (1998, 4).

Through analysis of indigenous feminist projects, some authors explore Islamism and Islamic movements as an alternative to Eurocentric liberal humanism and the maternalism of western feminist models. In addition, the essays in this volume expose tensions between local definitions of women's struggles and their reinterpretations through the processes of globalization, including diasporic movement of peoples, texts, and scholarship. Thus several essays draw on fieldwork in specific locales, such as rural Bangladesh, urban Pakistan, Palestinian refugee camps, and elite Yemeni households, to analyze women's empowerment and agency. Some essays explore the hybrid identity negotiations of underrepresented minority women, such as Shi'a Muslim women within Sunni dominant Pakistan or Muslim immigrant women in North America. Still others examine the ways in which women authors and their texts discursively construct Arab or South Asian Muslim women for local or western consumption. For example, the West's interest in Egyptian Nawal El Saadawi and Bangladeshi Taslima Nasrin is tied to its interest in and hostility toward Islam, for these women are often portrayed as lone crusaders against the patriarchy of their cultures, as victims of Islamic fundamentalism's repression of women, rather than as part of larger intellectual and feminist movements (Amireh, in this volume, 269). These cases expose the extent to which women's agency is circumscribed by the West's political and economic role in shaping the gender politics of the regions, as well as by its politically interested interpretations of women's lives. Altogether, these essays draw on current discourses circulating in news media, government policy, academia, publishing, and the global marketplace to analyze the power structures that circumscribe Middle Eastern and South Asian women's lives.

Islamic Feminism: Liberal Accommodation or Revolutionary Paradigm?

The first two essays by Valentine Moghadam and Anouar Majid examine the controversy surrounding Islamic feminism and its larger implications for global feminism and progressive movements. In "Islamic Feminism and

Its Discontents: Towards a Resolution of the Debate," Moghadam explores the potential for gender equality within an Islamic framework. Focusing on feminist debates and reformist activities within the Islamic Republic of Iran, as well as academic debates among expatriate Iranian feminists and leftists, the author elucidates various positions from recent writings in Persian and English by scholars and feminist activists. Moghadam then sets forth an alternative reading of Islamic feminism from a secular (Marxist-Feminist) perspective that examines the contributions of Iran's Islamic feminists, both independent and state feminists, to expanding women's rights, political access, and gender consciousness.

In analyzing the "promises and perils" of Islamic feminism, Moghadam critiques strategies that focus on the "correct" reading of Islamic texts and their use of the Quran as a universal standard. She draws an astute analogy between Iran's Islamic feminists and America's liberal feminists as reformists who seek gender equality within the prevailing political system. The author further critiques the limits of religious reinterpretation and calls for the separation of mosque and state to ensure the rights of all citizens irrespective of religious affiliation. Moreover, she asserts that Islamic feminism is influenced by Western feminism, and calls for a more expansive definition of global feminism that includes Islamic women.

In "The Politics of Feminism in Islam," Majid offers a more positive prognosis for Islamic feminism than does Moghadam. Situating his analysis within a broader critique of global capitalism and male-dominated Islam, Majid theorizes an Islamic feminism with a progressive, democratic, antipatriarchal, and anti-imperialist agenda as a potentially new revolutionary paradigm. The author argues for a critical redefinition of Islamic tradition and its assumptions about women, at the same time that he critiques the assumptions of Western human rights discourse, especially in regard to Muslim women. Throughout his essay, Majid surveys much writing by and about Arab and Muslim women to show how Muslim women are bound within the oppressive structures of imperialism, Orientalist discourse, and Islamic orthodoxy, thereby exposing the ways in which women's status has been determined by "the confrontation between the changing images of a hegemonic West and a defensive Islam" (71). In particular, he questions Muslim feminists such as Fatima Mernissi, who accept a capitalist model of human relations as a solution to Muslim women's liberation. In contrast, he points to Nawal El Saadawi's double-edged critique of Arab patriarchy and imperialism as more complex and relevant to an Islamic feminist politics. In addition, Majid criticizes the destructive effects of both capitalism and the imposition of nation-states on the third world and exposes the

West's promotion of human rights in the region as an attempt to ensure its own economic hegemony. He further argues that the Western construct of the "individual" central to human rights discourse is rooted in a "bourgeois definition of the human" (78) that contradicts Islam's emphasis on community and social justice.

In an attempt to resolve the crisis of Muslim identity created by modernity, especially regarding women, Majid argues for the renewed interpretation of Islamic texts and community consensus regarding those interpretations, as well as for the abandonment of Shari'a law and other reforms. Like Moghadam, the author points to women's movements in Iran working to redefine Islam based on more egalitarian interpretations of the tradition; however, he offers a much more enthusiastic assessment of the movement's potential for progressive change. According to Majid, this strategy reaffirms the indigenous, progressive elements in the culture as a "platform from which to resist global capitalism and contribute to a rich, egalitarian polycentric world" (87). He argues that a thoroughly redefined Islam in dynamic relation with other cultures is central to forming an Islamic feminist movement that resists both global capitalism and religious fundamentalism.

Power Paradoxes in Religious, National and Cultural Movements

Through fieldwork in Pakistan, Palestinian refugee camps, and Yemeni households, Mary Elaine Hegland, Julie Peteet, and Gabriele vom Bruck, respectively, analyze the gender negotiations of women within "local institutions and cultural processes" and their implications for women's agency and empowerment (Kandiyoti 1996, 19). In "The Power Paradox in Muslim Women Majales," Hegland examines the paradoxical power gained by women in Peshawar, Pakistan, through their participation in the religious rituals (*majales*) of their fundamentalist sect of Shi'a Islam. The author's fieldwork in Peshawar explores women's participation in and loyalty to their embattled, minority religious sect, when their service ironically both reinforces that sect's conservative powers and enables experiences that transform the women's self-images and worldviews. The Shi'a movement with its alternative power framework, she argues, brings women "both fundamentalism and freedom, as well as a female community both coercive and enabling" (97).

Hegland's analysis draws attention to her own cross-cultural research experience, as well as to the historical partition of Pakistan, which led to the dominance of religious over ethnic identity. In reviewing the social histories of the three main Peshawar Shi'a ethnic groups, Hegland shows how the expansion of the dominant Mohajir ritual, in the attempt to create a universalizing fundamentalist movement, has led to the decline in language and ritual styles of the other groups, thereby pulling women of all three ethnicities into a hegemonic, fundamentalist Shi'a community and worldview. Hegland asserts that despite the affirmation and social support women receive in these sex-segregated rituals, male domination is maintained by women acting as agents of patriarchal control. Moreover, although the rituals are inclusive of women from all classes, they maintain class elitism, since only the wealthy can act as ritual hosts and managers. Hegland concludes that through their participation in *majales*, women gain social mobility to travel, attend, and participate in these rituals, yet they also come under more social control and surveillance.

Hegland's research adds to previous analysis of women's contradictory roles during revolutionary movements, to demonstrate that despite conservative gender ideologies within these movements, women maintain the agency they have gained through their participation. Nevertheless, she argues that as Shi'a Muslims come under more attack in Pakistan by the majority Sunni's, Shi'a women are likely to maintain their loyalty to their sect above gender or ethnic interests.

In "Icons and Militants: Mothering in the Danger Zone," Peteet examines the paradox of mothering during nationalist conflict, here the Lebanese civil war and the first Palestinian *Intifada*. Peteet's analysis goes beyond feminist critiques of women as icons of the nation to explore the paradoxical role of mothering as simultaneously agential and limiting. Like Hegland, she is concerned with how women, through their processes of accommodation and resistance within male-dominated movements, "renegotiate cultural meaning and practices" (134). Through ethnographic research on Palestinian refugee women in Lebanon and the West Bank, Peteet examines how the nationalist discourse of "maternal sacrifice" offered women a platform from which to criticize the Palestinian Resistance movement and its leadership. Peteet argues that Palestinian women, through their negotiations of maternal practice and sentiment, have gained political agency and transformed the meaning of reproductive and caring labor. In particular, she shows how the context of war and national resistance transforms the essence of mothering and undermines the ability to mother safely. While poor, refugee women face the greatest dangers and acquire moral and social standing as well as political credentials for their struggles, Peteet asserts that middle-class activist women often characterize these women as "politically underdeveloped" and notes that the emerging Palestinian National Authority has failed to recognize their political participation. Peteet nevertheless demonstrates that motherhood in the context of nationalist resistance can be a politically militant role through which women gain a limited form of agency.

Vom Bruck's "Elusive Bodies: The Politics of Esthetics Among Yemeni Elite Women" draws on Judith Butler's notion of gender identity as a performative act to investigate the bodily practices of elite Yemeni women—unmarried sisters, wives, and mothers. While previous research on Muslim women's dress has focused primarily on veiling, this essay examines female bodily embellishment as linked to erotic and reproductive purposes, but also as a marker among women that signifies social status as well as the acquisition of feminine identity. The author argues that upon marriage, gender becomes more central to women's identity, marked by the transition from bodily concealment to adornment and embellishment, and is fully developed upon producing a child. Thus, vom Bruck asserts that unmarried women are "less gendered than wives and mothers" (162), and femininity is achieved rather than given.

Vom Bruck sets forth an historical analysis of attitudes about women's bodies within Islam in general, and the taboos that must be adhered to by Yemeni women collectively, to examine how the practice of these taboos marks status and communicates self-identity. She connects women's relational status within kinship structures to taboos on body exposure, including dress, self-naming, use of writing, voices and odors, as well as taboos on dress style and cosmetics. Women's social gatherings *(tafritah),* where married women display their attire, blur the distinction between public and domestic space, even as they enact competition and hierarchy between women. While the sex-segregated *tafritah* creates an all-women's sphere, vom Bruck, like Hegland, shows that this space is not free from the coercions of the patriarchal house, because women act on behalf of men in their scrutiny of other women. However, she claims that some women abstain from adornment as an act of resistance to specific gender regimes.

Fundamentalism, Modernity, and the Use of *Fatwa*

Elora Shehabuddin and S.M. Shamsul Alam offer alternative readings of the problematic use of *fatwa,* a decree or legal judgment based on Islamic texts, within Bangladeshi society. Shehabuddin's essay, "Contesting the Illicit: Gender and the Politics of *Fatwas* in Bangladesh," investigates national, urban-based debates about the rising incidents of *fatwas* against impoverished Muslim women in rural areas. Contrary to prevalent notions of Islam as being fundamentally incompatible with women's rights, the author draws on extensive research to demonstrate that there is little distinction between secularist and Islamist agendas. Their often overlapping interpretations of "modernity, development, Islam and feminism" perpetuate an elitist vision of society that negatively impacts impoverished rural women, who are the primary targets of *fatwas* (203). Shehabuddin's alternative reading of the *fatwa* problem shows how rural women negotiate between Islamist and secularist agendas to regulate their social, economic, and political behavior. In particular, the author examines the controversial role of nongovernmental organizations (NGOs), and she implicates the ineffective state in its failure to provide the poor with basic necessities and protections, as well as the local power elite who use *fatwas* to maintain their eroding power within a context of profound political transformation currently taking place in Bangladesh.

In his essay, "Women in the Era of Modernity and Islamic Fundamentalism," Shamsul Alam examines the *fatwa* against Bangladeshi writer Taslima Nasrin—"the female Salman Rushdie"—within the broader context of the debate between Islamic fundamentalism and modernity. The author argues that this false duality has closed off the possibility for "gendered subaltern self-representation" (236) and overlooks the continuity of patriarchal relations within both "traditional" and modernist discourses. Focusing on the heterogeneity of Islamic discourse, Alam situates the rise of Bengali Islam within the specific historic conflicts that have shaped Bengali national identity. He asserts that as Bangladesh was transformed from a secular state with independence from Islamic Pakistan in 1971, to an Islamized state responding to colonial modernity, *fatwa* became a tool used by both Islamic fundamentalists and modernists to control women. Alam questions how women can express their identities and political concerns outside the realm of the state. He goes on to analyze the writings of Nasrin as a subversive act of gendered self-representation that critiques both nationalism/modernity and Islamic fundamentalism and asserts sexuality and politics as central to women's liberation in Bangladesh.

Muslim Women's Discursive and Identity Negotiations in the Diaspora

While the previous essays address how women's agency is constrained by local processes and structures of family, community, and state, the final two essays examine diasporic Muslim women and their ambivalent reception in the West, through their writings and lived experiences. Alam's examination of the local reception of Nasrin's writing provides a useful backdrop to Amal Amireh's essay "Framing Nawal El Saadawi: Arab Feminism in a Transnational Frame," which discusses the Egyptian feminist writer and her canonization in the West. Amireh's case study of El Saadawi's reception is particularly relevant to this collection because it foregrounds the problematic readings of Third World feminists by the West. Furthermore, El Saadawi is praised by Majid for her anti-imperialist stance, and she has been dubbed by Susan Sontag the "Arab Taslima Nasrin." Amireh argues that the favorable reception of El Saadawi's writing in the West is governed by the asymmetry of power in first-world/third-world relations, and differs greatly from El Saadawi's reception in the Arab world. The author demonstrates that the Egyptian feminist is not always in control of her voice and image, and although El Saadawi struggles against misappropriation, she is often complicit in the West's reading of her. Amireh examines both academic and nonacademic writings about El Saadawi, as well as the differences between her original Arab writings and their English translations, to show how the context of reception shapes, and often distorts meaning. She argues for new methods of reading Arab women writers (or third-world women in general) that historicize writers and readers and examine the context of production and reception. Amireh asserts that these methods more adequately address the power imbalance in such cultural exchanges and work to counter the "persecuted feminist" image of Arab and Muslim women writers that has become popular in the U.S. media and classroom.

Focusing on Muslim women in Canada, Shahnaz Khan's "Muslim Women: Negotiations in the Third Space" further problematizes the prevailing, restrictive discourses of Orientalism and Islamism that construct the "Muslim Woman" and shape Muslim women's agency as well as their strategies of resistance. Returning to the debate about Islamic feminism, Khan, like Majid, is concerned with dismantling "monolithic assumptions about the Muslim in the First World" (306) and exploring the possibility of feminist politics within the category of Muslim. However, while Majid seeks a progressive Islamic politics within a redefined Islamic tradition, Khan seeks it in the hybridized, contemporary urban space of the diaspora. The author draws on Homi Bhabha's theory of "the third space"—a space where the individual's negotiation of contradictory demands and polarities effectively creates a hybridized subjectivity. Through ethnographic research Kahn explores how diasporan Muslim women in Canada construct hybrid forms of agency within the structural bind of Islamist, Orientalist, and multiculturalist discourses. The stories of Karima, an Arab Muslim immigrant from Iran, and Iram, an East Indian Muslim immigrant from Uganda, capture the heterogeneity of Muslim identity. Their case studies further emphasize that culture and religion play an important, but not exclusive, role in defining identity. Khan acknowledges the ambivalence and disorientation experienced by Muslim minority women, and argues that recognition of this ambivalence, alongside a dynamic definition of culture, the separation of prevailing Islamist and Orientalist discourses, and progressive interpretations of Islam, would further women's struggle for agency and identity in contemporary diasporic communities.

Conclusion

Modernity has brought about an identity crisis among the formerly colonized peoples of the Middle East and South Asia, in particular, and among Muslims, in general, who may seek a form of alternative modernity that is not contingent on embracing westernization. Yet as Abu-Lughod has argued, it is time to move beyond the East/West binary that has clouded much analysis of Muslim women and to "fearlessly examine the processes of entanglement" (1998, 16). In a similar gesture, Edward Said's post–9/11 essay, "The Clash of Ignorance" offers a resounding critique of "unedifying labels like Islam and the West, . . . [which] mislead and confuse the mind . . . " and fail to address "the interconnectedness of innumerable lives, 'ours' as well as 'theirs'" (2001, 12–13). Although the move beyond these deeply ingrained binarisms is challenging, the essays included here engage in the kind of complex analyses of identity, gender, nation, class, tradition, and modernity necessary to a clearer understanding of the lives of Middle Eastern and South Asian women. Most importantly, they explode constraining categories and contribute to a more expansive definition of feminism—a feminism that understands the global interconnectedness and diverse social realities of many of the world's women at the turn of the millennium.

Third World Feminist Studies
Evergreen State College
Olympia, Washington

References

Abu-Lughod, Lila, ed. 1998. *Remaking Women: Feminism and Modernity in the Middle East*. Princeton, N.J.: Princeton University Press.

Alexander, M. Jacqui, and Chandra Talpade Mohanty, eds. 1997. *Feminist Genealogies, Colonial Legacies, Democratic Futures*. New York: Routledge.

Butler, Judith. 1997. *The Psychic Life of Power: Theories in Subjections*. Stanford, Calif.: Stanford University Press.

Grewal, Inderpal, and Caren Kaplan, eds. 1994. *Scattered Hegemonies: Postmodernity and Transnational Feminist Practices.* Minneapolis: University of Minnesota Press.

Huntington, Samuel. 1993. "The Clash of Civilizations." *Foreign Affairs* 72(3): 22–28.

Kandiyoti, Deniz. 1988. "Bargaining with Patriarchy." *Gender and Society,* vol.2, no. 3: 274–289.

———. 1996. "Contemporary Feminist Scholarship and Middle East Studies." In *Gendering the Middle East,* 1–27. Syracuse, N.Y.: Syracuse University Press.

Mahmood, Saba. 2001. "Feminist Theory, Embodiment and the Docile Agent: Some Reflections of the Egyptian Islamic Revival." *Cultural Anthropology* 16(2): 202–236.

Said, Edward W. 2001. "The Clash of Ignorance." *The Nation,* October 22, 11–13.

Valentine M. Moghadam

Islamic Feminism and Its Discontents: Toward a Resolution of the Debate

F ew debates among expatriate Iranian feminists and leftists have been as contentious as those centered on *Islamic feminism*. The very term as well as its referent are subjects of controversy and disagreement. Can there be such a thing as a feminism that is framed in Islamic terms? Is Islam compatible with feminism? Is it correct to describe as feminist or even as *Islamic feminist* those activists and scholars, including veiled women, who carry out their work toward women's advancement and gender equality within an Islamic discursive framework? Can the activities of reformist men and women—who situate themselves within the broad objectives of the Islamic Republic of Iran and seek the improvement of the status of women—be described as constituting an Islamic feminism? Or are they reinforcing and legitimizing the state's gender policy? And are those expatriate feminist scholars who report positively on *Islamic feminism* correct to promote the phenomenon?[1] These are among the

For very helpful comments on two early drafts I am grateful to Ali Akbar Mahdi, Ziba Mir-Hosseini, Afsaneh Najmabadi, Nayereh Tohidi, Haleh Vaziri, two anonymous reviewers, and the journal editors. I thank Mohamad Tavakoli-Targhi for the many discussions we have had on the issues raised in this article. Thanks also are due to my graduate assistant, Kate Moritz, for help in reformatting the article. The analysis and any errors are mine.

[1] "Islamic feminists" are publishers, writers, academics, lawyers, and politicians, many of whom are associated with the women's press in Iran. Most are part of the reform movement, which since 1997 has been led by President Mohammad Khatami, but their activities predate his election. They include Shahla Sherkat, editor of *Zanan* (Women); Azam Taleghani, a member of the Islamic Republic's first parliament and editor of *Payam-e Hajjar* (Hagar's message) who tried to run for president in 1997 but was barred because of her sex; Faezeh Hashemi, a daughter of former president Hashemi-Rafsanjani who owned the newspaper *Zan* (Woman), which was shut down by the authorities in the spring of 1999 because of the publication of a controversial cartoon and letter; Zahra Rahnavard, prerevolutionary journalist, wife of former prime minister Mir-Hossein Mousavi, and professor at Al-Zahra University, who has criticized discrimination against women in the pages of the establishment magazine *Zan-e Rouz* (Today's woman); Maryam Behrouzi, former member of parliament and responsible for some successful prowomen legislation during the presidency of Hashemi-Rafsanjani; Jamileh Kadivar, university professor, head of the Association of Women Jour-

vexed questions that have emerged in various writings and that have been met by divergent responses.

This article provides an introduction to the debate and to its main protagonists. I focus on the Iranian debate, although there has been a wider and long-standing debate among feminists within Middle East women's studies regarding veiling and Islamic identity, feminisms among Arab/Muslim women, orientalism, universalist values, and cultural relativism.[2] Given the contentious nature of the debate and the tendency toward misrepresentation of positions, a concern for balance and clarity motivates this article. It is an attempt to contribute to dialogue and understanding and to help move the Iranian debate forward by identifying the strengths and weaknesses of the two main positions and the gaps that need to be addressed. I am also concerned with the definition and meaning of feminism, its applicability to Muslim societies, and the need for a more inclusive and cross-cultural understanding of feminism and the global women's movement.

I begin by providing some background to the debate through an overview of the Iranian Revolution, the role of leftists in it, the gender regime instituted following the revolution, some comments on the expatriate community, and recent political developments in Iran. I then turn to the perspectives of the scholars involved in the debate. Finally, I discuss the

---

nalists, elected member of a city council (in 1999) and of the Sixth Parliament (in the spring of 2000), sister of a prominent reform theologian and wife of a reformist cabinet minister; and scholars of Islam such as Monireh Gorji. Also included are Massoumeh Ebtekar and Mahboubeh Ommi (also known as Abbas-Gholizadeh), the editors of the women's studies quarterly, *Farzaneh* (Sage), notwithstanding their critiques of Western feminism and defense of Iran's clerical governance. (See, e.g., Ebtekar 1995–96 on the Fourth World Conference on Women and the editors' defense of "religious discourse, that of Islam in particular" in the preface to the same issue.) The term has sometimes been used to include secularists who work closely with the Islamic feminists and publish in their magazines, notably the feminist lawyers Shirin Ebadi and Mehrangiz Kar and the publisher and critic Shahla Lahiji, who owns Roshangaran Press. Other secular or independent feminists may be found among the editors and writers of the newer journals, *Hoghough-e Zanan* (Women's rights), *Negah-e Zanan* (Women's perspective), and *Jens-e Dovvom* (Second sex).

[2] For a sympathetic view of Islamic feminism as the wave of the future, see Badran 1999. Cooke 2001 describes how Arab/Muslim women, both secular and religious, are creating Islamic feminism through literature. For sympathetic approaches to veiling, see Hoodfar 1993; and Karam 1996, 1997. A critical approach is provided by Shahidian 1997, among others. For contrasting views on the analysis of the status of women in the Arab world, see Ghoussoub 1987, 1988; and Hammami and Rieker 1988. For critiques of orientalism and cultural relativism and a defense of universalist values, see Moghadam 1989a, 1993c, 1994b; Afkhami 1995; and Mayer 1995.

issues that are taken up by Islamic feminists and stake out my own perspective on the debate and on Islamic feminism itself.

The revolution and its aftermath: An overview

In 1979, Iran's monarchy was replaced by an Islamic republic, whose ruling clerics immediately instituted radical political and social changes. A broad revolutionary coalition that included an array of political groups (leftists, nationalists, and Islamists) and social forces (women and men of the middle classes, the intelligentsia, the working class, and the urban poor) brought about this change in regime. As early as the spring of 1979, however, the revolutionary coalition began to break down over the political direction of the new republic, and a mini–civil war took place that only ended in 1981 (or, in some accounts, 1983). Thus, it may be said that Iran had two revolutions. The first, the populist revolution in which leftists were quite prominent, ended the monarchy and brought about a republic. The second, the Islamic revolution, marginalized or eradicated leftists and liberals and instituted a draconian cultural-political system characterized by the rule of a clerical caste, the application of Islamic law to the areas of personal status and crime, and compulsory veiling for women (Moghadam 1989b, 1994a). During the 1980s, leftists—whether of the communist or Muslim variety—were purged from jobs, forced underground, compelled to flee Iran to escape arrest, imprisoned, subjected to torture, executed, and assassinated. In Europe and the United States, as well as in the former socialist bloc countries, a large expatriate community of Iranian communists, monarchists, liberals, Muslim socialists, and feminists began to form.[3]

The Islamic Republic of Iran (IRI) instituted other measures that greatly diminished the legal status and social positions of women. It banned women from serving as judges, discouraged women lawyers from practicing and other women from becoming lawyers, and excluded women from many fields of study, occupations, and professions. It repealed leg-

---

[3] The communists were associated with organizations such as the Tudeh Party, Fedayee, Paykar, and Rah-e Kargar. Of these, many continue to call themselves leftists or social democrats. The monarchists, whose U.S. stronghold is in Los Angeles, call for the resumption of the monarchy under the late Shah's eldest son. The liberals were those associated with the main nationalist party, the National Front, which had been part of the first revolutionary government but which was quickly sidelined by Ayatollah Khomeini and his associates. The Muslim socialists are members or supporters of the Iranian Mojahedin. After the revolution, the communists and the Mojahedin were the main targets of the Khomeini regime's repression. For an elaboration, see Moghadam 1987.

islation, known as the Family Protection Act of 1967 and 1973, which had restricted polygyny, raised the age of marriage for girls, and allowed women the right to divorce. The Islamic regime all but banned contraception and family planning. It waged a massive ideological campaign that celebrated Islamic values and denigrated the West, extolled women's family roles, and championed *hejab* (Islamic modest dress) as central to the rejuvenation of Islamic society.[4]

The full effects of the Islamic Republic's definition of women's place came to light when the results of the 1986 national census of population and housing were analyzed. These included increasing fertility and population growth, a decline in female labor force participation, particularly in the industrial sector, lack of progress in literacy and educational attainment, and a sex ratio that favored males. Clearly, religio-politics had resulted in an extremely disadvantaged position for women; it had reinforced male domination; it had compromised women's autonomy; and it had created a set of gender relations characterized by profound inequality.[5]

In the 1990s, however, the combination of a number of factors served to undermine several of the most egregious policies of the Islamic Republic and reverse its program on women, family, and gender relations. The changes occurred after the death of Ayatollah Khomeini, during the presidency of Ali Akbar Hashemi-Rafsanjani, and in the context of a program for economic liberalization, integration into the global economy, and the (re)establishment of capitalist society.

The first set of factors that shaped the trajectory of the Islamic Republic and its gender regime pertain to the social structure and the nature of Iran's Islamic ideology. In the 1980s Iran had a sizable modern middle class and working class whose members had relatively high rates of literacy and educational attainment. Iran has had a relatively long experience with modernization and economic development, and women's roles were somewhat varied in prerevolutionary Iran. Iranian modernization certainly affected expectations and aspirations within Iranian society, resulting in considerable resistance to strict Islamization.[6] Significantly, it may also have shaped the values and vision of many Islamists. Two important ideologues of the Islamic Republic, the late Ayatollah Morteza Motahhari and the late Ali Shariati, were part of the school of Islamic modernism.

---

[4] For an elaboration of these early events, see Tabari and Yeganeh 1982; and Neshat 1983.

[5] For an elaboration, see Moghadam 1993b, chap. 6.

[6] For an account of women's resistance narrated by women themselves, see Esfandiari 1997, esp. chap. 5.

Their thinking on women was contradictory and problematical, but they claimed to espouse women's rights; "both men found it necessary to show that Islam did not stand in the way of women's education, work, and participation in social life or stunt the personal development of women" (Esfandiari 1993, 16). Neither Motahhari nor Shariati opposed women's employment, although Motahhari, whose wife was a schoolteacher, did call for sex segregation in the workplace. Many of the officials of the Islamic Republic, including some of the clerical leaders, have higher education, are from the middle class, and favor industrialization, foreign investment, and economic growth.

The second set of factors was the long war with Iraq (1980–88) and the mobilization of all Iranian men. This created some employment opportunities for educated women in the public sector, particularly in health, education, and (to a lesser extent) public administration. These jobs went to ideologically correct women, but their very presence suggested both the determination of women and the flexibility of the Islamic regime. Third, while women were discouraged from assuming public roles, they were not formally banned from the public sphere; moreover, the regime rewarded Islamic women by allowing them to run for parliament and giving them jobs in the civil service. As early as the IRI's first parliament in 1980 there were four women members, at least two of whom—Azam Taleghani and Maryam Behrouzi—became known as Islamic feminists. Many of the women parliamentarians and women civil servants came to make demands on the government for equality and greater opportunity. Fourth, although working-class women were the most adversely affected by the early employment policies, a small contingent continued to work in factories, whether out of their own need and aspirations or because the employers could not find men to replace them. Women in such occupations served to negate the ideal of full-time motherhood and notions of the inappropriateness of factory work for women.

Fifth, evidence of increasing fertility in a situation of declining government revenues, indebtedness due to the war with Iraq, and increasing unemployment and poverty alarmed the authorities. Thus, following the death of Khomeini, the government reversed its opposition to family planning and embarked on a vigorous campaign to stabilize population growth through the widespread distribution of contraceptives to married women and men. In May 1994 the streets of Tehran were filled with signs promoting the campaign, linking small families to a higher quality of life and healthier children.[7]

---

[7] Personal observation. For an elaboration, see Moghadam 1998, chap. 7.

Sixth, as a result of agitation by activist Islamic women, restrictive barriers to women's educational achievement and their employment were removed. In 1992 the High Council of the Cultural Revolution adopted a set of employment policies for women. This new directive, while reiterating the importance of family roles and continuing to rule out certain occupations and professions as Islamically inappropriate, encouraged the integration of women in the labor force and directed attention to their interests and needs. The government also changed its policy on women and the legal profession, and during the 1990s the field of law became more open to women. In April 1993 there were 2,661 registered lawyers in Iran, including 185 women.[8] The law of 1371/1992 allowed for the employment of "women legal consultants" in the special civil courts. In 1997 the judiciary began to employ some twenty women holding degrees in law who would work as investigation judges, court counselors, and deputies/assistant judges.[9] Since the 1990s there has been a steady increase in women's share of government employment, though this may reflect the deterioration of government wages and the increasing participation of men in the private sector. The number of public-sector employees was nearly two million in 1994, of which 603,000, or about 31 percent, were women. The ministries of education and health employed most of these women (43.8 percent and 40 percent, respectively), and nearly 34 percent of them had university degrees.[10] By 1996, fully 38 percent of civil servant employees were female.

As a result of both its own economic imperatives and the repeated requests of women advocates, the government undertook a number of measures pertaining to women and work, including vocational training for rural women. A bill was passed in 1992 to guarantee equal payment of new year bonuses for male and female civil servants. Rafsanjani's government encouraged the participation of women in scientific and technical fields such as medicine, pharmacology, midwifery, and laboratory work—"which is more suitable to their physiological make-up" (Islamic Republic of Iran 1992)—and established quotas of 25 percent female in the fields of neurology, brain surgery, cardiology, and similar specializations.[11] Meanwhile, women's access to secondary schooling and higher education increased steadily over the decade.

In the realm of politics, the increasing visibility of women has been a

---

[8] See Lawyers Committee for Human Rights 1993, 44.
[9] See Islamic Republic of Iran 1994, 15; and Moghadam 1998, 163.
[10] See Bureau of Women's Affairs 1995, 45–46.
[11] See Moghadam 1998, 164.

gradual but noticeable trend. During the 1995 parliamentary elections, nine female members of parliament were elected to the Majlis; women's affairs offices were established in each ministry and government agency; and numerous nongovernmental (or rather quasi-governmental) organizations dealing with women's concerns were formed. Speeches by the women parliamentarians attest to changing and more assertive attitudes, with language that is less specifically Islamic and more compatible with what may be called "global feminism." Maryam Behrouzi, for example, stated, "We don't believe that every social change is harmful. Cultural refinement of some traditions, such as patriarchy (*mardsalari*), anti-woman attitudes (*zan-setizi*), and humiliation of women (*tahghir-e zanan*) must disappear. These have been fed to our people in the name of Islam" (quoted in *Zan-e Rouz* 1994, 4).

In the latter part of the 1990s, a new trend emerged in Iran: a broad-based social movement for the reform of the Islamic Republic. This movement—comprised largely of students, intellectuals, and women—has called for civil liberties, political freedoms, women's rights, and a relaxation of cultural and social controls. The reform movement has been behind the proliferation of a dynamic (albeit beleaguered) press, the 1997 election of the liberal cleric Mohammad Khatami, and the outcome of the parliamentary elections of February 2000, in which reformists made sweeping gains. Intellectuals have issued open letters and penned articles deemed seditious, and several prominent writers and dissidents have been jailed or murdered. In an audacious move in July 1999, university students protested against state repression and called for an acceleration of President Khatami's calls for civil society and democracy in Iran, only to be met by violent assaults by Islamist vigilantes.[12] Most of the Islamic feminists discussed in this article are associated with the reform movement, although they have not engaged in similar forms of collective action.

The Islamic Republic's gender regime has certainly evolved since the 1980s. In 1997, the newly elected President Khatami named Massoumeh Ebtekar, a U.S.-educated lecturer and an editor of the women's studies journal *Farzaneh*, as vice president in charge of environmental affairs. Culture Minister Ayatollah Mohajerani then appointed Azam Nouri as deputy culture minister for legal and parliamentary affairs. Interior Minister Abdollah Nouri followed by naming Zahra Shojai as Iran's first director-general for women's affairs, described in the Iranian media as a

---

[12] For an elaboration of the July 1999 protests by university students and of the reform movement in Iran, see the special issues of the *Journal of Iranian Research and Analysis* (Zanganeh 1999, 2000).

long-time women's rights activist, a professor at al-Zahra University in Tehran, and a member of the interior ministry's Women's Commission. Shojai would be responsible for issues such as social policies for women and violence against women. These were the first women to serve in top government posts since the 1979 revolution, and they proceeded to work with the reformist women parliamentarians who won seats in the February 2000 Majlis elections. It is the interpretation of these political developments, and the contributions of activist Islamic women to liberalization and reform, that is at the heart of the debate on Islamic feminism.

The debate: Viewpoints of the protagonists

Those involved in the debate on Islamic feminism form two opposing camps. On the one side are those who explore the possibilities that exist within Islam and within the IRI concerning women's interests. Chief among them are three feminist social scientists educated in Iran and the West, two of whom have deep roots in the Iranian left and the women's movement. Afsaneh Najmabadi, educated in both the United Kingdom and the United States, is a professor of women's studies in New York; Nayereh Tohidi is a U.S.-trained professor of women's studies in California; Ziba Mir-Hosseini is a Cambridge-educated social anthropologist based in London. In the 1970s and 1980s Tohidi and Najmabadi were active in the left-wing anti-Shah student movement and later in the antifundamentalist and feminist movements. Najmabadi was a founding editor of the expatriate feminist journal *Nimeh-ye Digar* (The other half). Tohidi, who traveled to Iran several times in the 1990s, is in close contact with feminists in Iran and, like Najmabadi, often publishes in the Iranian women's press. Mir-Hosseini, along with British filmmaker Kim Longinotto, produced the acclaimed 1998 documentary film *Divorce Iranian Style* and most recently has filmed a documentary on runaway girls in Iran.

In the opposite camp are those who argue vehemently against the possibility that activists and scholars operating within an Islamic framework, especially in contemporary Iran, may be accurately described as "Islamic feminists." Islamic feminists and their expatriate academic supporters, they argue, either consciously or unwittingly delegitimize secular trends and social forces. They maintain that the activities and goals of "Islamic feminism" are circumscribed and compromised, and they contend that there cannot be improvements in women's status as long as the Islamic Republic is in place. This group similarly includes Western-educated feminist social scientists, one of whom is a man, with deep roots in the left and in the women's movement. Haideh Moghissi teaches women's studies in Canada, Shahrzad Mojab holds a university administrative post in Canada, and Hammed Shahidian teaches sociology in the United States. Shahidian's articles have appeared in U.S. sociology journals and in the women's press in Iran. All three situate themselves on the secular left of the Iranian political spectrum.

In defense of Islamic feminism

Although writings on women and gender in the Islamic Republic were almost uniformly critical during the 1980s, a change of tone and style could be discerned after 1990.[13] Several studies began to argue that reforms and policy shifts were occurring in the Islamic Republic, that an incipient women's movement was under way, and that Muslim women activists were behind many of the changes. In the early 1980s, the writings of Parvin Paidar (sometimes under the name Nahid Yeganeh) suggested that Islamic women and left-wing women had some of the same concerns regarding the legal status and social positions of women and that these could lead to future alliances. "On the political front," she wrote, "we must situate ourselves in the mainstream of debates and dialogues. In making our alliances and voicing our oppositions, we cannot rely on pre-conceived ideas about ideologies such as Islam. Islamic political forces should always be assessed in relation to the overall political scene" (Yeganeh 1982, 70). At the time, however, her writings did not engender the kind of harsh debate that has developed since the mid-1990s. The debate proper on Islamic feminism may be said to have begun in February 1994, when Najmabadi gave a talk at the School of Oriental and African Studies, University of London, in which she described Islamic feminism as a reform movement that opens up a dialogue between religious and secular feminists. A Persian-language article ensued, and at least two English-language essays contain her views (Najmabadi 1995, 1997, 1998).

In her talk, Najmabadi focused on the women's magazine *Zanan* and the quarterly *Farzaneh*, both published in Tehran. *Zanan*, which was founded in 1992 by Shahla Sherkat, the former editor of the establishment women's magazine *Zan-e Rouz*, had become by 1994 the major voice for reform in the status of women. In the magazine's inaugural issue, Sherkat writes, "We believe that the key to the solution of women's problems lies

---

[13] Representative of critical studies were Afshar 1985; Moghadam 1991; Tohidi 1991; Najmabadi 1994. For the tone and style of the 1990s, which emphasized resistance and empowerment, see Moghadam 1993b; Ramazani 1993; Afshar 1996; Tohidi 1997a, 1997b; Najmabadi 1998; Poya 1999.

in four realms: religion, culture, law, and education. If the way is paved in these four principal domains then we can be hopeful of women's development and society's advancement" (*Zanan* 1992, 2). Each issue of the magazine has sections and articles on these four areas. *Farzaneh* is an academic journal of women's studies and research and less radical in its approach and its implications than *Zanan*. Najmabadi argued that Islamic feminists—and especially the editor and writers of *Zanan*—are open to Western feminism. Their translation and publication of the writings of Western feminists proves this. She described how articles in *Zanan*—particularly a series of articles that appeared in the initial issues—challenge orthodox Islamic teachings on the differential rights and responsibilities of women and men by claiming women's right to equality. She explained that part of her enthusiasm for Islamic feminism, and especially for *Zanan*, lay in her belief that they have entered a common ground with secular feminists in their attempts to improve women's legal status and social positions.

In her writings, Najmabadi discusses how Islamic feminists have come to insist that gender discrimination has a social rather than a natural (or divine) basis and how this could open the door to new possibilities for gender equality. Moreover, Sherkat and similar women, well versed in the Qur'an and who refer directly to the Qur'an in their writings, have raised the issue of the right to *ijtehad* (independent reasoning, religious interpretation) and the right of women to reinterpret Islamic law. Najmabadi writes, "At the center of *Zanan*'s revisionist approach is a radical decentering of the clergy from the domain of interpretation, and the placing of woman as interpreter and her needs as grounds for interpretation" (1998, 71). This, she feels, challenges one of the foundational concepts of the Islamic Republic: deference to the rulership of the supreme jurisprudent, or the *velayat-e faghih* (71). Another reason for Najmabadi's celebration of Islamic feminism (again, as articulated in *Zanan*) is her belief that it has opened up a new space for dialogue between Islamic women activists and reformers and secular feminists, thereby breaking down the old hostile divide between secular and religious thought. She maintains that *Zanan* could bridge the divide between Muslim women and women of the religious minorities—though she does not elaborate on this point or provide any empirical examples (77).

Najmabadi further elaborates her hopeful prognosis regarding Islamic feminism in two essays in which she explains the views of the cofounders of the women's studies journal *Farzaneh*. Her interpretation of several essays by Ebtekar and Mahboubeh Ommi suggests that the two are open to an emancipatory program for women, and one that is not necessarily exclusively grounded in Islam (Najmabadi 1997, 392, 1998, 81).

Like Najmabadi, Mir-Hosseini offers a careful analysis of the writings of *Zanan*, and she was the first to point out that the author of the early revisionist Islamic writings was a cleric, Mohsen Saidzadeh, who was writing under a female pseudonym.[14] But her analysis of gender and Islamic feminism in Iran goes even further, and she may be said to hold the "strong thesis" on Islamic feminism. In her writings, she focuses on new discourses on gender among Islamic theologians, the challenging of Islamic family laws by ordinary women, and the emergence of reform-minded Islamic feminists. Mir-Hosseini argues that an unpredicted outcome of the Islamic revolution in Iran has been to raise the nation's gender consciousness. "Whatever concerns women—from their most private to their most public activities, from what they should wear and what they should study to whether and where they should work—are issues that have been openly debated and fought over by different factions, always in highly charged and emotional language" (1996b, 143). She is mainly concerned with the paradoxical ways that the whole process has come to empower women and to create a popular feminist consciousness.

Mir-Hosseini has written most extensively about how family law, and in particular marriage and divorce, have constituted a contested arena. The official discourse promotes domesticity and motherhood for women as ideal roles, and the constitution promises to guard the sanctity of the family. Yet, the return to Sharia law gives men a free hand in divorce and polygamy. This "in effect subverts the very sanctity of the family as understood by women, thus going against the Constitution's promise" (Mir-Hosseini 1996b, 149). She then argues that many Muslim women who had at the beginning genuinely, albeit naively, believed that under an Islamic state women's position would automatically improve became increasingly disillusioned by the new discriminatory and patriarchal discourses and policies. These included establishment women such as Zahra Rahnavard, Azam Taleghani, and Monireh Gorji. Meanwhile, under the editorship of Sherkat, *Zanan* became the principal forum for the discussion of the injustices of current Sharia interpretations and their application to civil codes. In *Zanan* and elsewhere, feminist lawyers Mehrangiz Kar and Shirin Ebadi delineate the problems and legal tangles that women confront in terms of both the substance of the law and its implementation.[15]

[14] Mir-Hosseini 1999 elaborates on Sa'idzadeh's views (and those of other reformist as well as conservative clerics).

[15] Kar and especially Ebadi have written extensively on legal matters in the liberal monthly magazine *Jameh-e Saalem*, and they have lectured in the United States and Europe.

The Islamic Republic's failure to deliver on its promise to honor and protect women, Mir-Hosseini argues, has led to the emergence of the Islamic feminist challenge, or as she puts it, "[to] an indigenous, locally produced, feminist consciousness" (1996b, 162). This consciousness and challenge, she suggests, led to amendments to the divorce law in 1992, whose spirit is to make divorce less accessible and more costly to men. It has led to the widespread use of concepts such as *mardsalari*, which refers to male dominance and patriarchy. And it has led to the proliferation of social analyses by and about women and gender, particularly in *Zanan*. Mir-Hosseini has traced the evolution of these analyses in *Zanan* from the hesitant voice of the magazine's beginning, to the assertion of a *fiqh* (Islamic jurisprudence) voice, particularly with the series of articles written by the cleric Mohsen Saidzadeh in favor of equality for women and men and the reform of Sharia laws (1996a, 1998, 1999). She shows how the emerging Islamic feminist perspective rejects the orthodox view of complementarity of rights—a notion that emphasizes gender differences in rights and obligations and sees their source in both natural and divine law. And like Najmabadi, she sees *Zanan*'s willingness to publish the lawyer Kar as a sign of the magazine's "willingness to join forces with secular feminists to protest against the gender biases of a law which is derived from the Sharia." She deems this development "novel in post-revolutionary politics" (Mir-Hosseini 1996a, 318).

In *Islam and Gender*, Mir-Hosseini provides a detailed account of three Islamic perspectives on and debates about women and gender: traditionalist, neotraditionalist, and modernist. Drawing on her extensive fieldwork and taped interviews with leading clerics, she shows the similarities and differences among the three perspectives, the extent to which "the woman question" preoccupies them, and "the avenues they are opening for dialogue and change within the framework of Islam" (1998, 277). She concludes that the gender debates in Iran have "nurtured not only a new school of jurisprudence, which is slowly trying to respond to social realities, but also a new gender consciousness" (1998, 279).

Nayereh Tohidi is well known in Iranian expatriate circles for her many Persian-language writings and lectures on politics and women, from her early days as a left activist to the present. Her articles in the 1980s tended to be very critical of the Islamic Republic and of its gender policies. During the 1990s her writings shifted from an emphasis on the forms of gender oppression in Iran to the empowerment of Muslim women and the possibilities for reform within the Islamic system in Iran. Taking a cue from Deniz Kandiyoti's (1988) concept of "bargaining with patriarchy," she argues that women are able to renegotiate gender roles and codes and to find "a path of compromise and creative synthesis" (Tohidi 1997b, 106). She explains how her visits to Iran during the 1990s, and in particular her interviews and observations, compelled her to shift her focus from repression to resistance and empowerment. Moreover, she lists a number of scholars who, like herself, have changed their mode of inquiry, mainly on the basis of empirical research. Her views are expounded in a number of Persian-language journals and in a Persian-language book (1997a, 1997b), but Tohidi also publishes in English. She asserts that "secular feminists, democrats, and liberals have not been alone in contesting the state's ideology and politics on gender issues. Many proponents of Islam are playing an important role in the reformation of women's rights in an Islamic context" (1998, 285).

In a book that she has coedited, Tohidi writes approvingly that women in the Muslim world are fighting and strategizing against two sets of pressures, "one stemming from the internal patriarchal system and the other emitted by those forces seen as external, threatening people's national and cultural boundaries." She describes one of those strategies, "the recently growing phenomenon of 'Islamic feminism,'" a movement of women who "have maintained their religious beliefs while trying to promote egalitarian ethics of Islam by using the female-supportive verses of the Qur'an in their fight for women's rights, especially for women's access to education." Echoing Mir-Hosseini, she notes that Islamic feminists undermine the clerical agenda both within and outside the Islamist framework in a number of ways: "by subtly circumventing the dictated rules (e.g., reappropriating the veil as a means to facilitate social presence rather than seclusion, or minimizing and diversifying the compulsory hijab and dress code into fashionable styles), engaging in a feministic *ijtehad*, emphasizing the egalitarian ethics of Islam, reinterpreting the Qur'an, and deconstructing Sharia-related rules in a women-friendly egalitarian fashion (e.g., in terms of birth control, personal status law, and family code to the extent of legalizing a demand for 'wages for housework')" (1998, 283–85).

Tohidi warns that "secular feminists should differentiate between those Islamic women who are genuinely promoting women's rights and hence inclusionary in their politics from those who insist on fanatic or totalitarian Islam" (287). She echoes the feminist lawyer Kar in stressing that a "reformist or women-centered interpretation of religious laws should be considered not as an alternative to secular and democratic demands but as a component of more holistic social change" (288). Elsewhere, she elaborates on the necessary interaction of religious reinterpretation and secular thought and activism toward modernity and democracy in Iran (1999).

The case against Islamic feminism

Haideh Moghissi complains that "it has become fashionable to speak sympathetically and enthusiastically about the reformist activities of Muslim women, and to insist on their independence of thought. . . . The message is that a new road has been opened up for women—Muslim and non-Muslim alike—to gain equal rights to men: a road based on feminist interpretations of Islamic sharia laws" (Moghissi 1998, 42). This is problematical, she writes, for several reasons. It obscures the fact that in a country like Iran, Islam is not a matter of personal spiritual choice but rather a legal and political system. "Islam in political rule is incompatible with the cultural pluralism that is after all the prerequisite of the right to individual choice" (43).

Although critical of those "apologists of the Islamic government and uninformed observers" who attribute legal changes in the Islamic Republic to "the enlightenment of conservative Islamists" (1995, 251), she does not directly claim that there have been no achievements by Islamic feminists in Iran. In fact, she refers to the opportunities afforded to Islamic women and to the accomplishments of the female political elite. Without properly attributing these ideas to previous authors, she notes that the Islamic Republic's gender ideology faces the imperatives of a capitalist system, which requires sexual desegregation, and that the clerical state tries to accommodate the demands of activist women (1995, 252).[16] But then she opines that the "exaggerated reports" about recent legal gains by women, and the role of Islamic feminists in bringing them about, divert attention away from societal opposition to the economic, social, and cultural conditions brought about by nearly two decades of Islamization. It serves to strengthen the legitimacy of the Islamic system in Iran and "weakens the struggle of women inside Iran" (Moghissi 1998, 43). She does not explain how this occurs.

A central point is that the term *Islamic feminist* has been used in "inaccurate" and "irresponsible" ways. Almost all Islamic and active women are designated Islamic feminist, Moghissi asserts, "even though their activities might not even fit the broadest definition of feminism" (1998, 42). Although she herself does not define feminism, Moghissi complains that the term *Islamic feminism* encompasses members of the female political elite who believe in the Sharia and its prescribed gender

---

[16] The argument about capitalist contradictions facing the Islamic Republic is contained in Moghadam 1988, 1993b, chap. 6. The argument about accommodating the demands of activist women is made in Tohidi 1994 and in her other writings. I make the same point in the above works.

rights and roles, such as three former female parliamentarians who were responsible for two reactionary bills. Another criticism is that the term and the emphasis on the achievements of those believing women who reinterpret the Qur'an obscure the political, ideological, and religious differences among Iranian women and mask the valiant efforts of socialists, democrats, and feminists to work toward secularism (Moghissi 1997).[17] In her 1999 book, which is largely a collection of previously published essays, she writes of "the masterful manipulation of observers by the fundamentalists" (104). As in her Persian-language article, Moghissi singles out expatriate feminist authors, finds faults with their analyses, and labels them. But whereas in her *Kankash* article she deemed them "neoconservative," in her book she brands them "postmodernists" and "cultural relativists." She writes, "Charmed by 'difference' and secure from the bitter fact of the fundamentalist regime, outsiders do them [Iranian women and men] a disservice by clinging to the illusion of an Islamic path" (1999, 121).[18]

Hammed Shahidian similarly argues that the politics of "Islamic feminism" is problematical, whether in Iran or elsewhere. Like Moghissi, he argues that the emphasis on the achievements of Islamic women obscures the contributions of the left and secularists in the face of continued Islamist repression in Iran. (Ironically, Shahidian, like Moghissi, has published essays exceedingly critical of the left.)[19] In one article he refers to a "deepening identity crisis" among secular Middle East feminists and approvingly quotes two Iranian left-wing feminists: "Some women have found the pull towards a full or partial reconciliation with Iranian-style fundamentalism stronger. A trend is now developing among some Iranian feminists . . . to stand back and consider Islamic fundamentalism as opposed to stand up and fight against it." Shahidian adds that "this is a keen prognosis about the emerging conciliatory regard for 'Islamic feminism,'" and he implies that academic supporters of Islamic feminism have given up the

[17] I am among those criticized by Moghissi in that article (and elsewhere). The article does not define "neoconservative," does not distinguish between the active leftists and non-leftists among "Iranian Academic Feminists," and does not explain how secularists, democrats, and so on have been harmed by academic feminist support for Islamic feminism.

[18] In her book Moghissi shifts, without explanation, from the label "neoconservative" to the label "postmodern." Once again, she does not distinguish between those academic feminists who have been inspired by postmodernism (e.g., Najmabadi) and those who have not (Tohidi, Mir-Hosseini, and myself).

[19] See Shahidian 1994; and Moghissi 1993, 1996. For a more sympathetic treatment of the Iranian left, see Moghadam 1987; and Ashtiani and Moghadam 1991.

"critical edge" that he finds so appealing in his discipline, sociology (1999, 318).

Dismissive of attempts by Arab scholars such as Fatima Mernissi and Aziza Al-Hibri and the Pakistan-born Riffat Hassan to craft a feminist theology and reinterpretation of Islamic texts, Shahidian argues that these attempts are futile, given the strength of conservative, orthodox, traditional, and fundamentalist interpretations, laws, and institutions. He is especially critical of a growing trend in Middle East women's studies wherein authors justify Muslim women's veiling, domesticity, moral behavior, and adherence to Islamic precepts as signs of individual choice and identity (Shahidian 1997).[20] Even if we do not accept the notion of "false consciousness," he asks, is it not incumbent on scholars to situate and understand actors' views and perceptions within the broader social, cultural, political, and economic context? Political repression, cultural conservatism, and the social control of women characterize this context, he notes. For these reasons, Shahidian not only argues that Islamic feminism is an oxymoron but also that it has wider ramifications even beyond the Iranian left and Iranian society. Although he does not elaborate on this point, he asserts that Islamic feminism and its defense "affects the women's movement and the Left worldwide" (1998b).

Shahidian notes that Islamic feminists in Iran have been attentive to and influenced by Western feminism. But he is critical of them for neglecting key issues of sexuality, veiling, and religious law (1998b). His involvement in the debate on Islamic feminism extends to participation in an exchange with Iranian sociologist Nahid Motiee in the pages of *Zanan*. Shahidian criticizes Motiee's defense of the family and raises questions about her and other Islamic feminists' understanding of patriarchy, gender, and sexuality, including homosexuality (1998a).[21] He concludes that Islamic feminism fails to offer a liberating alternative to the dominant Islamic discourse and practice of gender and sexuality.

Whereas Shahidian has been especially critical of Tohidi, Shahrzad Mojab has focused on Najmabadi's writings on Islamic feminism. In an article published in the Persian-language magazine *Arash*, Mojab criticizes Najmabadi for suggesting that *Zanan* is the new "democratic forum" and that it can help to feminize democracy. She disputes Najmabadi's hopeful

[20] Shahidian's article on the politics of the veil is in part a critique of an article by Azza Karam (Karam 1996) that sympathetically reports on Egyptian women's veiling.

[21] In a personal communication (March 7, 2000, Cairo), Nahid Motiee, a sociologist who has researched the growth of female-headed households in Iran, told me that her strong defense of the family was influenced by what she perceived as Shahidian's own extreme views.

prognosis about the reinterpretation of Islamic texts and stresses that the ruling religious elite can dismiss, delegitimize, or prohibit radical or feminist reinterpretations. What Iran's Islamic feminists have achieved is, at any rate, quite limited in content and consequence. Real change—real democratization—will come about outside of the religious framework, writes Mojab (1999).

Some Iranian leftists in exile have been very vocal in opposing Islamic feminism. Left-opposition newspapers and magazines have carried articles describing the phenomenon and rejecting it as illusory or as legitimizing Islamic rule. Representative of this line of thought is an editorial titled "The Limits of Islamic Feminism" in *Iran Bulletin* (Kia 1994), an English-language magazine published in England with ties to the socialist group Rah-e Kargar. The basic premise is that no reform is possible in an Islamic legal and political system where "the very structure of power is male dominated to an absolute degree, backed by the Constitution, an all male clerical system ruling the country, and a Shari'a written for an era long past its sell-by date." The author, M. Kia, argues that the Islamic reformist discourse is not identical to liberation theology but derives from "a religion in which the role of women is clearly stated." This stated role includes women's inferior status with respect to marriage, divorce, child custody, inheritance, and court witnessing, the ban on women judges, and mandated veiling. The article notes that under pressure from women a debate has been under way and some political changes have been introduced, but the reforms have been limited and do nothing more than return Iranian gender codes to their prerevolutionary situation, which is still considerably behind most countries with similar economic status. Any reform movement or discourse that is carried out within the framework of Islamic law and that takes for granted the legitimacy and permanence of an Islamic state and of Qur'anic edicts is at best a very limited project and at worst a way of legitimizing the Islamic legal, political, and moral framework. With respect to Islamic feminism, "it would thus seem rather naïve to place too much hope in the 'internal' opposition to effect significant change in the conditions of women in Iran" (Kia 1994, 20–21).

Another argument, made mostly against the academic supporters of Islamic feminism, has surfaced in a number of Iranian seminars and conferences, mainly on the part of left-wing expatriates who remain affiliated with proscribed political organizations and therefore have not traveled back to Iran since the revolution. They complain that proponents of Islamic feminists—insisting as they do on the need for fieldwork, empirical research, and direct experience in Iran—delegitimize the analyses and perspectives of exiles. As such, they effectively close off debate and silence the critics of social conditions, gender relations, and Islamic feminism in Iran.[22]

The criticism of Islamic feminism is not limited to left-wing circles. Mahnaz Afkhami is a liberal feminist based in the Washington, D.C., area. Well known for her activism and eloquence, she was president of the Iran Women's Organization before the revolution; during much of the 1990s she was executive director of the Sisterhood Is Global Institute, a transnational feminist network. Speaking for herself and several other Iranian feminists, she said, "Our difference with Islamic feminists is that we don't try to fit feminism in the Qur'an. We say that women have certain inalienable rights. The epistemology of Islam is contrary to women's rights. But you can use what you need to [to advance women's positions]. I call myself a Muslim and a feminist. I'm not an Islamic feminist—that's a contradiction in terms."[23]

Islamic feminism: An assessment and alternative view

The Iranian debate on Islamic feminism certainly reflects the fragmentation of the Iranian left in exile. But it is probably best understood as part of three broad and at times overlapping debates and political realities. The first pertains to Islamic fundamentalism, including its origins, gender dynamics, and contradictions; the second to the IRI, including its gender regime and political evolution; and the third to the definition of feminism and the nature of women's movements around the world. In the interstices lies an ongoing debate within the expatriate Iranian left concerning the extent of reform possible within the Islamic Republic.

Fundamentalism, the Islamic Republic, and feminism

In the 1980s and 1990s, many of those who were grappling with the perplexing phenomenon of Islamic fundamentalism were Middle Eastern academic women (like myself) who were writing in North America and Europe. Politics and disciplinary training alike informed our approaches. We approached the problem of Islamic fundamentalism from a political position (whether socialist, feminist, or liberal), but we also sought to distance ourselves from Eurocentric and orientalist approaches. It was very important to refute orientalist charges that Islamic fundamentalism was the inevitable political expression of the Muslim world and to counter

---

[22] This argument surfaced at the seventh annual conference of the Iranian Women's Studies Foundation, which took place in Seattle in June 1996.

[23] Mahnaz Afkhami, interview by author, Washington, D.C., November 21, 1999.

cultural relativist arguments that criticism of gender practices in non-Western cultures was inappropriate and an imposition of Western values. At the same time, many of us who were social scientists used our disciplinary tools to analyze relations, institutions, and processes in Muslim societies (e.g., Kandiyoti 1990; Moghadam 1993a). Historical and comparative methods, for example, suggested similarities between Islamic fundamentalism in the Middle East at the end of the twentieth century and American Protestant fundamentalism in the early twentieth century. Both movements occurred in the context of the contradictions of modernity and modernization, including growing secularization and changes to family structure. (A difference between the two, of course, is that Islamic fundamentalism occurred in the regional context of Middle East politics, including the intractability of the Palestinian-Israeli problem, and the international context of economic recession and growing inequalities.) Scholars were also interested in the differences among Islamist movements (e.g., Iran, Afghanistan, Turkey, Algeria) and in the evolution of political Islam. In the late 1990s, a consensus developed that the wave of movements for political Islam that had swept over the Middle East and North Africa was subsiding, although the legacy of Islamic fundamentalism remains to be fully understood.

A parallel and interrelated debate has centered on the evolution of the Islamic Republic in the 1990s. Has the regime shown a capacity for reform? Is the IRI moving in a capitalistic, bourgeois direction that may augur legal reforms and changes in social relations (including gender relations and laws about women and the family)? Or is the Islamic Republic mired in a crisis that only complete systemic transformation can resolve? Again, Iranians have approached these questions both politically ("subjectively") and academically ("objectively"). Most of the expatriate oppositional press and some books highlight the political repression, violations of women's human rights, the archaic political system of clerical governance, and economic inefficiencies to insist on the impossibility of fundamental reform and change (e.g., Behdad and Rahnema 1995; Abrahamian 1999).[24] Other publications have documented reforms in the political system, economic policy, and foreign policy and progress in the spheres of education and infrastructural development that have occurred since the late 1980s (e.g., Ehteshami 1995; Khosrowkhavar 2000).

A third issue relevant to the debate on Islamic feminism pertains to the definition of feminism and the nature of women's movements world-

[24] The oppositional press includes left-wing periodicals as well as an array of liberal, conservative, and monarchist magazines and newspapers.

wide. As two scholars have noted, "'Feminism' is a contested term even in the present, and historical literature is full of kinds of feminists who would surely have had a hard time finding common ground: Nazi feminists and Jewish feminists, Catholic feminists and Islamic feminists, socialist feminists and utopian feminists, social feminists and equity feminists, imperial feminists and national feminists" (Rupp and Taylor 1999, 363). In this connection, a number of questions have been posed. Is "feminism" a Western ideology? What should women's rights movements and organizations that eschew the label *feminist* be called? Are those who promote the advancement of women de facto feminists?[25] Is feminism defined and understood only through the writings and actions of Anglo-Americans? What of the writings and actions of feminists from developing countries? Can a more inclusive "global feminism" be developed that draws on the writings of scholars from around the world as well as from the activities of women's movements and organizations?[26]

The debate on Islamic feminism is linked to the above three debates. We have seen how some Iranian feminists have shifted their focus from the unrelenting oppression of women in the IRI to an appreciation of resistance, empowerment, and change. It is in this context that they now analyze the activities of Iran's Islamic feminists, who have been responsible for some legal reforms beneficial to women in the Islamic Republic. In the opposite camp, the detractors of Islamic feminism reject the possibilities for any improvements in women's conditions or any reform of the Islamist system in Iran. On the other hand, as we have seen with Moghissi, they can argue, rather inconsistently, that the clerical state has undertaken legal reforms as concessions to women activists but that the proponents of Islamic feminism exaggerate the potential of Islamic feminism. In general, the detractors of Islamic feminism refuse to concede the few successes that Islamic feminists have made in overturning some discriminatory policies that were adopted in the early years of Islamization, mainly in the areas of employment and education. As such, they essentially deny women's agency in the Islamic Republic. They also dismiss the reform movement in Iran, with which many of the Islamic feminists are associated, as unimportant or futile. Finally, they seem to define *feminism* essentially

---

[25] For an elaboration of "de facto feminism," see Misciagno 1997.

[26] Feminists who seek to elaborate a more inclusive, global feminism include Charlotte Bunch and Roxanna Carillo (1990); Angela Miles (1996); and Val Moghadam (1996, 2000). Amrita Basu previously critiqued the idea of a global feminism (1995), but now she endorses it (personal communication and various public lectures).

as Anglo-American radical feminism and appear to reject the idea of an emerging global feminism.

An alternative analysis

The vast gulf that exists between the two camps calls for an alternative analysis of Islamic feminism and of the debate. In my view, there can be no doubt of the importance of the writings and public pronouncements of "Islamic feminists" such as Sherkat, Taleghani, Faezeh Hashemi, and Jamileh Kadivar. *Zanan*, *Zan-e Rouz*, and the short-lived *Zan*, along with the secular feminist journals *Hoghough-e Zanan*, *Jenss-e Dovvom*, and *Negah-e Zanan* constitute a lively and widely read women's press, which has succeeded in making highly visible the "question of women." For example, in 1997 *Zanan* organized and reported on a roundtable discussion titled "What Are the Most Important Problems of Women in Iran?" Involving academic Farideh Farhi, lawyer Mehrangiz Kar, and reformist Abbas Abdi, the discussion touched on such issues as the reform movement in Iran, the limited nature of women's rights, and the need for the press to enjoy more freedoms (*Zanan* 1997a). Another roundtable discussion by academics on the same subject expounded somewhat more moderate views. Here, Qolamabbas Tavassoli, Homa Zanjanizadeh, and Nassrin Mossafa emphasized the importance of the family and of ensuring that gender role changes do not disrupt the family (*Zanan* 1997b). Clearly, the women's press, and especially *Zanan*, provide a forum for the articulation of diverse views, including those that are officially unpopular. As such, the women's press and those Islamic feminists associated with it are playing an important role in broadening the discursive universe of the Islamic Republic and in expanding legal literacy and gender consciousness among their readership. Also noteworthy is that the Islamic feminists who run *Zanan* and *Farzaneh* publish the writings of secular feminists.

The rereading of the Islamic texts is a central project of Islamic feminists. Out of their own religious conviction, Sherkat, Behrouzi, Gorji, and the former cleric Sa'idzadeh (now defrocked) engage in new interpretations of Islamic texts in order to challenge laws and policies that are based on orthodox, literalist, or misogynist interpretations. Other Islamic feminists such as Faezeh Hashemi boldly insist on the need for women judges and on more equitable inheritance law. As such, Islamic feminists are addressing some of the fundamentals of Islamic doctrine and of the gender system in Iran.[27]

---

[27] A similar argument was made in a special issue of *Hamahang*, an expatriate left-wing newspaper published in Canada, focusing on feminist struggles in Iran. It draws parallels

Along with secular feminists (e.g., Kar 1999), Islamic feminists seek to improve women's status within the family and thus to revise Islamic family law. They point out the injustice of those sections of Iran's civil code that result in women's inferior status and subordinate position in the family. They also engage in theological reinterpretation to support the view that genuine Islam, as opposed to patriarchal interpretations, holds women in esteem and calls for an egalitarian status for them within the family and in the society. *Zanan*'s position is that men's headship of the household is a male construct and, like other male privileges attributed to Sharia laws, has its roots in the culture and customs of the time of revelation (Mir-Hosseini 1996a, 315). As early as 1992, *Payam-e Hajjar*, published by Taleghani, had an article titled "Are Men Superior to Women?" that examined certain passages from the Qur'an that are usually interpreted as indicating men's dominion over women.[28] The author, Zahra Ibrahimi, sought to argue otherwise, from an Islamic perspective. She offered a practical recommendation as well: "the legislators of the Islamic Republic . . . add an article to the civil code, stipulating that men do not have the right to beat women" (1992, 36).

As a result of pressure from Islamic feminists, parliament and government bodies passed legislation to support working mothers, to allow unmarried women to study abroad, and to permit war widows to retain custody of their children and to receive financial compensation. The 1992 amendments to the divorce law enabled the court to place a monetary value on women's housework and entitle her to *ujrat al-mithl* (wages in kind) for the work she did during marriage—provided, however, that divorce is not initiated by her or is not caused by any fault of hers. A law was passed in 1997 requiring that payment of the *mahr* (dower) be in-

---

between Islamic feminism and Christian and Jewish feminisms, stresses the antifundamentalist essence of Islamic feminism, and criticizes Moghissi for dogmatism. See Ne'mati n.d.

[28] For example, verse 34 of sura Nisa in the Qur'an: "Men have authority over women because God has made the one superior to the other, and because they spend their wealth to maintain them. Good women are obedient. They guard their unseen parts because God has guarded them. As for those from whom you fear disobedience, admonish them and send them to beds apart and beat them; then if they obey you, take no further action against them. God is high, supreme" (see *The Koran* 1993, 64.) Imam Ali's sermon 79 in *Nahj al-Balaqeh* has helped to shape gender norms among Shia Muslims: "O people, women are deficient in belief, inheritance and wisdom. Their deficiency in belief is due to not praying and fasting during menses; their deficiency in wisdom is that witness of two women equals one man and in inheritance is that their share is half of men's. Therefore, avoid bad women and beware good ones; do not follow their good advice and actions so as not to encourage them to spread bad advice and actions." Such verses are said to demonstrate the subordinate status of women in the family, i.e., vis-à-vis their husbands.

dexed to inflation, thus creating a disincentive for unilateral divorce by men. Islamic feminists drafted a bill that would provide for more equitable inheritance for women and men—though it was defeated by parliament in 1998. They have objected to the penal code for its discrimination against women, whereby the "blood money" of a woman is half that of a man. An increasingly larger number of women have run for and been elected to parliament and local councils.

Some Iranian feminists, notably the lawyer Shirin Ebadi, have been actively involved in the democratic struggle in Iran and engaged in political debates in both the women's press and the intellectual press. Among Ebadi's many activities is her role as legal counsel to the family of the murdered dissidents Daryoush Forouhar and Parvaneh Esfandiari-Forouhar. In a May 1999 interview in Stockholm, Ebadi spoke of "this challenge [in Iran] between modernity and orthodoxy, between a group that is after safeguarding traditions and the other one that is struggling for more freedom." She said that the most urgent need is "reforming the laws concerning people's freedoms in social, political, individual, and religious domains" (Haeri 1999). In an article in *Jens-e Dovvom*, she describes the discriminatory laws women face, notes that the government of President Khatami has been unable to overturn them, but adds that his government at least has provided a more open atmosphere within which to discuss issues concerning women's equality, democracy, and modernity (Ebadi 1999). In a talk given to an Iranian expatriate gathering in London on March 11, 2000, Ebadi criticized the Islamic penal code, *Qessas*, and pointed to the ways that it both encouraged political killings and protected killers of those deemed anti-Islamic. It should be noted, too, that *Zanan* reported on the July 1999 assault against student protesters and boldly printed the image of a bloodied shirt on its front cover (*Zanan* 1999).

Independent and state feminists

The Islamic discourse that Islamic feminists utilize is both genuine—an expression of their religious convictions—and a strategic attempt to acquire legitimacy that also serves to broaden the base of support for women's rights in the IRI. But to address an issue raised by Moghissi: Who exactly may be deemed an "Islamic feminist"? Here it may be useful to identify some distinct groups. Independent feminists (e.g., Sherkat and Ebadi) maintain a distance from the organs of state power and work closely with secular feminists such as Kar, the critic and publisher Shahla Lahiji, and sociologist Nahid Motiee, as well as expatriate Iranian feminists. Independent feminists and other women's rights activists revolve around

Zanan, *Houghough-e Zanan*, and *Jens-e Dovvom*, among other examples of the women's press. State feminists are associated with government or parliament. In addition to having government or parliamentary positions (e.g., Ebtekar, Shojai, Behrouzi, Gorji, Hashemi, Parvin Ma'arufi, Jaleh Jelodarzadeh), they may be involved with the establishment women's press (e.g., Rahnavard's association with *Zan-e Rouz*, Ommi's association with the Islamic women's studies journal *Farzaneh*). State feminists appear to be to the right of the independent feminists on cultural and gender issues. Some, for example, stress the importance of the cohesion of the family, stating that motherhood and domesticity keep the family together and society morally upright.

What independent and state feminists have in common is their rereading of the Qu'ran, their determination to contribute to the feminization of the political process, and their campaign for the modernization of family law. Their position on political and economic issues remains unclear and undeveloped; they have not formulated perspectives on economic development, poverty elimination, the welfare state, or civil society.

Among both independent and state feminists in the IRI are believing women who seek to counter patriarchal religious interpretations and highlight egalitarian or woman-centered understandings. I am sympathetic to the discursive strategy of these Islamic feminists, but I am concerned about the focus on the "correct" reading of the Islamic texts. A reasonable concern is that, so long as Islamic feminists remain focused on theological arguments rather than socioeconomic and political questions, and so long as their point of reference is the Qur'an rather than universal standards, their impact will be limited at best. At worst, their strategy could reinforce the legitimacy of the Islamic system, help to reproduce it, and undermine secular alternatives. But this worst-case scenario very likely will not materialize, because most Islamic feminists combine their religious reinterpretations with a recognition of universal standards, such as the UN's Convention on the Elimination of All Forms of Discrimination against Women (CEDAW). Nevertheless, it is indeed the case that Islamic feminists, and especially the state feminists, are situated within and firmly accept the legal framework, institutions, and discursive universe of Islam and the IRI. For example, Jamileh Kadivar—reformist, parliamentarian, and professor—staunchly defended "Islamic human rights" at a contentious conference in Berlin in early April 2000. A year earlier, however, she had incurred the wrath of conservatives by calling for an abrogation of men's right to unilateral divorce and polygamy. Such inconsistencies are common among Islamic feminists.

In some ways, Iran's Islamic feminists are not substantially different from liberal feminists, particularly those in the United States, who work within the existing political system and seek to improve women's positions though the discursive framework of liberal capitalism. Of course, the substance of their respective gender critiques is different, and they work within two entirely different political and legal environments. But both groups of feminists work within and maintain the legitimacy of their respective political systems. Shahidian has criticized Iran's Islamic feminists for their failure to take up such issues as homosexuality and personal autonomy. And yet, U.S. liberal feminists have not called for economic and political transformation. The demands for sexual rights and equal opportunities in education and employment are entirely compatible with the capitalist system. What liberal feminists have not called for is a change in the system of taxation and in development policy that would alter American foreign policy and the distribution of wealth, transforming the lives of low-income women in the United States and elsewhere. In fact, one may suggest provocatively that those Islamic feminists who question the exclusive right of clerics and the *faqih* to interpret the Islamic texts and to define and implement Islamic jurisprudence are more subversive to the existing political system than are their U.S. liberal-feminist counterparts.

The analogy between Iran's Islamic feminists and liberal feminists in the United States has not been made elsewhere, although I believe it to be an apt one. Another pertinent argument, made by Tohidi, Najmabadi, Ne'mati, and others, concerns the parallels between the theological project of Iran's Islamic feminists and that of Christian feminists. But are they similar? Anne Sofie Roald explains the difference between them, and it suggests the limitations of Islamic feminism in its present phase. Christian feminist theologians such as Rosemary Reuther, Phyllis Bird, and Elisabeth Shussler Fiorenza "are part of an established scientific tradition within Christian theology" (Roald 1998, 30). This historical-critical method allows them to "perceive the Bible as written by human beings and in particular by men" (35). This is "an assumption which is not possible in an Islamic exegesis." Islamic feminist theologians seek to evaluate Islamic sources, criticize the patriarchal interpretation of Islamic sources, and stress the equality of men and women in the Qur'an. Their method "concentrates mainly on textual analysis and thus works methodologically in search of evidences to establish laws and regulations suitable for modern society" (40). Roald concludes that "the interpretation of the Islamic sources by women is a new project and the next decades will show us whether this project has any future" (41). In Iran, while some reformists argue for period-based interpretations of the Qur'an, most seek to high-light the egalitarian tendencies within it as a way to frame contemporary legislation. None so far has suggested the fallibility of the Qur'an.

It is, at any rate, very difficult to win theological arguments. There will always be competing interpretations of the religious texts, and the power of the social forces behind it determines the dominance of each interpretation.[29] In this respect, I agree with Mojab on the limits of religious reinterpretation. Thus, although religious reform is salutary and necessary, it is important to acknowledge its limitations. Women's rights and human rights are best promoted and protected in an environment of secular thought and secular institutions, including a state that defends the rights of all its citizens irrespective of religious affiliation, and a civil society with strong organizations that can constitute a check on the state. I will return to this issue at the conclusion of this article.

Statements made and positions taken by some state feminists illustrate the promises and perils and the strengths and weaknesses of Islamic feminism. Ebtekar—cofounder of the women's studies journal *Farzaneh* and high-ranking official in the Khatami government—visited the Afghan city of Mazar-e-Sharif (before it fell to the Taliban) to speak to Afghan women. She assured them that "your sisters in the Islamic Republic are taking measures to establish Islamic human rights of women in the world which will contribute to the improvement of the status of women and provide progress in all areas for the Moslem communities around the world" (Heinrich 1998). But what are Islamic human rights? How do they differ from rights enshrined in the Universal Declaration of Human Rights or in CEDAW—both of which were drafted by persons from various national, cultural, and religious backgrounds? What are the rights of minorities, and in what ways can there be equality for all citizens, in an Islamic legal

[29] Many Islamic feminists are keen to show that men and women are equal and that women are respected in the Islamic texts. Yet other scholars from the Muslim world have pointed out that in Islam the male-female relationship is assumed to be highly sexual, that women are considered to have sexual power over men that needs to be controlled by veiling, that permanent marriage is a sale, and that temporary marriage (as practiced in the Shia Iranian tradition) is a lease of female sexuality. In an original and provocative article, Fatemeh E. Moghdam (1994) argues that the Islamic practice of *mahr*, or dower, represents the sale of female sexuality, and that the commoditization of female sexuality through *mahr* reinforces Muslim women's subordination within the family and their economic marginalization in the labor force. Turning to Christianity, it should be noted that two hundred years after the Christian world's Enlightenment and a long process of secularization, American Southern Baptists passed a resolution in 1998 calling on wives to defer to their husbands in all family matters. In Israel, the Orthodox and patriarchal interpretation of Judaism is the dominant one, backed by the state.

system that is premised on differences between men and women and between Muslims and non-Muslims?

Faezeh Hashemi, daughter of the former president Ali Akbar Hashemi-Rafsanjani (1990–97), is an outspoken advocate of women's rights, especially the right of women and girls to engage in athletics. A member of the past parliament, she had been an extremely popular candidate, winning one million votes. (She lost her seat in the February 2000 elections.) In a remarkable act, she marched in solidarity with students during the July 1999 protests. In Rakhshan Bani-Etemad's film within a film *Banoo-Ye Ordibehesht* (The May lady), she boldly states that the problems of women in Iran result from the fact that all the judges are men and that there are no women judges in Iran. In a 1997 interview she stated that "we generally agree that the role of women on the Iranian political scene has improved in the last years but still there are some basic problems such as an Iranian female official cannot leave the country without her husband's permission. Is this not a basic obstacle to the basic right of a woman, whether official or non-official?" In response to a question about national reconciliation, she was adamant that all Iranians regardless of political views had a place in the country and its system: "I think the Iranian people belong to Iran and live in Iran and tolerated all the problems in the last 17 years and even went to the war-fronts. Even though they might not have even been a Muslim or a Hezbullah, they might have only done that due to their national sentiments and due to their love for their country" (Hashemi 1997).

That she is a defender of the existing political system, albeit of its reformist wing, is evident. In the same interview, Hashemi continues,

> They should still be respected as a resident as long as they do not act outside the legal framework. We have a constitution and this constitution has set freedom for them and as long as the law is respected, the government should also respect them. The law must confront illegalities. No social strata should be put under pressure just because one day they might do something wrong. I respect all the people in Iran, regardless of their ideologies. For me there is no difference. An administration can only be successful when this national unity is maintained, if not then the administration itself will be the first victim.

On the issue of veiling, she is adamant, if contradictory. Referring to Turkey, she said, "I think that unfortunately in some countries Western norms are imposed on women. Hijab is an indisputable symbol for Muslim women. Muslim women should not be deprived. Although Turkey is an Islamic country, women are thrown out of universities because of Hijab" (Hashemi 1997). She makes no reference to the fact that in Iran veiling is compulsory rather than a freely chosen mode of dress or expression of identity. Nor does she refer to the fact that Iran's constitutional provisions on freedom of association and on the prohibition of torture have been routinely and systematically violated over the years. Subsequently, Hashemi changed her views on veiling. In the run-up to the parliamentary elections of February 2000, she declared that *hejab* should be voluntary and not mandatory. This was the boldest challenge yet to religious orthodoxy, state policy, and patriarchal norms.

Hashemi and other Islamic feminists sometimes refer to the goals of democracy, civil society, and equality for women and religious minorities. However, to the extent that they raise these issues, their discussion of them tends to be very general and nonthreatening.[30] In fact, Iran's constitution—as well as its family law and penal law, both based on the Shariat—will have to undergo complete revision, if those objectives are to be achieved. Moreover, the building of civil society calls for a specific kind of state. Civil society presupposes a state that enforces universal legal norms and guarantees protection of civil and human rights regardless of gender, religion, ethnicity, and class. An Islamic state cannot and will not undertake this because it defines citizenship rights on the basis of sex and religion.

Conclusion: Toward civil society and global feminism

Does Islamic feminism challenge or reinforce the fusion of religion and politics/law? Najmabadi celebrates *Zanan* for its receptivity to non-Islamic writers, which she sees as blurring the divide between religious and secular thought (1998, 77). And yet there is a need for separation of mosque and state, for a secular political system, and for a deepening of secular thought, even though there are different paths to and models of secularism and Iran will have to develop its own.

The efforts of believing women of the monotheistic faiths to subject their religious texts to a feminist rereading, or to locate and emphasize the women-friendly and egalitarian precepts within their religious texts, are to be supported. This is a legitimate and historically necessary strategy to improve the status of women and to modernize religious thought. In

[30] The notable exception is Shirin Ebadi, whose articles on politics and the law in *Jameh-e Saalem* have been rather audacious.

this respect, my position is different from that of Moghissi and Shahidian, who dismiss feminist theology and deny its wider implications. And yet, one cannot insist, as some Islamic reformists do, that the Islamic arguments are the only ones that matter and that change will occur only as a result of the reform movement within Islam. Islam in Iran may be experiencing a kind of Reformation, but what will be equally if not more important for long-term social change in Iran (and elsewhere in the Muslim world) is an Enlightenment. As such, the contributions of nonreligious thinkers and activists, whether inside or outside Iran, will continue the process of democratization and building of civil society that was initiated by the Constitutional Revolution earlier in this century.[31] In any event, it is clear that despite the changes of the 1990s, the IRI is mired in a political, economic, and cultural crisis that will only be overcome by major changes to its system of governance. The continuing battle between conservatives and reformists (including Islamic feminists) attests to this.

What are some elements of a system of governance and a legal system that could ensure greater social, gender, religious, and ethnic equality? Some of these changes have been suggested by certain intellectuals within the reform movement.[32] Here I will offer some needed changes from a secular feminist (Marxist-feminist) perspective. Religious doctrine should not be the basis of laws, policies, or institutions. Iran's constitution (or any other constitution) should not state that "Islam [or Christianity or Judaism or Hinduism] is the official [or state or national] religion." Family law should not derive from religious texts, whether in Iran or in Israel. Blasphemy laws should be removed, and religion should be the subject of historical and critical inquiry. All citizens should be equal before the law, with equal rights and obligations. Civil, political, and social rights of

---

[31] The Constitutional Revolution in Iran was an incomplete project that began with radical elements and ended in the first Pahlavi dictatorship. For an elaboration, see Afary 1996.

[32] Reformists have written on the need for civil society, democracy, and freedom of the press (an Islamic democracy) in such magazines as *Hamshahri, Iran-e Farda, Jame'eh, Jame'eh Saalem, Salam, Neshat,* and others. None, however, goes so far as to call for a secular political system. This is partly because such a discussion is currently illegal and partly because many reformists are attached to the Islamic system, which they seek to make more open and thus more conducive to their political power ambitions. One prominent intellectual who has combined a radical reinterpretation of Islam with an equally radical interrogation of clerical governance and the need for democracy, civil society, and freedom of expression is Abdolkarim Soroush, whose writings have appeared in *Kiyan* and elsewhere. Much of the left considers him unacceptable because of his role in the Islamic cultural revolution of the early 1980s. And yet, his philosophical writings appear to be innovative and important. For an elaboration of his writings, see Boroujerdi 1996; and Vahdat (in press).

citizens should be protected by the state and by the institutions of civil society. This includes worker participation in decision making and an active role for independent unions, professional associations, citizen groups, and so on. It should be noted that Islam, like other monotheistic religions, does have humane, compassionate, and egalitarian aspects. These may *inspire* civil codes, political processes, social policies, and economic institutions. For example, the social justice foundations of religious thought represent an important balance to the harsh discipline of the capitalist market. The ban on usury in Islam and Catholicism is in conflict with capitalism's creation of wealth through nonproductive financial transactions and speculation, and this, to my mind, is progressive and should be emphasized. Religious belief should be respected, and religious institutions should have a place in civil society, but religion should not dominate the state and the law.

I end by asking whether Islamic feminism is indeed feminism. Is Islamic feminism an indigenous alternative to secular or Western-inspired feminism? Is it an oxymoron, a contradiction in terms? Or is it part of the already diversified and colorful spectrum of the transnational women's movement and a contributor to a "global feminism"? There is no question that Islamic feminists have been inspired by the writings and collective action of feminists from the West and the third world. Any reading of the women's press in Iran reveals that Iranian women activists and scholars, including those who define themselves as Muslim or Islamic and eschew the label "feminist," engage with transnational feminism. In a thought-provoking book, Patricia Misciagno argues for a "bottom-up" or materialist approach to feminist identity that hinges on women's praxis rather than their ideology. She defines "de facto feminist praxis" as "activity that runs counter to the ideology of patriarchy, even while not directly addressing the issue of patriarchy as an ideology" (Misciagno 1997, 70–71). Similarly, Leila Rupp and Verta Taylor note that "a concentration solely on ideas ignores the fact that feminists are social movement actors situated in an organizational and movement context" (1999, 364). Their historical study shows that "the meaning of feminism has changed over time and from place to place and is often disputed." They emphasize the need to understand "what women (or men) in a specific historical location believed" but also "how they constructed, sometimes through conflict with one another, a sense of togetherness" (364). Feminist disputes, they argue, "take place within a social movement community that, as it evolves, encompasses those who see gender as a major category of analysis, who critique female disadvantage, and who work to improve women's situations." They conclude by asserting that "in every group, in every place, at every time, the meaning of 'feminism' is worked out in the course of being and doing" (382).

The above analysis sheds light on our question and points the way toward a resolution of the debate on Islamic feminism. For if feminism has always been contested, if feminists should be defined by their praxis rather than by a strict ideology, and if a feminist politics is shaped by its specific historical, political, and cultural contexts, then it should be possible to identify Islamic feminism as one feminism among many. Indeed, in my view, it is not particularly useful to create absolute boundaries between Islamic feminism, Western feminism, Latin American feminism, African feminism, Jewish feminism, and so on. In the same way that liberal, socialist, Marxist, radical, cultural, and postmodern feminisms (not to mention equality and difference feminisms, and first- and second-wave feminisms) are part of the feminist tradition, so are the various regional manifestations part of the evolving political philosophy of feminism and the social movement of women. At the beginning of the new millennium what appears to be emerging is a global women's movement and a philosophy that not only draws on the feminist "classics" but also reflects the social realities and concerns of women in various parts of the world. To a very great extent, the Beijing Platform for Action, adopted at the end of the Fourth World Conference on Women in September 1995, is a manifesto of the global women's movement. It describes the problems facing the vast majority of the women of the world and prescribes a set of actions to solve the problems involving government, international agencies, nongovernmental organizations, and the women's movement. That the Platform for Action was finally agreed on by governments and women's organizations after many disagreements confirms the multifaceted nature of global feminism and the capacity of the world's women to overcome some ideological and class differences and agree on measures necessary for women's equality and empowerment.

Feminism is a theoretical perspective and a practice that criticizes social and gender inequalities, aims at women's empowerment, and seeks to transform knowledge—and in some interpretations, to transform socioeconomic structures, political power, and international relations. Women, and not religion, should be at the center of that theory and practice. It is not possible to defend as feminist the view that women can attain equal status only in the context of Islam. This is a fundamentalist view, not one compatible with feminism. And yet, around the world there will be different strategies that women will pursue toward empowerment and transformation. We are still grappling with understanding and theorizing those diverse political strategies. In light of this, it serves no purpose to insist on a narrow definition of feminism, as Moghissi and Shahidian appear to do. And when one recalls the difficult period that the Iranian left went through after the Revolution, when disunity and fragmentation reigned, it seems obvious that harsh attacks and denunciations of some feminists by other feminists is hardly the way forward. This can only impede rather than contribute to dialogue, knowledge, coalition building, and collective action.

Women's Studies Program
Department of Sociology
Illinois State University

References

Abrahamian, Ervand. 1999. *Tortured Confessions: Prisons and Public Recantations in Modern Iran*. Berkeley: University of California Press.

Afary, Janet. 1996. *The Iranian Constitutional Revolution, 1906–1911: Grassroots Democracy, Social Democracy, and the Origins of Feminism*. New York: Columbia University Press.

Afkhami, Mahnaz. 1995. "Introduction." In *Faith and Freedom: Women's Human Rights in the Muslim World*, ed. Mahnaz Afkhami, 1–17. Syracuse, N.Y.: Syracuse University Press.

Afshar, Haleh. 1985. "Women, State, and Ideology in Iran." *Third World Quarterly* 7(2):256–78.

———. 1996. "Islam and Feminism: An Analysis of Political Strategies." In *Feminism and Islam: Legal and Literary Perspectives*, ed. Mai Yamani. New York: New York University Press.

Ashtiani, Ali, and Val Moghadam. 1991. "The Left and Political Islam in Iran: A Retrospect and Prospects." *Radical History Review* 51:27–62.

Badran, Margot. 1999. "Toward Islamic Feminisms: A Look at the Middle East." In *Hermeneutics of Honor: Negotiating Female "Public" Space in Islamicate Societies*, ed. Asma Afsaruddin, 159–88. Cambridge, Mass.: Harvard University, Center for Middle Eastern Studies.

Basu, Amrita. 1995. *The Challenge of Local Feminisms: Women's Movements in Local Perspective*. Boulder, Colo.: Westview.

Behdad, Sohrab, and Saeed Rahnema, eds. 1995. *Iran after the Revolution: Crisis of an Islamic State*. London: I. B. Taurus.

Boroujerdi, Mehrzad. 1996. *Iranian Intellectuals and the West: The Tormented Triumph of Nativism*. Syracuse, N.Y.: Syracuse University Press.

Bunch, Charlotte, and Roxanna Carillo. 1990. "Feminist Perspectives on Women in Development." In *Persistent Inequalities: Women and World Development*, ed. Irene Tinker, 70-82. New York: Oxford University Press.

Bureau of Women's Affairs. 1995. *National Report on Women in the Islamic Re-*

public of Iran: Prepared for the Fourth World Conference on Women. Tehran: Bureau of Women's Affairs.

Cooke, Miriam. 2001. *Women Claim Islam: Creating Islamic Feminism through Literature.* New York: Routledge.

Ebadi, Shirin. 1999. "Gender Equality through the Lens of Modernity and Tradition." *Jenss-e Dovvom* (2), Khordad 1378 (May): 31–38 (in Persian).

Ebtekar, Massoumeh. 1995–96. "Reflections on the Fourth World Conference on Women: The Process and the Issues." *Farzaneh: Journal of Women's Studies and Research* 2(7):93–104.

Ehteshami, Anoushiravan. 1995. *After Khomeini: The Iranian Second Republic.* London: Routledge.

Esfandiari, Haleh. 1993. "Iran: Women and Parliaments under Monarchy and Islamic Republic." *Princeton Papers in Near Eastern Studies* 2.

———. 1997. *Reconstructed Lives: Women and Iran's Revolution.* Washington, D.C., and Baltimore: Woodrow Wilson Center and Johns Hopkins University Press.

Ghoussoub, Mai. 1987. "Feminism or the Eternal Masculine in the Arab World." *New Left Review* 161 (January–February): 3–13.

———. 1988. "A Reply to Hammami and Rieker." *New Left Review* 170 (July–August): 107–9.

Haeri, Safa. 1999. "Civil War a Real Danger if Khatami Bows to Extreme Demands." Available on-line at http://www.iran-press-service.com/articles/ebadi_2459921.html.

Hammami, Reza [Rema], and Martina Rieker. 1988. "Feminist Orientalism and Orientalist Marxism." *New Left Review* 170 (July–August): 93–106.

Hashemi, Faezeh. 1997. "Interview with Faezeh Hashemi." *ASAHI Shimbun* (Tokyo), February 6. Available on-line at http://www.zan.org/lit2.html.

Heinrich, Mark. 1998. "Women's Day Focus on Afghan, Algerian Abuses." Available on-line at http://www.europa.eu.int/en/comm/echo/womensday/press/press52.htm.

Hoodfar, Homa. 1993. "The Veil in Their Minds and on Our Heads: The Persistence of Colonial Images of Muslim Women." *Resources for Feminist Research* 22.

Ibrahimi, Zahra. 1992. "Are Men Superior to Women?" *Payam-e Hajjar*, Shahrivar 1371 (September): 30–36 (in Persian).

Islamic Republic of Iran. 1992. *Employment Practices for Women in the Islamic Republic of Iran.* Tehran: High Council of the Cultural Revolution.

———. 1994. *Zan va Towse-eh: ahamm-e eqdamat-e anjam-shodeh dar khosus-e banovan pas az pirouzi-ye enqelab-e Eslami* (Women and development: Measures taken on behalf of women after the victory of the Islamic revolution). Tehran: Shura-ye Hamhangi-ye Tablighat-e Eslami.

Kandiyoti, Deniz. 1988. "Bargaining with Patriarchy." *Gender & Society* 2(3): 274–89.

———, ed. 1990. *Women, Islam, and the State*. New York: New York University Press.

Kar, Mehrangiz. 1999. "The Legal Status of Iranian Women." Paper presented at the Dialogue and Action between the People of Iran and America (DAPIA) meeting, Cyprus.

Karam, Azza. 1996. "Veiling, Unveiling, and the Meaning of the Veil." *Thamyris* 3(2):219–36.

———. 1997. "Essentialized Veiling: Static Symbolism Revisited." *Thamyris* 4(2): 338–46.

Khosrowkhavar, Farhad. 2000. "Toward an Anthropology of Democratization in Iran." *Critique*, no. 16 (Spring): 3–30.

Kia, M. 1994. "The Limits of Islamic Feminism." *Iran Bulletin* 8 (January–March): 20–21.

The Koran. (1956) 1993. Trans. N. J. Dawood. London: Penguin.

Lawyers Committee for Human Rights. 1993. *The Justice System of the Islamic Republic of Iran*. New York: Lawyers Committee for Human Rights.

Mayer, Ann Elizabeth. 1995. "Cultural Pluralism as a Bar to Women's Rights: Reflections on the Middle Eastern Experience." In *Women's Rights, Human Rights: International Feminist Perspectives*, ed. Julie Peters and Andrea Wolper, 176–88. New York: Routledge.

Miles, Angela. 1996. *Integrative Feminisms: Building Global Visions, 1960s–1990s*. New York: Routledge.

Mir-Hosseini, Ziba. 1996a. "Stretching the Limits: A Feminist Reading of the Sharia in Post-Khomeini Iran." In *Feminism and Islam: Legal and Literary Perspectives*, ed. Mai Yamani, 285–319. New York: New York University Press.

———. 1996b. "Women and Politics in Post-Khomeini Iran: Divorce, Veiling, and Emerging Feminist Voices." In *Women and Politics in the Third World*, ed. Haleh Afshar, 142–69. London: Routledge.

———. 1998. "Rethinking Gender: Discussions with Ulama in Iran." *Critique: A Journal for Critical Studies of the Middle East* 13 (Fall): 46–59.

———. 1999. *Islam and Gender: The Religious Debate in Contemporary Iran*. Princeton, N.J.: Princeton University Press.

Misciagno, Patricia S. 1997. *Rethinking Feminist Identification: The Case for De Facto Feminism*. Westport, Conn.: Praeger.

Moghadam, Valentine M. 1987. "Socialism or Anti-imperialism? The Left and Revolution in Iran." *New Left Review* 166 (November–December): 5–28.

———. 1988. "Women, Work, and Ideology in the Islamic Republic." *International Journal of Middle East Studies* 20(2):221–43.

———. 1989a. "Against Eurocentrism and Nativism: A Review Essay on Samir Amin's *Eurocentrism and Other Texts*." *Socialism and Democracy* 9 (Fall/Winter): 81–104.

———. 1989b. "One Revolution or Two? The Iranian Revolution and the Islamic Republic." In *Socialist Register 1989: Revolution Today, Aspirations and Re-*

alities, ed. Ralph Miliband, Leo Panitch, and John Saville, 74–101. London: Merlin.

———. 1991. "The Reproduction of Gender Inequality in Muslim Societies: A Case Study of Iran in the 1980's." *World Development* 19(10):1335–50.

———, ed. 1993a. *Identity Politics and Women: Cultural Reassertions and Feminisims in International Perspective.* Boulder, Colo.: Westview.

———. 1993b. *Modernizing Women: Gender and Social Change in the Middle East.* Boulder, Colo.: Lynne Rienner.

———. 1993c. "Rhetorics and Rights of Identity in Islamist Movements." *Journal of World History* 4(2):243–66.

———. 1994a. "Islamic Populism, Class, and Gender in Postrevolutionary Iran." In *A Century of Revolution: Social Movements in Iran,* ed. John Foran, 189–222. Minneapolis: University of Minnesota Press.

———. 1994b. "Reform, Revolution, and Reaction: The Trajectory of the 'Woman Question' in Afghanistan." In *Gender and National Identity: Women and Politics in Muslim Societies,* ed. Valentine Moghadam, 81–109. London: Zed.

———. 1996. "Feminist Networks North and South." *Journal of International Communication* 3(1):111–26.

———. 1998. *Women, Work, and Economic Reform in the Middle East and North Africa.* Boulder, Colo.: Lynne Rienner.

———. 2000. "Transnational Feminist Networks: Collective Action in an Era of Globalization." *International Sociology* 15(1):57–84.

Moghdam, Fatemeh E. 1994. "Commoditization of Sexuality and Female Labor Force Participation in Islam: Implications for Iran, 1960–1990." In *In the Eye of the Storm: Women in Post-revolutionary Iran,* ed. Mahnaz Afkhami and Erika Friedl, 80–97. Syracuse, N.Y.: Syracuse University Press.

Moghissi, Haideh. 1993. "Women in the Resistance Movement in Iran." In *Women in the Middle East: Perceptions, Realities, and Struggles for Liberation,* ed. Haleh Afshar. New York: St. Martin's.

———. 1995. "Public Life and Women's Resistance." In Behdad and Rahnema 1999, 251–67.

———. 1996. *Populism and Feminism in Iran: Women's Struggle in a Male-Defined Revolutionary Movement.* New York: St. Martin's.

———. 1997. "Populist Feminism and Islamic Feminism: A Critique of Neo-Conservative Tendencies among Iranian Academic Feminists." *Kankash* 13: 57–95 (in Persian).

———. 1998. "Women, Modernity, and Political Islam." *Iran Bulletin* 19–20 (Autumn/Winter): 42–44.

———. 1999. *Feminism and Islamic Fundamentalism: The Limits of Postmodern Analysis.* London: Zed.

Mojab, Shahrzad. 1999. "Women Undertaking *Ijtehad* (independent religious interpretation): Hoping for a Feminizing Democracy." *Arash* 70, Khordad 1378 (June): 48–52 (in Persian).

Najmabadi, Afsaneh. 1994. "Power, Morality, and the New Muslim Womanhood."

In *The Politics of Social Transformation in Afghanistan, Iran, and Pakistan,* ed. Myron Weiner and Ali Banuazizi, 366–89. Syracuse, N.Y.: Syracuse University Press.

———. 1995. "Years of Hardship, Years of Growth." *Kankash* 12 (in Persian).

———. 1997. "Feminisms in an Islamic Republic." In *Transitions, Environments, Translations: Feminisms in International Politics,* ed. Joan Scott, Cora Kaplan, and Debra Keates, 390–99. London: Routledge.

———. 1998. "Feminism in an Islamic Republic: 'Years of Hardship, Years of Growth.'" In *Islam, Gender, and Social Change in the Muslim World,* ed. Yvonne Y. Haddad and John Esposito, 59–84. New York: Oxford University Press.

Ne'mati, Payman. N.d. "A Critique of Haideh Moghissi's Perspectives on Islamic Feminism." *Hamahang,* no. 7, special issue on women in Iran.

Neshat, Guity, ed. 1983. *Women and Revolution in Iran.* Boulder, Colo.: Westview.

Poya, Maryam. 1999. *Women, Work and Islamism: Ideology and Resistance in Iran.* London: Zed.

Ramazani, Nesta. 1993. "Women in Iran: The Revolutionary Ebb and Flow." *Middle East Journal* 47(3):409–28.

Roald, Anne Sofie. 1998. "Feminist Reinterpretation of Islamic Sources: Muslim Feminist Theology in the Light of the Christian Tradition of Feminist Thought." In *Women and Islamization: Contemporary Dimensions of Discourse on Gender Relations,* ed. Karin Ask and Marit Tjomsland, 17–44. Oxford: Berg.

Rupp, Leila J., and Verta Taylor. 1999. "Forging Feminist Identity in an International Movement: A Collective Identity Approach to Twentieth-Century Feminism." *Signs: Journal of Women in Culture and Society* 24(21):363–86.

Shahidian, Hammed. 1994. "The Iranian Left and 'The Woman Question' in the Revolution of 1978–79." *International Journal of Middle East Studies* 26(2): 223–47.

———. 1997. "The Politics of the Veil: Reflections on Symbolism, Islam, and Feminism." *Thamyris* 4(2):325–37.

———. 1998a. "Feminism in Iran: In Search of What?" *Zanan* 40:32–38 (in Persian).

———. 1998b. "Islamic Feminism Encounters Western Feminism: An Indigenous Alternative?" Paper presented at the Women's Studies 1998–99 Seminar on Globalization, Gender, and Pedagogy, Illinois State University, Normal.

———. 1999. "Saving the Savior." *Sociological Inquiry* 69(2):303–27.

Tabari, Azar [Afsaneh Najmabadi], and Nahid Yeganeh [Parvin Paidar], eds. 1982. *In the Shadow of Islam: The Women's Movement in Iran.* London: Zed.

Tohidi, Nayereh. 1991. "Gender and Islamic Fundamentalism: Feminist Politics in Iran." In *Third World Women and the Politics of Feminism,* ed. Chandra Talpady Mohanty, Ann Russo, and Lourdes Torres, 251–67. Bloomington: Indiana University Press.

———. 1994. "Modernity, Islamization, and Women in Iran." In *Gender and National Identity: Women and Politics in Muslim Societies,* ed. Valentine M. Moghadam, 110–47. London: Zed.

———. 1997a. *Feminism, Democracy, and Islamism in Iran.* Los Angeles: Ketabsara (in Persian).

———. 1997b. "'Islamic Feminism': A Democratic Challenge or a Theocratic Reaction?" *Kankash* 13:106 (in Persian).

———. 1998. "The Issues at Hand." In *Women in Muslim Societies: Diversity within Unity*, ed. Herbert Bodman and Nayereh Tohidi, 277–94. Boulder, Colo.: Lynne Rienner.

———. 1999. "Gender, Modernity, and Democracy." *Jenss-e Dovvom*, pts. 1 and 2, 1378 (3–4) (in Persian).

Vahdat, Farzin. In press. *God and the Juggernaut: Iran's Intellectual Encounter with Modernity.* Syracuse, N.Y.: Syracuse University Press.

Yeganeh, Nahid [Parvin Paidar]. 1982. "Women's Struggles in the Islamic Republic of Iran." In Tabari and Yeganeh 1982, 26–74.

Zanganeh, Hamid, ed. 1999. "Student Unrest." Special issue of *Journal of Iranian Research and Analysis*, vol. 15, no. 2.

———. 2000. "The Sixth Majles Election." Special issue of *Journal of Iranian Research and Analysis*, vol. 16, no. 1.

Zanan. 1992. Issue no. 1, 1370 (February).

———. 1997a. No. 33.

———. 1997b. No. 35.

———. 1999. No. 54.

Zan-e Rouz. 1994. 30 Mehr 1373 (November).

The Politics of Feminism in Islam

The gender question should be reexamined, as the gender revolution was
intended in Islam but never took off. It was aborted arguably for two
reasons: a) mainstream Islam turned royalist from the Ummayids [first
ruling Islamic dynasty] onwards, and the harem developed and became
more secluded as a more aristocratic version of Islam developed, and b) the
doors of ijtihad [intellectual effort] closed and the gender revolution was
thereby aborted.
— Mazrui 1993, 533

We strongly affirm that feminism strives for the broadest and deepest
development of society and human beings free of *all* systems of
domination.
— Sen and Grown 1987, 19

Recent ideological shifts in Western capitalist countries have impelled
many Muslim intellectuals to examine the discourses of feminism and
human rights in the Islamic world and explore indigenous models of
emancipation for the masses in general and women in particular. While the
widely held assumption that women have been historically persecuted
by all patriarchal cultures is, to a large extent, incontestably true, the
discourses of Western[1] feminism, largely shaped by gender relations in

I would like to thank the anonymous reviewers who read my manuscript in its various
phases and the editorial staff at *Signs* for their thoroughly competent work. It should be noted
that this article is part of a larger attempt to rethink post-Eurocentric possibilities by exploring
alternatives rooted in other human traditions. I hope the reader manages to differentiate
Islam as a rich tradition with complex and contradictory legacies from the political extremism
espoused by parochial militants. The goal is not to let extremists monopolize the rich vocabulary of Islam and create a one-dimensional image of the religion. Yet both religion and image
can only be fully comprehended if situated in a wider global context where inequalities produce excesses and distort realities. Finally, one does not have to be religious to explore Islamic
possibilities in post-Eurocentric and postcapitalist arrangements. Reading others through
one's cultural and personal lenses needs to be tempered by a commitment to a critical, non-
hegemonic multiculturalism.
    [1] I am using the term *West* to refer to a somewhat identifiable cultural/economic matrix
that includes mostly Europe and its settler population overseas. The native populations and
those, such as Africans, who were forced into exile occupy a more complex place within

Christian capitalist cultures and by the exhausted paradigms of Western social thought, have hindered a more subtle appreciation of women's issues under Islam. This is because "the relationship between Islamism and 'women's rights' is often presented in an unusually heated environment," a situation that leads to "short cuts in analysis" (Burgat 1993, 101). Describing the current Islamic resurgence as a strategic component in the South's (Third World) attempt to contest Western hegemony in the domains of culture and ideology, Burgat is rather suspicious of "the ideological repositioning of the South [and its confinement] into the analytical ghetto of 'misogyny,' or with even less nuance, an 'apartheid' which is erected as a central and absolute principle 'explaining' the [Islamist] phenomenon" (101). Indeed, the rather vociferous discourses of Western feminism and human rights have far-reaching consequences for Muslim peoples, especially as "the social status of women constitutes one of the terrains on which the invasion of Western references has disturbed the dynamic of the internal normative evolution of the universe of Islam" (104). While one must expose Islamist ideologies to rigorous criticism and categorically reject all coercive and intolerant practices espoused in the name of religion, the recovery of a long-obfuscated egalitarian Islam together with an effort to reconceptualize a progressive Islam for the future are necessary undertakings if one is to go beyond a negative critique of homogenized Islamic cultures and rethink a possible indigenous path to women's emancipation.

In this article I argue that a critical redefinition and a thorough reassessment of Islamic traditions, including contesting several entrenched but Islamically questionable assumptions about women, are the proper platform on which to conduct dialogues and movements of liberation in the Islamic world today. Islamic societies are products of history; they bear the imprints of time and change. To rely uncritically on old canonical documents as the foundation of a new Islamic revival would run counter to the best tendencies in Islamic intellectual history. In fact, even certain aspects of the Prophet's life have not always been translated into general practice among Muslims. After carefully studying the Prophet Mohammed's relationships with women, and implying that his marriage to the six-year-old 'Aisha

---

the Western social order, as do the working classes and political minorities who have been marginalized by the ruling elites. While the West is ultimately a secular ideological concept born out of Europe's multiple crusades against the Other, the Westernization of non-European elites started as a deliberate policy designed to enhance the interests of colonial powers and maintain their hegemony over their colonies. For a very good analysis of the meaning and impact of the West, see Latouche 1989 and Von Laue 1987.

(consummated when the bride was nine) has not set a legal precedent in Islamic countries, Leila Ahmed wonders "whether the religion is to be allowed to remain permanently locked into replicating the outer forms of the specific society into which it was revealed, or whether the true pursuit and fulfillment of the Islamic message entails, on the contrary, the gradual abandonment of laws necessary in its first age" (1986, 677). Although the answer to such a proposition should be fairly simple (at least to progressive elements within the Islamic tradition), a practical solution has remained dauntingly elusive, especially as Islam evolved from an initial phase of tolerance to the gradual marginalization of women and their enclosure in the dark world of a theologically illegitimate patriarchy. This debilitating climate of oppression needs to be shattered through a revolutionary understanding of Islam and the restoration of "early Sufi and Qarmati thought," long eclipsed by a conservative, male-dominated clerical Islam (691). Only through the retrieval of this emancipatory tradition, Ahmed convincingly argues, would Muslim women "not be compelled to make the intolerable choice between religious belief and their own autonomy and self-affirmation" (679).

Yet as problematic as clerical Islam are the ideologically suspect discourses of unexamined Western social science theories. Marnia Lazreg (1988) has clearly demonstrated the bankruptcy of exhausted paradigms for interpreting the Middle Eastern and North African worlds and criticized both U.S. and "Eastern" feminists for failing to represent the heterogeneity and complexity of Arab[2] societies. Not only do U.S. feminists often assume that in order for Arab women to become real feminists they must dissociate themselves from Arab men and their own culture, but their attitude is often informed by an unmistakable bias against Islam (85, 88). Indeed, many Arab women become complicitous allies in propagating this reductionist interpretation of their societies; passing for social criticism, their "personal confessions" are often given a conspicuous forum in the West, even while these Arab women themselves are transformed into representatives for the millions of women on whose behalf they were never allowed to speak (89). The fetishization of Islam, Lazreg explains, obscures "the living reality of the women and men subsumed under it" and erases "the socioeconomic and political context within which it unfolds" (95). Hence, a contrapuntal reading (to use Edward Said's [1993] recently popularized metaphor for keeping the dialectical formations of cultural

---

[2] Whenever I use the word *Arab,* I do so only to reflect the original designations in my references. Epistemological confusions are one of the pitfalls of studying Islamic societies today (see n. 3 below).

consciousness firmly in mind at all times) of the feminist project in Islam seems to be indispensable if one is not to isolate any analysis from the global currents that both inform it and could, in turn, be influenced by it.

Since neither global capitalism nor a male-dominated and historically entrenched version of Islam is conducive to a genuinely liberating Islamic[3] culture, the feminist project is challenged with the monumental task of contesting both orthodoxies simultaneously and dialectically. The feminist question in Islam is necessarily implicated in the crosscurrents of several contestatory discourses and ideologies, including women versus the patriarchy within Islamic communities, the secular West versus Islam, why certain forms of Islam are politically more acceptable to the West than others, the specificity of the Islamic feminist project, and the various ideological tendencies within Islamic thought itself. Therefore, a careful articulation of an Islamically progressive agenda—democratic, antipatriarchal, and anti-imperialist[4]—might provide the impetus for a new revolutionary paradigm. This new Islamic consciousness, firmly rooted in usable traditions but uncompromisingly universal in outlook, can redefine the very meaning of Islam without abandoning the parameters of the faith. Syncretically arranged and engaged in permanent dialogue with the progressive agendas of other cultures, its ultimate goal is a culturally "polycentric" world (to use Samir Amin's [1990] expression) founded on economic socialism and gender equality. This conception of Islam alone is capable of legitimizing feminism in the Islamic world by posing a formidable challenge for clerical, orthodox Islam, which has stubbornly refused to extend more freedoms to women and minorities.

Indeed, it is in response to this new threat and the tenuous position

---

[3] The common use of the adjective *Islamic* to refer to civilizations or cultures shaped, in varying degrees, by the religion of Islam is theoretically confusing, if not outright misleading, as the late Marshall G. S. Hodgson argued in the introduction to his magnum opus, *The Venture of Islam* (1977). For Hodgson, the adjective *Islamic* must be restricted to the purely religious, while the more accurate *Islamicate* refers not only to the religion of Islam but also "to the social and cultural complex historically associated with Islam and the Muslims, both among Muslims themselves and even when found among non-Muslims" (59). Despite the fact that this eminent scholar made a compelling argument for the need to coin new terminology to deal with the history of "Islamdom," older prejudices continue to determine the questions asked by, and consequently the outcomes of, scholarship on Islam.

[4] I use the word *imperialism* here consciously, although expressions such as *neocolonialism*, *postcolonialism*, and others have been used frequently in recent literature. The usefulness of the term *imperialism* was the topic of a roundtable forum at the December 1992 meeting of the American Historical Association; the papers are published in *Radical History* 57 (Fall 1993): 7–84. Terms such as *postimperialism* have been suggested, but, in the final analysis, *imperialism* continues to describe adequately the underlying structures of present global and human relations.

of *clerical* Islamic (neocolonial) regimes that Western governments have resorted to the discourses of democracy and human rights (especially the rights of women) to contain the liberating possibilities of cultural alternatives. For, as I will argue, the West's promotion of human rights in the Third World is a strategy whose final aim is to stabilize political entities to facilitate the free circulation of goods and services. The U.S. policy of "low-intensity democracy" aims at creating a polyarchy that oversees "formal democratic institutions" able to channel people's grievances and "diffuse the sharpest social tensions" (see Robinson 1994). It surely needs no repeating that the existing global capitalist system has no intention of reducing poverty or creating a more humane and egalitarian civilization (see Sachs 1995). Because capitalism is structurally incapable of creating equality (see Amin 1990), committed feminists must look beyond mere reformism and toward radically different, indigenous, and pluralistic alternatives. A progressive Islam, empowered by the equal status and dynamic contributions of women and extending full rights to minorities, is therefore one way to break away from Eurocentric structures and redynamize progressive non-Western traditions in a genuinely multicultural world.

The West's crusade against Islam has been joined by Westernized Muslim writers such as Tahar ben Jelloun, Driss Chraibi, and the Indian-born Salman Rushdie, who have all attempted to depict Islam as a reactionary force that has set back or destroyed the freedoms of women and writers and eclipsed the traditions of non-Arab peoples. Such claims have proven to be controversial, lucrative, and reflective of the writer's entrapment in mainstream Western perceptions of Islam. Ben Jelloun's treatment of gender in *The Sand Child* (1989) and *The Sacred Night* (1991a), for instance, earned him the prestigious Goncourt literary prize and persuaded American publishers to make his fiction available to English-speaking readers for the first time. The novels are about gender repression and sexual mutilation in an obdurately unenlightened Islamic society. In *The Sand Child,* Hajji Ahmad Suleyman, an aging patriarch with seven daughters, in an attempt to save his honor and protect the inheritance of his children from his two scheming brothers, decides that his next newborn will be a boy, regardless of the actual sex of the baby. His name will be Ahmed. A daughter is then born into this fate, at a time of nationalist struggle for independence, suggesting that the anticolonial resistance is informed by a strong patriarchal ideology. The boy's circumcision is faked, and as the girl begins to reach puberty her chest is "bandaged with white linen, pulling the bands of cloth so tight that [she] could hardly breathe. It was absolutely vital that no breasts should appear" (24). Ahmed goes through all sorts of social contortions to hide her femininity (including a fake marriage) before she lifts the veil on her true identity and enters yet another universe of violent repression.

Ben Jelloun's improbable tale of the grotesque would seem to confirm the West's suspicion that Islam is hostile to women and inhospitable to their demands for change and freedom. In fact, John Erickson has stated that "nowhere in Maghrebian literature is the problem of sexuality more graphically explored, with all of its ties to much more extended social and political problems, and linked more indissolubly with literary revolt" than in *The Sand Child* (1993, 48). Ben Jelloun, according to Erickson, sets out to undermine the "structuring values in Islamic societies" (59). It is true that Ben Jelloun would have liked his female protagonist to be "held back by no religion" and to move freely from "myth to myth" (1991a, 64); however, as a longtime resident of France, the author knows that immigration to the West is not necessarily a solution for the oppressed and persecuted girl. Indeed, his later novel *Les yeux baisses* (1991b) does problematize the migration of a Berber girl from a High Atlas village to Paris, presenting an even bleaker picture of the predicament of Muslim women within existing global arrangements. Fleeing her old, murderous aunt, the young Moroccan woman finds little relief in the gray, cold, noisy, and crowded French metropolis, where she joins her immigrant father. She awakens to her sexuality and begins to flirt with a handsome Portuguese boy, but she also loses her religious convictions and is shocked by her discovery of anti-Arab racism. Unable to return to the confining village culture she left behind and condemned to remain the Other in France, the young girl struggles throughout the novel to construct a positive identity, her eyes downcast ("les yeux baisses") mostly out of oppression, not respect. The net of oppression has been enlarged to include the cruelties of tradition, state neglect, immigration, and the damaging legacy of colonialism. Ben Jelloun's "veiled narrative" enables him, however, to avoid closure, leaving the predicament of Muslim women unsettlingly suspended.

I cite the case of Ben Jelloun's recent fiction to illustrate the complex impact feminism has had on certain Muslim novelists. Are women to be given their rightful place in the canon only if Islam is depicted in the broadest orientalist strokes?[5] Is it possible to champion women's rights while

---

[5] Orientalism is a complex and controversial concept. Perhaps the best way to describe it is as a body of knowledge — initially shaped by Christian Europe's prejudice against Islam and gradually taking the form of objective scholarship (philology, anthropology, and, in the United States, social sciences) — that is ahistorical, unevolving, and, consequently, essentialist (Said 1979, 92–110). The Orient is "less a place than a *topos*" (117), which means that it is a product of discourse, an epistemological category, a catalog of *idees reçues* codified and available to merchants and conquerors who seek to assuage their consciences (123–48). Such

simultaneously extricating progressive Islam from the deadwood of orthodoxy and the biased interpretations of much of Western scholarship? Islam
has been used in so many contradictory ways that one cannot accept, as
both orthodox jurists and orientalists have, a monolithic definition of this
religion. (Said has warned us against this repeatedly.) During the Arab
world's struggle for independence, for instance, the nationalist bourgeoisie
used Islam to rally the masses for the liberation of their occupied land and
to preserve capitalism (or, in other instances, state socialism). This form of
Islam was obviously infused with a patriarchal spirit (a problem that has
afflicted many a revolutionary movement in the twentieth century),[6] although its anti-imperialist thrust was unmistakably liberating. And it was
imperialism that, paradoxically, "created the objective basis for both the
development of women's struggles and the integration of women into the
more general national struggle against colonialism" (Salman 1978, 28–
29). But if women were temporarily liberated from the shackles of a stifling
Islamic orthodoxy by imperialism, they were eventually recontained by a
new Islamic consciousness that refused to grant them more rights, despite

---

an Orient is discursively silent and unable, from the beginning, to "represent itself"; now,
incorporated into Western cultural and economic systems, it passively "participates in its own
Orientalizing" (324–45). Orientalism is also the *distribution* of geopolitical awareness into
aesthetic, scholarly, economic, sociological, historical, and philological texts" (12), a world
divided into the "good" West and the "bad" Orient, so to speak. Orientalism is a paradoxical
scholarship that seeks an "objective" knowledge of the natives but is enshrined in "the principle of inequality" (151). Thanks to the work of Billie Melman, we now know that
the negative connotations associated with "orientalism" are mostly the result of particular
Western masculinist perceptions of the Orient. European women travelers who had an intimate — not imagined — knowledge of women's lives were able to "de-hegemonize" the Orient
through the exclusively feminine genre of "harem literature." For them, "the *orientale*, as a
fixed category of promiscuous feminine sensuality, was supplanted by 'oriental women,'
whose *sameness* to middle-class Western women was repeatedly emphasised" (Melman 1992,
311–12). In fact, English travelers and authors of harem literature may very well have been
the first to detect the insidious effects of orientalism. Julia Sophia Pardoe, author of *The City
and the Sultan and the Domestic Manners of the Turks in 1836* (1837), a classic of harem literature, defined orientalism in very much the same terms as we know it today: "The European
mind has become so imbued with ideas of Oriental mysteriousness, mysticism and magnifi-
cence, and it has been so long accustomed to pillow its faith on the marvels and metaphors
of tourists, that it is to be doubted whether it will willingly cast off its old associations, and
suffer itself to be undeceived" (quoted in Melman 1992, 99).

[6] See, e.g., Margaret Randall's critique of socialist revolutionary movements' failure to
allow for an autonomous feminist agenda in her book, *Gathering Rage* (1992). Randall argues
that the fate of socialism ultimately depends on how women are treated in epochs of revolution and beyond. "I believe," she writes, "that in each of the revolutionary experiments the
failure to develop an indigenous feminist discourse and a vital feminist agenda impeded the
consolidation that would push an otherwise more humane society forward" (160).

their heroic struggle to preserve the sanctity of Islam itself. The new nationalist regimes were thus ensnared by more contradictions, for they had copied the colonial model of the nation-state, subscribed to a multitude of international organizations controlled by former colonialists, and accepted their neocolonial status, while perpetuating a stagnant, apolitical, and mostly reactionary version of Islam. Such a complicated situation, with a variety of discourses (some legitimized by the state to suit its needs), has made an accurate reading of the Islamic sociopolitical context difficult and can be approached only from a dialectical position that recognizes the specificity and historicity of Islamic cultures and the impact of global capitalism on them.

The prominent feminist sociologist Fatima Mernissi, however, has accepted the capitalist model of human relations; she goes beyond the cautionary approach and indeterminate position of Ben Jelloun's fiction to argue quite forcefully for a bourgeois notion of democracy and individual liberties as the foundations for any Arab nation that aspires to genuine sovereignty and development.[7] Mernissi agrees that the situation of women in

[7] I am using the concept of "bourgeois democracy," although Marx is not known to have used this expression and, in fact, favored universal suffrage — wherever possible — as a strategic move to wrest power from the capitalist ruling class and its attendants. Indeed, Marxian socialists believed in this strategy until Lenin problematized it in his polemical argument with Kautsy. But Marx was fully aware that the grand freedoms granted by the bourgeoisie are, in the final analysis, heavily circumscribed by legal trappings, such as the often appended proviso of *"exceptions made by law"* or the prohibitive expense of making oneself heard. In "The Constitution of the French Republic Adopted November 4, 1848," published in 1851, Marx scathingly denounced the nullifying effect of legal and economic systems on freedom in bourgeois societies: "This trick of granting full liberty, of laying down the finest principles, and leaving their application, the *details,* to be decided by subsequent laws, the Austrian and Prussian middle-classes have borrowed from their French prototypes. . . . The middle class can be democratic in *words,* but will not be so in deeds — they will recognize the truth of a principle, but never carry it into practice" (quoted in Hunt 1984, 171). Before the collapse of the Soviet Union, many scholars, probably sobered by the Soviet nightmarish experiment, continued to argue for "reformism" within the democratic system as a useful strategy toward achieving socialism (see Miliband 1977; and for a brief history of the polemic surrounding the Marxist view of democracy, see the entry "democracy" in Bottomore [1983] 1991, 133–34). But now in the post-Soviet era, the question of whether capitalism is compatible with popular democracy is posed with a heightened sense of urgency, especially as corporate capitalism has reduced public freedoms, even in the most advanced industrialized economies, to hollow statements propagated by an increasingly privatized media. In these circumstances, the erosion of human rights should be of equal concern to U.S. intellectuals who choose to focus on Third World countries and ignore the "Brazilianization" of their own society. While the managerial techniques of "lean managment" have increased the profit margins of corporations and stockholders, the wave of "downsizing" continues unabated and is further aggravating social imbalances in the United States (see Head 1996).

Morocco must be understood in relation to both the cataclysmic changes affecting that country and the redistribution of social space in it, and she keeps the distinct histories of West and East firmly in mind, especially those regarding the treatment of women (see Mernissi [1975] 1987a). She also understands that colonialism has had the unintended effect of retarding the legitimate struggle of women by subsuming it in an uncritical Islamic ideology of resistance. In the final analysis, however, Mernissi is clearly in favor of a United Nations definition of human rights and democracy. In *La peur-modernite* (1992), she repeats the familiar orientalist thesis that only a secular modernity would be able to lift Arabs from their long and deadly paralysis, although she avoids blaming Islam itself. She even admits that Islam is the "symbolic capital" of the wretched (80–83) and the voice of the proletariat in the struggle against the beneficiaries of international capitalism (in the modern Arab state poor children go to the Qur'anic school, while the children of the upper classes attend kindergarten [110–12]). Thus, as has always been true, the oppressed derive from Islam a powerfully inspiring impulse for justice (see Hourani 1991, 137). Yet Mernissi dismisses this Islamic legacy as dated in the contemporary era and suggests, instead, that it must give way to a secular civil society, democratically organized, that protects individual freedoms. For the lack of democracy leads to a host of social ills, including immigration to the "very paradoxical" West (Mernissi 1992, 78).

Mernissi's reflections on the position of women throughout much of Islamic history imply that democracy and individual freedoms were abolished with the advent of Islam, when the Prophet Mohammed destroyed polytheism in Mecca and replaced it with an uncompromising (but benevolent) monotheism. Describing democracy as a form of *shirk* (disbelief through associating another deity with Allah), she calls for the reestablishment of the culture of polytheism that had reigned in Arabia in the pre-Islamic period and thus, in a striking parallel with Rushdie's *Satanic Verses* (1989), redefines the *Jahiliya* (the pre-Islamic period; literally, the time of ignorance) as an exciting era of discussion and human rights. According to Mernissi's metaphor, Muslims are on a crusade to veil anything that threatens their faith, whether it be Western democracy, history (associated here with polytheism and powerful goddesses), or simply any form of change. Islam is depicted as fundamentally antihistorical and antifeminist, a religion that has totally eradicated the *Jahiliya* from consciousness. In fact, Islam has even launched the new patriarchal calendar of the *Hijra* (Mernissi 1992, 170–71), which, like the Qur'anic school, has relevance only to those who are poor and abide by the faith; for it is Western time that regulates transactions in the global village. Mernissi still (intuitively) believes in an Arab takeoff (196) and criticizes the West's essentialization of Muslim women despite their remarkable accomplishments in the past few decades (206, nn. 247–48). However, her methodology desacralizes the Qur'an by reducing it to a mere historical document in *Le harem politique* (1987b), showing that it was produced in a series of human negotiations in which God always intervened — rather diplomatically — on behalf of the Prophet. For her, adopting secularism means further demystifying the transcendental process of revelation and solving all social issues through the powers of human agency, not by an uncritical resort to the male-constructed texts of Islam.

Mernissi's rereading of Islamic history — a project she considers necessary to demystify the regnant but dubious misogynist myths — can be remarkably perceptive and invigorating. If parliaments in Islamic countries are harems that exclude women from any meaningful political participation and that allow men to decide the fate of women, their roots are in the beginnings of the caliphal state, legitimized by the aristocratic principle of *bay'a* (pledge of allegiance), in which the caliph is "veiled" from the people he governs, the *'amma* (a rather derogatory word for the masses of people, akin to what the French call "le petit peuple") (see Mernissi 1990). Through brilliant etymological connections, Mernissi stretches the symbolism of the veil to include the realm of politics, demonstrating with astonishing perspicacity the erosion of political freedoms with the consolidation of the early empires based on ethnic and gender exclusions. (Arabhood and maleness were initially indispensable criteria for the position of caliph, but while the Arabhood requirement would eventually be contested, the criterion of maleness never was.)

The caliphal state (symbolized by the Friday sermon [*khotba*] and the inscription of the name of the caliph on coins) was thus to become an exclusively masculine domain, although women were allowed to rule in specific instances. However, this practice contradicted the Prophet's insistence on converting the mosque — outside of prayer time — into a democratic, public space and using the Friday *khotba* as a sort of brief public report on the affairs of the state (123–27). With the advent of the caliphal state, this mosque-based popular democracy was gradually drained of its content (130, 132) and transformed into an oppressive institution for women, who were — in clear violation of the Prophet's practice — discouraged from attending mosques (136). Closing the mosque and veiling women therefore amount to closing the political arena to democratic participation and veiling resistance to authoritarianism (140–41). Restoring women to the political arena thus becomes the necessary condition for restoring the long-eclipsed democratic spirit to Islam.

While Mernissi's reinterpretation of Islamic history does indeed challenge the unimaginative, orthodox stranglehold of the still-powerful *ulama* (religious scholars), she, like the male elites she questions, remains conspicuously silent on the bases of power in the late twentieth century. If the *ulama* are the co-opted intellectuals of feudal, patriarchal regimes in the Islamic world, late capitalism has created its own set of privileged intellectuals and theories, which, I contend, have not been sufficiently examined by Muslim feminists or Western scholars writing on feminism in the Islamic world. When Mervat Hatem (1987), after surveying scholarship on Middle Eastern women, called Mernissi "very weak" because of her "largely unsuccessful" attempt to link "the textual with the historical" and "the sexual with the economic" (816), she should have specified the context she was referring to, since Mernissi is, in fact, quite capable of historicizing Islamic texts. Mernissi's failure to understand "the material and social systems of particular epochs" is less likely an ideological strategy (as is the case with the *ulama,* who obfuscate meanings to marginalize women) than the result of the enormous task of conceptualizing a method for examining the various interlocking factors of oppression synchronically. For Hatem, such a method should be able to account for gender within a Marxist reading of social formations (818). And while Mernissi has strategically fought for the integration of women into a more democratized political process, it is now equally crucial to move beyond the false essentialization of women as ideologically neutral and examine the ways socioeconomic systems enhance or reduce the freedoms of both sexes in an increasingly globalized environment.

The struggle in the Islamic world today is, in fact, over democratizing decision making and wresting the state from the hands of regimes that have ossified religion and turned it into a tool of political control. Even the Islamic movements that now openly challenge the legitimacy of the state do not seem to object to democratic political structures, provided that they do not hinder the application of Islam (see Krämer 1993, 5). In other words, despite their lack of clearly articulated readings of canonical texts and the history of Islamic societies generally, and their inability to outline a coherent vision of the future, many revivalist movements share the same general aspirations of liberating Muslim people from the dependencies imposed on them in the modern period. The widespread fear that Islam cannot open genuine spaces for democratic practice cannot be justified by historical precedent. Mernissi herself has shown—despite her occasional privileging of the pre-Islamic period—that a popular form of mosque-centered democracy existed during the Prophet's time and that it was the caliphal political system that violated the early Islamic principles.[8] Hence, depending on how it is done, and from which ideological perspective, the recovery of an Islamic past, thoroughly cleansed of the residue of centuries of male-dominated interpretations, can be useful to women fighting for freedom in the Islamic world. Some of the feminists mentioned in this article (such as Mernissi) have already taken the step of dusting off the pages of history, and it is now the task of other Muslim and socialist feminists to build on these monumental efforts.[9]

Nawal El Saadawi's feminist and "contrapuntal" critique of Arab patriarchy was, in fact, remarkably comprehensive almost two decades ago, when she subjected all grand narratives to uncompromising critique without using the mantle of "culture" to disguise distinct power relations: imperialists are imperialists, and pathological Muslim men who find satisfaction in the mutilation of women's bodies are just that (see El Saadawi 1980). Like Mernissi, she implies that the orthodox version of Islam enshrined in the *Shari'a* has curtailed the freedoms and power enjoyed by women during not only the pre-Islamic period (*Jahiliya*) but also the early stages of Islam, when women like 'Aisha, the youngest of the Prophet's wives, exercised a high degree of authority and independence (125–31). Undoubtedly, legalized clerical Islam privileged the male through the sanction of men's polygamy and the insistence on women's monogamy (which could mean the legalization of prostitution for the benefit of men). It also adopted some Christian motifs, such as the separation of body and soul, which El Saadawi views as one of the greatest afflictions of the human race, for it associates sexuality with sinfulness and tends, as in Christianity, to emphasize a cult of virginity that not infrequently leads to frigidity (149–50, 120–21). Women have thus come to be associated with *fitna* (chaos) and pleasure, which are "contradictory, and in terms of logic, mutually exclusive conceptions" (137), but which seem to have conditioned Arab men's ambiguous attitude and inhibited their adequate examination of the tragedy of women in their cultures (165, 167). The Arab man's honor, as Ben Jelloun dramati-

[8] However, as Leila Ahmed (1992) and Weibke Walther (1993) have shown, many aspects of the caliphal system were borrowed from major pre-Islamic civilizations.

[9] There is a tacit understanding among Marxists that, while the Islamic struggle against imperialism needs to be supported, the reactionary tendencies of the petite bourgeoisie (the main support base of Islamic revivalist movements today) must be rigorously critiqued (see Marshall 1988). Although I believe that no emancipatory system can be complete without a thorough understanding of capitalism, I must stress that Islam is a broadly defined philosophy of life rather than the set of narrowly defined principles proposed by certain militants. With the exception of a few rules in the Qur'an, one can negotiate any ideology within the wide and amorphous parameters of the faith. In the medieval period, Islam "permitted many schools of thought, great freedom of thought, and tremendous development of philosophical and scientific thinking" (Rodinson 1981, 66).

cally illustrates in *The Sand Child* and *The Sacred Night,* still depends on the compliance and domination of women, although the patriarchal family is increasingly weakened by the modern state, which renders many precolonial practices and other concepts of honor impractical (207; also see Mernissi 1987a, 172–73).

El Saadawi's indictment of the unholy global alliance of Western imperialism and reactionary Islamic jurisprudence and customs to maintain the inferior status of women is, however, complex enough to allow for a progressive and recuperable Islamic agenda. She calls on Western feminists to understand that "in underdeveloped countries, liberation from foreign domination often still remains *the* crucial issue" and that women in the Arab world are more interested in it than in freedom of speech and belief, "male chauvinism," or copying the social models of affluent Western societies: "In its essence, the struggle which is now being fought seeks to ensure that the Arab peoples take possession of their economic potential and resources, and of their scientific and cultural heritage so that they can develop whatever they have to the maximum and rid themselves once and for all of the control and domination exercised by foreign capitalist interests. They seek to build a free society with equal rights for all and to abolish the injustices and oppression of systems based on class and patriarchal privilege" (ix–x). Thus, El Saadawi took the unfashionable stance of seeing the Islamic revolution in Iran as essentially liberating and as reminiscent of an "early Islam [that] laid the first foundations of what might be called Primitive Socialism," which would later be eclipsed by a successive line of rulers, beginning with "Osman Ibn Affan, the Third caliph of the Muslims and head of the Ommayad dynasty in Damascus" and ending with American imperialism and its agents in the Arab world (iii). Given El Saadawi's insistence on preserving Arab people's "cultural heritage" free of the deculturing tendencies of capitalism, she calls for (and applies) a methodology that would "visualize the links between the political, economic and social remoulding of society, and the cultural, moral, psychological, sexual and affective remoulding of the human being" (xvi). It is not possible, El Saadawi argues, "to separate the sexual and emotional life of people, and their economic life," for "any separation is artificial and will lead to ideas that are incomplete, shallow and distorted" (182).[10]

---

[10] Evelyne Accad (1991), by contrast, singles out macho Mediterranean Arabs and (especially Marxist) feminists who subsume sexual pleasure under the overriding imperative of class struggle and cultural liberation as culprits in retarding women's emancipation in the Arab world. For Accad, a healthier attitude toward sexuality (love, pleasure) will temper other passions and bring civil war in Lebanon to an end. Thus, a liberated sexuality should be treated as fundamental in the nationalist struggle of the Lebanese — and other Arab — peoples

I   I   I

An example of the shallow debate that has characterized the question of feminism in Islam is the issue of the veil as a token of women's repression. For the Western media, the picture of the veiled woman visually defines both the mystery of Islamic culture and its backwardness.[11] Despite its close association with Islam, the veil is in fact an old eastern Mediterranean practice that was assimilated by Islam in its early stages of expansion. In the two suras in the Qur'an that refer to the veil, not only is there no specific mention of veiling the face but certain parts of the body in fact are assumed to be visible (see Walther 1993, 69–70). Women in pre- and early Islamic Arabia actively contributed to social and economic life, and only through the gradual absorption of other civilizations into the world of Islam was the "ethical vision" of the new religion—a vision that is "stubbornly egalitarian, including with respect to the sexes" (Ahmed 1992,

---

(237–60). Strange as this theory may seem (for the fate of Lebanon was and still is entangled in regional and global contestations for hegemony and sovereignty), the equation of feminism with a Western-style mode of existence has been the most conspicuous public assumption in some North African countries. Paris-based periodicals such as *Jeune Afrique* never tire of promoting the image of superficially Westernized women as liberated. But free sexuality has its downsides too, as the recent heartwrenching autobiography of Ken Bugul (the pseudonym for Marietou M'Baye) clearly shows. Once she arrives in Europe, Bugul realizes that virginity in Africa tied her to an "entire generation of mores and traditions" and that sexuality and culture are, in the final analysis, inseparable. "Sexuality is culture and atmosphere," wrote the uprooted Senegalese woman (Bugul 1991, 48, 52).

[11] Claire Dwyer (1991–92) has discussed "the fetishisation of the veil as the signifier of both Oriental women and of the Orient" in her astute study of photographic representations of Islam. She notes the West's fascination with the veil and demonstrates how it has come to "represent a whole constellation of meanings over time—mystery, exoticism, forbiddeness [*sic*], sensuality, sexuality, backwardness, resistance, domination, passivity, religious fundamentalism" (8). This all-signifying motif, inherited from an enduring legacy of orientalism, is also an apt metaphor both for the West's perpetual attempt to undress Muslims and make them available to its gaze and for Muslims' equally obdurate resistance to such crude efforts. Lazreg (1988) states that "the persistence of the veil as a symbol that essentially stands for women illustrates the difficulty researchers have in dealing with a reality with which they are unfamiliar" (85). Even Mernissi has been convinced, despite her protestations, by French and German editors to put the word *harem* in the title of her books to enhance their marketability. It is almost as if the West wants to hold onto an image of an archaic Islam that has been radically transformed by modernity. Otherwise, how is one to explain the fact that the ratio of women to men college professors in Iran was higher than Germany's in 1986 (19 percent and 17 percent, respectively) or that the same ratio in Egypt in 1986 (28 percent) was higher than that of the United States in 1980 (24 percent) and France in 1987 (23 percent)? (See Mernissi 1992, 206–7, 209, and n. 10.)

63)—gradually eclipsed. From the birth of Islam in Arabia to the rise of the Abbasids, the position of women seemed negotiable; however, as Islam expanded, non-Arab prejudices against women were written into Islamic law (many theologians who later developed and interpreted the *Shari'a* were of non-Arab stock [Walther 1993, 6–7, 60–61]), and the egalitarian message of early Islam was conveniently forgotten. It was this "legal and social vision of establishment Islam [that] gave precedence to women's obligations to be wives and mothers" (Ahmed 1992, 66). Even the few misogynist elements in the *hadith* (sayings attributed to the Prophet) may have been influenced by Muslims' contact with Christian asceticism, especially since Islam, unlike the belief widespread in Christendom for so long, never asserted that "women have no soul" (Walther 1993, 51). Because it was the ancient Middle East and not Arabian customs and early Islamic practices that provided the prototype for harems adopted by the Abbasids and later dynasties (94), Leila Ahmed strongly suggests that had the earlier "ethical voice" been heard, "it would have significantly tempered the extreme androcentric bias of the law, and we might today have a far more humane and egalitarian law regarding women" (1992, 88).

Still, the erosion of women's rights, enforced by a male-constructed law, did not silence or immobilize women entirely; nor were men equally content with the subordinate status of their female partners. Mernissi has written an entire book (1990) about women who managed to rise to political leadership despite the odds against them, and Ibn Battuta, the renowned Moroccan traveler from Tangier, was impressed by the large number of women who still attended prayers in the mosque when he was in Shiraz (Mernissi 1990, 135). Indeed, Afsaneh Najmabadi (1993) has convincingly demonstrated that many Iranian women (especially those from the upper class) were learned and cultured well into the modern period and that the image of premodern Iranian women as illiterate and silent (because veiled) is a modernist distortion of traditional women's real lives. Because the orality of premodern culture required a homosocial setting where no male presence was allowed, Muslim women told their own uncensored stories, completely unconcerned with the prudish repressive values that were later ushered in with modernity. Muslim women in Islamic Spain of the eleventh and twelfth centuries (who were admittedly freer than their counterparts in the East) displayed an astonishing measure of erotic freedom in their public poems and their own personal lifestyles (see Walther 1993, 144–49). Even the premodern veiled women of polygamous harems were both sexually and economically freer than their European contemporaries. When Lady Mary Wortley Montagu traveled to Turkey in the eighteenth century, she wrote that she "never saw a country where women may enjoy so much liberty, and free from all reproach as in Turkey" (quoted in Melman 1992, 87).

Indeed, as late as the nineteenth century, English women continued to report on the superiority of Turkish women in almost every sphere of social life, including hygiene, economics, and legal rights. In her *Women of Turkey, and Their Folklore* (1893), the first complete ethnographic study of women in the Middle East, Mary Lucy Garnet praised Muslim women and launched a bitter attack on Christian misogyny, "the Liberal state," and "the movement for universal suffrage"; she even made an astonishing critique of John Stuart Mill, who, in his *Subjection of Women,* failed to distinguish among the status of women in various cultures (see Melman 1992, 106–7).

The harem did not prevent Egyptian women from conducting business and international trade within the Islamic ecumene prior to Western encroachment. Allied with the *'ulama,* women exercised sufficient control over their lives "to go to courts and sue, for divorce, for business deals, for unpaid loans, i.e. for exactly the same things as men (except that men could repudiate their wives and women had to sue for divorce)" (Marsot 1996, 39). There is also evidence that some women beat their husbands and appeared "unveiled in public" (40). With the Westernization of social institutions under Mohammed 'Ali, however, the major trade routes "to and from the Hijaz, Syria and the rest of the Ottoman Empire" were reoriented toward Europe, eroding Muslim women's access and economic independence (41–44). Similarly, while traditional, veiled women told stories with what today might be considered pornographic content and, at the same time, made copious references to Islamic texts to bolster their arguments, this discursive freedom was veiled by modern women who sanitized their descriptions with the help of the exalted language of science and frequent references to European writers and women (Najmabadi 1993, 487–504).

Iran's anxiety to catch up with the West and to liberate itself from the curse of backwardness led to the establishment of a new educational system privileging science and including "courses on home management, education of children, hygiene, fine arts and crafts, and [in some instances, French] cooking" (507). The chaste woman was to become the one who propelled her country into the future, erasing obsolete traditional practices and relating to her husband the way European and American women did: "The woman of modernity, thus crafted through the construction of a veiled language and a disciplined de-eroticized body, as well as through the acquisition of scientific sensibilities, could now take her place next to her male counterpart in public heterosocial space. Instead of being envisaged as a threat to social order, her very disciplined language and body became the embodiment of the new order. Unlike her traditional Other who was scripted not only illiterate but crudely sexual, a shrew if not a whore, she could now be imagined unveiled" (Najmabadi 1993, 510). This hollow conception of freedom advanced by women trapped in the discourse of modernity would, ironically, be taken at face value by the Islamists in the post-1970s period, when the veil was mistakenly revalorized as the true symbol of chastity (511–12). And while women's general condition has deteriorated since the advent of the caliphal state, one must make a similar effort of painstaking differentiation and sort out the good men (such as the Andalusian and Moorish philosophers Ibn al-'Arabi [1165–1240] and Ibn Rushd or Averroes [1126–98]) who, in contradistinction to the proverbially harsh 'Umar al-Khattab (the second of the four Righteous Caliphs) and the influential Khorasan-born scholar/philosopher Abu Hamid al-Ghazali (1058–1111), strongly argued for the emancipation of women (see Walther 1993, 40).

Hence, within the temporal and spatial world of Islam, the position of women and male attitudes toward them were determined by a variety of social factors, not least of which was ethnicity. Yet, despite these variations, the fact remains that women — until the shock of European imperialism unleashed new agendas and turned them into a contentious topic of debate — had been increasingly confined in private spaces and harems and could only socialize in certain circumstances, such as in the *hammams* (public baths). It is rather tragic that the emergence of the status of women as an issue of major social concern would be ensnared by the reigning discourses of modernity and its antithetical defensive Islamic response. Often, both discourses fail to register the subtle nuances of history, and both demonstrate an inadequate grasp of the centrifugal forces that have been shattering world cultures in the modern period.

Muslim women's entrapment in a false debate may well have started, Ahmed contends, with the publication of Qasim Amin's book *Tahrir Al-Mar'a* (The liberation of women) in 1899. Amin, who was unabashedly apologetic for European genocidal wars and colonialism, used the pretext of the veil, as the British had done before him, to launch an assault on Islam, despite Victorian England's own patriarchal attitude toward British women. The book was subsequently suspected of playing into the hands of British colonialism and its designs on Islam, and it prompted a strong defense of the veil and other un-Islamic practices as irrevocably indigenous. The publication of Amin's book and the reaction to it became a "precursor or prototype" of the ensuing debate that mired the feminist agenda in larger and more confusing issues of cultural and political sovereignty:

> Amin's book then marks the entry of the colonial narrative of women and Islam — in which the veil and the treatment of women

epitomized Islamic inferiority—into mainstream Arabic discourse. And the opposition it generated similarly marks the emergence of an Arabic narrative developed in resistance to the colonial narrative. The veil came to symbolize in the resistance narrative, not the inferiority of the culture and the need to cast aside its customs in favor of those of the West, but, on the contrary, the dignity and validity of all native customs coming under attack—the customs relating to women—and the need to tenaciously affirm them as a means of resistance to Western domination. (Ahmed 1992, 163–64)

European hostility and orientalism, then, fundamentalize Islam into a defensive orthodoxy and largely dictate the cultural agenda of the Muslim peoples, since "it is Western discourse that in the first place determined the new meanings of the veil and gave rise to its emergence as a symbol of resistance" (164). The process of Western hegemony stimulates reactionary tendencies within Islamic cultures and delays women's emancipation from the clutches of clerical Islam. Because the most privileged and Westernized classes in Arab society eagerly surrendered to the cultural imperialism that was an integral part of the colonial process, the disinherited masses resorted to Islamic doctrine, even the most obscurantist practices, as a form of resistance to the perceived onslaught on their identity. Positions were thus dangerously polarized and hardened.

That it was Egyptian and Iranian upper-class women who first condemned native customs as backward, proclaimed the superiority of the West, and uncompromisingly equated unveiling with liberation is not only historically ironic but also reveals the class structure of the Islamic world today. Many upper-class women who advocate unveiling may only be interested in conforming to trends in international fashion, which, like the veil of old, are inaccessible to the poor (see Walther 1993, 208). While the class appropriation of veiling has shifted from the upper classes to the lower ones, the meaning and symbolism of a woman's dress in the Islamic world today is still determined by regional attitudes, inherited legacies, and the negotiation of identity within the hegemonic structures of capitalism. Still, whether veiled or not, women's conditions are determined not by the clothes they wear, but by the degree to which they manage to forge an identity for themselves that is not manipulated by the (often male-constructed) discourses of modernity or religious authenticity.

When, on January 8, 1936, Reza Shah Pahlevi (r. 1921–41) decreed compulsory unveiling in public places, associating Muslim women's traditional attire with residual backwardness, he mindlessly "inflicted pain and terror" on many women accustomed to the symbolism of the veil (see Milani 1992, 28, 35). While unveiling women was then seen as a symbolic act of the nation's resolve to catch up with modernity, the oil-based "sultanistic state" of Muhammad Reza Shah, no longer relying on its traditional base of support among social elites, simply resorted to repression in order to accomplish the same goal of modernization. Under this regime, women's rights became royal grants (see Najmabadi 1991, 59, 60, 63). The revolt against the dictatorial powers of the late Shah was thus accompanied by a general repudiation of the West, stretched by Islamic militants to associate veiling with the fight against imperialism. As Iran has tried to come to terms with the challenge of the West for more than a century, and as state ideologies of emancipation have shifted from nationalist modernity to sultanistic authoritarianism to "the moral purification of a corrupt society" (Najmabadi 1987, 203), women's status has been determined largely by the confrontation between the changing images of a hegemonic West and a defensive Islam. This larger conflict has complicated the agenda for Muslim women, and in this seemingly interminable civilizational tension Muslim feminists find themselves caught, as Ahmed eloquently puts it, between the two "opposing loyalties" of sex and culture, "forced almost to choose between betrayal and betrayal" (quoted in Kandiyoti 1991, 7).

Decreeing veiling or unveiling, however, does not make women willingly transform themselves overnight, en masse, for the sake of new ideologies (see Milani 1992, esp. 19–45). Just as many women today have resisted veiling and continue to read it from a modernist perspective, some early Islamic feminists resisted the ideologies of modernity by arguing for a gradualist approach, claiming that it was still premature to do away with the veil, given men's unenlightened attitudes and upper-class women's interest in (Western) fashion only — instead, feminists such as Malak Hifna Nassef (1886–1918) focused on promoting education and abolishing polygamy (see Ahmed 1992, chap. 9). If this discourse of Islamic "female affirmation" — widely shared by influential Islamic organizations such as the Muslim Brethren — is still, according to Ahmed, "mostly unchronicled" (195), it may be because the dominating currents of Western feminism partake in many of the assumptions of Western secularism and orientalist legacies, as well as other liberal bourgeois values (such as a dehistoricized notion of human rights and an implicit acceptance of the bourgeois political apparatus as a reliable mechanism for negotiating the grievances of the exploited).

In its reappearance in the past two decades, however, the veil acquired a new symbolism and cannot be read within the set of symbolic earlier binarisms described by Najmabadi. In countries where the veil is not mandated, many women choose it both as a reaction to the failed bourgeois nationalist program of the postindependence era (although there is still a great deal of male coercion) and as part of the mainstream, middle-class rejection of the secular ideologies that have dominated public life. Veiling cannot, in these historical circumstances, "be constructed as regressive" (Ahmed 1992, 244) and must be seen as the younger women's recuperation and affirmation of their heretofore marginalized identity.[12] Islamic dress is "the uniform of arrival" (225), the latest stage in a long struggle against colonialism and the postcolonial elites who, although politically secular, continue to impose a false Islamic orthodoxy on the people they govern. The veil is a reminder that most Islamic societies are still part of the global neocolonial order and that the collective process of liberation through the recuperation of a mutilated identity is far from complete. The response the veil elicits is thus, to a large extent, a symbolic statement about continuing class struggle in the Islamic world: hence Ahmed's call for the same multilayered, anti-imperialist position already practiced by feminists such as Nawal El Saadawi in *The Hidden Face of Eve* (1980).

I I I

This feminist position, however, requires an examination of the validity of secularism as a project in the Islamic world. While establishing a secular political structure finally may not be problematic (as long as it remains a technical matter and does not infringe on basic Islamic values it is not likely to elicit much resistance), the secularization of the Revelation and of the Prophet's life has been universally rejected, if not condemned, by the Islamic world (as the case of Rushdie amply demonstrates) and cannot be the basis of any emancipatory social movement in the Arab and Islamic worlds. Secularism, the separation of state and church, is, historically, a Western phenomenon, originating as much from the schisms that afflicted the church as from the post-Enlightenment period (see Lewis 1991, 14, 17; and Esposito 1992, 199–203). It cannot be superimposed on a culture in which human agency is constantly negotiating its boundaries with those of the Revelation, in which accommodation to divine intent is a fundamental principle. But this is precisely the agenda of secular elites in remolding Islamic countries, and, because of it, a new form of orientalism has emerged to equate the re-Islamization of secularized discourses with a new barbarism that aims at throwing these countries back into a medieval obscurantism.

---

[12] Professional Muslim women in Turkey have been fighting the ban against wearing headscarves at work. The fact that the Turkish Bar Association's 1985 dress code prohibits headscarves means that secularism has a superficial hold on Turkish society and can be maintained only by decree. See Bohlen 1995.

Few Western(ized) scholars have questioned the validity of secularism as a global project, although it is well known that the concept is the intellectual product of a specific moment in European history. Moreover, even fewer scholars have examined the fundamental imperialism of the epistemology of secularism, which Abdulwahab al Masseri has cogently exposed.

> Secularism is not a separation between religion and the state, as propagated in both western and Arab writing. Rather, it is the removal of absolute values — epistemological and ethical — from the world such that the entire world — humanity and nature alike — becomes merely a utilitarian object to be utilized and subjugated. From this standpoint, we can see the structural similarity between the secular epistemological vision and the imperialist epistemological vision. We can also realize that imperialism is no more than the exporting of a secular and epistemological paradigm from the western world, where it first emerged, to the rest of the world. (al Masseri 1994, 403)

At a time when the reigning ideology of capitalism has desacralized all of human life for the sake of a destructive acquisitiveness, the need to open up noncapitalist spaces is more urgent than ever. The insistence on establishing an alternative social imaginary makes Islam appear as the perennial threat it has always been,[13] especially because, as Burgat has suggested, Islam may well be the most authentic voice of the South in its struggle against the Western-inspired and racially informed hegemonic aims of transnational capital.[14] Whatever the case, it has become quite clear that the nationalist secularist model of the postindependence period has utterly failed to emancipate the people and is now seen as a dismal failure (see Esposito 1992, 15–16, 22–23).

---

[13] Most recently, even while the project of the Enlightenment is increasingly being questioned, the reconfiguration of the world into civilizations rather than ideologies is gaining more attention. Samuel Huntington's 1993 essay "The Clash of Civilizations?" elicited a spirited response and launched a worldwide discussion. The intractability and endurance of Islam in the face of overwhelming odds (modernity, genocide in Bosnia, superior Western military power, and unabated orientalism) may have led to this renewed interest in the study of civilizations. The attempt to replace the red menace with a green one in the United States is still under way, despite the proliferation of scholarship that rejects the simplistic reduction of different movements and ideologies into an undifferentiated radicalism. For a recent example, see Sciolino 1996. Of course, this is also another ploy to distract attention from growing global inequities and a corresponding socialist critique of a new world order increasingly shaped by multinational corporations.

[14] See also Mazrui 1990, 219. Transnational corporations are segregating the world into a new apartheid, with the North controlling most of the world's resources (see Falk 1993).

Dominant Western secular ideologies must therefore be questioned and resisted where viable traditions of social organization can lay the framework for a more humane and egalitarian society.[15] If Islam is increasingly seen as the outstanding (and enduring) example of this alternative, then a vigilant resistance to the sort of monolithism persistently denounced by Edward Said and to the partiarchal extremism that seeks to subvert the progressive and prophetic essence of Islam must continue to guide all attempts at emancipatory reform. For Islam is primarily a cosmopolitan culture that, since its inception, has preached the sort of ethnic and religious tolerance that many Western societies are still trying to achieve,[16] although it has long failed to eradicate certain social and political inequities based on class, gender, and religion. In fact, the upheaval that Islam underwent with the advent of European colonialism may have strained social relations further and exacerbated un-Islamic patriarchal practices, for colonial subjects were bewildered by two worldviews and could only escape the resulting confusion either by embracing one or the other or by vacillating in the middle and never formulating a position of their own.

The institutionalization of the nation-state (an outcome of a secular epistemology) is in itself a form of cultural aggression against Islam and other cultures that share in the communal traditions of kinship and honor.[17] Furthermore, the nation-state has had catastrophic effects on much of the Third World, where thousands of culturally autonomous communities were subjugated through the tyranny of dictatorships and parasitic bureaucracies, often financed and upheld by metropolitan centers. Indeed, no agency has succeeded in oppressing the peoples of the Third World more successfully than the state with its wide-reaching apparatuses of social and political control and its affiliation with international organiza-

[15] Certain Western environmentalists are also critical of the Enlightenment as a social project and are increasingly sacralizing nature to protect it from the destruction that befell it with the advent of objectification (see Morin 1989).

[16] The cosmopolitan Islamicate society is the successor to a variety of cultures and high civilizations that had existed at the strategic heart of the "Oikoumene"—the Nile-to-Oxus region, which, by the end of the Axial age, had become culturally a rather distinct area. Hellenistic, Indic, Irano-Semitic, and, later, Roman and Sasanid traditions converged to give the birthplace of the early Islamic empires, already at the heart of a large mercantile nexus, a very urban outlook (see Hodgson 1977, 103–45). The tolerance of minorities such as Jews in Islamdom has been duly noted by Bernard Lewis (1984), and the coexistence of all three monotheistic faiths in Islamic Spain (al-Andalus) is frequently mentioned. For a classic example, see Lane-Poole (1886) 1990.

[17] Many years of scholarship on Africa have led Basil Davidson (1992) to conclude that the nationalist elites turned their backs on their own traditions and usable past and finished the project of colonialism by establishing Eurocentric models of governance (nation-states).

tions designed to further the conquest of the poor through debt and other economic schemes. The case of the Arab Gulf states, in all their mythical splendor, is a concrete illustration of this new world order where natural wealth, if not carefully managed by unscrupulous financiers, leads inexorably to dependency and erodes the simple but self-sufficient economies that once granted autonomy to these societies.[18] The rejection of certain Western secular models in the age of late capitalism is consequently a survival imperative for Muslim people, not just a fanatical reaction to "progress."

Yet, despite its enduring strengths, Islam is now incontestably challenged by the universalized ideology of modernity and cannot resist its interpellating discourses simply by rationalizing the *Shari'a* or by proving the infallibility of the Qur'an in the Revelation's consistency with modern scientific discoveries (see Hoodbhoy 1991). The resumption of *ijtihad* (intellectual effort) and the differentiation of the ethico-religious from the existing socioeconomic (in the granting of equal divorce rights and the elimination of polygamy) appear to be necessary steps in creating a more equitable and inclusive public space for Muslim women (Esposito 1982, 116, 108). The restoration of what Esposito calls "the dynamic relationship of *ijtihad* and *ijma'* [consensus]" (1982, 124, 133), which to me suggests innovation within tradition, is an equally urgent undertaking to avoid other superficial configurations and can only be achieved through an indigenous and progressive educational system, not the bifurcated one that has disoriented students and alienated the ruling elites from the people they govern. Esposito contends that "Islamic history, if correctly understood, has a lesson for the conservatives and reformers. It offers a picture of a dynamic, changing, adaptive religious tradition. A fuller appreciation

---

[18] Mazrui calls them "camel-and-date" economies (1990, 72). The depletion of Saudi wealth has been widely reported in recent years, especially since the Gulf War. Kuwait, Iraq, Libya, and Algeria have all been weakened through internal destabilization, sanctions, boycotts, or war. Still, all of these countries are cash-crop economies that are condemned to failure in the long run because of their utter dependency on the West — unless they opt for new economic and political models. For an examination of how the West enriches itself while the Arabs are being impoverished by the sale of petroleum, see Sarkis 1993. A few years ago, the *New York Times* reported on the depletion of Saudi money (see Engelberg 1993; Gerth 1993; *New York Times* 1995). Also see the *Economist* 1995 for the austerity measures the frail kingdom has taken. Yet, despite the impoverishment of Saudi Arabia, the United States has managed to secure more than $10 billion in Saudi contracts for its aircraft and communications industries and thus to revive major sectors in its troubled economy. See Andrews 1994; Sims 1994; and Bryant 1995. Meanwhile, Kuwaiti investments have been completely mismanaged and have led to the loss of billions of dollars. See the case of Kuwaiti investment in Spain in Cohen 1993.

of the real as well [as] idealized Islamic past can provide the understanding and means or methodology for Islamic responses to the challenge of modernity as Muslims once more repeat the process of Islamization — to develop a viable political, legal, and economic model of society and to draw all available data and practices, but to do so in light of the *Qur'anic* principles and values" (1982, 134).

Esposito's recommendation, however, may well entail a critical reading of the *Shari'a* itself, which has been the basis of gender relations and classical family law and has also been codified and jealously guarded by conservative religious scholars (*'ulama*) since the tenth century. Despite the undeniable progressive elements in early Islam (acknowledged by El Saadawi, Ahmed, Mernissi, Walther, and others), the *Shari'a*, largely unquestioned to this day, has continued to enforce the prevailing traditional roles of women. This may be why Mernissi anticipated that social struggles in the Arab world will be over civil rights (1992, 205).[19] The problem is that proponents of this political alternative assume that bourgeois democracy (a participatory or parliamentary system that assumes the existence of classes vying for political control) is inherently liberating, although it is clear that the ideology of pluralism is being used to contain oppositional forces in much of the Third World.[20] Arguing for civil rights as a reliable

[19] In countries such as Morocco, the personal status code (known as the Mudawwana) that regulates family law was amended in 1993 to extend more rights to women, and lively debates are still being held on this issue (see *Le Matin du Sahara* 1996). The precarious situation of women in the family law codes of the Maghreb and Turkey cannot always be attributed to Islamically based discriminatory practices, however. Sometimes the position of women in these countries is determined by the larger Mediterranean ethos of machismo and the cult of honor (see Mayer 1995b). In fact, not only was the Tunisian Code of Personal Status enacted in 1956 the most modern in the Arab world but its divorce provisions "were ahead of many contemporaneous divorce laws in Western countries" (Mayer 1995b, 434). But again, granting more liberties for women is sometimes part of the government's plan to use women as a showcase of modernization and resist the threat of fundamentalism (441).

[20] Several Arab states, such as Egypt, are busy introducing a watered-down notion of "civil society" (based on a government-sponsored pluralism) that would contain the rising forces of discontent, expressed, as has been the case historically, in the language of Islam (see Beinin 1992; and Ibrahim 1993). The creation of bourgeois states in the Middle East is the new focus of the U.S. Agency for International Development (AID), a policy consistent with the United State's recent emphasis on expanding markets (see Miskin 1992). The National Endowment for Democracy is another "independent, non-governmental foundation which receives a grant from Congress every year for the purpose of strengthening democracy around the world." Official sponsorship of such a venture reveals the extent to which "democracy" is ideologically deployed to serve U.S. interests abroad. (It is estimated that the Clinton administration spent more than $725 million on "democracy-related programs" in fiscal 1995.) See Samuels 1995, 48. But despite its rhetorical commitment to democracy, the United States is, in fact, wary of the democratization of Middle Eastern societies, since such a process cannot

basis for a legitimate feminist movement in the Islamic world today not only dismisses the weight of tradition and culture (and thus paradoxically partakes in the same antihistoricism of which Islam is accused) but also discourages any attempt at conceptualizing and building genuine movements of resistance to the "global revolution of Westernization" (Von Laue 1987).

The proposition that religion and state be separated is a tenuous one in the world of Islam, for its impact would be superficial and would benefit — as it has until now — only those opportunistic and superficially Westernized elites who have maintained patriarchal regimes in the Arab world and beyond. Still, Arab states have not been able to adhere fully to the text of the 1948 Universal Declaration of Human Rights (UDHR) because the tension between, on one hand, Islamic teachings and the religious principles of the *Shari'a* and, on the other, the legitimization of individual human rights in a secular framework of social relations proved, in the long run, to be irresolvable. In her detailed study of major Islamic documents dealing with human rights issues, Ann Elizabeth Mayer (1995a) concludes that, despite the fact that Islam initially provided unprecedented rights to women (94), all of the documents fail to elevate women to an equal status with men and fail to meet the basic standards of the UDHR and the Convention on the Elimination of All Forms of Discrimination against Women (CEDAW).[21] To the extent that Mayer suspects patriarchal, neocolonial regimes of concocting these "schemes" in order to stifle dissent (163, 177) and to legitimize, through the deceptive use of modern terminology, the archaic Islamic tenets of the *Shari'a,* her argument remains strong and credible. However, when she avoids any meaningful discussion of either the last eight articles in the UDHR dealing with economic rights or the utter failure of Western capitalist societies to implement other "human rights" documents such as the International Covenant on Economic, Social and Cultural Rights (1966), she privileges the monadic, nebulous individual supposedly free from physical coercion by the state but trapped in a violent economic system that ruthlessly distorts the very meaning of humanity, freedom, and happiness.

---

be guaranteed to serve the vital interests of the United States in the region. "The worry is that anti-American, militantly Islamic regimes might replace the durably autocratic but pro-American governments of Egypt, Saudi Arabia, and many gulf states." See Miller 1996, 50.

[21] Mayer's study includes the Iranian Constitution of 1979, the Universal Islamic Declaration of Human Rights, the Azhar Draft Islamic Constitution, the Cairo Declaration, the Saudi Basic Law, certain policies of the Sudanese government, and other writings by influential intellectuals such as the Iranian Sufi Sultanhussein Tabardeh and the Pakistani scholar Mawdudi.

I am not implying that the political is absolutely and mechanistically determined by the economic (a margin of autonomy always exists [see Hindess 1980, 52], but whether it works in the interests of the working class and the poor is still not clear). I too think that expanding the sphere of political freedom is still strategically indispensable, but to regard this as an end in itself, or to assume that political rights (e.g., freedom to vote) will be translated into better social conditions, is a dubious proposition, especially in this advanced epoch of capitalism characterized by relentless corporate warfare on public security. Marx himself preferred democracy to other political systems, but he had no doubt that freedom of contract under postslavery capitalism was still a form of enslavement. In *The Holy Family* (1845), he explained this paradox succinctly: "The *slavery of civil society* is *in appearance* the greatest *freedom* because it is in appearance the fully developed *independence* of the individual, who considers as his *own* freedom the uncurbed movement, no longer bound by a common bond or by man, of the estranged elements of his life, such as property, industry, religion, etc., whereas actually this is his fully developed slavery and inhumanity" (quoted in Hunt 1984, 165). This tension between freedom and exploitation is precisely the reason Marx thought capitalism irredeemable and proposed communism as the most civilized system of human relations.

If the crisis of the Muslim is one of identity, the solution does not lie in accepting a bourgeois definition of the human, but in examining the historical and cultural background of the prevailing (Western) capitalist equation of the individual with an "autonomous, contract-making self," where the "self" is conceived of as property (Joseph 1993, 22–26). Mayer herself makes detailed and legalistic (i.e., textual) comparative analyses of Islamic and Western laws and concludes that the current notion of international human rights is based on "Western traditions of individualism, humanism, and rationalism and on legal principles protecting individual rights" (1995a, 38). The indifference to Islamic law in the drafting of international human rights documents was probably prompted by the West's assumption of its own superiority and by the fact that "Islam is overwhelmingly the religion of Third World countries" (39). Although for Mayer the topic of Islam is still mired in historical antagonisms, the secondary literature on human rights is too weak to elucidate the issues, and "dealing with Islam is like stepping into a minefield" (14), she is convinced that "Islam is not the cause of the human rights problem endemic to the Middle East" (1995a, xvii). However, instead of tackling the epistemological and ontological differences that fuel the tension between the Islamic and Western views of society and the individual, she devotes most of her book to taking officially sponsored documents to task for failing to be consistent with the international laws ratified by Islamic governments. There is nary a word on the complicity of Western governments in supporting undemocratic regimes,[22] and there is no examination of the United Nations's structure; in short, Mayer's legalistic approach in comparing texts (although this is a strategy she uses for enlarging the sphere of freedoms in Islamic societies) turns her book into an ahistorical document of limited value to the perennial struggle of Muslim peoples against the secular ideologies of the West.

For instance, Mayer fails to examine how the notion of the "individual" in Islam is inextricably tied to the spiritual and socioeconomic welfare of the community, as Mahmood Monshipouri (1994) has shown: "The atomized and 'private' individual, abstracted from the social and political context of his or her surroundings, is a product of the rationalizing aspects of modernization and the spread of science and technology" (217). Or, as al Masseri further explains, the "individual," according to the model propagated by Western capitalism, is

> a set of abstract needs defined specifically by monopolies, advertisement and fashion companies, and by several entertainment industries. In this context, the individual is no more than a unit reduced to a receptor of heavy instructions from public institutions that have no individuality and no value other than augmenting profit. These institutions resemble an absolute state that has appointed itself as an absolute power and that has remodelled individuals so that they could play the roles or perform the functions assigned to them. To talk of human rights (in the abstract) is, therefore, to continue the

[22] The cases of Saudi Arabia and Indonesia are revealing. Saudi Arabia's petrodollars sponsor a significant portion of the arms industry in the United States. Between 1990 and 1994, Saudi Arabia committed $30 billion for the purchase of American weapons. For this reason, a human rights lawyer in New York was told by U.S. officials that human rights and democracy are not a U.S. concern in that country. See Cockburn and Cockburn 1994; and Miller 1996. Britain, the United States, and other major Western countries continue to have friendly relations with the Indonesian government despite its well-documented genocidal war against the non-Muslim people of East Timor. According to Mark Curtis, "Britain has sold arms worth more than $350 million to Indonesia, and has in place agreements to sell an estimated $3.5 billion more" (1995–96, 52). President Suharto, the military-backed dictator of Indonesia, was given preferential treatment in Washington when he visited in October 1995. To its credit, the *New York Times* acknowledged the double standard of the U.S. government on human rights issues. While the presidents of China and Cuba are either snubbed or shunned, Suharto is embraced because his "wildly corrupt" country is "sitting on the ultimate emerging market." He has had the savvy to deregulate the economy, open the market to foreign investors, and heroically restrict the notoriously aggressive Japanese to one-quarter of that market. See Sanger 1995.

original assault on the intermediary institutions that began in the Renaissance and left humanity completely naked before the state and its institutions. (1994, 412–13)

While Monshipouri dismisses the pressure of the West on Islamic societies as a simplistic form of cultural imperialism that rests on "the amorphous assumption of value diffusionism" (1994, 225), he proposes that only an internal evolution that emphasizes economic rights is likely to work (225). Such a system would be consistent with the aspirations of Third World peoples, expressed in the New International Economic Order (NIEO), and with the fundamental precepts of Islam. "Muslim perspectives on universal human rights," he points out, "have traditionally revolved more around themes of social justice than of individual freedoms" (237). Indeed, like many Marxists who have advocated a synthesis of civil and economic rights, Monshipouri argues for an entente between Islam and the secular West: "In the final analysis, just as the Islamic views and traditions on certain fundamental human rights ought to evolve in keeping with the modern world, so too the Western liberal traditions (those belonging to the Lockean praxis) must be complemented by necessary additions compatible with the global evolution of economic rights" (238).

Muslim identity, as one interview with mostly Muslim Arab intellectuals revealed (see Dwyer 1991), is often privileged over individual rights. Since, in Islam, "the conceptual basis [of rights] is teleological and their ethical foundation theological" (Monshipouri 1994, 218), the boundaries of individual freedom are determined not by secular law but by divine decree. Even the idea of freedom itself is defined by the late Sudanese scholar Mahmoud Mohamed Taha in transcendental terms as being primarily secure in one's innermost being (Taha 1987).[23] The rights to autonomous identity and self-determination have solidified the Arab states' position—despite their varying degrees of complicity with the reigning international order—toward the Western-inspired human rights charter precisely because bourgeois democracies assume the sovereignty of the individual, not the community (see De Brie 1991; Khamlishi 1993). The incompatibility of Islamic principles and secular assumptions, together with the Third

[23] Taha writes: "An individual can never achieve absolute individual freedom as long as he is divided within himself, with one part at war with the other. He must restore unity to his being, so that he may be at peace with himself, before he can attempt to be at peace with others. One cannot give what he does not have. One can be at peace with himself when the conscious is not in conflict and opposition with the unconscious" (1987, 110). And such a state, he explains, can only be achieved through the agency of Islam (111). Margaret Randall comes to a similar conclusion: "Authentic power comes from a fully developed sense of self, possible only when both individual and collective memory is retrieved" (1992, 171).

World's resistance to Western hegemonic aims, complicated the 1993 Conference on Human Rights in Vienna, although minorities and particularly women seem to have benefited from an expanded definition of rights (see Riding 1993a, 1993b). It is perhaps not surprising, given the current definition of human rights in the West, that women would emerge as beneficiaries, while entire peoples do not have the right to determine their own cultural and economic agendas.[24] For this reason, neocolonialists will continue — partly through the agency of individualism — to discredit non-Western conceptions of rights, and the debate over feminism in Islam will continue to be implicated in larger ideological struggles. But remembering that gender and gender difference are products of history and are "reproduced through complex moralities, idioms and structures" (Joseph 1993, 26) may allow the feminist agenda to take center stage now and not wait, as Iranian feminist Nayereh Tohidi cautions us against, until "the days after the revolution," or the time — which has yet to dawn — when ideological and cultural binarisms (colonizer/colonized) are dismantled. To chart out an acceptable "cartography" of struggle, feminists need to engage Dorothy Smith's "relations of ruling" strategy, which designates a totalizing approach to the multifarious but interlocking practices of power (Smith 1987, 3),[25] although I still do not think that Tohidi's Western secular model of social relations is ultimately effective in Islamic societies (see Tohidi 1991).

If gender hierarchies were more fluid in the precolonial period (Joseph 1993, 23), then to claim that Islam is essentially undemocratic and "patriarchal"[26] is ideologically suspect, because it freezes the history of Muslim peoples and downplays the impact of imperialism on gender relations in Islamic countries (Sadowski 1993). The recent popularity of civil society as "the new analytical tool that will unlock the mysteries of the social order" (Seligman 1995, 200) has not only obscured the cultural foundations of this concept in European Reason and Christian Revelation, but it also dangerously posits the duplication of very specific cultural evolutions of

[24] At the time of the conference in Vienna, the United States had not ratified the Covenant on Economic, Social, and Cultural Rights and was thus seen as having double standards (see Stephens 1993).

[25] Smith writes: "'Relations of ruling' is a concept that grasps power, organization, direction, and regulation as more pervasively structured than can be expressed in traditional concepts provided by the discourses of power. I have come to see a specific interrelation between the dynamic advance of the distinctive forms of organizing and ruling contemporary capitalist society and the patriarchal forms of our contemporary experience."

[26] Bernard Lewis has shown that this concept of the "father" is essentially a Christian one (1988, 17, 64–70).

Western Europe and the United States in parts of the world that have undergone different historical experiences and the populations of which respond to different markers of identity. It also assumes the inevitability of capitalism as a system of social relations, since "it was in the modern era, with the nascent capitalist economy and the freeing of the individual from traditional and communal ties, that the problem of squaring individual and social goods and desiderata achieved a new saliency. The modern ideas of civil society developed by Locke, Ferguson, Smith, and Hutcheson (and, to some extent, Shaftesbury) were all attempts to posit a solution to the new problem of the social order that emerged at the end of the seventeenth century" (Seligman 1995, 205). Moreover, the notion of civil society "is based on a gendered distinction between public [male] and private [female] domain" and "is now being challenged in the West by feminists and people of color." Consequently, "its uncritical application to Third World countries and the uncritical use of the relative existence of components of civil society as measures of 'modernity' or progress are highly problematic" (Joseph 1993, 24).

While women are inevitably caught up in the "political-cultural battleground" of Muslim societies, and all "political and cultural projects are gendered" (Moghadam 1994, 3, 9), there is no reason to believe that secularized discourses are indispensable for the emancipation of women from the tyranny of a male-dominated Islam. The case of Algeria is a glaring instance of how secular modernization in the postindependence period has been primarily mimetic, restricted to a vacuous political discourse, since the Family Code, based on the precepts of the *Shari'a,* has continued to regulate gender and family relations. Cherifa Bouatta (1994) and Doria Cherifati-Merabitine (1994) present the *moudjahidates* (women who valiantly fought for independence)[27] as symbols of the Algerian woman who

---

[27] *Moudjahidates,* the term used to describe women freedom fighters in Algeria, is representative of the schizophrenic imagination afflicting secular nationalists in the Arab world. The "usurpation" and "illicit secularization" of religious referents (such as *umma*) reveal the extent to which secular projects are hopelessly imprisoned in a Qur'anic vocabulary and make it quite clear that modernist ideologies have failed significantly to alter prerevolutionary cultural patterns in postcolonial Algeria, notwithstanding the modernist rhetoric of the elites (see Addi 1989; and Michalon 1994). This should not be surprising, since it was through Islam that the bedouin culture of Arabia was both spread and superseded. And though Arabism existed as a sentiment before 1914, it was through the confrontation with the Turks (the Arabs' Other) that Arab nationalism was born and consolidated. This reversal to a superficially constructed ethnicity was inspired by the European concept of nation. For a good discussion of the untenable doctrines of traditional Arab nationalism, see the "Dossier special" in *Qantara* (*magazine des cultures arabes et mediterraneenne*) (November–December 1995). For a discussion of false epistemologies in the discourses of Arab nationalism, see Salame 1995.

was betrayed by the promise of the revolution. But contrary to Bouatta's implication, it was the postcolonial secular system that permitted the marginalization of women by maintaining the supremacy of men. Women were to be legitimated as equals not through secular legislative measures (although the Algerian Constitution affirmed women's equality) but through their heroic struggle against French imperialism. If they were able to conquer previously closed (because sacralized) spaces, it was because the regressive codes of a patriarchal Islam had so clearly failed to defend the country (see Cherifati-Merabitine 1994). In other words, it was the national struggle against imperialism that brought women out of their confined, privatized social spaces into the public sphere, where their contributions would be crucial for the liberation of Algeria. It is not clear at all that the modernist project embraced by the secular elites immediately after independence included a concrete agenda for relinquishing male privilege and sharing social and political responsibilities with women.[28] And that has been so not because of a deliberate conspiracy but because of the contradictory nature of Algerian society in the postcolonial period. Political will, in this case, has not been able to eradicate a more profoundly entrenched culture of Islam and kinship. And it is partly this irresolvable contradiction that has thrown Algeria into its current impasse.

I I I

The failure of both modernist ideologies and clerical Islam indicates the need for a third way that is both indigenous and progressive, a way that was charted out by the late Mahmoud Mohamed Taha (opportunistically executed for challenging orthodox beliefs) in his still largely unread manifesto *The Second Message of Islam* (1987). Taha's argument is serious and, if widely discussed, might provoke a debate rooted in what Esposito calls "a consistent Islamic rationale" (1982, 102). Taha and his disciple Abdullahi Ahmed An-Na'im, however, go further than any mainstream reformer to call for the total elimination of the *Shari'a* (since it is inherently inegalitarian and patriarchal and cannot be altered beyond certain limits) and the creation of a new law based on Meccan Revelation (i.e., before the Prophet's flight [*hijra*] to Yathrib, later Medina, an event that inaugurated the Islamic calendar and that, in Mernissi's view, set back the freedoms of women and reinstated them at the point zero of history). Although extremely controversial, such an arrangement would not necessarily be un-Islamic, for the

---

[28] Judith Miller reported that, by 1987, Algerian women "constituted only 3.3 percent of the paid work force. The average woman had eight children" (1992, 6). It was clear to her that the Algerian francophone males were paying only "lip service" to women's rights.

Shariʿa is "a situational, not a transcendental law" (Engineer 1992, 9). If the Revelation could adapt to the specific historical period of Arabia's transition into a new Islamic order, then it makes little intellectual sense to canonize the interpretations of orthodox *ʿulama* into an antihistorical immutability.

Both Taha and An-Naʿim use the method of *naskh* (abrogation) to retrieve the earlier, abrogated verses of the Meccan Revelation, which (unlike the later, ethnic-specific messages revealed to the Prophet during the process of *umma* building) are more egalitarian and universal in spirit (Taha 1987, 21).[29] Taha's "Second Message" is an Islamically derived critique of both the stagnation of Islamic scholarship and the failure of "industrialized Western civilization . . . to reconcile the needs of the individual with the needs of the community" (39, 52–53). The first message of Islam was the preparatory phase (including the gentle censorship of certain unacceptable practices and the implicit maintenance of others) for the eventual emancipation of all peoples through a revolutionary reading of the Qurʾan. This, according to Taha, is the only solution for enlightened Muslims who reject both orthodox interpretations of Islam and the corrosive program of Western secularism. As An-Naʿim says in the introduction to Taha's book, the best way to combat the obscurantism of Islamic extremism today is not through an equally irrational recourse to secular ideology but through reforms that "would make Islam a viable modern ideology" (Taha 1987, 28). Taha's conception of the "Good Society" as economically socialistic, politically democratic, and founded on the equality of men and women is both consistent with Islamic principles and the only way out of the cultural impasse facing Muslims today (153).

An-Naʿim (1990) states, at the outset, that the reconstructed *Shariʿa* should be based on the same Islamic foundations, since "Islamic identity" is "essential for the political viability of the proposed reforms" (xv). In fact, An-Naʿim reads the actual Islamic resurgence as an expression of "the right to self-determination" (14), including the (misguided) attempt to reinstate the *Shariʿa* as the binding law in social relations (6–7). Yet the historical *Shariʿa* is proving too inflexible to meet the legitimate aspirations of women within the political framework of the nation-state (whose existence

---

[29] This argument is significantly different from the one recently advanced by Asʿad Abu-Khalil (1993a), who claims that the inferiority of women is unequivocally stated in the Qurʾan and the *hadith* and that it cannot be dispensed with either by conservative clerics or women revisionists. AbuKhalil places Mernissi in this apologetic school and argues finally that Islam is incompatible with both democracy and gender equality (see AbuKhalil 1993a, 3–22). While AbuKhalil argues for lifting "the hegemony of Muslim laws," he wants to see these replaced by secular status laws (1993b, 239–45).

An-Naʿim takes for granted [7–8], for it seems that the concept "is now firmly and irrevocably established throughout the Muslim world" [72]), which means that the *Shariʿa,* not being divine, must be challenged from within an Islamic context if women and religious minorities are to enjoy their constitutional rights as citizens and members of a nation-state. Indeed, the time has come to dispense with the privileging of the Muslim male over women and religious minorities and to adopt the "principle of reciprocity" or the golden rule that "one should treat other people as he or she wishes to be treated by them" as the "common normative principle" of universal standards of human rights — or, alternatively, "those rights to which human beings are entitled by virtue of being human" (162–63, 164). But since the *Shariʿa*'s sanction of slavery and discrimination on the grounds of religion and gender conflict with these basic principles, Islam is harmed by its continued unmodified implementation.

While I do not agree with An-Naʿim's premise that the nation-state will (or should) endure as a form of political and social organization in the Islamic world and elsewhere, I share his criticism of the West for not laying the groundwork for the execution of the lofty principles it preaches and for refusing to eradicate the conditions of inequality and oppression, within both its metropolitan centers and semicolonies. Any agenda that seeks the emancipation of women in the Islamic world must examine the implications of its program at a variety of interlocking levels if it is not to be co-opted by the dehumanizing effects of the global capitalist system. In this case, a positive sense of identity works to ensure continued resistance to the destructive effects of commodity culture.[30]

I   I   I

Now, then, is the time to dispel the entrenched belief that the religion of Islam acts as a barrier to women's fulfillment outside of men's arbitrary control, and to acknowledge that it is a male-manipulated interpretation of Islam, often encoded in an increasingly irrelevant *Shariʿa,* that has allowed orientalist prejudices to persist in the West and among Westernized Muslim elites (see Said 1981, 161). A thoroughly redefined Islam, in dynamic relation with other cultures, must be preserved as a viable alternative to the unrelenting process of Westernization and the sometimes extremist practices of fundamentalists. Ultimately, both practices threaten the Islamic cultures that sustain the identities of both women and men. While the term *Islam* itself may evoke strong (mostly negative) reactions among

---

[30] David Rieff calls Islam the last credible force of resistance left to the superfluous globalism of American culture (1993–94, 77).

Westernized Muslims, feminism must still be understood as "a mode of intervention into *particular* hegemonic discourses" and not as a universal response to an assumed universal patriarchy (see Mohanty 1991, 53–54). The common denominator of victimization that certain Western feminists have ascribed cross-culturally erases the complexities, pluralities, and historical specificities of different cultures; its monolithic assumptions are therefore akin to those of orientalism. This is why "sisterhood cannot be assumed on the basis of gender" but "must be forged in concrete historical and political practice and analysis" (Mohanty 1991, 58; see also 71–74). Moreover, as Lazreg has put it, "to think of feminism in the singular is sociologically inappropriate" (1988, 101).

The egalitarianism inherent in what Leila Ahmed calls "the ethical voice of Islam" (1992, 88) is one reason "Muslim women frequently insist, often inexplicably to non-Muslims, that Islam is not sexist. They hear and read in its sacred text, justly and legitimately, a different message from that heard by the makers and enforcers of orthodox, androcentric Islam" (66). This voice must now be retrieved through a radical reform of the *Shari'a* and the resurrection of *ijtihad* as the basic core of a dynamic Islamic scholarship. The Prophet's wives (despite the highly publicized portions of Rushdie's *Satanic Verses,* which may appear to be outrageously demeaning to women) could stand as a new model of womanhood in Islam, for it is now well known that several of his wives challenged male supremacy and, as widows, took an active interest in public and political affairs. Several, such as 'Aisha, Umm Salama, and Umm Habiba, were renowned for their "intellectual qualities," and 'Aisha is said to have been one of the principal sources of 2,210 *hadiths* (see Morsy 1989, 19–20).[31] In short, once it becomes clear that "there is a general thrust towards equality of the sexes in the *Quran* [sic]" and that several verses, such as the (in)famous one on polygamy, were "contextual" justifications, not "normative" ones, and that therefore their "applicability must be seen as dated, not for all times to come," a progressive reform can proceed simultaneously with the harnessing of energy needed to resist the increasing marginalization of the world of Islam and the Third World generally.[32] And because the Qur'an

[31] Magali Morsy (1989) offers a useful study of the Prophet's wives. Ahmed posits that the comparative freedom enjoyed by the first generation of Muslim women reflected the persistence of Jahiliyan mores in early Islam, a freedom that was eventually eroded as clerical Islam began to cast a stifling and gloomy shadow on the fate of women (see Ahmed 1986).

[32] "International" institutions such as the IMF and World Bank and trade agreements such as NAFTA and GATT are designed to benefit the rich at the expense of the poor. On how these institutions perform their nefarious tasks in concrete reality, see the issue of *Race and*

intervenes rather ambiguously in the social sphere (Morsy 1989, 32, 163–64), the forms of social relations would be negotiable if men were to be guided (forced?) back to the true spirit of Islam, long frozen into a debilitating orthodoxy.

In fact, the process seems to have begun in parts of the Islamic world. In the Islamic Republic of Iran, a country governed by a male clerical elite, there is now a thriving intellectual debate over how to challenge repressive laws from within the Islamic tradition itself. Incredible as it may sound, "no other group has been as determined and resourceful in challenging the various economic, social and cultural obstacles that have been placed in its way as have been Iranian women under the Islamic Republic" (Banuazizi 1994, 7; Kian 1996; Mir-Hosseini 1996).[33] The emerging Islamic feminists in Iran are challenged "to maintain a delicate balance between reclaiming a national identity, reaffirming progressive elements of the indigenous culture, and the struggle to create a democratic, just, and coherently developed society" (Tohidi 1994, 142). Similar efforts are taking place in other parts of the Islamic world.[34] Indeed, the scope of the Islamic feminist movement is so large and thoroughly revolutionary that it may well be one of the best platforms from which to resist the effects of global capitalism and contribute to a rich, egalitarian polycentric world.

When the Moroccan writer Leila Abouzeid captured the hypocrisy of the postcolonial ruling classes in her novella *Year of the Elephant* (1989) by exposing the predicament of Zahra, a traditional guerrilla fighter against French colonialism whose husband rejects her upon independence for a younger, more modern woman, she made her protagonist seek strength in tradition and Islam, not in some ill-digested and amorphous ideology of modernity without resonance among the people. Contrary to ben Jelloun's suggestion in *The Sand Child* and *The Sacred Night*, Abouzeid defines Morocco's nationalist movement of resistance to colonialism as a liberating epoch for women; it is modernized elites who have subverted this

---

Class: A Journal for Black and Third World Liberation on "the new conquistadors" (July–September 1992); Ridgeway 1993, 15–16; and Bello, Cunningham, and Rao 1993–94.

[33] Banuazizi (1994) also describes the dynamic intellectual climate in Iran, which, in many ways, is superior to that of the days before the Islamic revolution. Even unorthodox, if not quite radical, religious ideas are now widely discussed. See Adelkhah 1995; and Wright 1995. Iranian films, "increasingly admired at international film festivals" (Brooks 1996), are severely critical of the government despite the puritanical code to which they are subjected. For more information on the emerging Iranian cinema, see Cheshire 1977.

[34] For a good overview of Muslim women's attempt to articulate a progressive agenda within Islam, see Yamani 1996.

potentially egalitarian project by pursuing the mirage of Westernization in the postcolonial era. Despite her profound disillusionment, Abouzeid's protagonist, Zahra, continues to pray, to wear the *djellaba*, and, as a committed revolutionary, to wait for the day when this neocolonial order will be replaced by a new independence that allows cultures to negotiate their destinies in their own vocabularies.

Humanities Department
University of New England

References

Abouzeid, Leila. 1989. *Year of the Elephant: A Moroccan Woman's Journey toward Independence,* trans. Barbara Parmenter. Austin: University of Texas, Center for Middle East Studies.

AbuKhalil, As'ad. 1993a. "Toward the Study of Women and Politics in the Arab World: The Debate and the Reality." *Feminist Issues* 13(1):3–22.

———. 1993b. "A Viable Partnership: Islam, Democracy and the Arab World." In *Altered States: A Reader in the New World Order,* ed. Phyllis Bennis and Michel Moushabek, 239–45. New York: Olive Branch Press.

Accad, Evelyne. 1991. "Sexuality and Sexual Politics." In *Third World Women and the Politics of Feminism,* ed. Chandra T. Mohanty, Ann Russo, and Lourdes Torres, 237–50. Bloomington and Indianapolis: Indiana University Press.

Addi, Lahouari. 1989. "De la democratie en Algerie." *Le Monde diplomatique,* October, 9.

Adelkhah, Fariba. 1995. "L'offensive des intellectuels en Iran." *Le Monde diplomatique,* January, 20.

Ahmed, Leila. 1986. "Women and the Advent of Islam." *Signs: Journal of Women in Culture and Society* 11(4):665–91.

———. 1992. *Women and Gender in Islam: Historical Roots of a Modern Debate.* New Haven, Conn.: Yale University Press.

Amin, Samir. 1990. *Delinking: Towards a Polycentric World.* London and Atlantic Highlands, N.J.: Zed.

Andrews, Edmund B. 1994. "AT&T Wins $4 Billion Saudi Project." *New York Times,* May 10, D1, D7.

An-Na'im, Abdullahi. 1990. *Toward an Islamic Reformation: Civil Liberties, Human Rights, and International Law.* Syracuse, N.Y.: Syracuse University Press.

Banuazizi, Ali. 1994. "Iran's Revolutionary Impasse: Political Factionalism and Societal Resistance." *Middle East Report* 24(6):2–8.

Beinin, Joel. 1992. "Aspects of Egyptian Civil Resistance." *Middle East Report* 22(6):38–39.

Bello, Walden, Shea Cunningham, and Bill Rau. 1993–94. "IMF/World Bank: Devastation by Design." *CovertAction* 47:44–47.

Ben Jelloun, Tahar. 1989. *The Sand Child,* trans. Alan Sheridan. New York: Ballantine.

———. 1991a. *The Sacred Night,* trans. Alan Sheridan. New York: Ballantine.

———. 1991b. *Les yeux baisses.* Paris: Seuil.

Bohlen, Celeste. 1995. "Turkish Lawyers Are at Center of a Battle over Muslim Head Coverings for Women." *New York Times,* November 12, sec. 1, 12.

Bottomore, Tom, ed. (1983) 1991. *A Dictionary of Marxist Thought.* 2d rev. ed. Oxford: Blackwell.

Bouatta, Cherifa. 1994. "Feminine Militancy: *Moudjahidates* during and after the Algerian War." In *Gender and National Identity: Women and Politics in Muslim Societies,* ed. Valentine M. Moghadam, 18–39. London and Atlantic Highlands, N.J.: Zed.

Brooks, Geraldine. 1996. "In Iran, Quiet Films Can Speak Volumes." *New York Times,* January 28, sec. 2, 9, 21.

Bryant, Adam. 1995. "Saudis Sign $6 Billion Deal with Boeing and McDonnell." *New York Times,* October 27, D4.

Bugul, Ken. 1991. *The Abandoned Baobab,* trans. Marjolijn de Jager. New York: Lawrence Hills.

Burgat, François. 1993. *The Islamic Movement in North Africa,* trans. William Dowell. Austin: University of Texas, Center for Middle Eastern Studies.

Cherifati-Merabitine, Doria. 1994. "Algeria at a Crossroads: National Liberation, Islamization and Women." In *Gender and National Identity,* ed. Valentine M. Moghadam, 40–62. London and Atlantic Highlands, N.J.: Zed.

Cheshire, Godfrey. 1997. "The Iranian Who Won the World's Attention." *New York Times,* September 28, sec. 2, 11, 18.

Cockburn, Leslie, and Andrew Cockburn. 1994. "Royal Mess." *New Yorker,* November 28, 54–72.

Cohen, Roger. 1993. "Big Wallets and Little Supervision." *New York Times,* September 28, D1, D20.

Curtis, Mark. 1995–96. "Hawks over East Timor: Britain Arms Indonesia." *CovertAction* 55:52–56.

Davidson, Basil. 1992. *The Black Man's Burden: Africa and the Curse of the Nation-State.* New York: Times Books.

De Brie, Christian. 1991. "Champ libre au modèle libéral et démocratique." *Le Monde diplomatique,* November, 22–23.

Dwyer, Claire. 1991–92. "'Ninja Women': The Representation of Muslim Women in the West." *Intertwine* (Journal of the Association of International Students at Syracuse University), 8–13.

Dwyer, Kevin. 1991. *Arab Voices: The Human Rights Debate in the Middle East.* Berkeley and Los Angeles: University of California Press.

Economist. 1995. "Saudi Arabia's Future." *Economist,* March 18–24, 21–25.

El Saadawi, Nawal. 1980. *The Hidden Face of Eve.* London: Zed.

Engelberg, Stephen. 1993. "U.S.-Saudi Deals in 90's Shifting Away from Cash toward Credit." *New York Times,* August 23, A1, A6.

Engineer, Asghar Ali. 1992. *The Rights of Women in Islam.* New York: St. Martin's.

Erickson, John D. 1993. "Veiled Woman and Veiled Narrative in Tahar ben Jelloun's *The Sandchild.*" *boundary 2* 20(1):47–64.

Esposito, John. 1982. *Women in Muslim Family Law.* Syracuse, N.Y.: Syracuse University Press.

———. 1992. *The Islamic Threat: Myth or Reality?* Oxford and New York: Oxford University Press.

Falk, Richard. 1993. "Global Apartheid: The Structure of the World Economy." *Third World Resurgent* 37 (September): 15–16.

Gerth, Jeff. 1993. "Saudi Stability Hit by Heavy Spending over Last Decade." *New York Times,* August 22, 1, 12.

Hatem, Mervat. 1987. "Class and Patriarchy as Competing Paradigms for the Study of Middle Eastern Women." *Society for Comparative Studies of Society and History* 29(4):811–18.

Head, Simon. 1996. "The New Ruthless Economy." *New York Review of Books,* February 29, 47–52.

Hindess, Barry. 1980. "Marxism and Parliamentary Democracy." In *Marxism and Democracy,* ed. Alan Hunt, 22–54. London: Lawrence & Wishart.

Hodgson, Marshall G. S. 1977. *The Venture of Islam: Conscience and History in a World Civilization.* Vol. 1, *The Classical Age of Islam.* Chicago: University of Chicago Press.

Hoodbhoy, Pervez. 1991. *Islam and Science: Religious Orthodoxy and the Battle for Rationality.* London and Atlantic Highlands, N.J.: Zed.

Hourani, Albert. 1991. *A History of the Arab Peoples.* Cambridge, Mass.: Harvard University Press, Belknap Press.

Hunt, Richard N. 1984. *The Political Ideas of Marx and Engels.* Vol. 2, *Classical Marxism, 1850–1895.* Pittsburgh: University of Pittsburgh Press.

Huntington, Samuel. 1993. "The Clash of Civilizations?" *Foreign Affairs* 72(3): 22–49.

Ibrahim, Saad Eddin. 1993. "Crises, Elites, and Democratization in the Arab World." *Middle East Journal* 27(2):292–305.

Joseph, Suad. 1993. "Gender and Civil Society." *Middle East Report* 23(4): 22–26.

Kandiyoti, Deniz, ed. 1991. *Women, Islam and the State.* Philadelphia: Temple University Press.

Khamlishi, Muhammed. 1993. "Al-'arabu, al-'ilmaniyya wa huququ al-insan." *Anoual,* August 11–14, 7.

Kian, Azaden. 1996. "Des femmes iraniennes contre le clergé." *Le Monde diplomatique,* November, 8.

Krämer, Gudrun. 1993. "Islamist Notions of Democracy." *Middle East Report* 23(4):2–8.

Lane-Poole, Stanley. (1886) 1990. *The Story of the Moors in Spain.* Baltimore: Black Classic Press.

Latouche, Serge. 1989. *L'occidentalisation du monde: Essai sur la signification, la portée et les limites de l'uniformisation planetaire.* Paris: Editions la Decouverte.

Lazreg, Marnia. 1988. "Feminism and Difference: The Perils of Writing as a Woman on Women in Algeria." *Feminist Studies* 14(1):81–107.

Lewis, Bernard. 1984. *The Jews of Islam*. Princeton, N.J.: Princeton University Press.

———. 1988. *The Political Language of Islam*. Chicago: University of Chicago Press.

———. 1991. "Secularism in the Middle East." Rehovat, Israel: Weizmann Institute of Science.

Marshall, Phil. 1988. "Islamic Fundamentalism — Oppression and Revolution." *International Socialism* 40 (Autumn): 1–51.

Marsot, Afaf Lutfi al-Sayyid. 1996. "Entrepreneurial Women in Egypt." In *Feminism and Islam: Legal and Literary Perspectives*, ed. Mai Yamani, 33–47. New York: New York University Press.

al Masseri, Abdulwahab. 1994. "The Imperialist Epistemological Vision." *American Journal of Islamic Social Scientists* 11(3):403–15.

Le Matin du Sahara et du Maghreb. 1996. "Les participants qualifient de positifs les amendements de 1993." *Le Matin du Sahara et du Maghreb*, January 7, 2.

Mayer, Ann Elizabeth. 1995a. *Islam and Human Rights: Tradition and Politics*. 2d ed. Boulder, Colo.: Westview.

———. 1995b. "Reform of Personal Status Laws in North Africa: A Problem of Islamic or Mediterranean Laws?" *Middle East Journal* 49(3):432–46.

Mazrui, Ali. 1990. *Cultural Forces in World Politics*. Portsmouth, N.H.: Heinemann.

———. 1993. "Islam and the End of History." *American Journal of Islamic Social Sciences* 10(4):512–35.

Melman, Billie. 1992. *Women's Orients: English Women and the Middle East, 1718–1918*. Ann Arbor: University of Michigan Press.

Mernissi, Fatima. (1975) 1987a. *Beyond the Veil: Male-Female Dynamics in a Modern Muslim Society*. Rev. ed. Bloomington and Indianapolis: Indiana University Press.

———. 1987b. *Le harem politique: Le Prophète et les femmes*. Paris: Albin Michel. Trans. Mary Jo Lakeland as *The Veil and the Male Elite: A Feminist Interpretation of Women's Rights in Islam,* Reading, Mass.: Addison-Wesley, 1991.

———. 1990. *Sultanes oubliees: Femmes chefs d'État en Islam*. Casablanca: Editions le Fennec. Trans. Mary Jo Lakeland as *The Forgotten Queens of Islam*. Minneapolis: University of Minnesota Press, 1993.

———. 1992. *La peur-modernite: Conflit Islam démocratie*. Paris: Albin Michel. Trans. Mary Jo Lakeland as *Islam and Democracy: Fear of the Modern World*. Reading, Mass.: Addison-Wesley, 1992.

Michalon, Thierry. 1994. "L'Algerie des cousins." *Le monde diplomatique*, November, 1, 16–17.

Milani, Farzaneh. 1992. *Veils and Words: The Emerging Voices of Iranian Women Writers*. Syracuse, N.Y.: Syracuse University Press.

Miliband, Ralph. 1977. *Marxism and Politics*. Oxford: Oxford University Press.

Miller, Judith. 1992. "Women Regain a Kind of Security in Islam's Embrace." *New York Times*, December 27, sec. 4, 6.

———. 1996. "At Hour of Triumph, Democracy Recedes as the Global Ideal." *New York Times,* February 18, sec. 4, 1, 5.

Mir-Hosseini, Ziba. 1996. "Stretching the Limits: A Feminist Reading of the Shari'a in Post-Khomeini Iran." In Yamani 1996, 285–319.

Miskin, Al. 1992. "AID's 'Free Market' Democracy." *Middle East Report* 23(4): 33–34.

Moghadam, Valentine M. 1994. "Introduction and Overview: Gender Dynamics of Nationalism, Revolution and Islamization." In *Gender and National Identity: Women and Politics in Muslim Societies,* ed. Valentine M. Moghadam, 18–39. London and Atlantic Highlands, N.J.: Zed.

Mohanty, Chandra Talpade. 1991. "Under Western Eyes: Feminist Scholarship and Colonial Discourses." In *Third World Women and the Politics of Feminism,* ed. Chandra Mohanty, Ann Russo, and Lourdes Torres, 51–80. Bloomington and Indianapolis: Indiana University Press.

Monshipouri, Mahmood. 1994. "Islamic Thinking and the Internationalization of Human Rights." *Muslim World* 84(3–4):217–39.

Morin, Edgar. 1989. "Pour une nouvelle conscience planétaire." *Le Monde diplomatique,* October, 18–19.

Morsy, Magali. 1989. *Les femmes du Prophète.* Paris: Mercure de France.

Najmabadi, Afsaneh. 1987. "Iran's Turn to Islam: From Modernism to a Moral Order." *Middle East Journal* 41(2):202–17.

———. 1991. "Hazards of Modernity and Morality: Women, State and Ideology in Contemporary Iran." In Kandiyoti 1991, 48–76.

———. 1993. "Veiled Discourses—Unveiled Bodies." *Feminist Studies* 19(3): 487–518.

New York Times. 1993. "Saudis without Dollars." *New York Times,* August 25, A14.

Randall, Margaret. 1992. *Gathering Rage.* New York: Monthly Review Press.

Ridgeway, James. 1993. "Trade Imbalance." *Village Voice,* March 30, 15–16.

Riding, Alan. 1993a. "Rights Forum Ends in a Call for a Greater Role by UN." *New York Times,* June 26, 2.

———. 1993b. "The West Gets Some Tough Questions." *New York Times,* June 20, sec. 4, 5.

Rieff, David. 1993–94. "A Global Culture?" *World Policy Journal* 10(4):73–81.

Robinson, William I. 1994. "Low Intensity Democracy: The New Face of Global Domination." *CovertAction* 50:40–47.

Rodinson, Maxime. 1981. *Marxism and the Muslim World,* trans. Jean Matthews. New York: Monthly Review Press.

Rushdie, Salman. 1989. *The Satanic Verses.* New York: Viking.

Sachs, Ignacy. 1995. "Contre l'exclusion, l'ardente obligation du codéveloppement planetaire." *Le Monde diplomatique,* January, 12–13.

Sadowski, Yahya. 1993. "The New Orientalism and the Democracy Debate." *Middle East Report* 23(4):14–21.

Said, Edward. 1979. *Orientalism.* New York: Vintage.

———. 1981. *Covering Islam: How the Media and the Experts Determine How We See the Rest of the World.* New York: Pantheon.

————. 1993. *Culture and Imperialism*. New York: Knopf.

Salamé, Ghassan. 1995. "Le nationalisme arabe: Mort ou mutation." In *Le déchirement des nations*, ed. Jacques Rupnik, 183–212. Paris: Seuil.

Salman, Magida. 1978. "Arab Women." *Khamsin* 6:24–32.

Samuels, David. 1995. "At Play in the Fields of Oppression." *Harper's* 290 (May): 47–54.

Sanger, David E. 1995. "Real Politics: Why Suharto Is In and Castro Is Out." *New York Times*, October 31, A3.

Sarkis, Nicolas. 1993. "L'inquietante baisse des revenus du pétrole." *Le Monde diplomatique*, February, 6.

Sciolino, Elaine. 1996. "Seeing Green. The Red Menace Is Gone. But Here's Islam." *New York Times*, January 21, sec. 4, 1, 6.

Seligman, Adam B. 1995. *The Idea of Civil Society*. Princeton, N.J.: Princeton University Press.

Sen, Gita, and Caren Grown. 1987. *Development, Crises, and Alternative Visions: Third World Women's Perspectives*. New York: Monthly Review Press.

Sims, Calvin. 1994. "Saudi Sales Should Brighten Aircraft Makers' Dark Days." *New York Times*, February 17, C2, D1.

Smith, Dorothy. 1987. *The Everyday as Problematic: A Feminist Sociology*. Boston: Northeastern University Press.

Stephens, Beth. 1993. "Hypocrisy on Rights." *New York Times*, June 24, A23.

Taha, Mahmoud Mohammed. 1987. *The Second Message of Islam*, trans. and with introduction by Abdullahi Ahmed an-Na'im. Syracuse, N.Y.: Syracuse University Press.

Tohidi, Nayereh. 1991. "Gender and Islamic Fundamentalism." In *Third World Women and the Politics of Feminism*, ed. Chandra Mohanty, Ann Russo, and Lourdes Torres, 251–67. Bloomington and Indianapolis: Indiana University Press.

————. 1994. "Modernity, Islamization and Women in Iran." In *Gender and National Identity: Women and Politics in Muslim Societies*, ed. Valentine M. Moghadam, 110–47. London and Atlantic Highlands, N.J.: Zed.

Von Laue, Theodore. 1987. *The World Revolution of Westernization: The Twentieth Century in Global Perspective*. New York: Oxford University Press.

Walther, Wiebke. 1993. *Women in Islam*, trans. C. S. V. Salt. Princeton, N.J.: Markus Weiner.

Wright, Robin. 1995. "Shaking the Foundation of Islam." *Portland Press Herald*, January 30, 2A.

Yamani, Mai, ed. 1996. *Feminism and Islam: Legal and Literary Perspectives*. New York: New York University Press.

The Power Paradox in Muslim Women's *Majales:*
North-West Pakistani Mourning Rituals as Sites of
Contestation over Religious Politics, Ethnicity, and Gender

During revolutions, rebellions, and movements, women are often called on to serve contradictory roles. They are asked to perform work— political, communicative, networking, recruiting, military, manual— that generally goes beyond the society's usual gender restrictions. At the same time, women serve as symbols of movement identity, unity, commitment, and righteous entitlement. To fit into this idealized symbolic image, individual women must fulfill often "traditional" or even exaggerated "feminine" behavioral and attitudinal requirements, such as loyalty, obedience, selflessness, sacrifice, and "proper" deportment: all in all, they are to put aside any personal aspirations and wishes for self-fulfillment and give their all to promoting the values and interests of their nation, revolutionary movement, or social group.

In serving the revolution, group, or movement, women gain skills, experience, and awareness of their own capabilities. However, they are to place all of this at the disposal of the revolutionary movement or, more precisely, its male leaders. Then, when the struggle is over and they are no longer needed, the female Algerian and Palestinian freedom fighters, the French and Iranian revolutionaries, and the American "Rosie the Riveters"

For funding my research in Pakistan, I am grateful to the Fulbright Commission. For their generosity in allowing me to take a year of leave and providing me with supplementary research funds, I thank the administration and the members of my department at Santa Clara University. I owe much to my students at the University of Peshawar, where I taught as part of my Fulbright fellowship, and to other Peshawar Shi'a friends for their generous assistance and companionship. Their names have been changed to protect their privacy. For creative, constructive comments, I am grateful to Catherine Bell, Michelle Brunet, Maria Cattell, Sima Fahid, Marilyn Fernandez, Dorothea French, Shahla Haeri, Pat Higgins, Diane Jonte-Pace, Barbara Molony, Seyyed Vali Reza Nasr, David Pinault, Nayereh Tohidi, and George Westermark, and especially to Diane Dreher, Erika Friedl, and Jean Hegland, who generously gave dedicated support and detailed attention to several drafts. To my wonderful research assistants, Michelle Brunet and Caprice Scarborough, many thanks.

[*Signs: Journal of Women in Culture and Society* 1998, vol. 23, no. 2]

are all supposed to go home and revert to earlier, narrower gender roles, as if all of their experiences had not happened and nothing had changed.

But of course things do change. In spite of increased pressures to serve their group selflessly during times of agitation and to promote their group's values devotedly, women do *not* abnegate all sense of selfhood. Within the tight constraints of their loyalties, they manage to maintain agency. Their experiences and what they have learned from them about themselves, society, and possibilities for change do not disappear but are incorporated into their self- and worldviews and may play a part in further personal and social transformation.

In this article, I examine a situation where women in Peshawar, Pakistan, as part of a religious/political movement, were passionately loyal to their deprecated religion and threatened religious group. With all their hearts, they wanted to serve their embattled religious sect. And yet, in spite of their dedication to their religion and religious movement, they used their service experiences to consider and transform their self-images and worldviews.

Many Americans might assume these Pakistani Shi'a Muslim women, caught up in a religious fundamentalist movement, to be so much controlled by their attachment to their culture's values and constraints that they become passive subjects, lacking selfhood and actor status. This view may be due to the fact that the women are Middle Eastern, Muslim, and religious fundamentalists. Any one of these three identities might imply that a woman is so attached to or embedded in her social grouping and its values that she capitulates entirely and is incapable of agency. True, dedicated as they are to their beleaguered religious group, they are not willing to question openly its values or tenets by obviously straying outside of its gender boundaries. My field research demonstrates that through their summer 1991 women's religious rituals (*majales*), Shi'a women in Peshawar, Pakistan, carried out crucial outreach work among Shi'a from various ethnic backgrounds, assisting their mobilization into the unified Shi'a movement.[1] In conducting this political work, they did not threaten central Shi'a values or gender expectations: they worked under male guidance in sex-segregated female groups and wrapped themselves in proper purdah veils while traveling to and from women's religious rituals.

While conducting their political and symbolic Shi'a movement work, however, the Peshawar women simultaneously furthered their own mo-

---

[1] Peshawar, a city of some three million inhabitants in northwestern Pakistan, is capital of the North-West Frontier Province (NWFP). It is located not far from the Khyber Pass leading into neighboring Afghanistan.

bility, freedom of action, and personal development. The paradoxical demands on women of the Shi'a movement—that they should be capable
political workers as well as obedient, pure, self-abnegating, covered, and
secluded symbols of the strength and rectitude of the Shi'a religion and
movement—provided a gender situation with some fluidity and dynamic
potential. In spite of what outsiders might think and what movement adherents and political/religious leaders might attempt to project, gender—
even for members of a fundamentalist Shi'a movement—is not immutable
or unmalleable.

During my field research in Peshawar in the summer of 1991, Shi'a
women engaged in subtle gender negotiation and modification through
the practice of their religious mourning rituals—the *majales*. Through this
religious ritual work, the women generated paradoxical power. Their significant political outreach and consolidation work made them valuable political resources—and thus all the more important to contain and control.
But their travels around the city and even to other cities to attend *majales;*
their developing performance, social, and leadership skills; their experiences with diverse people and situations; and their growing awareness of
their capabilities presented them with opportunities to think differently
about themselves, women in general, and women's place in society. It is
ironic that the *majales* brought women *both* fundamentalism *and* freedom
as well as a female community *both* coercive *and* enabling. Investigation of
1991 Shi'a women's *majales* in Peshawar reveals how women, no matter
how loyal to their social group's values, religion, and aims in troubled
times, may nevertheless find means for self-development—and thus potentially also for an evolving self- and worldview and for gender transformation—through the very practice of their group service.

The martyrdom of Imam Husein generated Shi'a Muslims' central myth
and paradigm as well as these mourning rituals, which hold such profound
significance for contemporary Pakistani Shi'a women.[2] Although the reigning caliph's army killed Imam Husein and his followers thirteen hundred
years ago, the martyrs' struggle and plight still influence believers' worldviews and political stances at present. After their A.D. 680 conquest, the
victors marched the captive womenfolk from the Karbala plains, south of
present-day Baghdad, to Damascus, the caliph's capital. Zaynab, Imam

---

[2] Sunni (the majority in most Muslim countries) and Shi'a are the two main groups of
Muslims. Shi'a, with their belief in intercession between God and humanity through the
Family of the Prophet, *Imam*s (successors to the Prophet), and *imamzadeh* (descendants of
the *Imam*s), are roughly analogous to the Catholic branch of Christianity. Similar to Protestant Christians, orthodox Sunnis do not accept intermediation or spiritual hierarchy, although
many among the Sunni masses do.

Husein's sister, initiated the Shi'a mourning rituals by courageously lamenting and recounting the martyrdom story along the way and even at
the caliph's court. Since then, the lamentations have been elaborated into
passion plays, chants and hymns, ritual self-flagellation, processions, and
narrations. With the profound spiritual and emotional meanings that they
hold for believers, these rites of lamentation are also politically charged.
Adherents use them for expressing Shi'a identity, making political statements, and contesting political power. Although the efficacy of Shi'a
mourning rituals in political competition and conflict has been documented,[3] their implications for ethnic and gender politics have been
neglected.

My Peshawar study investigated connections among religious rituals,
ethnic identity, and political hegemony. The *majales* provided a medium
for Indian immigrant Shi'a to monopolize ritual process. In the Shi'a unification effort, Indian-Pakistani, or Mohajir (refugees from India), Shi'a
were propagating their own ritual style, religious interpretation, and language — Urdu — at the cost of those from other Shi'a ethnic groups, such
as Pukhtun and Persian-speaking Qizilbash.

Regarding gender politics, my research explored the paradoxical effects
of women's rising commemorative ritual participation for their self-
actualization and autonomy. Although women played a central part in
knitting together Shi'a from various ethnic groups, and thereby gained
mobility and a heightened sense of community, they were also exposed to
intrusive social coercion and Shi'a activists' increasingly fundamentalist attitudes. The Shi'a movement's alternative power framework thus
brought women constraints and losses as well as new freedoms. Because
both female and male Shi'a organizers sought to use women's intensified
ritual devotion for their own ends, women's ritual involvement became a
contested resource in the subtle struggle over gender power.

To develop the analysis, I first contextualize my research on women's
majles (sing. of *majales*) in Shi'a political history, Peshawar gender attitudes, and my own cross-cultural research experience. After introducing
the concept of alternative power frameworks, I go on to review the social
histories and divergent ritual practices of the three main Peshawar Shi'a
ethnic groups and then analyze the expansion of Mohajir ritual influence
and the Mohajir-dominated Shi'a fundamentalist movement. Finally, I dis-

[3] In addition to Gustav Thaiss's (1972, 1973, 1978) sagacious work in prerevolutionary
Iran, other examples of *Moharram* rituals commemorating the passion of Imam Husein as
sites of political competition, conflict, or struggle over change are provided by Peters 1956;
Jayawardena 1968; Hegland 1983a, 1983b; Good and Good 1988; Singh 1988; Freitag
1992; Ram 1994; and Thaiss 1994.

cuss the paradoxical power that women *majles* participants generate and speculate about where the contradictory forces might lead Shi'a women.

Power politics, gender politics, and Peshawar women's *majales*

The 1979 Iranian Revolution strengthened Shi'a identity not only in Iran but in other countries as well.[4] My interest in the connections between Shi'a religious rituals and power contention was first aroused during my field research in Iran, which began in July 1978, just as the Iranian revolutionary movement was gathering force. A Fulbright fellowship to Pakistan in the fall of 1990 offered the opportunity to further probe connections between Shi'a ritual and politics. However, my teaching and research in Peshawar were rudely interrupted in mid-January 1991 by the pre-Gulf War evacuation of Americans. In July I was able to return, just in time for the anniversary rituals of Imam Husein's martyrdom. Shahida, a former student from the University of Peshawar, took me to her Mohajir neighborhood public Huseiniyyah Hall, launching me into the summer's round of women's *majales* and my research on the ethnic and gender politics of Imam Husein mourning ceremonies. At each *majles,* women invited me to a future *majles* in their own home or told me about others and urged me to attend. During the next two months, I spent most of my time scurrying around the city to women's rituals and interviewing Shi'a men and women.[5]

Few ethnographers have studied Shi'a women's rituals;[6] male researchers

---

[4] Iran is the only country where Shi'a Muslims are the majority and also control the government. Shi'a are a minority in most other Muslim countries, such as Bahrain, Kuwait, Saudi Arabia, Pakistan, Lebanon, and Afghanistan. Although most Iraqis are Shi'a (about 55 percent), the government is Sunni controlled. As Nayereh Tohidi reminded me, Shi'a are the majority in newly independent Azerbaijan, formerly a republic of the USSR, although the government is secular. A large minority in Tajikistan is Shi'a as well. Among the many studies of Shi'a are Keddie 1983; Mottahedeh 1985; Cole and Keddie 1986; Rizvi 1986; Cole 1988; Hasnain 1988; Loeffler 1988; Norton 1988; Schubel 1991, 1993; Pinault 1992a, 1992b; Nakash 1994; and Walbridge 1996.

[5] See Hegland 1995, 1997, in press for more discussion of my research experience.

[6] For materials on the variety of ritual practices among Shi'a women, such as pilgrimage and *sofreh* (meals donated to the saints to request or thank for assistance), I refer the reader to the work of Anne H. Betteridge (1985, 1989), based on fieldwork in the southwest Iranian provincial capital, Shiraz, and Azam Torab (1996), based on Tehran research. The Ferneas' (1978) article about Muslim women's religious practices includes a vivid description of Shi'a women's mourning gatherings, which Elizabeth Fernea attended, in a small town of southern Iraq. Elizabeth Fernea's well-known book, *Guests of the Sheikh: An Ethnography of an Iraqi Village* (1989), contains gripping portrayals of *Moharram* activities by southern Iraqi Shi'a. In

have no access to the sex-segregated women's gatherings. Even with the entrée provided by my students, going on my own to rituals was difficult for me, because I did not know what reaction to expect from fervent Shi'a practitioners, particularly in the aftermath of Desert Storm. The American offensive against their fellow Iraqi Muslims had horrified and infuriated Pakistanis, and Saddam Hussein's genocidal slaughter of Iraqi Shi'a after the war and American inaction sorely grieved Pakistani Shi'a.

As an American, therefore, I was reluctant to attend *majales* where I might not know anybody and sometimes had to compel myself to go. My second *majles,* the *'Ashura* ritual at a large Qizilbash home, was the most nerve-racking for me.[7] A student's brother guided me through alleys and deposited me at the passageway leading to the women's upstairs balcony. (My student could not come with me, much to my regret; her conservative family did not allow their womenfolk out even to attend sex-segregated religious rituals.)

I slowly moved up the steps, emerging into the crowd of women already seated on the floor as close as possible to the lattice looking down on the courtyard below, where all the action would take place. All faces looked at me in wonder and then turned to murmur questions and speculations to their neighbors. I gathered the courage to find a space to sit and, eventually, even talk a little to the women around me. Hidden from male sight up on the latticed balcony, we women listened to the sermon and then crowded in to watch the men's spectacular grieving and bloody self-flagellation following the entrance of the white horse representing Imam Husein's bereaved steed.

Later, I realized I need not have been so apprehensive. As I attended more rituals and became acquainted with the regulars so that I could join in the chatting and community feeling, my comfort level rose. Although I am concerned about many implications of religious fundamentalisms and cannot entirely share these women's worldviews, during my visits I concentrated on trying to understand them. People did not query me on my opinions that summer but rather focused on expressing their own. In char-

---

contrast to city and town women's access to mourning rituals, Erika Friedl (1989) found Shi'a women in a southwest Iranian village lacking their own rituals and able only to watch the men while veiled and crouching unobtrusively on rooftops. Women were likewise excluded from *Moharram* processions in a settlement of about three thousand (in 1978–79) near Shiraz (Hegland 1986b).

[7] *'Ashura,* meaning "tenth" in Arabic, refers to the tenth of the Muslim lunar month *Moharram,* commemorated as the martyrdom anniversary.

acteristic anthropological "participant observation" research practice, I participated in their *Moharram* experiences as fully as possible while observing attentively.

As a Western, liberal woman, I saw this situation to be marked by a religious ideology and related sociopolitical stances that severely confine women. Indeed, I had come to the North-West Frontier Province (NWFP) precisely because I wanted to study gender dynamics and women's coping mechanisms under extreme conditions. Yet I wanted to focus not on women's confinement but, rather, on their attempts to create selves, lives, and communities to serve best their own interests and those of their loved ones and affiliates, under their limiting circumstances.

For several reasons, I felt a bond with these Shi'a women that somewhat mitigated the worldview discrepancies. We were all females together, and in both their cultural setting and my own Midwestern, Scandinavian Lutheran background, women were perceived as having commonalities and were expected to interact among themselves at social gatherings. Further, in both cultural environments, women were supposed to be "nice" and were responsible for reaching out to and including other women. Adding to my sense of belonging at Peshawar Shi'a women's ritual gatherings were my memories of similar Shi'a women's gatherings I had attended in Iran. With these women, I was furious at Saddam Hussein's brutality against the Iraqi Shi'a and greatly saddened by their plight. I too was distressed by discrimination and violence against Shi'a in Pakistan and elsewhere. My personal philosophy of concern about people suffering under inequality and unrightful power resonated with the Shi'a collective memory of Imam Husein and his small band's courageous battle against the tyrannical caliph's great forces. I grew intrigued with how these Pakistani Shi'a applied their paradigm of a persevering struggle between justice and evil domination to their current political situation, just as the application of this paradigm to the 1978–79 popular movement against the Shah's government had fascinated me in Iran.

In Pakistan's early history after the 1947 partition from India, Sunni-Shi'a conflict was not significant. The founders of Pakistan were largely secularists, and, in fact, Jinnah himself was a nominal Shi'a convert. In the early 1960s, however, Sunni religious leaders reacted to the Western-educated political elite's plans for a democratic, secular state with demands that Islamic principles must govern Pakistan (Ahmed 1987). *Moharram* clashes broke out between Sunni and those Shi'a opposed to a Sunni Islamic state. Shi'a supported President Ali Bhutto: his secular government and Shi'a connections (his wife was originally an Iranian Shi'a) portended tolerance for the Shi'a minority, some 15–20 percent of Pakistan's population. Then, with President Zia-ul-Haq's politically astute efforts at Islamization, Pakistani Shi'a became seriously disaffected (Keddie 1993). Many aspects of President Zia's 1979 reform package, Shi'a angrily pointed out, were derived from a Sunni school of law and were not in accordance with Shi'a religious law (Richter 1981, 153). Shi'a were particularly incensed that Zia planned to collect *zakat* (religious taxes) directly from bank accounts; Shi'a did not give religious taxes to the government but to Shi'a leaders (*mujtahids*). After widespread demonstration in 1980, Shi'a were exempted from the government *zakat* taxation, but Zia's rigid Sunni Islamization had alienated Shi'a and encouraged Sunni-Shi'a acrimony, resulting in the bloody *Moharram* 1986 rioting in Pakistani Punjab (Keddie 1995, 207–9). Peshawar Shi'a, still furious, told me that during that period extremist Sunni groups, fueled by Zia's press for Islamization and funded by Saudi donations, had attacked Shi'a mosques in the NWFP and had even desecrated the Qur'ans found inside.

Peshawar Shi'a had particular reason to feel outraged frustration against the government. The top-ranking Pakistani Shi'a cleric, Arif al-Hussaini, a Peshawar resident and ardent Khomeini supporter, had been assassinated in 1988; those responsible had still not been punished. Militant Shi'a, racked by thoughts of Arif al-Hussaini's martyrdom and his as-yet unapprehended assailant, were at loggerheads with militant Sunni. Inspired also by the Iranian Revolution and by the related growth of Shi'a religious transnationalism,[8] Peshawar Shi'a[9] were gaining self-consciousness, I found in 1991. Many believed that the Sunni Muslim government and majority population discriminated against and mistreated them. Shi'a leaders felt that a stronger political front could potentially pressure the Sunni government into better protection and sensitivity to Shi'a needs and demands. Consequently, they were working to unite the divergent Shi'a ethnic groups—Mohajir, Pukhtun, and Qizilbash—into one large alliance.

As is often the case, women played central roles in reaching out to other

---

[8] Shi'a present an opportunity to rethink the constructed boundaries for anthropological research and analysis. Some Shi'a leaders and communities spread around the globe—with their own languages, ethnic identities, nationalities, and variations in ritual practice—are finding means and motivations to develop closer ties and a greater sense of unity. We see not only the strengthening of Shi'a religious nationalisms within countries, but also the growth of Shi'a religious transnationalism.

[9] Studies of Shi'a in Pakistan are rare. See Ahmed 1987; Keddie 1993, 1995, 183–86, 208, 209; Sagaster 1993; Schubel 1993; and Hegland 1995, 1997, in press. I am grateful to David Pinault for providing me with Ursula Sagaster's article.

Shi'a ethnic groups and strengthening social connections, in this case, largely through women's ritual mourning gatherings.[10] Their task required increasing mobility and independence for *majles* attendance. By patronizing these mourning rites, they could spend time outside of the house in enjoyable social interaction, which was much appreciated by women ordinarily restricted to their homes by the stern Peshawar modesty code (purdah).[11]

It is difficult for contemporary American women to grasp the extent of Peshawar women's containment and suppression. Peshawar is the capital of the NWFP, homeland of the Pukhtun ethnic group, whose stark views of women's place are distilled in their ominous saying: "Women—either the house or the grave." Ideally, a female should go out of the house only twice during her lifetime: once when being conveyed as a fully veiled, arranged-marriage bride from her father's to her husband's extended household, and the second time when her dead body is carried from house to cemetery. Although few (if any) women actually attain this ideal, nevertheless they are secluded as much as possible. Schooling takes few out of the home; only some 3 percent of NWFP females are literate. When women do leave the home, their segregation from men is still rigid: even social occasions, such as weddings or funerals, are sex-segregated. Further, men of any standing have men's houses—separate buildings or set-aside rooms—for entertaining other males apart from their own households, so that their women need never be exposed to outsiders.

Generally, to be allowed out of the home, Peshawar females must have very good reason; be fully concealed with a body veil and, for most, a face shield; and be escorted by a male relative. The careful modesty normally necessary even for non-Pukhtun women—the majority male Pukhtun population expected rigid purdah for proper females—became even more important with the growing Afghan refugee population. Women venturing outside without the knowledge or permission of their supervising menfolk feared their men's suspicion and severe punishment, rival groups' political

---

[10] Hegland 1997 provides detailed discussions of Peshawar Shi'a women's ritual activities and their social bonding work in the Shi'a consolidation movement. For other analyses of women's social bonding work and its usefulness in politics, see Aswad 1967; Kaplan 1981; Joseph 1982, 1983; Hegland 1986b, 1990, 1991; di Leonardo 1987; and Peteet 1991.

[11] For informative discussions about the general situation of Pakistani women, see Eglar 1960; Papanek 1973, 1982, 1984, 1994; Rahat 1981; Ramazani 1985; Weiss 1985, 1990, 1992; Shaheed 1986, 1994; Rauf 1987; Mumtaz and Shaheed 1987; Mehdi 1990, Ewing 1991; Jalal 1991; Haeri 1993; and Mumtaz 1994.

or honor-motivated violence,[12] or harassment or worse, which any male "naturally" might commit against an unprotected woman.

Little wonder, then, that Shi'a women eagerly grasped the expanding latitude to travel far afield for women's religious gatherings. In addition to compelling spiritual reasons and sectarian loyalty, women tremendously enjoyed the adventure, socializing, and special refreshments at rituals. In spite of such attractions, though, their ritual participation confronted the women with problematic paradoxes: the Shi'a unification goal rather inevitably bolstered religious fundamentalism and group social pressure. Non-Mohajir women faced further drawbacks. As the Mohajirs' ritual style, religious approach, and language (Urdu) became predominant in the consolidated Shi'a movement, the languages and ritual/religious styles of Shi'a women recruited from other ethnic/linguistic groups, such as the Persian-speaking Qizilbash, were becoming lost to them.

Alternative power frameworks:
Opportunity *and* oppression

Several anthropologists have analyzed situations where women turn to another power framework in order to enjoy the alternative system's freedoms and benefits.[13] Embracing an alternative power framework and enjoying the freedom, opportunities, and mobility that it offers may also result in unsought and unforeseen restrictions and disadvantages (Abu-Lughod 1990). People may draw on several "spheres of action" in power manipulations and strategizing toward their own ends (Friedl 1991a; see also Friedl 1991b).

To gain affirmation, competence, status, religious reward, and self-assurance, Peshawar Shi'a women evaluated several power frameworks and juggled numerous aspects of their identities and affiliations, all with their respective diverging, converging, and overlapping discourses. For these women, religion, family, ethnicity, gender, and nationality were significant sources of identity and meaning. They faced the challenge of finding means to satisfy their socially constructed needs and aims in each discourse while threatening others as little as possible.

[12] Kidnapping and rape of opponents' womenfolk are not excluded from strategies of political competition in Pakistan. Perpetrators of such political violence against women have little fear of legal results: in order to bring the rapist successfully to conviction, a prosecutor would have to produce four male eyewitnesses to testify that the sexual encounter was indeed rape and not consensual, or else the female victim would be punished. See Haeri 1995b.

[13] See Cattell 1992. For additional examples of people turning to alternative power frameworks or organizing paradigms, see Bailey 1957, 1960, 1970; and Cohen 1969, 1981.

Choosing appropriate frameworks

For Shi'a women, attachments to family and religion were so critical and profound that they were not prepared to pursue social status, self-assertion, career, competence, or distinction through means considered illegitimate by religious teachings and cultural understandings about family. In Deniz Kandiyoti's (1988) terminology, Peshawar Shi'a women were not prepared to reject the "patriarchal bargain" of exchanging autonomy for support and protection. Given their existential situations, they had good reason for this stance: economic dependence, lack of other viable options, and the perceived impossibility of living without family and male protection meant that women could not opt to leave sternly patriarchal, religiously supported family authority. In addition, the powerful emotional, psychological, and spiritual ties connecting women with their religious community and Shi'a saintly figures made them understandably reluctant to resist openly their religious heritage's patriarchal components (Hegland, in press).[14]

Pakistanis, on the whole, seem less ready to question their religion than are people in many other Middle Eastern countries. Their reluctance is related to the proximity and history with India and its Hindu majority, among other factors. As part of their nationalistic as well as religious duty, Pakistani Shi'a and Sunni women have shared responsibility for upholding Islam — Pakistan's raison d'etre and the rallying focus against larger and more powerful India.[15]

Advantages for women in the Shi'a movement:
Freedom, mobility, women's community

For a number of reasons, then, Peshawar Shi'a women abstained from direct criticism or flagrant disobedience in order to pursue their own goals

[14] Nancy Tapper (Lindisfarne's) publications on Syrian elites (1988–89) and an Afghan Durrani Pukhtun tribal group (1991) and Patricia Jeffery's (1989) on Muslim shrine managers in India feature women who could not afford to leave the relative security of family ties and patriarchal protection and so felt forced to comply with patriarchal authority. Also see Rugh 1984; Altorki 1986; al-Khayyat 1990; Peteet 1991; MacLeod 1992a, 1992b; Joseph 1993, 1994; Arebi 1994; and Friedl 1994.

[15] This is not to claim that women completely refrained from any thoughts along these lines. With longer-term and more intimate interaction, enhanced experience and research skill, and the right opportunities (Keesing 1985), a field-worker might be able to hear indications of cynicism concerning religious gender teachings from these Peshawar Shi'a women. An illiterate, poor Iranian village woman confided to Friedl her strong suspicion "that religion, as preached and practiced, was not made by God but by men in order to suppress women!" (Friedl 1989, 133). All other village women with whom she spoke, Friedl reported, found it troubling to deal with the contradictions about women in their religion. Shi'a

(see Hegland, in press); rather, they appropriated the authorized *majles,* framing their ritual performances with their own interests.[16] They thereby fulfilled central responsibilities, avoided jeopardizing valued connections, and even won approval from male family and religious supervisors. The male president of the Peshawar Shi'a organization, for example, did not hesitate to acknowledge women's contributions to *Moharram* commemorations. They did more for Imam Husein than men, he said: women spent far more time attending *majales.* Indeed, they maintained connections with each other through less frequent ritual gatherings during the off-season but socialized with other females practically from morning to night, day after day, during the entire two-and-a-half-month annual mourning season. Women were thought to be more emotional and compassionate, more attached to the saints and their sorrowful deaths. The president praised his niece Shahida for her *noha* (mourning couplets) chanting fame. He promoted his sister Mahreen's preaching career and sponsored her *majles* rituals in the courtyard he owned, where Mahreen lived with two other unmarried sisters. The president and others intent on uniting Shi'a into a strong political pressure group recognized the importance of women's gatherings for reaching out to the Shi'a population.

With new opportunities come new trials

Able to transcend their narrow ethnic social neighborhoods through entering the consolidating, Mohajir-dominated Shi'a movement's wider feminine ritual arena, the Peshawar Shi'a women did not consider that the greater opportunity for spatial movement through the alternative power framework would entail greater oppression in other regards, particularly for Qizilbash women. Indian-Pakistani Shi'a maintained links with relatives in Hindu-dominated areas. They were accustomed to the intense ritual life, rather fundamentalist worldview, and careful restrictions on women's behavior that provided Shi'a in India with shelters and markers against the Hindu population. The consolidating Shi'a fundamentalist movement in Peshawar influenced Indian women immigrants but affected Qizilbash women all the more; Mohajir language and ritual style were overshadowing Qizilbash ritual practices.

Women from other language groups — such as Pukhtuns and Persian-speaking Qizilbash — who were attracted by the Shi'a fundamentalist

---

women in Peshawar were probably somewhat less inclined to ponder contradictions, or at least to verbalize such reflection.

[16] See Hegland in press for elaboration on how the women subverted *Moharram* rituals to construct their own meanings.

movement faced the demise of their own language in ritual practice and interethnic Shiʿa interaction. In the consolidation of Peshawar Shiʿa groups, Urdu, the language of the Indian Shiʿa, gained preeminence. Urdu, the national language of Pakistan, is used in the educational system and is the mother tongue of the Mohajirs, who had mostly come to Pakistan at the time of the partition in 1947 and maintained close ties with relatives and associates in India. Urdu was a natural choice as the Pakistani Shiʿa common language, because any Shiʿa who attended public school automatically studied in this language. The use of Persian, the mother tongue of the Qizilbash (a minority among a minority), thus was declining in Pakistan.

For similar reasons, the Mohajir ritual style was becoming more popular at the Qizilbash format's expense. As the consolidating Shiʿa fundamentalist movement gained force, Qizilbash women faced the extinction of their own ritual tradition: lyrical, gentle cultural performances. The Mohajirs were the most prominent Pakistani Shiʿa group, and, in addition, their more fervent, vehement, and fundamentalist preachings and practices better matched the influential Islamic Republic of Iran brand of Shiʿism and more emphatically responded to extremist Sunni Muslims in Pakistan. Just as their spectacular, passionate ritual processions distinguished Indian Shiʿa from the surrounding Hindu majority, their sensational rituals dramatically set off Pakistani Shiʿa from the surrounding majority Sunni population.

Shiʿa women attained gratifying social support and a sense of belonging by joining rituals, but only in exchange for submitting to peer surveillance and social pressure that enforced rigid behavioral expectations for women. The many sermons they heard decreed the essentializing fundamentalist Shiʿism that fueled Shiʿa self-identification in Iran and in Pakistan.[17] Indian Shiʿism's fundamentalist tendency, exacerbated by the explosion of sectarian violence and flourishing Hindu fundamentalism, spread to Pakistan through Urdu media, kinship networks, visiting, and clerical contact.

---

[17] Detailed discussion on the applicability of the term *fundamentalism* to Middle Eastern or South Asian Islamic religious movements can be found elsewhere. *Fundamentalism* is, in my belief, the best term available to refer to a reemphasis on religion, including a return to what are considered by adherents to be the fundamentals or basics of the religion, the need for their application in this-worldly life, and — therefore — efforts to influence politics. Fundamentalists generally consider standardized belief and behavior, principles of hierarchy and obedience, traditional gender roles, and restrictions on women to be basic to their religions. They claim support for their assertions from holy sources. Fundamentalisms will naturally vary in meaning and character according to situation and even from person to person — in spite of their belief that only one version of the truth is valid (Loeffler 1988).

Finally, extremist Pakistani Sunni fundamentalist rhetoric and violence against Shi'a, together with strong Sunni Islamist influence in government, further pushed Pakistani Shi'a into their own defensively fundamentalist entrenchment.

Religious fundamentalism—a power framework alternative to ethnic group resource and territory protection

Seyyed Vali Reza Nasr (1994, 1995) argues that many aspects of current Islamic fundamentalism originated during the partition process between Pakistan and India. Nasr sees Pakistani theologian/ideologue Mawlana Mawdudi as developing a Muslim fundamentalist perspective to safeguard the interests of Muslims within the Muslim state of Pakistan.

> Only if that [Muslim] majority would reaffirm its attachment to the fundamental tenets of the faith from which its identity was drawn would it safeguard its interests. . . . Fundamentalism was . . . the means for creating impregnable walls around the Muslim community. By interpreting Islam as an ideology for a vigilant community, by emphasizing puritanism, the exoteric dimensions of the faith, strict obedience to Islamic law narrowly interpreted, and by discouraging those customs and rituals that resembled Hindu practices or could serve as a bridge with Hinduism, Mawdudi moved to change the cultural milieu of Indian Islam as well as the context in which Muslims were encountering the political choices before them. . . . Fundamentalism, therefore, was at inception nothing more than radical communalism. (Nasr 1995, 126, 127, 128)

Anthropologists will see parallels between using fundamentalism to emphasize Muslim religious/cultural characteristics—and thereby to strengthen the boundary between Muslims and Hindus, between Muslim territory and Hindu territory—and Fredrik Barth's seminal work on ethnicity (see Barth 1969, introduction). Barth suggests that one way for an ethnic group to deal with contact and competition with another under conditions of change is to "choose to emphasize ethnic identity." And "the innovators may choose to emphasize one level of identity among the several provided by the traditional social organization."[18]

[18] Barth 1969, 33, 34. In his classic work on ethnicity, based on research among the NWFP Pukhtun, Barth explores the factors, such as visible markers and value orientations, that bring about and maintain or modify group distinctions, resulting in the persistence of ethnic groups. It is precisely conditions of contact, interaction, and competition over territory and resources, he argues, that lead to the generation or exaggeration of markers and value

Barth focuses on generative processes rather than essentialist entities in examining ethnicity. Borrowing his approach, one can postulate that Muslims who were in contact with Hindus under the divisive partition conditions would develop extreme forms of appearance, behavior, and value orientations to mark their identity and maintain the boundary between themselves and the surrounding Hindu population.

In partitioning India and Pakistan, the religious "level of identity" was emphasized over the ethnic. This process is repeating itself in Pakistan with the religious dichotomization between Sunni and Shi'a through the growth of fundamentalism and extremist groups in both branches of Pakistani Islam and, in correlation, deemphasizing ethnic identity among Shi'a groups.[19]

In earlier periods, Shi'a *Moharram* processions in India had been community events, with Hindus participating alongside Muslims (Cole 1988, 115–19; Freitag 1992). But as sectarian tension escalated before partition, *Moharram* rituals proclaiming Muslim identity and community carried explosive potential. Indian Shi'as' more dramatic rituals had reinforced their separate identity against the majority Hindus and their rich ritual calendar. Those Mohajir Shi'a migrating from India to Pakistan continued practicing their accustomed rituals, which were far more fervent than the rituals of local Qizilbash, who, having lived for generations in Muslim areas, had not faced a menacing Hindu majority. The Mohajir style of *majles* began to supplant their own informal, dispassionate performances and their less strict lifestyles. With barriers of language, ethnicity, and distinctive ritual practice between them and the wider fundamentalist Shi'a community eroding, Qizilbash women had more to lose in terms of attitudinal and behavioral latitude. Although embracing the Shi'a unification movement allowed Qizilbash females a way out of confinement to home and narrow social circle, they now had to deal with greater demands for conformity in dress and behavior and repeated ritual assertions in sermons and symbolism of feminine inadequacy and dependence.

Ethnic groups and women's divergent ritual practices

In the past, women in particular had been limited to religious gatherings in their own ethnic enclaves: Mohajirs, Qizilbash, or Pukhtuns. The Mohajirs had settled in the newer Sadar area of Peshawar during the 1947

---

[19] While Pakistani Shi'a are suppressing ethnic differences, thereby strengthening sectarian unity, other Pakistanis are engaging in ethnic conflict. Violence between natives and immigrants from India (Mohajirs) in Karachi, for example, has produced far more dead than the

partition of India. Most Mohajirs were from merchant families and generally lived well on proceeds from Sadar Bazaar area commerce.

Qizilbash Shiʿa had long lived in the Peshawar "Old City," where narrow, rambling walkways formed a maze between jutting walls that hid courtyards and homes. Originally of Turkish background, their forebears had been brought by the Persian shahs from Anatolia to serve in their administration and military. The Qizilbash had become Persianized during their long residence in that country (Roemer 1990). Qizilbash fought for the Safavid state of Persia and then were employed by Nadir Shah during his invasion of India in 1739 (Cole 1988, 41, 45). While traveling east in Persian service, the Qizilbash had become scattered along the way. A sizable group, still speaking an older version of Persian, lived in Peshawar's Old City. Most Qizilbash women who attended *Moharram majales* lived comfortable lives, supported by male family members' profitable occupations such as merchants or bankers.

Shiʿa are a religious minority among Pukhtun; most Pukhtun are Sunni Muslims. The Pukhtun, the ethnic group populating Pakistan's NWFP, were described as unruly and fierce by British colonial administrators. The present border between Pakistan and Afghanistan divides the Pukhtun homeland. More than two million Afghan Pukhtun refugees who fled Afghanistan during the recent war now live in Pakistan (Grima 1992, 3). As this ethnic group dominates in the NWFP of Pakistan, some Pukhtun who are asserting their identity and political power have been lobbying to change that province's name to Pukhtunistan.[20]

Pukhtun Shiʿa rituals

Among Shiʿa women of these three ethnic backgrounds, ritual practices differed dramatically. For Pukhtun Shiʿa, *Moharram* practices resembled some sufi groups' rituals. Male ritual performers in Pukhtun villages, enabled by their faith in Imam Husein's protection, put on spectacular demonstrations walking on coals or piercing themselves without negative effect. Pukhtun women practiced arduous facial self-flagellation, swinging their hands together from above to strike their cheekbones.

For several reasons, Pukhtun ritual practices were not as rapidly displaced by those of the Mohajirs as were Qizilbash rituals. Although Pukhtun Shiʿa living in Peshawar might attend rituals with non-Pukhtun, most Pukhtun Shiʿa lived in rural areas and were not exposed to Mohajir influence. Pukhtuns dominated in the NWFP and were thus generally more

[20] If this renaming should be done (although it is highly unlikely), each of the four provinces in Pakistan would carry the name of its predominant ethnic group.

influential than the small Qizilbash minority. Also, Shi'a zealots admired Pukhtun Shi'a because of their dramatic and arduous mourning practices and so did not target them for tactful missionizing, as they did the "lax" Qizilbash.

Mohajir Shi'a rituals

Mohajir women practiced strict mourning. They attended ritual sessions from morning to evening during the two and a half months of mourning, especially during the first ten days of *Moharram*. Going from one home in Sadar to another, they joined perhaps eight *majles* sessions a day. At mourning gatherings they maintained somber demeanor: they did not talk frivolously, smile, or laugh. They did not wear makeup, gold jewelry, or flamboyant hues of red, pink, orange, or yellow, but wore black on the most important mourning days and on lesser days wore reserved colors such as blue or green.

Mohajir *majles* sessions, conducted in Urdu, began with singing *marsia* (devotional or commemorative verses) while women sat on the floor, sometimes beating their chests. Then a preacher admonished the women about their Islamic duties. Her sermon ended in a martyrdom story while women wept and moaned and slapped chests or legs. After the sermon, women stood while different circles of young women vied to lead *noha* (mourning chants). All the women beat their chests in rhythm to the chanting, often with athletic swinging movements, stretching their arms up high and then flinging their hands back down for resounding blows to the chest. Finally, prayers were directed to the Prophet and other holy figures before the women sat down for a treat offered by the host.

Qizilbash Shi'a rituals

In contrast to their Indian counterparts, Qizilbash women modified their appearance and comportment very little for *majles* gatherings. Wearing bright clothing, makeup, jewelry, and cheerful faces to *majles* sessions, they chatted and laughed and did not change their normal behavior to step into mourning stance. Indian women therefore criticized them — although not to their faces — for their shocking lack of piety. Until recently, Qizilbash women had conducted their *majales* in their own Persian language. Sitting at ease on the floor, they sang or chanted lyrically about Imam Husein and his family while tapping themselves gently on the chest with one hand. The program might include a *rozah*, or story about Imam Husein's martyrdom. The audience joined in the choruses, but women did not weep or display a sorrowful air during the *rozah* recitation. Rather than frantic, heartrending grief and self-mortifying fealty exhibitions, Qizilbash rituals were quiet, poignant performances.

Mohajirs' encroaching cultural hegemony over Qizilbash

In 1991, women were attending more rituals than in the recent past, both in their own and other congregations, and another change was also taking place: the Indian *majles* model was prevailing over Qizilbash ceremonials. By 1991 Shi'a women and men were beginning to attend rituals of other ethnic groups in addition to their own, as Shi'a consolidated. They thereby emphasized sectarian identity and deemphasized ethnic identity. Increasingly, the ritual language was Urdu, the Indian immigrants' language. All over the city, Husein rituals began to replicate the Indian format characterized by extreme displays of grief, self-flagellation, and a more fundamentalist worldview. Women were central in the process of pulling different Shi'a ethnic groups into a cohesive unit, and, in conjunction with this unification work, their religious practices became altered. The Qizilbash women's informal ritual interaction and gentle cultural Persian-language performances were being replaced by the Mohajir passionate performances of mourning and fundamentalist sermons about Islamic duty, conducted in Urdu.

One reason for the recession of the Qizilbash performance mode was education. Although government education in Urdu facilitated Shi'a unity by providing Shi'a of various linguistic backgrounds with a common language, such unity came at the cost of diminishing the use of other languages. Qizilbash girls still spoke Persian at home, but in general, the use of that language was declining. Educated young Qizilbash women were now experts in Urdu mourning *noha* and *marsia*. Consequently, chants and songs in Urdu were replacing Qizilbash chants and songs in Persian.

Earlier, all female *majles* narrators among the Persian-speaking Qizilbash had been *rozah-khwani* (reciters of *Moharram* stories) rather than preachers who gave sermons in Indian-Pakistani fashion. But in 1991, only one woman still presented *rozah* in Persian. Shireen had begun performing not long before, when other aging female *rozah-khwani* had retired. At a *majles,* she would intone a story about the Karbala martyrs, interspersed with refrains joined by the audience, especially her daughters and nieces sitting at her feet. During such performances, there was no outpouring of grief, nor was there a sermon admonishing women of their Islamic duties. However, since Shireen delivered her *rozah*s in Persian, only Persian speakers could understand them. Consequently, Urdu-speaking hosts in the Mohajir Sadar Bazaar area did not ask Shireen to come and give performances, and no one else was training to deliver *rozah*s in Persian.

Language learning appeared to be going in one direction only, with Persian speakers learning Urdu but no Urdu speakers learning Persian. As more Urdu-speaking Mohajirs frequent the Old City Qizilbash rituals, and as more Qizilbash become comfortable in Urdu through education, the less welcome Persian *rozahs* will be.

All women who gave sermons in Sadar were Mohajirs and used Urdu. Government schooling in Urdu extended the audience for Urdu-speaking preachers, and literacy equipped these preachers to deliver orations based on the published views of Urdu language fundamentalist theologians. One afternoon I sat with Mahreen, the most prominent female Indian-Pakistani preacher, as she prepared to deliver a sermon, leafing through and studying first one and then another Urdu book from her small library.

Mahreen was training several Urdu-speaking Mohajir little girls to preach. The eldest sister of the talented Old City Qizilbash singing group spoke with Mahreen about bringing her own young daughter for training. Rather than asking a Persian-speaking *rozah-khwana* from her own Qizilbash background to teach her little girl, a Qizilbash mother was turning to Mahreen, an Urdu speaker of Indian origin. This is another indication of tradition shifting away from Qizilbash practices and toward the Urdu language and Indian Shi'a mode of mourning ritual that was pulling more and more women into the hegemonic, fundamentalist Shi'a community and worldview.

Freedom *and* fundamentalism

The Shi'a unification movement offered women mobility and autonomy. Women went to various *imambara* (the house or place of the Imam in Urdu: privately owned ritual spaces; *imambargah* in Persian) in their own area of the city—Sadar Bazaar area, a newer city section for the Indian women, and the Old City, or old part of Peshawar for the Qizilbash. Because women were needed to help consolidate the various Shi'a ethnic groups, they traveled elsewhere as well.[21] Increasingly, women commuted the fifteen to twenty minutes between the two city sections by bus, motorized rickshaw, or automobile to attend the other ethnic group's sessions. Someone told me of a woman who complained—or perhaps it was bragging—about the ten to fifteen young women in her extended family

---

[21] In Hegland 1995 and 1997, I document how some Shi'a men steered their female relatives in ritual performance and Shi'a consolidation activities. Men also marched in their own flagellation groups to mourning sessions in public Huseiniyyah Halls and the some one hundred *imambargah* in Peshawar's Old City district.

household who frequented *majales:* her bus expenses during the mourning months amounted to 50 rupees (about US$2.00 in 1991) a day. At the 1991 ninth of *Moharram* women's *majles* in Huseiniyyah Hall, the public mourning place in Sadar, most of the hundreds of women present were from the Old City or even from towns and villages surrounding Peshawar. That evening, the night before the tenth of *Moharram* — commemorated as the anniversary of Imam Husein's martyrdom — some Sadar Indian-Pakistani women went to the Old City. Like Qizilbash women, they walked, in the company of a few other women only, among the many Old City *imambargah* almost all night long.[22]

Thanks to the more relaxed mobility constraints, the outstanding performance group of Qizilbash sisters attended their first Indian *majles* at a Sadar home while I was present. They listened to the Urdu-language sermon and joined in the Urdu singing and chanting. Warmly welcomed, they stayed a while afterward and exchanged notebook *marsia* and *noha* materials with the host's teenaged daughter. The eldest Qizilbash sister taught at the University of Peshawar, where the host's daughter studied; the national educational system brought Shi'a from different ethnic communities into contact. Later, I saw these Qizilbash sisters perform in a courtyard *majles* hosted by Mahreen, the Sadar Indian-Pakistani woman preacher. The ability to converse with each other and sing and chant in Urdu enabled Shi'a groups of various origins and native languages to commemorate jointly Imam Husein's martyrdom.

Because of intermarriages between Peshawar Shi'a Mohajirs and people in their home Indian communities, women frequently went to India in order to visit relatives and joined *Moharram* rituals there. Travelers visited Iran as well. Women spoke to me enthusiastically of their pilgrimages to Iranian shrines and of their visit, in the company of male relatives and as guests of the Iranian government, to the 1991 commemorations of Ayatollah Khomeini's death anniversary. I met a young couple coming from India on their way to Qom, center of Shi'a learning in Iran, for religious schooling. At least one young woman from Peshawar was also studying at Zeynab University in Qom. Even locally, women's mobility expanded as a result of the Shi'a fundamentalist movement's recruitment of females through education: some females were students at the Iranian Cultural Center in Peshawar.

[22] Men did the same, but, instead of slipping unobtrusively through alleyways, they aggressively broadcast their progress with loud chanting and reverberating chest beating. With thunderous mourning announcing its arrival, each male troupe then put on a vigorous collective chest-beating exhibition in each *imambara* that it visited. Following, male hosts served the troupe refreshments.

Even more so than other women, female preachers were highly mobile. Demand for their services gave them a hectic mourning season schedule as well as a wide social network, respect and status, opportunities to study and speak, and even gustatory delights — ritual offerings of food to the martyred saints. Mahreen was surely one of the most sought-after and mobile women in Peshawar. Well-known female preachers might even be invited to speak in other cities, as was common for male preachers.

A number of single, childless, widowed, and even divorced women found in ritual an approved outlet for their energy. Religiously motivated, an active outside life brought women this-worldly power in terms of social support and freedom from household confinement. One woman, an outstanding performer with a beautiful voice, did not have children. Her *Moharram* singing was her profession, her calling, another woman explained; her strenuous schedule and highly regarded talent helped fill her childless days. One evening she was sick. Her feet had swelled up, she told me, because of so much walking from one *majles* to another. Her husband scolded her: "You're going to get terribly ill if you don't rest. Don't go tomorrow!" She tossed her head in the midst of telling the story. "I told him, 'I'm *going*.' And today I got up and got ready and I'm *just fine!*"

This singer's story, implying that with the Imam's mystical intervention the singer need not listen to her husband, expressed an outrageous sentiment for a Muslim woman, who is charged with obeying her husband. It is ironic that if Mahreen or another preacher of Indian background gave the sermon at the *majles* that this soloist insubordinately attended, she would hear there much about the obligation of pious women to submit themselves entirely to their husbands. She defied her husband for the opportunity to hear that she must not defy him.[23]

This singer's ritual-wrought defiance exemplifies the paradoxical nature of feminine ritual-shaped freedoms. Involved with the Shi'a movement, which offered an alternative power structure and entrance into a wider world, Peshawar Shi'a women encountered mounting fundamentalism and the androcentrism permeating *Moharram* ritual symbolism and organization.[24] Fundamentalist sermons taught women their Islamic duties, such as modesty and *hejab*, or covering; separation from unrelated men; and obedience to husbands. Only near the conclusion of her sermon did a Mohajir preacher turn to the Karbala martyrs. During the almost three months of mourning in 1991, Sadar Shi'a women generally heard several

[23] I am grateful to Diane Dreher for noting this paradox.
[24] In Hegland 1997 and in press, I discuss the negative influences of androcentric rituals and fundamentalist pressures at greater length.

Mohajir-style, fundamentalist sermons a day and some during other times of the year as well.

Community *and* coercion

Women aimed at forming a female ritual community as large and unified as possible, cutting across ethnic, linguistic, class, and even sectarian lines. To this end, the Shi'a women attempted to be inclusive, welcoming anyone who came to a *majles,* no matter what her background. They included members of all language groups by making sure there were some chants or songs in the mother tongue of all present. Pukhtun women were usually in a small minority at Mohajir- and Qizilbash-hosted rituals, but at one point or another, other women would call out, "Now one in Pukhtu, let's do one in Pukhtu."

Even professional singing girls, who were generally looked down on as low-class and lacking in moral constraint, were not turned away. At a *majles* in Mahreen's courtyard, several singing girls started a song at the same time as another group. Leaders waved the others quiet. When I questioned my student Shahida later, she said people had not wanted the singing girls to feel ashamed. At another ritual some half of the females present were sing-ing girls. A young relative of the host mockingly sang a phrase in the nasal, tinny tones supposed to be the singing girls' style. An older woman repri-manded her, and she was quiet. During *majales,* ritual managers attempted to suppress judgmental attitudes toward singing girls, who otherwise could never enter these courtyards.

In actuality, ritual insiders enjoyed advantaged economic standing and pious reputations, and ritual leaders all the more so. However, an appar-ently open and warmly accepting feminine ritual community—character-ized by the appearance of class inclusiveness that ritual regulars so carefully fostered—helped attract higher attendance and the larger community's favor.

As part of their incorporating behavior, women refrained from overtly criticizing others, choosing rather to guide through praise and example. Although Shireen, the Qizilbash *rozah-khwana,* told me in private that the plastic flower decorating the hair of one sister in the eminent Qizilbash singing group offended her, she did not show her disapproval. She also was disturbed that an older Qizilbash woman, a *seyyid* and informal ritual leader, frequently made mistakes even in Persian verses.[25] Asking me to turn off the tape recorder, Shireen spoke quietly into my ear. The woman

---

[25] *Seyyid*s are descendants of the Prophet Mohammad in the male line (through his daugh-ter Fatima and her husband Ali, since the Prophet Mohammad had no surviving sons).

even said *rahem* (womb), which, Shireen said, "has a bad meaning," when the word was supposed to be *raheem,* meaning mercy. Shireen did not say anything to the woman, though; *seyyids* must be respected, she explained. Even when a woman stumbled noticeably while reading from the Qur'an, there were no raised eyebrows or words of reproach.

Ritual performance seemed to be failure-free; thus, women's *majales* provided a safe arena for developing performance and social skills. *Majles* participation helped women to form a sense of self and identity through comparison and regulated competition with others. They developed autonomy through travel, organizing, and leadership in the women's community (Hegland 1997). The few women who were married into another Shi'a ethnic group were particularly well situated to practice mobilizing and administrative skills. An Old City Qizilbash woman was married to a Pukhtun man from the NWFP town of Parachinar. She and her daughter were active in both Qizilbash and Mohajir ritual schedules. With the woman's sister, they sponsored a huge gathering at the large Old City Huseiniyyah Hall that women from all ethnic backgrounds attended. When some Parachinar Shi'a men were killed during a procession, this mother-daughter team inflamed Qizilbash, Pukhtun, and Mohajir women.

The empowering affirmation, social support, and opportunities for personal development that women gained through ritual gatherings, however, were matched by coercion and a patriarchal worldview.[26] Even the mere reciting and going through ritual bodily motions brings its own coercions, as ritual practice theorist Catherine Bell notes: "One might retain one's limited and negotiated involvement in the activities of ritual, but bowing or singing in unison imperceptibly schools the social body in the pleasures of and schemes for acting in accordance with assumptions that remain far from conscious or articulate" (1992, 215).

Further, ritual dedication subjected women to female social group pressure and also to male domination even in the absence of males. Because *majales* were sex-segregated, males were generally not present; women themselves were in charge of surveillance, supervision, and management of other women, thus acting as agents of patriarchal control.[27] Women urged other women to attend *majales.* Once involved in rituals, women

---

[26] Because of fundamentalisms' androcentrism, declared reliance on holy texts, close-knit groupings, and required belief and behavior conformity, women operating within a fundamentalist framework can go only so far in creating autonomous space and extending mobility. Among the publications analyzing fundamentalisms' dangers for women are Hardacre 1993; Baffoun 1994; Hale 1994, 1996; Lawrence 1994; Mazumdar 1994; Papanek 1994; and Shaheed 1994.

[27] Paradoxically, scrutiny and coercion from other women helped women to be successful in the only way open to them within their existential framework's parameters.

were pressured to attend regularly. If someone did not show up at a certain ritual, women asked relatives and friends about the absentee and interrogated her at the next opportunity. My students had to have the excuse of exams to be absent. Even then, others criticized their failure to attend *majales*. The warmth and intimacy women received from fellow mourners made their scrutiny and social pressure all the more effective.

By following proper form throughout the course of a ritual, women hoped to earn approval and respect and were thus acutely conscious of other women's surveillance and extremely sensitive to the potentially pointed meaning even in brief glances. Quite unintentionally, I became a part of this process. At one Mohajir *majles,* Shahida's mother and her best friend exchanged knowing, amused looks after the mother gave a bellowing call for response during another woman's sermon. Then they noticed my eyes on them and immediately retreated into their solemn mourner roles.

Women were susceptible to other women's evaluations regarding their responsibilities for others' deportment as well. At a Qizilbash *majles,* one of the informal ritual leaders, a *seyyid,* felt my eyes on her as she beat herself with one arm, while holding her tiny granddaughter in the other. The little girl was not beating herself. Aware of my gaze (although here, too, I certainly did not mean to reproach), the grandmother took the child's hand, raised it high, and then slapped it back on the little chest. As the child became distracted, looked around, and forgot to beat herself after a few moments of compliantly striking her small bosom, her grandmother (still aware of my observation) repeated this action several times.

Even in the absence of males, women carried Peshawar society's patriarchal tenets and gender expectations into the ritual environment. There, through mutual surveillance and positive and negative commentary, which could be highly subtle or even projected, women managed each other and kept each other within the proper boundaries of their severely patriarchal world. The more prominent female ritual figures were all the more committed to the patriarchal order and earning their male family seniors' approval — and thus to their control functions as well. Female ritual seniors had gained their respected positions through upholding patriarchal cultural and religious values and took their responsibilities of monitoring others' compliance seriously.

All leading female *majles* preachers, performers, and hostesses were related to prominent male activists. Women were beholden to their male supervisors for opportunities to earn fame, freedom, performance competence, and social and spiritual power. These males directed their female relatives' religious careers. After hearing other women talk about her, I began to suspect Mahreen's brother of refusing her suitors in order to keep her single and preaching under his management. Mahreen's brother, a high-ranking Shi'a leader, owned the courtyard where she lived with her two other unmarried sisters and hosted her renowned *majales*. With his sons and other younger male kin, this brother carried in the huge kettles of *majlis* food and, after the formal service, dished it into platters that Mahreen's female guests distributed to mourners, now seated around long tablecloths quickly spread on sheeted courtyard floors. Male physical power carrying in the heavy kettles, financial power funding the meal, and social/cultural power monitoring women's behavior highlighted female subordination and dependency. The relatively great mobility that her brother allowed Mahreen for her preaching engagements did not mean that he also granted her self-rule. In fact, her famous preaching ability and associated roving made her all the more valuable and thus crucial to contain. Outstanding ritual and Shi'a movement contributions by no means freed women from patriarchal authority exerted either indirectly by female social group pressure or directly by male domination.

Although women emphasized *majles* participants' egalitarian status, in actuality, hierarchies of age, talent, education, piety, modesty, personality, activism, self-mortification, family size and composition, social clique, male relatives' positions, and wealth and class disrupted *majles* ideals and enabled elites to dominate the less powerful and subtly coerce them into acquiescing to the elite's ritual administration and control.

Although ritual managers — older, high-status women — allowed young women to shine in chanting and singing competitions, they quietly controlled the course of a *majles* by signaling to each other from back rows. They ruled on contested performance slots, decided when one ritual stage would end and another begin, and monitored behavior with glances and comments. More modest (fully covered and secluded), pious, talented, and assertive women enjoyed greater respect in the *majles* setting. Because these characteristics coincided with ritual status and power, women (or their male relatives) desiring higher Shi'a political positions sought to acquire them. Although other women wore merely the Pakistani *shalwar kamis* (loose pants and long tunic) and *dupata* (long rectangular scarf, put over hair when praying) at rituals, preachers kept themselves covered completely with black veils. The Qizilbash *rozah-khwana* and her daughters wore long black dusters over their clothing. This Qizilbash *rozah-khwana* was the only non-Pukhtun Peshawar woman whom I saw beating herself on the cheekbones. Her piety, modesty, *Moharram* story recitations, extreme self-mortification, and initiation of women's bus trips to out-of-city *majales* gained her leadership status and the respect of even her older sisters-in-law. As female singing circles were usually formed along matrilateral lines, women from families with a good number of sisters, daughters, cousins, or nieces who were talented, eager performers attained highest performance recognition. Preeminent women had large, extended families whose members, male and female, young and old, were all active in Shi'a rituals and organizations.

In earlier years women had learned mourning chants and hymns by heart. In 1991, though, it was no longer possible to be successful in Shi'a religious life without literacy. Women performers relied on their ability to transcribe the latest chants and hymns, learn, and then perform them, notebook held up for the chorale to read. Preachers prepared their sermons from published materials, and Qur'an and prayer reciters sat at the front of the group and read from a book resting on a black pillow.

Because only 3 percent of NWFP females are literate, Shi'a ritual performers' reading and writing abilities tell us much about their socioeconomic status. All female leaders were related to economically and politically powerful men. Although less obvious than male performers' and hosts' competition, women performers, hosts, and donors carried out status contestation as well.[28] They sought to have the largest and most resplendent shrines, shrine rooms, and battle standards in honor of Hazrat-e Abbas,[29] signs of their own and their family's economic and social success.

Prominent *majles* hosts must be wealthy. They need ritual space — a large separate building or courtyard with adjoining rooms and a room to house shrine and ritual paraphernalia. The Old City Qizilbash community alone boasted more than one hundred such ritual spaces. Shrines or ritual areas differed greatly from family to family and could be quite ostentatious. Some families dedicated an entire room to house battle standards, maybe a covered, thronelike preacher's seat, pictures, statues, candles, and other ritual items. Other families owned whole buildings built specifically for *majles* gatherings. Waiting for a *majles* to begin in one large courtyard, I accompanied other women into the large, separate room built to the side of the courtyard. There, surrounded by framed photographs of the Karbala shrines, black banners inscribed with invocations to the Karbala saints, and glass-protected Qur'an verses in exquisite calligraphy hanging on the walls,

---

[28] For an entertaining account of the strategies of one aggressively competitive chorale determined to capture a performance opportunity at a major *majles* of the 1991 season, see Hegland, in press.

[29] Hazrat-e Abbas, younger half-brother of Imam Husein, was martyred with him at Karbala.

the women lit candles placed on a long shelf in supplication to the Karbala martyrs.[30]

Aspiring ritual hosts could not stop at the one-time ritual space investment. Ritual status depended on regularly hosted gatherings featuring tea, betel leaves, pastries, or even meals feeding hundreds. Hosts required clean sheeting to cover the entire sitting area; serving dishes and utensils; drinking glasses and pitchers; long tablecloths; *Moharram* decorations and shrine items; cleaning, washing, and cooking assistance; transportation funds; and communication means. More prominent figures hosted ten-day ritual series representing *Moharram*'s first ten days, culminating in *'Ashura* (the tenth), commemorated as Imam Husein's martyrdom anniversary. Richer hosts served meals or even, for all-night chanting and self-flagellation sessions, a series of refreshments at breaks: first tea, then dinner, a midnight snack, and finally early morning breakfast.

Naturally, women relished the blessed offerings — the *tabarruk* — given by donors as thanks to a sainted member of Imam Husein's family or to request a specific favor or general health and well-being. The *tabarruk* refreshments did much to sweeten women's *majles* experience and whet their appetites for ritual participation. But as only the well-off could afford the treats that added so much to the *majles*'s attraction and convivial social interaction, the sense-satisfying refreshments reminded all present that their benefactors enjoyed a privileged temporal position and a gifting relationship with Imam Husein, Prince of Martyrs. Participating in *majales* hosted and funded by politically and economically powerful Shi'a meant that one had to accept the elites' ritual administration and interpretation and to recognize their social and political leadership (Hegland 1986a).

Although a few Shi'a Pukhtun landlord families sometimes sponsored a Peshawar *majles*, it was mainly affluent Mohajir and Qizilbash families who enjoyed devoting themselves and their resources to *imambara* and *majales*. Among both Mohajir and Qizilbash, the top Shi'a organizational officers and most ardent Shi'a activists were also among the very richest.[31] Shahida's uncle owned one tall building of Sadar Bazaar shops and was

[30] As Iranians do not have shrines in their homes, I found shrines of great interest, believing them to be derived through influence of Hindu practices in India. For description and discussion of Shi'ite shrines (in Hyderabad, India), see Naqvi 1987 and Pinault 1992a. Cole 1988 offers a fascinating historical treatment of *imambara* in northern India. See also Das 1992.

[31] Economic and political elites typically host, sponsor, and control *Moharram* rituals. Many publications document how the powerful use mourning plays, story recitations, processions, and self-flagellation sessions to demonstrate and fortify their positions. See nn. 3, 4, and 9.

planning to construct yet another commercial high-rise. The father of the Qizilbash sisters was a highly successful rug merchant and owner of a huge new Old City home with a top story courtyard open to the sky. The eldest sister was married to a prosperous young banker and vociferous Shi'a spokesman.

Both Shi'a urban business and commercial groups had brought capital from elsewhere — the Indian-Pakistanis, money from Indian merchant families, and the earlier Qizilbash settlers, money from their Persian or Afghan government connections or financial concerns. Most Mohajir and Qizilbash Shi'a continued to have incomes and living standards well above the Peshawar average.

Economic differences between Shi'a *majles* patrons and some non-Shi'a devotees were even more apparent. A great many women at the public Huseiniyyah Hall rituals were Pukhtun village women or even less prosperous Sunni women attracted by both free food and holy blessings. At one Sadar Huseiniyyah Hall women's *majles* I even recognized some young sweeper girls I had seen earlier gathering street brush. Less advantaged women sometimes came to private courtyard rites, licensed by the rule that no one should be prevented from entering. *Tabarruk* meals served to all comers at the public Huseiniyyah Halls and large courtyard ritual gatherings significantly supplemented poorer women's skimpy diets (and those of family waiting at home) and accentuated the great economic and political discrepancies between themselves and their Shi'a benefactors.

Sugar-coated power frameworks

An outsider might well wonder why Shi'a women accepted — in fact championed — the fundamentalist Shi'a movement; why Qizilbash women readily relinquished their own ritual cultural performance format, relaxed comportment, and language for Mohajir ritual mode; or why less favored Shi'a or even non-Shi'a bowed to Shi'a elites' ritual management, interpretation, and style, thus accepting (at least for the time being) their religious, social, political, and economic superiority. Why did women not overtly resist or critique these power frameworks and their constraints, disadvantages, and indignities?

In all three cases, the frameworks' advantages looked so appealing that women sought them out, believing that the rituals would enrich their daily lives, palates, opportunities, spirituality, and social circles. Becoming ritual and fundamentalist Shi'a activists brought women excitement, mobility, fame, artistic development, approval, and higher community status. Adding Urdu chants and hymns to their ritual repertoire and Mohajir *majales* to their ritual schedule made even less prominent Qizilbash women's religious and social lives all the more fulfilling. And, of course, both Shi'a and Sunni women at whatever political and economic level relished *tabarruk* refreshments and cherished the *majales*'s spiritual power. Shi'a women, to gain access to beloved and powerful rituals, an engaging social schedule, a sense of intimacy and community, and political connections, were all too happy to yield to elites' ritual management. Particularly because they lacked other ways to gain such inducements — because of severely restricted access to education, careers, nonreligious outside activity, and even opportunities to leave home seclusion — these Shi'a women found heightened *majles* involvement and the fundamentalist, standardizing Shi'a unification movement highly alluring.

Conclusion: Flourishing women's *majales*— paradoxical potential

Ritual contributions to Imam Husein and consolidating Shi'a from various ethnic backgrounds carried contradictory ramifications for Peshawar Shi'a women. In 1991, these women were gaining freedom with their expanding ritual activities. *Majles* gatherings provided them with opportunities for mobility; *majles* participation was a way to get out of the house without endangering their reputations. They were attaining mobility within Peshawar and taking buses to other cities for women's *majales* — without male escort. The Peshawar women were extending their worlds, but their wider-ranging mobility and ritual performances were allowed and abetted by men: their male supervisors defined the borders of their larger worlds.

On the one hand, women could spend time with friends, relatives, and neighbors and develop satisfying and stimulating performance relationships with a close circle of associates. On the other hand, the warm embrace of these associates provided greater opportunity for surveillance and social control over ritual participants. In turning to the wider Shi'a movement's alternative power structure, women were more often in contact with limiting symbolic representations of femininity and confining fundamentalist values and expectations regarding women's place. Yet so compelling were the alternative power frameworks' attractions that women overlooked the associated shortcomings and losses.

Given these observations, one wonders about the long-term outcome of Peshawar women's escalating *majles* attendance and promotion of Shi'a unification. How long can these Shi'a women — especially the out-of-line Qizilbash — resist conformity to the fully veiled dress, seclusion, and behavior dictated by Shi'a fundamentalism? Since their outstanding ritual contributions have not resulted in males handing over to them the power to define their own boundaries, what will happen should male family and religious authorities decide to tighten once again parameters on female mobility? Continued tension can be expected between the need for females to work as constructors of Shi'a community and as propagators of the Shi'a fundamentalist movement among women and the need to cloister and control females as a central aspect of fundamentalist Shi'a identity. Further, women can be expected to go on taking advantage of that paradoxical tension in their quest for a measure of independence, new vistas and experiences, and community.

Epilogue: The power paradox

Sadly, sectarian bloodshed has erupted in Pakistan each *Moharram* since my 1991 research, with the worst occurring in Punjab and then spreading to Karachi. In 1995, bloodshed began even before the *Moharram* mourning period — during Ramadan, the month of fasting for both Sunni and Shi'a, with yet another Karachi Shi'a mosque massacre on February 5 and two more on February 25 (see Burns 1995). Karachi turned into a chaotic sectarian battlefield. Hundreds of people there and in other Pakistani cities were killed in 1995 alone. According to journalist Ahmed Rashid (1995, 23), "The SSP [most violent of the extremist Pakistani Sunni parties] believes in a purely Sunni state and the physical elimination of all Shias. Its hate literature has flooded bazaars and schools. 'We believe the conflict between Shias and Sunnis can never be eliminated,' Azam [chief of the SSP and a Parliament member] said recently. 'We believe the Shias are not Muslims.'"

The Shi'a, in response, have organized into political groups, and some extremist Shi'a have committed violence against Sunnis. Emphasizing the need for dialogue and government intervention to prevent disaster, in a Shi'a publication Asif Hussein (1995, 2) pointed to the escalating seriousness of the sectarian crisis: "In turn, [the Shi'a] have created a group calling itself the Sipah-e-Muhammad (SMP), which now claims to have thirty thousand members. Its headquarters, in Lahore, is guarded by gunmen and they claim to have already retaliated against the SSP and vowed to counteract any further actions with equal force."

Because of the sectarian violence, many Pakistani Shi'a continue to perceive themselves as under siege and believe they must build from divergent Shi'a congregations and ethnic groups a garrison of fundamentalist Shi'a unity. One can therefore expect the contradictory tension inherent in the position of fundamentalist Shi'a women to escalate. Under such threatening conditions, women are all the more needed to reach out to different Shiʻa groups, weaving them together, and to propagate Shiʻa fundamentalism among women. Yet a primary symbol of Shiʻa fundamentalist identity is the seclusion and restriction of women. How will these paradoxical pressures play out? To recruit women, movement organizers must find ways to make activism appealing to women. Yet they must also be able to contain and control women and their work and abilities. To be competent roving spokeswomen and outreachers, women must be granted some mobility, autonomy, self-development, and community support. The more they gain, the more effective they can be for the Shiʻa movement, but also the more astute and the more prepared and powerful they will be if they get out of control and decide to take their abilities and passions in other directions. This power paradox inherent in women's *majles* activism conveys a mutable and malleable gender formation — even in this apparently gender-rigid environment — enabling women to seek subtly personal advancement as well as gender slippage and transformation.

Women supported the Iranian revolutionary movement, marching in revolutionary demonstrations — modeled after *Moharram* mourning processions — in numbers equal to men, only to face heightened modesty requirements and mobility restrictions under the ensuing Islamic Republic. Even in the Shiʻa fundamentalist Iranian Islamic Republic, however, women slip out of control and containment. Shahin Gerami (1994) found that middle-class Iranian women did not accept all of the teachings of the Islamic Republic officials about females and their place. Women answering her survey rejected sexual spacial segregation and thus also the belief that women should not work as they do not belong in public space. Some Iranian women are cultivating the means to dispute patriarchal religious authority — even within the pages of government-sponsored women's publications and on the panels of government-sponsored women's conferences.[32]

During the Iranian Revolution, and other revolution/movement/conflict/agitation periods from the French Revolution onward, women were allowed greater freedom, mobility, and leeway in order to assist in the struggle. "Afterwards, male ideologues try to edge them out of leadership and visibility," Erika Friedl observes. But it is not easy to do so. "As the Iranian case shows, women are not likely to be silenced completely or for long."[33]

In the short run Pakistani Shiʻa women will probably maintain loyalty

---

[32] I am grateful to Iranian friends for describing such.

[33] Erika Friedl, personal communication, March 20, 1996. I am grateful to her for urging me to make this point boldly and directly.

to their threatened community and thus be distracted from considering their own separate interests. But that will not be the end of the story.

Department of Anthropology/Sociology
Santa Clara University

References

Abu-Lughod, Lila. 1990. "The Romance of Resistance: Tracing Transformations of Power through Bedouin Women." *American Ethnologist* 17(1):41–55.

Ahmed, Munir D. 1987. "The Shi'is of Pakistan." In *Shi'ism, Resistance, and Revolution,* ed. Martin Kramer, 275–87. Boulder, Colo.: Westview.

Altorki, Soraya. 1986. *Women in Saudi Arabia: Ideology and Behavior among the Elite.* New York: Columbia University Press.

Arebi, Saddeka. 1994. *Women and Words in Saudi Arabia: The Politics of Literary Discourse.* New York: Columbia University Press.

Aswad, Barbara. 1967. "Key and Peripheral Roles of Noble Women in a Middle Eastern Plains Village." *Anthropological Quarterly* 40(3):139–52.

Baffoun, Alya. 1994. "Feminism and Muslim Fundamentalism: The Tunisian and Algerian Cases." In *Identity Politics and Women: Cultural Reassertions and Feminisms in International Perspective,* ed. Valentine M. Moghadam, 167–82. Boulder, Colo.: Westview.

Bailey, F. G. 1957. *Caste and the Economic Frontier.* Manchester: Manchester University Press.

———. 1960. *Tribe, Caste and Nation.* Manchester: Manchester University Press.

———. 1970. *Politics and Social Change: Orissa in 1959.* Berkeley: University of California Press.

Barth, Fredrik. 1969. *Ethnic Groups and Boundaries: The Social Organization of Cultural Difference.* Boston: Little, Brown.

Bell, Catherine. 1992. *Ritual Theory, Ritual Practice.* New York and Oxford: Oxford University Press.

Betteridge, Anne H. 1985. "Ziarat: Pilgrimage to the Shrines of Shiraz." Ph.D. dissertation, University of Chicago.

———. 1989. "The Controversial Vows of Urban Muslim Women in Iran." In *Unspoken Worlds: Women's Religious Lives,* ed. Nancy Auer Falk and Rita M. Gross, 102–11. Belmont, Calif.: Wadsworth.

Burns, John F. 1995. "Attack on Mosque Kills 11 in Pakistan." *San Jose Mercury News,* March 11, 5A.

Cattell, Maria. 1992. "Praise the Lord and Say No to Men: Older Women Empowering Themselves in Samia, Kenya." *Journal of Cross-Cultural Gerontology* 7(4):307–30.

Cohen, Abner. 1969. *Custom and Politics in Urban Africa: A Study of Hausa Migrants in Yoruba Towns.* Berkeley: University of California Press.

———. 1981. *The Politics of Elite Culture: Explorations in the Dramaturgy of Power in a Modern African Society*. Berkeley and Los Angeles: University of California Press.

Cole, J. R. I. 1988. *Roots of North Indian Shi'ism in Iran and Iraq: Religion and State in Awadh, 1722–1859*. Berkeley and Los Angeles: University of California Press.

Cole, Juan R. I., and Nikki R. Keddie. 1986. *Shi'ism and Social Protest*. New Haven, Conn.: Yale University Press.

Das, Neeta. 1992. *The Architecture of Imambaras*. Lucknow: Lucknow Mahotsava Patrika Samiti.

di Leonardo, Micaela. 1987. "The Female World of Cards and Holidays: Women, Families, and the Work of Kinship." *Signs: Journal of Women in Culture and Society* 12(3):440–53.

Eglar, Zekiye. 1960. *A Punjabi Village in Pakistan*. New York: Columbia University Press.

Ewing, Katherine P. 1991. "Can Psychoanalytic Theories Explain the Pakistani Woman? Intrapsychic Autonomy and Interpersonal Engagement in the Extended Family." *Ethos* 19(2):131–60.

Fernea, Elizabeth Warnock. 1989. *Guests of the Sheik: An Ethnography of an Iraqi Village*. New York: Anchor.

Fernea, Robert A., and Elizabeth W. Fernea. 1978. "Variation in Religious Observance among Islamic Women." In *Scholars, Saints, and Sufis: Muslim Religious Institutions since 1500*, ed. Nikki R. Keddie, 385–401. Berkeley: University of California Press.

Freitag, Sandria B. 1992. "State and Community: Symbolic Popular Protest in Banaras's Public Arenas." In *Culture and Power in Banaras: Community, Performance, and Environment, 1800–1980*, ed. Sandria Freitag, 203–28. Berkeley and Los Angeles: University of California Press.

Friedl, Erika. 1989. "Islam and Tribal Women in a Village in Iran." In *Unspoken Worlds: Women's Religious Lives*, ed. Nancy Auer Falk and Rita M. Gross, 125–33. Belmont, Calif.: Wadsworth.

———. 1991a. "The Dynamics of Women's Spheres of Action in Rural Iran." In *Women in Middle Eastern History: Shifting Boundaries in Sex and Gender*, ed. Nikki R. Keddie and Beth Baron, 195–214. New Haven, Conn.: Yale University Press.

———. 1991b. *Women of Deh Koh: Lives in an Iranian Village*. New York: Penguin.

———. 1994. "Sources of Female Power in Iran." In *In the Eye of the Storm: Women in Post-Revolutionary Iran*, ed. Mahnaz Afkhami and Erika Friedl, 151–67. Syracuse, N.Y.: Syracuse University Press.

Gerami, Shahin. 1994. "The Role, Place, and Power of Middle-Class Women in the Islamic Republic." In *Identity Politics and Women: Cultural Reassertions and Feminisms in International Perspective*, ed. Valentine M. Moghadam, 329–48. Boulder, Colo.: Westview.

Good, Mary-Jo DelVecchio, and Byron J. Good. 1988. "Ritual, the State, and the Transformation of Emotional Discourse in Iranian Society." *Culture, Medicine and Psychiatry* 12(1):43–63.

Grima, Benedicte. 1992. *The Performance of Emotion among Paxtun Women.* Austin: University of Texas Press.

Haeri, Shahla. 1993. "Obedience versus Autonomy: Women and Fundamentalism in Iran and Pakistan." In *Fundamentalisms and Society: Reclaiming the Sciences, the Family, and Education,* The Fundamentalism Project, vol. 2, ed. Martin E. Marty and R. Scott Appleby, 181–213. Chicago: University of Chicago Press.

———. 1995a. "Of Feminism and Fundamentalism in Iran and Pakistan." *Contention* 4(3):129–49.

———. 1995b. "The Politics of Dishonor: Rape and Power in Pakistan." In *Faith and Freedom: Women's Human Rights in the Muslim World,* ed. Mahnaz Afkhami, 161–74. Syracuse, N.Y.: Syracuse University Press.

Hale, Sondra. 1994. "Gender, Religious Identity, and Political Mobilization in Sudan." In *Identity Politics and Women: Cultural Reassertions and Feminisms in International Perspective,* ed. Valentine M. Moghadam, 145–66. Boulder, Colo.: Westview.

———. 1996. *Gender Politics in Sudan: Islamism, Socialism, and the State.* Boulder, Colo.: Westview.

Hardacre, Helen. 1993. "The Impact of Fundamentalisms on Women, the Family, and Interpersonal Relations." In *Fundamentalisms and Society: Reclaiming the Sciences, the Family, and Education,* The Fundamentalism Project, vol. 2, ed. Martin E. Marty and R. Scott Appleby, 129–50. Chicago: University of Chicago Press.

Hasnain, Nadeem. 1988. *Shias and Shia Islam in India: A Study in Society and Culture.* New Delhi: Harnam.

Hegland, Mary Elaine. 1983a. "Ritual and Revolution in Iran." In *Culture and Political Change,* Political Anthropology Series, vol. 2, ed. Myron J. Aronoff, 75–100. New Brunswick, N.J.: Transaction Books.

———. 1983b. "Two Images of Husain: Accommodation and Revolution in an Iranian Village." In *Religion and Politics in Iran: Shi'ism from Quietism to Revolution,* ed. Nikki R. Keddie, 218–35. New Haven, Conn.: Yale University Press.

———. 1986a. "Imam Khomaini's Village: Recruitment to Revolution." Ph.D. dissertation, Department of Anthropology, State University of New York at Binghamton.

———. 1986b. "Political Roles of Iranian Village Women." *MERIP (Middle East Report),* no. 138, 14–19, 46.

———. 1990. "Women and the Iranian Revolution: A Village Case Study." *Dialectical Anthropology* 15(2–3):183–92.

———. 1991. "Political Roles of Aliabad Women: The Public-Private Dichotomy Transcended." In *Women in Middle Eastern History: Shifting Boundaries in Sex and Gender,* ed. Nikki R. Keddie and Beth Baron, 215–30. New Haven, Conn.: Yale University Press.

———. 1995. "Shi'a Women of Northwest Pakistan and Agency through Practice: Ritual, Resistance, Resilience." *PoLAR (Political and Legal Anthropology Review)* 18(2):65–79.

———. 1997. "A Mixed Blessing: The *Majles* — Shi'a Women's Mourning Rituals in North-West Pakistan." In *Mixed Blessings: Religious Fundamentalisms and Gender Cross-Culturally,* ed. Judy Brink and Joan Mencher, 179–96. New York: Routledge.

———. In press. "Flagellation and Fundamentalism: (Trans)forming Meaning, Identity, and Gender through Pakistani Women's Rituals of Mourning." *American Ethnologist.*

Hussein, Asif. 1995. "Pakistan in the Grip of Terror." *Dialogue* (London), May, 2.

Jalal, Ayesha. 1991. "The Convenience of Subservience: Women and the State of Pakistan." In *Women, Islam and the State,* ed. Deniz Kandiyoti, 77–114. Philadelphia: Temple University Press.

Jayawardena, Chandra. 1968. "Ideology and Conflict in Lower Class Communities." *Comparative Studies in Society and History* 10(4):413–46.

Jeffery, Patricia. 1989. *Frogs in a Well: Indian Women in Purdah.* London: Zed.

Joseph, Suad. 1982. "The Family as Security and Bondage: A Political Strategy of the Lebanese Urban Working Class." In *Towards a Political Economy of Urbanization in Third World Countries,* ed. Helen Safa, 151–71. New Delhi: Oxford University Press.

———. 1983. "Working Class Women's Networks in a Sectarian State: A Political Paradox." *American Ethnologist* 10(1):1–22.

———. 1993. "Connectivity and Patriarchy among Urban Working-Class Arab Families in Lebanon." *Ethos* 21(4):452–84.

———. 1994. "Brother/Sister Relationships: Connectivity, Love, and Power in the Reproduction of Patriarchy in Lebanon." *American Ethnologist* 21(1):50–73.

Kandiyoti, Deniz. 1988. "Bargaining with Patriarchy." *Gender and Society* 2(3): 274–90.

Kaplan, Temma. 1981. "Female Consciousness and Collective Action: The Case of Barcelona, 1910–18." In *Feminist Theory: A Critique of Ideology,* ed. N. Keohane, M. Rosaldo, and B. Gelpi, 55–76. Chicago: University of Chicago Press.

Keddie, Nikki R., ed. 1983. *Religion and Politics in Iran: Shi'ism from Quietism to Revolution.* New Haven, Conn.: Yale University Press.

———. 1993. "The Shi'a of Pakistan: Reflections and Problems for Further Research." Working Paper no. 23. G. E. von Grunebaum Center for Near Eastern Studies, University of California, Los Angeles.

———. 1995. *Iran and the Muslim World: Resistance and Revolution.* London: Macmillan.

Keesing, Roger. 1985. "Kwaio Women Speak: The Micropolitics of Autobiography in a Solomon Island Society." *American Anthropologist* 87(1):27–39.

Al-Khayyat, Sana. 1990. *Honor and Shame: Women in Modern Iraq.* London: Saqi.

Lawrence, Bruce B. 1994. "Woman as Subject/Woman as Symbol: Islamic Fundamentalism and the Status of Women." *Journal of Religious Ethics* 22(1):163–85.

Loeffler, Reinhold. 1988. *Islam in Practice: Religious Beliefs in a Persian Village.* Albany, N.Y.: SUNY Press.

MacLeod, Arlene Elowe. 1992a. *Accommodating Protest: Working Women, the New Veiling, and Change in Cairo.* New York: Columbia University Press.

———. 1992b. "Hegemonic Relations and Gender Resistance: The New Veiling as Accommodating Protest in Cairo." *Signs* 17(3):533–57.

Mazumdar, Sucheta. 1994. "Moving Away from a Secular Vision? Women, Nation, and the Cultural Construction of Hindu India." In *Identity Politics and Women: Cultural Reassertions and Feminisms in International Perspective,* ed. Valentine M. Moghadam, 243–73. Boulder, Colo.: Westview.

Mehdi, Rubya. 1990. "The Offence of Rape in the Islamic Law of Pakistan." *International Journal of the Sociology of Law* 18(1):19–29.

Mottahedeh, Roy. 1985. *The Mantle of the Prophet: Religion and Politics in Iran.* New York: Simon & Schuster.

Mumtaz, Khawar. 1994. "Identity Politics and Women: 'Fundamentalism' and Women in Pakistan." In *Identity Politics and Women: Cultural Reassertions and Feminisms in International Perspective,* ed. Valentine M. Moghadam, 228–42. Boulder, Colo.: Westview.

Mumtaz, Khawar, and Farida Shaheed. 1987. *Women of Pakistan: Two Steps Forward One Step Back?* London: Zed.

Nakash, Yitzhak. 1994. *The Shi'is of Iraq.* Princeton, N.J.: Princeton University Press.

Naqvi, Sadiq. 1987. *Qutb Shahi 'Ashur Khanas of Hyderabad City.* Hyderabad: Bab-ul-Ilm Society.

Nasr, Seyyed Vali Raza. 1994. *The Vanguard of the Islamic Revolution: The Jama'at-i Islami of Pakistan.* Berkeley and Los Angeles: University of California Press.

———. 1995. "Communalism and Fundamentalism: A Re-examination of the Origins of Islamic Fundamentalism." *Contention: Debates in Society, Culture, and Science* 4(2):121–39.

Norton, Augustus Richard. 1988. *Amal and the Shi'a: Struggle for the Soul of Lebanon.* Austin: University of Texas Press.

Papanek, Hanna. 1973. "Purdah: Separate Worlds and Symbolic Shelter." *Comparative Studies in Society and History* 15(3):289–325.

———. 1982. "Purdah in Pakistan: Seclusion and Modern Occupations for Women." In *Separate Worlds: Studies of Purdah in South Asia,* ed. Hanna Papanek and Gail Minault, 190–216. Columbia, Mo.: South Asia Books.

———. 1984. "False Specialization and the Purdah of Scholarship — A Review Article." *Journal of Asian Studies* 44(1):127–48.

———. 1994. "The Ideal Woman and the Ideal Society: Control and Autonomy in the Construction of Identity." In *Identity Politics and Women: Cultural Reassertions and Feminisms in International Perspective,* ed. Valentine M. Moghadam, 42–75. Boulder, Colo.: Westview.

Peteet, Julie. 1991. *Gender in Crisis: Women and the Palestinian Resistance Movement.* New York: Columbia University Press.

Peters, Emrys L. 1956. "A Muslim Passion Play: Key to a Lebanese Village." *Atlantic Monthly* 198:176–80.

———. 1972. "Shifts in Power in a Lebanese Village." In *Rural Politics and Social Change in the Middle East,* ed. Richard Antoun and Iliya Harik, 165–97. Bloomington: Indiana University Press.

Pinault, David. 1992a. "Shi'a Muslim Men's Associations and the Celebration of Muharram in Hyderabad, India." *Journal of South Asian and Middle Eastern Studies* 16(1):38–62.

———. 1992b. *The Shiites: Ritual and Popular Piety in a Muslim Community.* New York: St. Martin's.

Rahat, Naveed-i. 1981. "The Role of Women in Reciprocal Relationships in a Punjab Village." In *The Endless Day: Some Case Material on Asian Rural Women,* ed. T. S. Epstein and R. A. Watts, 47–81. Oxford: Pergamon.

Ram, Haggay. 1994. *Myth and Mobilization in Revolutionary Iran: The Use of the Friday Congregational Sermon.* Lanham, Md.: University Press of America.

Ramazani, Nesta. 1985. "Islamization and the Women's Movement in Pakistan." *Journal of South Asian and Middle Eastern Studies* 8(3):53–64.

Rashid, Ahmed. 1995. "The Great Divide: Shias and Sunnis Battle It out in Pakistan." *Far Eastern Economic Review* 158(10):24.

Rauf, Abdur. 1987. "Rural Women and the Family: A Study of a Punjabi Village in Pakistan." *Journal of Comparative Family Studies* 18(3):403–15.

Richter, William L. 1981. "Pakistan." In *The Politics of Islamic Reassertion,* ed. Mohammed Ayoob, 141–62. New York: St. Martin's.

Rizvi, Saiyid Athar Abbas. 1986. *A Socio-Intellectual History of the Isna 'Ashari Shi'is in India.* Vols. 1–2. Canberra: Ma'refat.

Roemer, Hans R. 1990. "The Qizilbash Torcomans: Founders and Victims of the Safavid Theocracy." In *Intellectual Studies on Islam: Essays Written in Honor of Martin B. Dickson,* ed. Michel M. Mazzauoi and Vera B. Moreer, 27–39. Salt Lake City: University of Utah Press.

Rugh, Andrea B. 1984. *Family in Contemporary Egypt.* Syracuse, N.Y.: Syracuse University Press.

Sagaster, Ursula. 1993. "Observations Made during the Month of Muharram, 1989, in Baltistan." In *Proceedings of the International Seminar on the Anthropology of Tibet and the Himalaya,* ed. Charles Ramble and Martin Brauen, 308–17. Zurich: Ethnological Museum of the University of Zurich.

Schubel, Vernon. 1991. "The Muharram Majlis: The Role of a Ritual in the Preservation of Shi'a Identity." In *Muslim Families in North America,* ed. Earle Waugh, Sharon McIrvin Abu-Laban, and Regula Burckhardt Qureshi, 118–31. Edmonton: University of Alberta Press.

———. 1993. *Religious Performance in Contemporary Islam: Shii Devotional Rituals in South Asia.* Columbia: University of South Carolina Press.

Shaheed, Farida. 1986. "The Cultural Articulation of Patriarchy: Legal Systems, Islam and Women in Pakistan." *South Asia Bulletin* 6(1):38–44.

———. 1994. "Controlled or Autonomous: Identity and the Experience of the Network, Women Living under Muslim Laws." *Signs* 19(4):997–1019.

Singh, Kelvin. 1988. *Bloodstained Tombs: The Muharram Massacre 1884.* London: Macmillan.

Tapper (Lindisfarne), Nancy. 1988–89. "Changing Marriage Ceremonial and Gender Roles in the Arab World: An Anthropological Perspective." *Arab Affairs* 8(1):117–35.

———. 1991. *Bartered Brides: Politics, Gender and Marriage in an Afghan Tribal Society.* Cambridge: Cambridge University Press.

Thaiss, Gustav. 1972. "Unity and Discord: The Symbol of Husayn in Iran." In *Iranian Civilization and Culture,* ed. Charles J. Adams, 111–19. Montreal: McGill University, Institute of Islamic Studies.

———. 1973. "Religious Symbolism and Social Change: The Drama of Husain." Ph.D. dissertation, Washington University.

———. 1978. "Religious Symbolism and Social Change: The Drama of Husain." In *Scholars, Saints, and Sufis: Muslim Religious Institutions since 1500,* ed. Nikki R. Keddie, 349–66. Berkeley: University of California Press.

———. 1994. "Contested Meanings and the Politics of Authenticity: The 'Hosay' in Trinidad." In *Islam in the Age of Postmodernity,* ed. Akbar Ahmed and Hasting Donnan, 38–62. London: Routledge.

Torab, Azam. 1996. "Piety as Gendered Agency: A Study of *Jalaseh* Ritual Discourse in an Urban Neighbourhood in Iran." *Journal of the Royal Anthropological Institute* 2(2):235–51.

Walbridge, Linda. 1996. *Without Forgetting the Imam: Lebanese Shi'ism in America.* Detroit: Wayne State University Press.

Weiss, Anita M. 1985. "Women's Position in Pakistan: Sociocultural Effects of Islamization." *Asian Survey* 25(8):863–80.

———. 1990. "Benazir Bhutto and the Future of Women in Pakistan." *Asian Survey* 30(5):433–44.

———. 1992. *Walls within Walls: Life Histories of Working Women in the Old City of Lahore.* Boulder, Colo.: Westview and Pak Books.

J u l i e   P e t e e t

Icons and Militants: Mothering in the Danger Zone

t is crucial to theorize the relation among mothering, nationalism, and conflict in such a way as to go beyond the now familiar nationalist formulation of women as icons of the nation and recent critiques of that conflation.[1] An ethnographic approach, examining how this relation is experienced and simultaneously renegotiated in meaning by Palestinian women in refugee camps and villages, may help to carry the issue in a new direction. In her review essay on motherhood, Ellen Ross concludes that studies of motherhood are "in the process of moving from the margins to the center of feminist discussion, the mother increasingly a subject rather than a distant, looming object" (1995, 413). I approach Palestinian activist mothering as a paradoxical practice that is simultaneously agential and limiting but one that may present an analytical potential for identifying previously ambiguous forms of subjectivity and creative agency.

In building a case for this paradox, I elicit the multiple meanings and purposes to which a central cultural notion — sacrificial and activist maternal sentiment and practice — held by Palestinians (and often ethnographers) to occur naturally, has been construed, managed, and yet simultaneously transformed in moments of intense and prolonged conflict.[2]

Shorter versions of this article were presented at the conference Redefining Motherhood: Mothers, Politics and Social Change in the Twentieth Century, Dartmouth College, Hanover, N.H., May 14–16, 1993, and as a Mellon Lecture at the University of Michigan, Ann Arbor, November 1, 1993. I would like to thank the participants for their helpful comments. I am particularly indebted to Ellen Fleischmann, Shiva Balaghi, Rosemary Sayigh, and the anonymous readers for *Signs* for their judicious readings of this article and the good advice they offered. Research for this article was made possible by a Fulbright Islamic Civilization Research Award for fieldwork on gender and the political culture of the intifada in the occupied West Bank in 1990. My research in Palestinian refugee camps in Lebanon involves multiple visits spanning the periods 1980–82 and 1993, 1994, and 1995 and, by and large, has focused on gender and nationalism. Research during the last period was funded by an Advanced Research Award from the Social Science Research Council.

[1] Chatterjee 1989; Baron 1993; Sen 1993; Lazreg 1994.

[2] Since 1948, the Palestinians have been fragmented geographically. More than half of the population lives in the diaspora, while the remainder resides in the West Bank and Gaza Strip and Israel. Research for this article dealt with Palestinian refugees resident in Lebanon since 1948 and the Palestinian population of the West Bank, occupied in 1967.

[*Signs: Journal of Women in Culture and Society* 1997, vol. 23, no. 1]

Palestinian women, both in Lebanon during the civil war (1975–91) and in the West Bank during the intifada (1987–93), responded to this conflation of mothering with nationalism and acted within its parameter while asserting their own demands and claims on, as well as critiques of, the polity. Accommodation and resistance to cultural complexes are not mutually exclusive categories. Their simultaneity can be what propels the renegotiation of cultural meaning and practice.

Women as icons of the nation, a widespread image in Palestinian literature, art, and political rhetoric, is a cultural construct;[3] its message was recoded by women as self-affirming political agency that they deployed to press for rights. During the periods of Palestinian national struggle in Lebanon (1968–82), which I refer to here as the "Resistance era," and more recently in the West Bank and Gaza Strip (1990s), women have been engaged actively in the process of reconstituting the meaning of motherhood. When they engaged in defense of their communities as mothers they acted in reference to culturally dominant and highly charged symbols of maternal sentiment and behavior. Yet a transformation in meaning was occasioned by a praxis that, while culturally sanctioned, subverted the space and meaning traditionally associated with maternal practice.

In the dominant masculinist order of what constitutes Palestinian nationalist action, the political status of mothers has been shrouded, as often as not, in ambiguity. Mothers engaged with this nebulous classificatory order, simultaneously challenging, accommodating, and reinterpreting it. A central point of this article is to investigate how the practice of maternal activism and the discourse of sacrifice carved out a space of political validation. I argue that with the defeat and evacuation of the Palestinian Resistance Movement from Lebanon in 1982, maternal sacrifice became a validating position from which to launch a critique of the movement and its leadership. With the transition to a highly circumscribed form of autonomy in the West Bank and Gaza in the 1990s, maternal practice and sacrifice have become components of feminist demands for equal rights.

I suggest that a pronounced discourse of mothers as national icons intersected with a particularly situated maternal practice, and that both have been mobilized to empower and constrain women. A female practice and emotion were transformed in a way that empowered mothers as political actors but did not challenge the gendering of either citizenship or caring labor. The national movement endowed the "mothers of the martyrs" with the status of national icons and yet did not consider this particular form of

---

[3] For example, in painting, the land is often configured as a woman. In poetry, Palestine is variously referred to as the mother or the lover.

national being and participation as grounds for equality of citizenship.[4] Maternal sacrifice was categorized as belonging to the realm of the "natural." Yet women rescripted motherhood to make claims to citizenship in a future state in such a way that motherhood would be recognized as a socially productive activity warranting state support and recognition. In those areas of Palestine (limited portions of the West Bank and Gaza Strip) now under the authority of the Palestinian National Authority, the discourse of maternal action has been deployed to demand access to state-level (or quasi-state-level) resources. The particularly feminine practice of motherhood acquired a political status that mothers conceived as empowering (but not transformative). The feminine was valued, although, as I suggest, in highly incongruous ways.

Gender and conflict

Although the subject of this article is motherhood, the subject itself is located within a set of interlocking issues that include nationalism, protracted conflict, political activism, and the construction of femininity and masculinity. A critical point of departure in this project is the anthropological and feminist literature on motherhood and conflict. Until recently, anthropologists seldom questioned maternal sentiment as constructed and contingent, engaging in what Catherine Lutz and Lila Abu-Lughod call a "strategy of essentializing emotions" (1990, 3). Maternal sentiment was assumed to be a human universal, premised on the biological process of birth.[5] An interdisciplinary range of recent feminist studies has diluted and held up for questioning the conflation of motherhood with peace, sacrifice, and nurturing.[6] Feminist anthropologists have critiqued the concept of the "moral mother" and its association with pacifism (di Leonardo 1985). In a critical departure from Sara Ruddick's notion of maternal thinking as derived from maternal practice (1989), Nancy Naples argues that the social experience of oppression generates maternal activism in African-American

---

[4] Palestinians commonly refer to those who have died for the national cause as martyrs and to mothers who have lost children as mothers of martyrs. Martyrs tended predominantly to be young men or boys because most of those who fought in sustained military campaigns were males. On the infrequent occasions when a female did die in battle, her mother would henceforth be known as a mother of a martyr.

[5] While anthropological texts noted differences in practice, with few exceptions (Mead 1935), maternal sentiment was rarely addressed directly. Thus one can assume that maternal sentiment was held to be standard or taken for granted.

[6] See, among others, di Leonardo 1985; hooks 1990; Collins 1994; Scheper-Hughes 1992; Bailey 1994; Kaplan 1994. See also Elshtain 1987; Ruddick 1989.

communities that "challenges essentialist interpretations of mothering practices" (1992, 457–58).

At the same time, however, anthropologists have explicitly questioned the notion of an essential, nurturing maternal sentiment in societies experiencing conflict and extreme poverty (Turnbull 1972; Scheper-Hughes 1992). Such situations can unsettle cultural notions of maternal sentiment and behavior, or make them impossible to perform, and thus point to the highly situated, lived experience of motherhood.[7] Nancy Scheper-Hughes's (1992) monumental ethnography of mother love and infant death in a Brazilian shantytown points to the embeddedness of mothering, and the situatedness of emotions, under economic and cultural constraints. Archetypes of motherhood and mother love are "anything *other* than natural and instead represent a matrix of images, meanings, sentiments, and practices that are everywhere socially and culturally produced" (Scheper-Hughes 1992, 341).

In spite of cultural diversity and widely varying political economies in the Arab world, cultural notions of motherhood, and of mothers as sacrificial and devoted, are to a degree consistent.[8] Islamic discourse elevates mothers to near saintliness and exhorts believers to honor mothers.[9] Generativity and femininity are inextricably intertwined; birthing and mothering are pivotal, registering femininity and female social adulthood.

To begin to frame the ways in which gender and conflict intersect one needs to ask various questions. To speak of war/peace and masculine/feminine spaces and orientations without specifying what type of warfare is being engaged in and what, historically, has been the association, if any, between war and gender in a particular culture is to engage in dubious

[7] In Colin Turnbull's then shocking 1972 ethnography of the Ik of eastern Africa, hunger had undermined nearly all social bonds, including that of mother-child. Social disintegration occasioned by famine undermined human relationships based on cultural notions of love and commitment, including mother-child and familial ones, those often cast as most natural. Turnbull wrote that "what the Ik are telling us is that these qualities are not inherent in humanity at all, they are not a necessary part of human nature" (1972, 289).

[8] See the poet Fedwa Tuqan's autobiography (1990) for a poignant revelation of her emotional neglect by her mother. Such displays of truthfulness about negative experiences of being mothered are rare in Arabic discourse.

[9] Examples may be found in the *hadith,* or sayings attributed to the Prophet Mohammed. One such saying is "Paradise lies under the feet of mothers" (quoted in Abu-Lughod 1993, 45). Another example from the *hadith* is this story: "A man came to God's Messenger and said, 'O Messenger of God, who is most entitled to the best of my friendship?' The Prophet said, 'Your mother.' The man said, 'Then who?' The Prophet said, 'Your mother.' The man further said, 'Then who?' The Prophet said, 'Your mother.' The man said again, 'Then who?' The Prophet said, 'Then your father.'" (127).

generalization. Does official war discourse point to an expansionist, offensive war or a defensive war to protect and defend communities? This question is complicated by the proclivity of the military and governments to package expansionist and offensive operations as defensive ones. Does a militaristic ethos and a masculine identity tied to it precede and therefore in some way contribute to the launching of war (Enloe 1993)?

Historically, Palestinians did not directly conflate war-making activities with manhood. Indeed, under the Ottomans, Palestinian peasants tried to escape military conscription, finding little honor or future in the military. Masculine honor was more associated with one's cleverness in evading conscription. In historicizing this discussion, I am not attempting to say that Palestinians have a standard reference point of masculinity in which violence is absent. Violence does index masculinity but not in ways often discussed in analyses of Western militarism and gender where war can be a test space for masculinity.[10]

Rather, Palestinian masculinity references abilities to protect, defend, and sustain home and family, whether this protection demands militancy or social astuteness.[11] In both Lebanon and the West Bank, sites of organized and prolonged Palestinian resistance, the willingness to die has been more significant than the willingness to kill. In the Lebanon era (1968–82), where armed struggle assumed symbolic and social prominence as an assertion of a willingness to sacrifice and an ability to organize to fight, women were not excluded on the grounds of unfitness.[12] In fact, among Palestinians, the space of combat and violence was not defined as exclusively male. Indeed, these spaces were those in which mothering took place and are why, as I suggest, Patricia Hill Collins's (1994) notion of "othermothering" and the conceptualizations of the home as a site of resistance (hooks 1990) in African-American communities resonate in this context.

A common denominator in the Western feminist peace literature locates women's peace activism in the practice of mothering (Ruddick 1989). In their article on feminism and peace, Karen Warren and Duane Cady (1994) fail to look beyond the American and European context to other

[10] See Enloe 1983; Theweleit 1993.

[11] Just as significant, masculinity in this cultural context is a matter of acquiring particular forms of knowledge and social skills. Knowing the point at which an insult warrants a riposte is one such important index of adult masculinity (Bourdieu 1977, 11–12). Concern with masculinity in the Arab Middle East is of increasing interest to anthropologists; see Abu-Lughod 1986; Kandiyoti 1994; Peteet 1994; Gilsenan 1996.

[12] Cynthia Enloe has argued persuasively (in a Western context) that women "must be denied access to the 'front,' to 'combat,' so that men can claim a uniqueness and superiority that justify their dominant position in the social order" (1983, 15).

parts of the world where women engage in a variety of forms of militancy and where nationalist politics are still a prominent framework for communities and for the practice of mothering. In a critical vein, Alison Bailey (1994) suggests that an examination of the diverse conditions in which women mother and the concomitant variable meanings of mothering would add more complexity to these rather simplistic formulations.

The home as front

For Palestinians, during the revolt of 1936–39 and the wars of 1948–49 and 1967, the home was the front.[13] Blurring of home and front further collapsed distinctions between feminine and masculine spaces in conflict. The continuous violation of the home—the violent entries, searches, and demolitions, common features of both British and Israeli occupations of Palestine—and the bombings, sieges, and massacres of civilians in the 1970s and 1980s in the camps in Lebanon quickly cast aside notions of home as a space distant from conflict. This blurring suggests that the *ideology* of the home as a private, sheltered space distant from the conduct of warfare may be more historically and culturally relevant to post–Civil War America, where subsequent wars have been fought elsewhere and where white, middle-class abodes are distant from conflict. Sometimes, however, a critical space in that "elsewhere" is located in the West. African-American feminist bell hooks (1990) has called the home in black communities a "site of resistance" in the struggle against racism and poverty, and Collins (1994) argues that many of women's community activities place them in the position of "othermothers"—a kind of mothering writ large in communities facing poverty and discrimination.

In a manner that resonates cross-culturally, Palestinian mothers in camps in Lebanon often acted politically and militantly to ensure a future where, as they often opined, "our children will grow and thrive in safety and equality."[14] Since the 1967 occupation of the West Bank and Gaza Strip, women have been active in organizing demonstrations and marches

[13] The war of 1936–39 pitted the indigenous Palestinian Arab population against both the British and the Zionists; the war of 1948–49 between the Palestinians and the Israelis resulted in the exile of the Palestinians and the establishment of the Israeli state; the Six-Day War of 1967 between Israel and Syria, Egypt, and Jordan resulted in the occupation of the remaining areas of Palestine—the West Bank and Gaza Strip—and the Syrian Golan Heights and the Egyptian Sinai Peninsula.

[14] In her work on the Sandinista revolution, Margaret Randall talked with women engaged in military activities who had left behind children. While not a decision made easily, one woman said of her decision: "It may seem ironic, but part of my decision was precisely because of my children. I believed that by doing my part I would be helping to bring about a better world for them, and other children like them" (1981, 122). The Argentinean writer

to protest the detention and mistreatment of their children and husbands. In Lebanon, both in the pre-Resistance era (before 1968), when the camps were under the control of the Lebanese government and army, and after the departure of the Resistance in 1982, when the camps were exceedingly vulnerable to attacks from various militiamen, mothers organized small but vocal demonstrations and marches to protest the arrest or disappearance of their sons and husbands. What they were protesting was the disruption and chaos of everyday domestic life occasioned by the disappearance of loved ones as well as concern for their well-being. Public expressions of love and care for husbands, not easily pronounced, were voiced in a discourse in which children were the point of reference. "Who will provide for the children?" was a common lament of women relatives of those who disappeared.

Mothers from the refugee camps were acting within the parameters of cultural convention when they protested these assaults on the community. Indeed, they acted to sustain and to ensure a safe climate for the performance of caring labor, thus ultimately upholding the gendered order of society.

Mothering in the war zone: Icons and militants

Having set out some of the theoretical and critical issues that frame mothering, in this section and the next, I explore ethnographically the practice and meaning of mothering in situations of violence and nationalist politics. How do women manage maternal practice and sentiment in situations where conflict is endemic? What kinds of decisions and choices must they make in this space of violence and death, and how are they rendered meaningful? By exploring how they manage the tension between cultural sentiments of maternal protection and nurturance and a political situation that gives them little choice but to see some of their children die early and violent deaths, I argue that reproductive and caring labor has acquired new public and militant meanings.

Two places and historical moments in Palestinian history—pre-1982 Lebanon, also known as the "Resistance era" to refer to a period in Palestinian history (1968–82) characterized by a high level of political and military autonomy and the flourishing of cultural forms focused on an ethos of militancy, and the West Bank during the intifada (1987–93)—constitute the analytical fields and temporal zones I discuss. I conducted interviews with more than fifty women and engaged in extensive, long-term

---

and activist Alicia Partnoy writes about taking up political activism for the sake of her child's future (1986, 13).

participant observation in both communities. For the most part, women were eager to tell their stories, especially in postwar Lebanon, where the camp in which I worked is inhabited by a large number of widows and mothers of martyrs. In the West Bank, and more recently in Lebanon, my two children accompanied me in the field. Being a mother made for an atmosphere where certain assumptions about maternal sentiments were taken for granted. As a mother, I was expected to understand maternal sentiment and the possibility of loss.

In what follows, I detail the practice and multiple discourses of motherhood to try to tease out the ways in which women simultaneously incorporated and upheld, critiqued and challenged dominant cultural images and political policies. I interweave a discussion of official nationalist and women's discourse into the two Palestinian temporal-spatial moments, not to draw an artificial distinction between imagery and action, but to question how they engage with and intrude upon one another. A key issue here is to elaborate on how women, as agents and subjects, negotiate the meaning of official, nationalist, maternal imagery.

Women, particularly mothers, as iconic representations of the nation are not unusual in nationalist movements.[15] In protracted military conflict, with its attendant losses of life, women, in particular the mother of the martyr, symbolize life giving, or national generativity, loss, and sacrifice. Celebrating women's reproductive potential often is the ideological gloss on subordination; yet women can call upon it for a culturally potent and resonant framing of demands. In contemporary Palestinian formulations of gender, becoming a mother is the fulfillment of womanhood and the attainment of femininity. Once a woman is a mother, she is assumed to be focused largely on that task. Militant women (nonmothers) were usually unmarried or married to activist men who supported their political participation. Mobilization campaigns focused on the unmarried, who were categorized as potentially ripe for recruitment. The relationship between formally activist women and mothers in the camps was often tense, in spite of their common support for the resistance movement. Differentially positioned in the resistance movement, the mothers were categorized by the activists as "prepolitical" and highly unlikely to reach a stage, on a unilinear trajectory, of political commitment and knowledge (Peteet 1991). This categorization left older women with children in an ambiguous position vis-à-vis political activism. I suggest that activist mothering, and the meanings with which it was endowed, crafted a less ambiguous space where women could be both activists and mothers.

[15] Chatterjee 1989; Baron 1993; Sen 1993; Lazreg 1994.

Armed struggle in Lebanon (1968–82)

When I first conducted fieldwork among Palestinian women in Lebanon in the late 1970s and early 1980s, I was often asked how many children I wanted. When my response was "only two," most women were shocked. One woman poignantly exclaimed, "But what if they die? Then you'll have none!" Such an exchange pointed starkly to the ever-present possibility of death with which mothers in the refugee camps lived.

In the camps, militancy stood out as a dominant and pervasive cultural theme and social practice. Often poor and of peasant origin, women designed spaces for themselves on the home/front as activists in political groups and as mothers and housewives informally affiliated with the resistance movement. During the civil war in Lebanon (1975–91) the home and front were hardly distinguishable for mothers in the camps, as they strove to shelter and provision their children in conditions of extreme danger. Thus, it was a space in which a new practice and discourse of motherhood, not always congruous with official imagery, were played out.

In the context of exile and continued crisis, reproductive capabilities were increasingly connected to larger communal political concerns by an official discourse that cast mothers as repositories of a nationalist reproductive potential and as sacrificial icons. These representations were particularly pronounced for women in the camps who were of peasant origin, given the elevation of the peasantry to the level of authentic representatives of Palestinian culture (see Swedenburg 1990). However, as I argue in this section and the next, mothers themselves engaged in a similar discourse but deployed it in such a way as to validate motherhood as a political practice in itself. Mothering, and the sacrifices and hardships it entailed, was the ground on which to make gendered claims for political and social rights and for a critique of the resistance. Conflict was an arena in which female consciousness was activated as mothers strove to maintain domesticity in the face of danger. In doing so, they were demanding what they perceived to be their due rights in a gendered division of labor (Kaplan 1982; Peteet 1991).

Throughout the 1970s and early 1980s, nationalist ideology had widespread currency in the refugee camps. Alternative or counterdiscourses circulated less easily, their muteness a recognition of their then political marginality and ability to arouse social opprobrium. A state of war demands certain forms of silence and thus is hardly encouraging of dissonant voices.

Official nationalist ideology and discourse could be read in the publications of the various bodies and institutions of the Palestine Liberation Organization (PLO), heard in interviews with and speeches of its officials, and easily culled from everyday political discussions. In a very general sense, it posited that women could contribute to the Palestinian cause by bearing children and participating in the national struggle. Political participation was defined in a highly domestic manner. In speeches, Yasir Arafat, chairman of the PLO, often declared that mothering was equivalent to participation in national struggle and was enough to ask of women. Speeches by local leaders were often addressed to "brothers and sisters, mothers of martyrs, workers, students." "Mothers of martyrs" was a sort of category, a way of classifying and thus rendering meaningful maternal sacrifice and giving it public recognition. Nor was political activism to impinge upon domestic arrangements. In the late 1970s, Munir Shafiq, a high-ranking member of Fateh, had an article printed in *shu'un filastinniyya* (1977), a publication of the PLO, in which he declared that the mobilization of women for nationalist action should not impair their performance of domestic tasks nor should men be called upon to share in housework in situations of women's activism.[16]

Perhaps the clearest expression of official nationalist discourse on women can be read in the Palestine National Charter Adopted by the Fourth Palestine National Assembly, 1968 (1979), which states that national belonging is based on patrilineal descent. Article 4 asserts that Palestinian identity is "transmitted from father to son" (119). Palestinians are defined in Article 5 as those Arab citizens living in Palestine up to 1947 and "anyone born to a Palestinian father after that date" (119–20). It seems that before 1948, one was a Palestinian by virtue of living in the geopolitical entity known as Palestine, whereas with displacement, patrilineal descent assumed prominence in the transmission of national identity. For those in exile, blood lines seem to replace presence on the land in the reproduction of identity.

There are a number of problems entailed in drawing a distinct line between women's discourse and an official nationalist one, for women activists did not form a separate movement. They were members of nationalist organizations, and the General Union of Palestinian Women (GUPW) was composed of women from these very same organizations. Official nationalist discourse is itself neither uniform nor unambiguous. What makes for ambiguity and imbrication is that the GUPW embodied nationalist discourse on motherhood in its texts and public pronouncements. As part of the nationalist movement, the GUPW was enabled yet simultaneously constrained by its nationalist ideology and structures. While women's discourse, in its multiplicity of forms, could hardly be said to be hegemonic,

---

[16] Fateh is the largest and most powerful political group in the PLO.

neither was it unitary. It was diverse and multivocal, ranging from the women in the camps who were the mothers of the fighters and the martyrs and were neighborhood activists, to the feminist discourse of the more formally affiliated activists and the urban, middle-class women often spatially distant from the front. Yet recognizing the field of meaning of motherhood in national crisis and of mothers as icons of sacrifice was a common thread. What distinguished these discourses was the tendency of many women in official positions to categorize activist mothers as politically underdeveloped (or prepolitical) and therefore of limited political value.

The civil war in Lebanon (1975–91) propelled many women to participate in a wide variety of ways. During the civil war, camp mothers could be mobilized easily during crises to cook and provide nursing care. For example, Um Nabil, a refugee in Lebanon since 1948, had a long history of political activism. In Lebanon, she often visited the military bases, taking food to "my sons," as she called them, and offering to wash and mend their clothing. She was the mother of several activists and a martyred son and had participated in the 1936–39 revolt in Palestine. At that time, she used to hide in her house guerrillas fleeing the British. The extension of a kinship frame further blurred home/front boundaries.

During the Lebanese civil war, the Israeli invasion of 1982, and the series of camp battles with Lebanese Shiite militia during the 1980s, each of which involved sustained shelling, air raids, sieges, and massacres, women had to gather children as well as the elderly quickly and decide whether to stay put or go to the underground shelters. During prolonged stays in often hot and overcrowded shelters, provision had to be made to secure food, water, and milk for the children. The daily routine of sustaining and nurturing children was subject to serious and deadly disruption. In the besieged Tel al-Zaʿter camp, an unknown number of women died trying to provide water for their children, obtained only under gunfire and shelling.[17] A young woman who survived the siege described the deadly context in which caring for children unfolded:

> We couldn't get water or food, and children were dehydrated. Ten women would go out for water; only two or three would come back. They died — there was no solution: either their children died of thirst or their mothers died under the shells and bullets. . . . One woman

[17] Tel al-Zaʿter was a large Palestinian refugee camp located in largely Christian East Beirut. During the Lebanese civil war, it was besieged for nine months and subsequently overrun by the rightist Phalangist militia. Hundreds were massacred during the fall of the camp and the exodus of its inhabitants.

was killed in front of me. She was balancing a bucket on her head when a bullet hit her. Still holding the water container with one hand, the other hand on her chest where the bullet had entered, she slowly sank down. There was no choice: either children died of thirst or their mothers died trying to get water. (Peteet 1991)

Mothering in this context evokes Collins's notions of "othermothering" and "motherwork" (1994) and reiterates the need to locate the position from which women engage in mothering (Bailey 1994). In this instance, insuring survival rather than simply nurturing was the essence of mothering.

During crises, caring labor was politicized and pressed into national public service, a process that expanded its range of meaning. Listening to women talk, one acquired a sense of how they perceived and categorized their daily caring labor. Daily household chores were cast as a form of "struggle" (*nidal*), and those who carried them out were "strugglers" (*munadilin*). To survive and maintain the family in crises referenced national participation.

Women in the camps often rhetorically stated that it was a national duty to bear many children to replenish wartime losses. In all likelihood, women did not make reproductive decisions on the basis of a perceived national need, but by conceptualizing and categorizing fertility and reproduction in these terms—the same terms as in national discourse—they cultivated a sense of contribution and commitment to the national struggle. In doing so, they located their reproductive abilities in a national political context. While a nationalist discourse celebrated them as icons of the nation, emblematic of the suffering and losses of the Palestinian people, mothers were crafting an agential location for themselves in a movement that did not directly recruit them or position them as crucial actors, but simply celebrated their reproductive potential.

Women spoke of giving birth and nurturing children as signifying political praxis. At a 1981 women's seminar (*nadwi*) in the camps, there was much grumbling about rationing and inadequate public services. Um Mohammad, a survivor of Tel al-Za'ter who lost several sons to warfare, commented, "We Palestinian women, we have a '*batin askari*'" ("military womb"; figurative meaning: we give birth to fighters). A woman who had lost her husband and four sons in Tel al-Za'ter, explained with resignation, "We Palestinian women, we give birth to them, we bring them up, and we bury them for the Revolution." A middle-aged woman, complaining about rationing of foodstuffs and fuel in the camp and how all women were contributing to the revolution, stood up defiantly at a women's seminar and declared, "I'm giving the Israelis a hit, too — my four sons and my husband are guerrillas!" (Peteet 1991). In these kinds of expressions women articulated their reproductive and caring labor with national struggle, although perhaps more by force of circumstances than choice. Women were framing claims to rights on the basis of maternal practice.

As emblems of the nation and its ability to reproduce itself, women's actions encoded key cultural components of resistance. To remain in the camps during attacks, a risky venture, was a highly valued action. The concept of *sumud* (steadfastness) had great resonance among refugees in Lebanon. Staying put was a defiant, positive action that proclaimed history would not be repeated. Mothers exemplified *sumud* when they remained in the camp shelters during attacks. Had the women and children left the camps, the empty domestic space they left behind would have signaled defeat and fragmentation.

Funerals were another key component of women as national emblems and their actions encoding resistance. Funerals of martyrs were rituals that enacted a linkage between mothering, death or sacrifice, and the nation in a way that publicly stated and validated mothers' moral and political standing as othermothers.[18] Funerals dramatized sentiments that were decidedly celebratory, and thus defiant, in the face of death and collective loss and asserted community solidarity despite wrenching adversity. In one example, a parade-like procession wound its way through the camp streets and then proceeded down the wider city boulevards to the cemetery. Looming above the heads of the mourners were large placards, carried by youngsters, on which were mounted a photograph of the martyr. Women's ululations sounded throughout the procession and burial.

The recourse to symbols of weddings, such as ululation, inverted the symbolic and ritual practices that signified life and death. Considered the bravest of mothers and an exemplar of militant motherhood, Um Saleh had lost three sons in the civil war. Attending the funerals of many martyrs, she was centrally positioned in the front, ululating and often leading the

---

[18] Contemporary Palestinian rituals surrounding death take their cue from Islam. Mingling the secular and the religious, an *ayah* (verse from the Qur'an), which claims immortality for the martyr, is imprinted on posters carried in funeral processions: "You must not think that those who were slain in the cause of Allah are dead. They are alive and well provided for by their Lord" (sura 3, verse 169). Inscribed on the gravestones of those who died in *jihad,* the *ayah* has been incorporated into the mourning rituals for those who died for the national cause. There is a widespread popular belief that the martyr for Palestine ascends to heaven, just like the martyr for Islam. In Islam, the dead are washed and wrapped in a white linen shroud. Martyrs for Palestine, however, are neither washed nor wrapped. They are buried as they died: the state of purity effected by washing is achieved by death in martyrdom. The *fida'i* (guerrilla) is buried in a similar manner — "he is washed in his own blood."

procession. Her place at the front was a dramatic national symbolic state-ment of the mother (Palestine) as one who gives birth (generativity) to and buries (death) children and thus continues the cycle of life.

Palestinian women ululate at weddings as a sign of joy for the bride and groom, their new status, and the new life forthcoming. Ululating at the funerals of the youth who died in battle publicly attested to the honor of martyrdom and the eternal life that would follow. The mother of the mar-tyr lamented and wailed privately; her personal grief was not for public display.[19] Ululating at a funeral signifies an anomalous situation in the or-der of events such as premature death. Women ululate at the funerals of those who have died at a young age. But there is a difference between dying at a young age through accident and dying as a martyr, a meaning culturally renegotiated in the Resistance era. A mother ululated at the fu-neral of her son who died prematurely because she is going to miss ululat-ing at his wedding. When a mother ululated at the funeral of a martyr, she did so in a celebratory spirit for the eternal life and honor bestowed upon the martyr in Islam. It is equally important that she ululated in defiance at the forces that caused the death. Her position vis-à-vis her dead child was not only a private one; it took on a wider meaning, occurring as it did in the context of mothering in a zone of national conflict. Thus during the Resistance era, such traditions were endowed with new meanings both for the community, as participants, and for the women who ululated. Ululat-ing is a female expressive form, and in its new nationalist and more secular context, it signified women's willingness to put aside individual maternal feelings of grief and women's refusal to internalize and publicly accept de-feat. Attendees at funerals gave public, mournful recognition in their chorus to maternal feelings of loss and also assuaged loss by symbolically reiterating the mother as othermother: "O Mother of the martyr, rejoice, for all youth are your children." This was a public, highly ritualized display of the conflation of mothering with nationalist sentiment and the ideology of struggle and sacrifice.

Although the mother of the martyr may not have been active politically in the sense of belonging to an organization, nationalist discourse extolled her maternal sacrifice as a supreme political act. Mothers of martyrs were invited to attend resistance celebrations with the leadership, a public, sym-bolic display of a newly acquired stature in the community and a demon-

---

[19] Abu-Lughod has illustrated how Bedouin women's behavior at funerals — wailing and lamenting — expressive forms disapproved by Islam, are "powerfully implicated in the repro-duction of gender hierarchy" (1992, 196). In lamenting and wailing, women "publicly enact their own moral, and ultimately social, inferiority" (203).

stration of easy access to the resistance leadership. In Arab culture, visiting has powerful social connotations; who visits whom is a crucial index of status and social hierarchies.[20] Visits to the mothers of the martyrs by leaders and social committees offered a public recognition of the communal and sacrificial nature of mothering and its position in the national order.[21] Outpourings of sympathy and acts of respect served to cushion the loss. After losing a son, some women became quite visible and played an active political role in camp life as intermediaries between the leadership and women of less status, transmitting requests or appeals. It was said of them: "They have the ear of the Resistance." The recognition accorded the mother of the martyr epitomized the process by which the meanings of reproductive and caring labor had become enmeshed in the national political matrix and politically validated this particular form of mothering.

Thus in the Resistance era, it was a specifically located maternal practice, more akin to Collins's othermothering than to Ruddick's notion of maternal thinking deriving from practice, that defined the contours of political activism for some women. Women occupied a position in the order of national activism but one ranked as somehow less central than formal, masculinist militancy. Women were activists by virtue of their caring labor and the deadly sacrifice they endured. As I argue, their particular form of mothering became the grounds from which they later launched a critique of the Resistance movement and era.

With the 1982 defeat of the Resistance Movement in Lebanon, the brutal and deadly assaults on the camps during the second half of the 1980s, the establishment of the Palestinian National Authority in the West Bank and Gaza Strip, and the effective abandonment by the Palestinian leadership of the refugees in Lebanon, mothers elaborated a critique of the Resistance era and its leadership using the idiom of maternal sacrifice and its political meaning. While adhering to a hegemonic discourse that glorified maternal sacrifice, mothers did not let the national movement easily appropriate the

---

[20] The "rules" of visiting and its social significance are stated wonderfully and forcefully in an incident recounted by Tuqan. A visitor remarked to her aunt, "'Please come and honour us with a visit. We always visit you but you never visit us.' Her aunt arrogantly retorted, 'Listen, you've always visited us and we've never visited you. Why violate this rule now? What's happened to the world? Has everything been turned topsy-turvy?'" (1990, 31).

[21] The Palestinian Resistance Movement gave institutional and financial expression to the esteem in which martyrs and their families were held. Samed, the industrial concern of the PLO, was formed to provide employment to families of martyrs. Significantly, it was the first of the PLO social institutions to be established. Although monthly stipends are supposed to be paid to martyrs' widows and children and support is to be provided for their medical and educational needs, the system has been in disarray for more than a decade, and as a result women in Lebanon seldom receive a stipend.

meaning of their reproductive tasks. They deployed it as a platform from which to put forth strident demands and a virulent critique of the leadership. Their trust in the revolution to effect a positive outcome for their sacrifice was betrayed. Women did not deny the potency of maternal sacrifice; indeed, its rhetorical centrality underscored the shift in its meaning from celebration to critical agency.

In summer 1993, I met Um Ali. My friend Um Khalid, a well-known and respected women's leader in the camp, told me Um Ali was someone I should meet, for she was the mother of five martyrs. She shared with her only son a small, two-room, cinder-block house in Shatila camp.[22] The depressingly dark and sparsely furnished house resembled many of the newly constructed homes in a camp that had come back from the ruins of nearly two decades of war and whose residents were busily engaged in rebuilding. The walls were unpainted; the cinder-block walls cast a dark pall over the room, and the unfinished windows were covered with dark squares of roughly cut cloth. Hanging high on the wall above the cotton mats on the floor was a framed, glass-covered mat on which were affixed black-and-white photos of a middle-aged man and five young boys. I knew it was a picture of death. In the barely furnished homes of the widows, the pictures of dead husbands, sons, and daughters were ubiquitous — a constant reminder of Shatila's tumultuous history of massacre and prolonged sieges. Um Khalid had told me matter-of-factly: "Um Ali is a 'problem' or case. Her five sons and her husband were shot by the Phalangists in the massacre of 1982, and they made her watch. They told her she could keep her youngest son, who was then about twelve years old. Now she lives in that shack with her only son."

That summer I spent many afternoons at Um Ali's house. Um Khalid made a point of visiting her several times a week. Visiting Um Ali, as well as other widows and "mothers of martyrs," constituted an integral part of Um Khalid's informal social work in the camp. During visits to women who had lost children in war, a particular kind of narration occurred with some frequency. In what amounted to a critical narrative of the revolutionary era and leadership, women's experiences of loss were told metaphorically in terms of "blood and milk," calling forth bodily substances associated with birth, nurturing, and death, thus evoking the specificity of maternal sacrifice and the conflation of life and death. "We gave our blood

[22] Located on the outskirts of Beirut, Shatila camp was the site of a 1982 massacre by the South Lebanon Army and Phalangists, who were sponsored and logistically supported by Israel. In the mid-1980s, it was the site of a series of sieges by the Lebanese Shiite Amal militia that resulted in the nearly complete destruction of the camp.

and milk," Um Ali shouted angrily, "and look how we are living—we are barely able to feed ourselves." Mention of the recent Palestinian/Israeli peace accords, which paved the way for the establishment of a Palestinian authority in the West Bank and Gaza Strip (and postponed discussion of refugee issues to a later date), elicited a host of negative reactions such as, "We have been abandoned! We gave our children, and they [the PLO] have left us!"

Um Khalid did her best to help Um Ali. When Um Ali was eight months behind on her rent (her own house awaited repairs) and had not received her monthly martyr's family indemnity from the PLO's Office of Social Affairs for nearly two years, she was in despair: "If I had my sons and they each gave me money, I would be living comfortably." Um Khalid took her to ask for financial assistance from one of the few remaining Palestinian political leaders in Lebanon. He told them frankly, and without hesitation, that his office could not help. Next, the two women went to seek help from the PLO representative in Lebanon. They met him as he was leaving his house. Um Khalid asked him for money to repair Um Ali's house so she would not have to rent. He agreed and told one of his aides to give her $200 when she returned. When they returned to pick up the $200, the aide told her they did not have any money. According to Um Khalid, "Um Ali squatted on the ground and started crying. She could not walk from his house to the street. I calmed her down and told her, 'Do not ask for any more—have faith in God and he will provide.'" In talking about Um Ali's plight and her attempts to help, Um Khalid engaged in a running critique of the leadership and their abandonment of the Palestinians in Lebanon and those who had sacrificed so much for nothing.

In the near absence of a social service sector for the Palestinians in Lebanon since the PLO's 1982 departure, women like Um Khalid have taken upon themselves the task of identifying those in need and relaying this information to Shatila's popular committee.[23] Um Khalid's husband serves on the popular committee, and she conveys to him her concerns about particular widows. A small French delegation visited the camps and presented Abu Khalid with several hundred dollars for the popular committee. In a continuing attempt to assist Um Ali, the minute they were out the door, Um Khalid quickly and firmly told her husband: "That money is to go to Um Ali. She gave five sons to the revolution and look how she lives—in an unfinished shack!" Abu Khalid nodded in agreement with his

---

[23] Popular committees that function as a sort of municipality are present in each camp. They are composed of representatives from major factions of the PLO as well as several independents.

wife's critique of a failed revolution in which he was a participant and promised her that some of the money would go to Um Ali.

Maternal sacrifice as critique of the peace accords also finds women wielding their sacrifice not only as critique but as a marker of a particular identity. There is a popular consensus among Palestinians, especially in Lebanon, largely based on Israel's insistence that they will never allow the return of the refugees or pay them compensation, that the peace accords effectively legitimize their refugee status. Thus the Palestinian community in Lebanon feels abandoned and betrayed (Peteet 1995). In reference to the peace accords, Um Ali said scathingly: "We are not involved in this. We are the people from 1948. We benefit nothing. The only thing we got was to see our children put under the earth, our houses destroyed, and we became like gypsies. Abu Ammar [Arafat] just benefited his friends and people, not us . . . what does he care. . . . He took what he wanted for himself and his people. Not for us. We got nothing. The people of 1948 are the losers." For such women, maternal sacrifice and the disruption of domesticity resulted only in defeat and further distance from the peace process and the geopolitical and demographic core of Palestine and marked the emergence of an identity increasingly associated with the highly particular experience of exile (Peteet 1996). In the following section, I discuss how, in the 1987–93 uprising in the occupied territories, maternal activism took a slightly different course and had a markedly different outcome while retaining some similarities with the experience of mothers in Lebanon.

Intifada: Mothering in an era of civil disobedience

In this second ethnographic examination of the paradox of mothering during nationalist conflict, it is again apparent that women both accommodate and resist cultural expectations of maternal behavior and engage in a critique of the polity. Both the nature of civil disobedience and the repressive techniques that preceded and accompanied the uprising (1987) in the West Bank and Gaza Strip against Israeli occupation also blurred a home/front distinction. Violent entries and searches of their homes, often in the middle of the night, left most Palestinians with an intense sense of vulnerability, as did the long-standing Israeli policy of collective punishment.

Official discourse can be read in leaflets produced during the uprising.[24] A leaflet distributed March 8, 1988, and signed "Palestinian Women in the Occupied Territories," explicitly states one of the women's main roles in the uprising: "Mothers, in camps, villages, and cities, continue confronting

---

[24] Leaflets were clandestinely produced and distributed throughout the intifada. As one of the primary means of communication inside the occupied territories, they were documents that directed the uprising, indicating local resistance activities and announcing strike days.

soldiers and settlers. Let each woman consider the wounded and the imprisoned her own children." The signature on the leaflet indicates the difficulties of trying to distinguish sharply between nationalist and women's discourse. Of most significance, the leaflet puts into public circulation the notion of mothering as a national project that extends well beyond the home and the actual ties of kinship. In anthropological parlance and as a further instance of othermothering, mothers were to extend fictive kinship status to those injured in communal strife.

In the leaflets, women were a separate and marked category of persons and could be addressed and expected to act in specific ways. For example, leaflet number 3, dated January 18, 1988, is addressed to, among others, "O workers and *fellahin* [peasants], students, merchants, and women." Motherhood and sacrifice are recurring themes. Leaflet number 12, dated April 2, 1988, extols "the thousands of women who have miscarried due to noxious gas bombs and those whose husbands and sons are incarcerated in the Nazi prisons" (Mishal and Aharoni 1994, 78). Others, such as number 29, dated November 20, 1988, and marking the Declaration of Palestinian Independence, said, "Let the mother of the martyr rejoice, she has lifted her voice twice: first on the day of her son's death, and again on the day of the declaration of the state" (146). These kinds of statements reiterate national expectations of maternal sentiment and conflate women's "voice" with maternal sacrifice and the formation of the nation.

One of the most prominent and widely circulated images associated with the uprising is that of mothers saving boys from public beatings and arrest by the occupying forces. These dramatic and dangerous events put into relief othermothering in the context of a violence that easily overturns the semblance of a home-feminine/front-masculine equation. And it was precisely an act of maternal caring, extended communitywide, that was central in renegotiating the meaning of motherhood.

Beatings and bone breakings by the occupier were public spectacles that not only dramatized superior means of force and a willingness to use them; they were also attempts to infantilize (Theweleit 1993, 305) and, in doing so, humiliate the occupied. For Palestinians, as both participants and witnesses, the public inscription of bodily violence was a setting in which their moral qualities were juxtaposed dramatically with those of the occupiers. Reconstituting a moral self through enduring violence was a gendered process as well as one that heavily implicated class, which I critically examine below.[25] While women had been active in all areas of the uprising, there was a sort of division of labor by class and region. It was women in villages

---

[25] See Peteet 1994 for an extensive discussion of the infliction of bodily violence and its meaning for the attainment of masculinity.

and camps who were called on to intervene in these violent public spectacles. As both witnesses and defusers of violence, their practice was an intervention and an instance of othermothering.

During the uprising, mothers were popularly extolled as the "mothers of all Palestinians." The actions of Um Kamel are a case in point. She had been living since 1948 in the refugee camp where I did fieldwork and, since 1967, had experienced the usual litany of daily crises, insults, and violence that accompanies foreign occupation. Two of her homes had been demolished on the grounds that her sons were activists. Several children had been shot, one had died, and two sons had been in and out of detention and had been tortured during interrogation. Her husband was serving a ten-year prison sentence for resisting occupation.

In the camps, mothers like Um Kamel were attuned to the slightest sounds of trouble. They had established their own system of communication. When soldiers patrolled, the women would whistle or make bird sounds to warn one another of their approach or the advent of trouble. They changed signals every few weeks. Whenever Um Kamel heard the sounds of a confrontation between youths of the camp and the soldiers, she would rush to see what she could do. At great risk to herself, she intervened in these public dramas. When I asked why, she explained, "I feel each and every one of those boys is my son. If it were my son, I would want other mothers to try to protect him." They tug at the soldiers, exhorting and pleading with them to stop. Armed only with determination and their voices, they hurl insults that challenge the humanity of the occupier: "Has God abandoned you?" "Have you no compassion and pity?" "Aren't we human beings, too?" "Don't you have mothers and sons — how would your mother feel if you were treated this way — would you like to see your sons beaten like this?" "What kind of a people takes the land of another and then beats them when they protest?"

Thus the act of saving boys accomplishes several things: on a pragmatic level it may lessen the severity of a beating, and it can create a diversion affording boys the opportunity to escape. The noise and confusion it occasions can signal passersby and nearby residents to surround the soldiers and try to intervene or to bear witness. But most crucial, it juxtaposes moral qualities and practices in a publicly dramatic and witnessed form. Mothers acted as a collective moral representation of a community testifying to the abusive nature of occupation. I would argue, further, that the emotional discourse, the harangue that accompanies the intervention in a boy's beating, is a means of asserting moral and spiritual superiority. In crafting this superiority, women are not positing femininity or maternity as a superior position or essence; they are asserting the moral superiority of the community of Palestinians whose embodiment they represent.

Maternal activism was enacted in other spaces as well. Bodily interference and a running commentary were combined with the act of witnessing. Witnessing itself was a form of political practice, not a private, solitary act. What was witnessed was then told; it circulated through networks of kin and friends in the daily routine of receiving and making visits. On occasion, it was told to the foreign journalist or researcher and thus became part of a body of knowledge on Palestinian life under occupation. Mothers were called on to tell outsiders what they had seen, and in doing so, they became communal witnesses, a sort of oral archive, or repository of experiential, historical lore, and tellers of suffering. Telling was a way of taking back the violence inflicted upon them and working it creatively. As a means of constructing a historical narrative, one that had meaning within the community as well as on an international stage, it was an intervention. Mothering writ large, and its associated tactics of intervention as community defense and resistance, were later deployed to argue for women's rights.

Marginal icons and claims on the polity

At this early stage in the transition to a limited form of Palestinian self-rule in Gaza Strip and parts of the West Bank, one can only speculate as to the future contours of social policy and questions of citizenship. I think it is plausible to suggest that mothers, as a category of political actors—whether lauded as givers or savers of children—have been relegated to the margins of public policy. Their iconic status, as well as that of martyrs in general, has declined somewhat. Simply speaking, there are too many of them; once sacrosanct symbols have lost some of their potency. In policy debates, the women's movement has pushed to the forefront a critique of the marginalization of women and mothers (Giacaman, Jad, and Johnson 1996).

During the uprising, mothers were establishing a particularly gendered claim to belonging to the nation. They were reconstructing maternal selves as a gendered category of belonging to a nation. Through a gendered discourse—the harangue and the practice of othermothering, where "every one of those boys is my son"—mothers were refashioning a gendered way of relating to the nation and the state, one they insisted recognized different ways of being in the polity as compatible with equality.

Mothers were claiming equality of future citizenship on the basis of their particular work and sacrifice. Ultimately, their sacrifice is one step removed; they sacrifice their male progeny, who are powerfully implicated in their sense of self. They did so not solely because of maternal virtue or practices but because women considered reproductive labor and the sacrifices it entailed as a contribution to a common national future in which they did not wish to be marginalized. Yet their claims to citizenship have been on the basis not necessarily of a gender-neutral conception of citizenship but of a citizenship that recognizes gender difference.[26]

With the uprising having given way to a transitional period, women activists, not necessarily mothers, have begun orienting their energies to issues of policy and women's legal status. The GUPW's Declaration of Principles on Palestinian Women's Rights presented to Arafat in July 1994 made clear their agenda.[27] The declaration demanded complete equality of civil, political, educational, and work rights. The right to citizenship and its transmission to spouses and children is included, a radical demand in a region of the world where, with few exceptions, citizenship and its transmission follow patrilineal lines of descent and affiliation.

Principle 4 of the declaration demands "equality in work opportunities and wages, all securities and compensations, training and promotion, and in a woman's right to maternity leave and social services which enable her to combine her family duties and the responsibilities to participate in the public social life, with a special consideration for women in the countryside" (137). This statement clearly references women's maternal roles as not incompatible with "public social life" and incorporates a claim on the incipient state for social services in recognition of "her family duties." Indeed, such a claim locates maternal practice squarely in the public domain.

The social policy of the Palestinian National Authority has been the subject of a critique by women activists and intellectuals. The PLO document that provisionally sets out national social policy is the *General Program for National Economic Development, 1994–2000*. Some feminist critics find in it "an implicit structure for social entitlements that is gendered and discriminatory" (Giacaman, Jad, and Johnson 1996, 13). Entitlements are linked closely to market or paid labor participation, while other forms of productive activity such as informal labor sector participation and women's reproductive labor in the domestic arena are barely acknowledged. The document calls for state control of the nongovernmental organization sector, an arena in which women have played a predominant role. Mothers (or wives) of martyrs are relegated to the section on "vulnerable groups" (14). Destitute women are considered to be those without sons (or husbands) to support them, their domestic-based caring labor not recognized as labor worthy of entitlements. This "reenforces the assumed status quo, where

---

[26] Citizenship in most Middle East states is gendered. There is an imbalance not only in the kinds of rights men and women possess but in the kind of citizenship they possess.

[27] This document is reprinted in General Union of Palestinian Women 1994, 137–38.

women's needs and existence are viewed solely in terms of their linkage to men, family and kin" (14). Most striking here is the absence of secure entitlements derived from nationalist political activities. Such an inclusion would move mothers, whose political activism was maternal, from the category of vulnerable and destitute to a position where their particular forms of political participation would be accorded recognition. It is important to note that in the Middle East in general, where there are few social security programs, the elderly rely on sons (and daughters, although to a lesser extent) to support them.

Connecting fragments: The issue of class

Mothers as icons of the nation are a representation easily dislodged by an examination of the different ways women have connected motherhood to struggle and of the class nature of such a conflation. Whether in Lebanon or in the West Bank and Gaza, it has been poorer, usually refugee, women who confront chronic danger and crisis on a daily basis. Upon the loss of their children in battle, mothers have been consoled by women with similar experiences and others who were acutely aware of their own lack of immunity from such tragedies. The death of a son in battle was felt by the whole camp community as its loss, expressed in the common reference to martyrs as "sons of the camp." Few middle- and upper-middle-class, urban Palestinian mothers lose sons in battle. Distant from the centers of organized resistance in the camps, they do not share their loss with a community. A middle-class mother of a martyr wept openly and cried, "Why did my son have to die? Couldn't someone else do the fighting? My son was educated!" Such a statement could hardly have been uttered in public among camp women; to put oneself above others was to defy openly the prevailing sentiment of shared suffering.

Mothers in the camps in Lebanon pressed claims for services on the leadership on the basis of their maternal contribution to the cause — mothers sustained those men (and women) who fought, and they bitterly critiqued the Resistance for abandoning the mothers of the dead. The leadership has been unable to fulfill its promises of financial assistance and services for the families of the martyrs. During the intifada, a camp mother in the West Bank voiced a similar concern when we were discussing the legitimacy and effectiveness of the urban-based political leadership: "What do they know of suffering? Who are they to lead? They and their sons are not beaten, and they rarely go to jail. Their sons study here and abroad while *our* sons are beaten, shot and imprisoned!" Camp mothers' critiques angrily juxtaposed forms of mothering by class, and, in part, it was in those juxtapositions that women pressed claims for rights in the polity. Suffering and generativity were hallmarks of a mother's nationalist credentials but not her rights as a citizen. The Palestinian Declaration of Independence "renders special tribute to that brave Palestinian woman, guardian of sustenance and life, keeper of our peoples' perennial flame." Such a slogan now has a hollow ring to it.

Culturally sanctioned emotions and their enactment were highly class specific. In the Arab context, parental wrath (*ghadab*) has been described by Soroya Altorki as "covering a wide range of responses to filial disrespect and disobedience, from momentary anger and longer-lasting discontent to outrage and, in extreme circumstances, to rejection" (1986, 72). *Ghadab* could be effective in compelling the desired behavior. Some mothers swooned and declared their imminent death if children continued to pursue a certain line of behavior. The middle-class mother could wield *ghadab* to prevent a son from joining the resistance movement, but a camp mother rarely had recourse to such emotional enactments. Camp mothers deferred to conditions beyond their control, couching them in the honorable idiom of national sentiment. They were accorded honor and status in the community for their deference to the national cause in the face of the culturally sanctioned maternal emotion of protection, which was conceptualized as a "natural" quality of femininity and maternal sentiment. Supposedly natural emotions had been mastered in the face of national adversity. The "natural" in maternal, and its connectedness to the national, has obvious and undercutting class dimensions.

Conclusion

In the spaces of defeat in Lebanon, mothers of martyrs wielded their particular form of mothering and the sacrifice it entailed as a powerful critique of the Resistance era. They demanded that caring labor and othermothering be recognized as political rather than relegated to space on the margins of national politics—a space often characterized as "prepolitical." In Palestine, the women's movement has been seeking to influence policy such that gender difference is recognized in the concept of citizenship as the basis for organizing and distributing entitlements and rights. The policy they envision would recognize and compensate for the particular contributions of women as workers and as the mothers (and wives) of martyrs.

By deferring to national and community sentiments, women attain an honor and respect that they feel validate claims to rights, entitlements, and a critical voice. Their maternal practices during the years of conflict in Lebanon (1975–91) and in the intifada (1987–93) were at once culturally

accommodating and politically resistant. A discernable temporal and political distance separated the celebratory accommodation of sacrificial
motherhood and its deployment as critique of the leadership and resistance strategy.

Scheper-Hughes discusses the notion of "letting go" in a Brazilian shantytown where lower-class women must resign themselves to the death of
their children, a death that they believe is beyond their control (1992,
362–63). She refers to letting go in this context as a Catholic "holy indifference" (often misread by anthropologists as peasant fatalism). Among
the Palestinians I discuss here, largely former peasants now residing in refugee camps, "letting go" is a recognition of the powerful and destructive
forces that have shaped their lives and impinged on their ability to mother
safely and of the actions required to resist such forces. Lower-class women
have reconfigured maternal practice in a way that constitutes defiance of
these forces and yet is a creative act through which mothers acquire moral
and social standing as well as political credentials. Ironically, mothering
in this specific national and class context gives agency but simultaneously
embodies and delimits its space and meaning.

Department of Anthropology
University of Louisville

References

Abu-Lughod, Lila. 1986. *Veiled Sentiments: Honor and Poetry in a Bedouin Society.*
Berkeley and Los Angeles: University of California Press.

———. 1992. "Islam and the Gendered Discourses of Death." *International Journal
of Middle East Studies* 25(2):187–205.

———. 1993. *Writing Women's Worlds: Bedouin Stories.* Berkeley and Los Angeles:
University of California Press.

Altorki, Soroya. 1986. *Women in Saudi Arabia: Ideology and Behavior among the Elite.*
New York: Columbia University Press.

Bailey, Alison. 1994. "Mothering, Diversity, and Peace Politics." *Hypatia*
9(2):188–98.

Baron, Beth. 1993. "The Construction of National Honour in Egypt." *Gender and
History* 5(2):244–55.

Bourdieu, Pierre. 1977. *Outline of a Theory of Practice.* Cambridge: Cambridge University Press.

Chatterjee, Partha. 1989. "The Nationalist Resolution of the Women's Question."
In *Recasting Women: Essays in Indian Colonial History,* ed. Kumkum Sangari and
Sudesh Vaid, 233–53. New Brunswick, N.J.: Rutgers University Press.

Collins, Patricia Hill. 1994. "The Meaning of Motherhood in Black Culture." In

The Black Family: Essays and Studies, ed. R. Staples, 165–73. Belmont, Calif.: Wadsworth.

Elshtain, Jean Bethke. 1987. *Women and War.* New York: Basic.

Enloe, Cynthia. 1983. *Does Khaki Become You? The Militarization of Women's Lives.* Boston: South End.

———. 1993. *The Morning After: Sexual Politics and the End of the Cold War.* Berkeley and Los Angeles: University of California Press.

General Program for National Economic Development, 1994–2000. 1992. Department of Economics and Planning. Tunis: Palestine Liberation Organization.

General Union of Palestinian Women. 1994. "Declaration of Principals on Palestinian Women's Rights." *Journal of Palestine Studies* 24(1):137–38.

Giacaman, Rita, Islah Jad, and Penny Johnson. 1996. "For the Public Good? Gender and Social Citizenship in Palestine." *Middle East Report* 26(1):11–16.

Gilsenan, Michael. 1996. *Lords of the Lebanese Marches: Violence and Narrative in an Arab Society.* Berkeley and Los Angeles: University of California Press.

hooks, bell. 1990. *Yearning: Race, Gender, and Cultural Politics.* Boston: South End.

Kandiyoti, Deniz. 1994. "The Paradoxes of Masculinity: Some Thoughts on Segregated Societies." In *Dislocating Masculinity,* ed. Andrea Cornwall and Nancy Lindisfarne, 197–213. London and New York: Routledge.

Kaplan, Laura Duhan. 1994. "Woman as Caretaker: An Archetype That Supports Patriarchal Militarism." *Hypatia* 9(2):123–33.

Kaplan, Temma. 1982. "Female Consciousness and Collective Action: The Case of Barcelona, 1910–1918." In *Feminist Theory: A Critique of Ideology,* ed. Nannerl Keohane, Michelle Rosaldo, and Barbara Gelpi, 55–76. Chicago: University of Chicago Press.

Lazreg, Marnia. 1994. *The Eloquence of Silence: Algerian Women in Question.* New York: Routledge.

Leonardo, Micheala di. 1985. "Morals, Mothers, and Militarism: Antimilitarism and Feminist Theory." *Feminist Studies* 11(3):599–617.

Lutz, Catherine, and Lila Abu-Lughod. 1990. *Language and the Politics of Emotion.* Cambridge: Cambridge University Press.

Mead, Margaret. 1935. *Sex and Temperament in Three Primitive Societies.* New York: Dell.

Mishal, Shaul, and Reuven Aharoni. 1994. *Speaking Stones: Communiqués from the Intifada Underground.* Syracuse, N.Y.: Syracuse University Press.

Naples, Nancy. 1992. "Activist Mothering: Cross-Generational Continuity in the Community Work of Women from Low-Income Urban Neighborhoods." *Gender and Society* 6(3):441–63.

"The Palestine National Charter Adopted by the Fourth Palestine National Assembly, 1968." 1979. In Y. Harkabi, *The Palestinian Covenant and Its Meaning,* 119–24. London: Vallentine Mitchell.

Partnoy, Alicia. 1986. *The Little School: Tales of Disappearance and Survival in Argentina.* Pittsburgh: Cleis.

Peteet, Julie M. 1991. *Gender in Crisis: Women and the Palestinian Resistance Movement.* New York: Columbia University Press.

————. 1994. "Male Gender and Rituals of Resistance in the Palestinian Intifada: A Cultural Politics of Violence." *American Ethnologist* 21(1):31–49.

————. 1995. "'They Took Our Blood and Milk': Palestinian Women and War." *Cultural Survival* 19(1):50–53.

————. 1996. "From Refugees to Minorities: Palestinians in Post-War Lebanon." *Middle East Report* 26(3):27–30.

Randall, Margaret. 1981. *Sandino's Daughters: Testimonies of Nicaraguan Women.* Toronto and Vancouver: New Star.

Ross, Ellen. 1995. "New Thoughts on 'the Oldest Vocation': Mothers and Motherhood in Recent Feminist Scholarship: Review Essay." *Signs: Journal of Women in Culture and Society* 20(2):397–413.

Ruddick, Sara. 1989. *Maternal Thinking: Towards a Politics of Peace.* New York: Ballantine.

Scheper-Hughes, Nancy. 1992. *Death without Weeping: The Violence of Everyday Life in Brazil.* Berkeley and Los Angeles: University of California Press.

Sen, Samita. 1993. "Motherhood and Mothercraft: Gender and Nationalism in Bengal." *Gender and History* 5(2):231–43.

Shafiq, Munir. 1977. "Propositions on the Struggle of Women" (in Arabic). *shu'un filastinniyya*, no. 62, 200–227.

Swedenburg, Ted. 1990. "The Palestinian Peasant as National Signifier." *Anthropological Quarterly* 63(1):18–30.

Theweleit, Klaus. 1993. "The Bomb's Womb and the Gender of War (War Goes on Preventing Women from Becoming the Mothers of Invention)." In *Gendering War Talk*, ed. M. Cooke and A. Woollacott, 283–315. Princeton, N.J.: Princeton University Press.

Tuqan, Fadwa, ed. 1990. *A Mountainous Journey: A Poet's Autobiography*, trans. Olive Kenny and Naomi S. Nye. St. Paul, Minn.: Graywolf.

Turnbull, Colin. 1972. *The Mountain People.* New York: Simon & Schuster.

Warren, Karen, and Duane Cady. 1994. "Feminism and Peace: Seeing Connections." *Hypatia* 9(2):4–20.

Gabriele vom Bruck

Elusive Bodies: The Politics of Aesthetics
among Yemeni Elite Women

In memory of Amatullah al-Shami

Pierre **Bourdieu** notes, following Marcel Mauss (1979), that gender differences are revealed in ways of walking, looking, and even standing still; differences in posture and body demeanor "express a whole relationship to the social world" (1986, 192).[1] To these are added, he writes, "the deliberate modifications of appearance, especially by use of the set of marks — cosmetic (hairstyle, make-up, beard, moustache, whiskers etc.) or vestimentary — which, because they depend on the economic and cultural means that can be invested in them, function as social markers deriving their meaning and value from their position in the system of distinctive signs which they constitute and which is itself homologous with the system of social positions" (192). I take Bourdieu's analysis as a starting point to explore Yemeni women's deportment in relation to issues of personhood and social location. Bourdieu focuses on class and gender disparities, but he treats women as a homogeneous category (see Moore 1994, 78). My concern is to look at differences among women who share a position within the status hierarchy and to explore how female gender identity is articulated. All Yemeni women are defined relationally in terms of belonging to specific categories of men, but their status as unmarried sisters or wives is acted out through the way in which their body is displayed and modified. Sherry Ortner's (1981) analysis of women's positions within

The field research on which this article is based was conducted in the capital of the Yemen Arab Republic, San'a, and Sa'dah province from 1982 to 1986. The research was funded by the Studienstiftung des Deutschen Volkes, the German Historical Institute in London, and the Greater London Research Council. I have carried out further research among Yemenis in England. For a detailed account of how fieldwork was conducted, see vom Bruck 1991. Previous versions of the article were presented at the Centre for Cross-Cultural Research on Women of Oxford University in 1992 and the Seminar for Mediterranean Studies, Dartmouth College, in 1996. I have benefited from stimulating discussions with the participants of these seminars. I should especially like to thank Maurice Bloch, Alfred Gell, and Henrietta Moore for their comments.

[1] See also Bourdieu 1977, 89–94; Jenkins 1992, 75; Shilling 1993, 128.

[*Signs: Journal of Women in Culture and Society* 1997, vol. 23, no. 1]

conjugal relations and kinship relations in hierarchical societies is pertinent. She contrasts the cognatic type of kinship and marriage organization that occurs in Southeast Asia and Polynesia with patrilineal systems found in the cultures of South Asia. Her analysis of patrilineal systems would also apply to the Middle East. She argues that, irrespective of the differences between the two systems, "in marriage a woman's specifically *feminine* (as against generically human) attributes mainly centering on biological reproduction are highlighted" (1981, 400).[2] Ortner's point is significant because it sheds light on women's different attributions in two fundamental sets of relationships, namely, that of married couples and of brothers and sisters. In their analyses of gender in Middle Eastern cultures, anthropologists have predominantly focused on the married couple.[3] The issue of gender, however, is central to both types of relationships. The Yemeni material shows that in respect to their capacities and the performance of particular kinds of activities, two different kinds of female bodies — those of unmarried sisters and wives — can be distinguished. The symbolism of space, consumption, deportment, and bodily enhancement reveals that Yemeni women's diverse status is inscribed on their bodies and is physically experienced in a variety of ways. Unmarried sisters have not yet fully developed their gender potential; they are seen as incomplete (*naqisah*) and thus less gendered than wives and mothers. (By unmarried, I refer primarily to those women between the ages of fifteen and thirty-five; beyond age thirty-five Yemeni women rarely marry.) I argue that, upon marriage, gender becomes more central to a woman's identity, and gender is fully developed when she embarks on her reproductive career. Enhancement of the body by means of cosmetics and attire is contingent on her conjugal status. Bodily practices focusing on indulgence in conspicuous consumption and self-decoration indicate women's sexual and reproductive activities. These practices distinguish them from other women who abstain from these activities.

Studies of gender in the Middle East have been predicated on the notion of men and women as different kinds of persons. Alternatively, attention has been drawn to difference within either gender category. For example, several authors have explored coexisting or ambivalent notions of

---

[2] As Ortner 1981 notes, depending on specific cultural contexts, one dimension may be more prevalent than the other (400). It goes without saying that everywhere women are both kin and spouses. Throughout her life, a Yemeni woman is "in between," associated with her descent category by birth and with that of her spouse through marriage. As I explain later, more significance is attached to the conjugal bond.

[3] An exception is Suad Joseph (1994).

masculine identities.[4] Besides those writers who have focused on women's acquiescence to dominant ideologies while attempting to subvert them (Abu-Lughod 1986), some have examined women's diverse interpretations of cultural notions according to class and age.[5] As I explain, however, divisions among women according to class and generation might conceal discontinuities of gender attributions within these categories.

Janice Boddy (1982, 1989) has taken a different approach in her work on northern Sudan. According to Sudanese villagers, the recognition of physical difference does not automatically produce gendered bodies. Children are assigned male or female characteristics at birth according to their genitalia, but these are regarded as insufficient determinants of their gender identities. Gendering is achieved only through circumcision. Boddy shows that gender is socially induced, arguing that it is a process rather than a status. My concern is this process of gendering with respect to the female body.

Before elaborating on this issue, I would like to stress that in the Yemeni context gender is at the core of female personhood of both unmarried and married women. However, as I show below, their different gender identities are subject to different moral evaluations and have different implications for concepts of agency. Linda Nicholson (1994, 100) has suggested that an understanding of the meaning of woman requires the elucidation of a complex network of characteristics rather than a single one.[6] Notions of female gender can be informed either by concepts of femininity or by physical difference in relation to men. In Yemen, the activation of female fertility in marriage is what primarily defines a woman's femininity. As long as they have not entered the sexually productive phase of their lives, women are denied the distinctly feminine attributes with which married women, specifically those who have given birth to several children, are endowed. Special significance is attached to motherhood as an aspect of womanhood; birth is highly ritualized, and women's personal status derives mainly from motherhood.[7]

Yemenis do not assign a feminine identity to an unmarried woman, but in anticipation of her future role as a wife and mother, she is treated

[4] Wikan 1977; Cornwall and Lindisfarne 1994, 1995; Kandiyoti 1994; Lindisfarne 1994; vom Bruck 1996.

[5] Abadan-Unat 1981; Wikan 1982; Tapper 1983; Altorki 1986; Meriwether 1993; Mir-Hosseini 1996.

[6] On the problematic notion of "woman," see also Errington 1990, 7; Moore 1993, 200; Kandiyoti 1996, 5.

[7] On this issue, see Yanagisako 1979, 191; and Moore 1988, 25.

differently from an unmarried man. On the one hand, she is a member of the "house" whose corporate identity she shares. (In accordance with Yemeni kinship terminology, I use the term *bayt* [house] to describe patronymic descent categories of varying size.) All members are equally related to the founder of the house to which they belong and whose name they carry throughout their lives. On that level, differential gender attribution is played down. Those (married) women who conceal the potent symbols of sexuality and femininity, such as hair and pregnancy, from fathers and brothers emphasize their status as kin; this concealment almost implies a denial of their link to other men's houses.[8]

On the other hand, unlike her brothers, a woman "becomes" her spouse's *sharaf* (honor) and is therefore subjected to greater control. Once a girl reaches puberty, she is looked at with growing unease: there is great concern about appropriate suitors, and all effort is made that the girl's reputation will not be tarnished. As do others who are not sexually active within the confines of a conjugal relationship—for instance, divorcees—unmarried women pose a threat to the social order. All Islamic legal schools recognize both men's and women's libidinous energies, and sexual abstinence does not carry any positive moral value (Musallam 1983; Haeri 1994, 104). Because, in most circumstances, conjugality is the only permissible and desirable form of cross-gender interaction, fertile unmarried women are not as fully incorporated into the adult world as are married women.[9] The unmarried are marginal in the household of their kin, and they rarely acquire as much authority in the household as women who have produced children. Girls are aware that marriage raises a woman's personal status and that their movements are much more restricted than those of married women. As a girl once explained to me, "If I do not get married, I shall only be a servant in my brother's house. Being married is like holding a 'green card.'" However, in high-status families the unmarried are granted respect, and occasionally the advice of elderly unmarried women is sought in family matters. Married women are seen as less impartial than them. For example, a woman looking for a bride for her son is said to seek as much an obedient daughter-in-law as the happiness of her son.

Distinct moral codes and practices guide the lives of men and women, but in view of the diverse categorization of the female gender, it can be argued that these codes and practices define differences both between and within gender categories. The concept that the female body is endowed

---

[8] Note that married women among the Egyptian Awlad 'Ali veil from their fathers and uncles (Abu-Lughod 1987, 25).

[9] On this subject, see Mernissi 1975, 59; and Sanders 1991, 74.

with the capacity to provide a sensual stimulus for men accounts for restrictions on cross-gender interaction between persons who, according to Islamic law, are not in a degree of consanguinity that precludes marriage (*mahram*). This concept provides the rationale for camouflaging women's bodies in the presence of non-*mahram*. The majority of women of urban northern Yemen render their bodies inaccessible to the sensory perception of non-*mahram*. In other words, the body must not be communicated — it must not be seen, smelled, heard, or touched. As I explain, in some contexts the pattern of physical or symbolic separation of non-*mahram* is analogous to that of same-gender relationships such as those between married and unmarried women.

In the first part of this article, I focus on acts of "abstaining from," "protecting from," and "sealing off," which are oriented toward avoiding illicit relationships between non-*mahram*. In his study of Malagasy Muslims, Michael Lambek (1992) shows how persons are granted value through what they refrain from doing; the practice of taboos establishes who they are. Taboos are "acts of separation" that serve as boundaries "which are marked on, or within, or by means of the body" (Lambek 1992, 247–48). The classical writings on sexual segregation and the "honor code" focus on systems of values that define categories of persons in relation to status and gender.[10] However, Lambek's theory provides a more illuminating perspective on the Yemeni data. By showing that certain acts of denial serve partly to constitute persons, he creates a link between performative acts, gender, the body, and the person. Moreover, he argues that relations among different categories of persons are determined and communicated by these acts (see also Gell 1979).

Lambek is concerned with taboos as both practices and prescriptions. The relevance of Lambek's argument for Yemen is reinforced by his proposition that persons are "performatively constituted in part through the

---

[10] Several diverse aspects have been highlighted in this literature. Exploring the gendered nature of honor, Bourdieu explains the diverse connotations of honor among the Kabyle. The Kabyle distinguish between "*nif,* self-esteem or point of honour, and *h'urma,* honour, the entirety of that which is *h'aram* . . . all that is prohibited . . . or is sacred." Bourdieu emphasizes that as a system of values, honor is lived rather than clearly conceived (1965, 216, 231); see also Jenkins 1992, 40, 72. Abu-Lughod 1986 links honor to the "nobility of descent." She also analyzes honor in relation to the weak, who acquire moral worth through deference to those on top of the hierarchy (see also Gilmore 1982, 192). Honor is conceived as an aspect of the person (Wikan 1984, 636); for Gilsenan, "true honour" combines "act and being" (1996, 126). Nancy Tapper (1991, 15) suggests that honor and shame articulate an ideology of control that embraces relations of production and reproduction. She suggests that the primary referents of notions of honor and shame are gender and sexual differentiation (see also Eickelman 1989, 253; Delaney 1991, 38).

practice of their bodily taboos" (1992, 249, quote on 253). Because taboos are instrumental in creating persons, the body is the primary seat of the person (261). The taboos I explore involve the entity of women's bodies. Lambek notes that one feature of taboo practice is its gender specificity. Men and women observe different taboos, and the latter are expected to observe them more conscientiously. Taboos provide space for individual identification; practicing taboos is one way in which Yemeni women relate to specific cultural notions of male and female.

Lambek's argument can be situated in a tradition of theorizing that analyzes "woman" and "man" as categories that are constructed through specific practices and discourses. Judith Butler, for example, defines gender as a *"corporeal style,* an 'act,' as it were, which is both intentional and performative" (1990, 139).[11] She argues that persons only become intelligible through becoming gendered in accordance with specific normative criteria (16). "Sexed bodies" (135), or rather gender identities in a more general sense, are generated by a set of prohibitions that form the core of culturally specific "regulatory norms" (1993, 2, 55). Like Lambek, Butler stresses the constraining nature of performative acts (1993, 225). For both, however, the "performative" suggests a contingent construction of meaning. The meaning of acts of taboos may shift and involve resistance (Lambek 1992, 260–62). According to Butler, the compulsory practice that produces gendering, notably the embodiment of "norms," does not rule out subversion and instability (1990, 139; 1993, 231, 225). As I show, both adherence to taboos and abandonment of them at specific moments of the life cycle articulate processes of gendering. For example, brides who refuse to abandon taboos that must be observed by unmarried women are protesting against an undesired marriage arrangement.

While in the first part of the article I deal with taboos that must be adhered to by women collectively, in the second part I describe how, through the practice of taboos, women's status as unmarried sisters or wives is inscribed on and into the body. The unmarried must abstain from bodily enhancement and the consumption of stimuli. Studies of the skin as a symbolic artifact emphasize that dress and bodily adornment are central media that serve as status markers, and they shape and communicate self-identity.[12] Yemenis place great emphasis on different styles of bodily

[11] Butler does not have a singular or deliberate "act" in mind, but "reiterative and citational practice" (1990, 139). She stresses that bodily styles "have a history" and are never fully initiated by individuals (1993, 2).

[12] See Uberoi 1967; Turner 1969, 1980; Strathern and Strathern 1971; Strathern 1979; Knauft 1989; O'Hanlon 1989; Gell 1993; Maynard 1994; Hendrickson 1996; Tarlo 1996.

decorum in accordance with gender. Both men and unmarried women are supposed to exercise restraint in embellishing their bodies. Over the centuries, the *'ulama* (religious scholars) have discussed the kind and quantity of jewelry appropriate for a man. They disagree about whether a man might wear silk, gold, silver, or pearls (*Sharh al-Azhar* 1980, 1:177).[13] Men who shave all their facial hair might be depicted as *khanfus* (beetle), which has connotations of transvestism. The sight of men's earrings and long hair on the streets of London makes Yemeni visitors indignant, and some of my colleagues who are eager to establish their proper masculine credentials grow beards before they embark on field research in Yemen.

The "social skin" mediates relations between the body and the world (Comaroff and Comaroff 1992, 74), but features of social identity are not always central to aesthetic display. In her study of Hagen self-decoration, Marilyn Strathern (1979) stresses the relationship between physical appearance and inner qualities of the person. Hageners are aware that beautification might serve to conceal rather than highlight personal identity. Indeed the decorated dancer is painstakingly concerned to disguise his identity. Yet rather than camouflage his self, he reveals his inner qualities. In the Yemeni context, the visible signs women's bodies display are interpreted as signs of inner moral states. Both bodily disguise and embellishment are supposed to reveal these dispositions. Although sharing space with non-*mahram* requires body concealment, in the company of married women and husbands "decorated exposure" (James Faris, quoted in Strathern 1979, 242) carries positive moral implications. Thus depending on the social categories with which a woman is interacting, both bodily disguise and adornment are expressions of virtue and indices of legitimate decorum. A woman wears her moral disposition on her skin.

Differences between women are symbolically accentuated by the way they dress. Dress and sexual reproduction are obviously linked (Turner 1969, 57; 1980, 119; Knauft 1989, 251). While the common disguise of Muslim women's bodies and its links to gender, power, and sexuality have been the subject of much ethnographic inquiry, embellishment has been given far less attention (Kanafani 1983; Weir 1989). Huda Lutfi's (1991) intriguing article about medieval Muslim prescriptive literature

---

On the status-marking significance of dress and the practice of veiling in Yemen, see Mundy 1983.

[13] There is consensus among scholars that during prayer no wearing of jewelry is allowed. Imami (Twelver) Shi'i scholars such as Al-Khu'i (1985, 649) ruled that although a man should not wear golden rings or spectacle frames, he might have a gold crown fitted even for the purpose of adornment.

demonstrates that women's adornment has attracted the attention of scholars as an issue of both public and private morality. Yemenis explicitly perceive a nexus between female bodily embellishment and erotic purposes. A woman's adorned body marks out boundaries between her and non-*mahram* as well as between her and other women's unadorned bodies. Adornment is a means of sexualizing and feminizing the body, but the achievement of conjugal status is a prerequisite of adornment. Embellishment ideally correlates with (physiological) reproduction. A woman's ornaments are indices of potentialities that must be unfolded only in marriage. Like married women, the unmarried must be remote from the sensory experience of non-*mahram,* but they are not permitted to modify the body as a means of enhancing its sexual attributes. Their bodies must be distinct from bodies that signify their implication in sexual relationships, when enchantment through bodily embellishment takes on an obligatory dimension. Thus body decoration is central to the politics of reproduction, and reproductive status is central to female gender identity.

Writers have also stressed that control of body decoration establishes authority that can serve to maintain sets of sociopolitical relationships (Knauft 1989; Gell 1993). The unadorned body of the unmarried Yemeni woman is a sign of her marginal status. She is a *bint* (virgin, sister, daughter) and excluded from the daily gatherings of married women. The relation between the adorned and the unadorned body is hierarchical. As Lambek (1992, 249) notes, taboos can serve to objectify status and to establish hierarchical relationships between certain categories of persons. Status difference between unmarried and married women is tied to the latter's rights over bodily decoration and attire. Married women also have power to influence opinions about unwed girls by questioning their modesty and by criticizing their indulgence in self-enhancement.

The place of bodily enhancement and conjugality in the social construction of masculinity and femininity is different. Unlike a woman, who is referred to as a *bint* as long as she has not entered a conjugal relationship on reaching puberty, a man is no longer classified as a *walad* (boy) and can act as a self-governing entity. This excludes certain categories of men in dependent service as domestic staff, as well as barbers, tanners, blacksmiths, and so forth. They are likened to females by virtue of being "in need of protection." I have heard adult domestic staff referred to as *walad* (vom Bruck 1996). Conjugality is central to the definition of male personhood only insofar as producing offspring, particularly male offspring, is an attribute of adult status generally.[14] Like women, men are urged to

---

[14] On this point, see Launay 1995, 120.

marry so that their sexuality may be properly channeled. Marriage is *nisf wajib al-din* (half of your religious duty), and married people can expect more *ajr* (merit) in this and the other world.

It goes without saying that taboos observed by one category of people necessarily affect others. Both men and women must refrain from behavior that might produce contexts of seduction: women must not be seen, heard, or touched; men must not look at, hear, smell, or touch women who are not their *mahram*. Whether prescriptions about deportment such as body concealment victimize women, it must be borne in mind that taboos might restrict the behavior of others as much as the woman herself.[15]

It is clear that, because of the wide-reaching moral implications a woman's self-presentation has for her and her *mahram,* and the anxiety that surrounds every aspect of body management, the practices I examine are constitutive in the formation of female personhood and social identity. I do not make any claims about the extent to which these practices reveal women's inner selves, nor do I reduce female subjectivity to these practices.

Hierarchy and the manifestation of virtue

In this article, I refer predominantly to houses that constituted the elite of the Yemeni Imamate and that reside in the capital San'a.[16] The Imamate, which had been legitimized by Zaydi Islam — a branch of the Shi'a — was overthrown in a revolution in 1962. The Zaydi doctrine recognizes a living Imam (leader, ruler) who is a descendant of the Prophet Muhammad and distinguishes himself through erudition and piety. The doctrine stipulates that political authority be exercised in conformity with religious precepts; "rising" (*khuruj*) against oppression and injustice is explicitly sanctioned. The elite derived their legitimacy primarily through descent from distinguished Muslim authorities and religious and legal knowledge. Many of these preeminent houses were and are landed, but wealth was less significant as a marker of high status than noble ancestry and erudition. Claims to social and political supremacy were based on genealogy, learning, and

---

[15] This point was made by Buckley and Gottlieb 1988, 9, with respect to restrictive rules surrounding menstruation. On discussions of body concealment and female subjugation, see Mernissi 1975, 142–44; Marsot 1978, 270; Kandiyoti 1988, 283; 1991, 18; Ahmad 1992, 144–68; El-Solh and Mabro 1994, 7–9; Haeri 1994, 108; Hessini 1994, 47–55; Badran 1995, 48, 55; Hoodfar 1995; Macleod 1996, 118–52; Mir-Hosseini 1996, 153–55.

[16] The elite was made up of the *sadah* (sing. *sayyid*), who trace descent to the Prophet Muhammad and who recruited the ruler (Imam), and the *qudah* (sing. *qadi*), who derived their status from their (or their forebears') occupation as government-employed judges. Members of these social categories monopolized state offices and prestigious positions.

moral worth or virtue. The discourse of moral worth embodied in descent lines and displayed in everyday social conduct informed relationships from the top to the bottom of the sociopolitical hierarchy.

Elite women were among the few who received an education. The great majority of their families disapproved of their labor outside the house. In the 1960s, nursing and teaching were the only respectable professions open to these women. Women of low status sold produce in the market and served at coffee shops frequented by male customers, activities regarded as inherently disreputable. The notion of shame associated with women's market activities becomes intelligible when one considers that neither high-status women nor *ulama* were supposed to enter the market. The degree to which women shared physical space with non-*mahram* depended on their position in the status hierarchy rather than merely the economic means available to their families. Bourdieu (1986) links the diversity of lifestyles to the material capital different classes have at their disposal. In the case of Yemeni high-status women, the question was not how much privacy their *mahram* could afford them, but how much privacy their status demanded to maintain. An impoverished scholar would have forfeited much of his honor had he sent his wife or daughter to sell or buy goods in the marketplace.[17]

Since the 1962 revolution, changing power constellations have been characterized by an expansion of the bureaucracy and by the emergence of a modern commercial sector. Men of tribal background, from whose ranks most leaders of the republic have been drawn, have acquired important political positions and wealth. The former ruling houses have lost much of their political power, but they continue to belong to the higher echelons of Yemeni society. They have invested in secular education and have begun to occupy innovative professional niches such as computer science and engineering. Their preoccupation with propriety, accommodated in a legalistic discourse by which all kinds of behavior are rationalized, is a crucial factor in the reproduction of this elite. Indiscretion by either men or women might diminish the elites' moral authority. Strict adherence to moral principles is anchored in the Zaydi doctrine that this elite has represented and that, throughout the history of the Imamate, lent itself to an activist interpretation of piety (vom Bruck 1993). This adherence is regarded as an obligation toward those ancestors who embody a scholarly tradition on which both social position and identity have been based. Zaydi law requires that women give their consent to marriage. Elite families place the least pressure on women to get married or to remarry when

---

[17] Wealth disparities accounted for internal ranking within status categories.

they refuse to do so. Maintaining their image as good Muslims is given precedence over release from the financial burden these women represent.

In recent decades, women of the old elite have attended secondary schools and universities. The majority of middle-aged women do not carry out salaried labor. Younger women who are employed as civil servants and as schoolteachers tend to contribute little to the family income; they invest their money in real estate or spend it on personal luxuries and servants. Their decisions regarding expenditure are guided by two principles: they argue that the Qur'an requires men to provide for them and that women do not want to be accused of neglecting their households. In San'a, most women now enter the market, but foodstuffs and *qat,* a mild narcotic chewed regularly by the majority of adults, are purchased by men.[18] San'a is thus one of the few cities in the world where women are not seen carrying heavy shopping bags.

Women's body management: Taboo practice

Irrespective of their pursuit of salaried labor and the wealth they own, women can rarely act as self-governing agents. Women are constituted relationally by virtue of being *hurmah. Hurmah* is linked linguistically to terms such as *haram* (forbidden, sacred, prohibited). *Hurmah* is often used as a synonym for wife (*zawjah*), but generally women are categorized as *hurmah* because they are "in need of protection." By definition, *hurmah* is a relational category; it must be established whose *hurmah* a woman is. The man to whom a woman belongs (father, brother, or husband) is obliged to provide for her. Being *hurmah* is conceived as an attribute of a woman's vulnerability, a notion through which her dependency on men is rationalized.[19] Disregarding certain moral codes might challenge her status as *hurmah* and thus jeopardize her livelihood and reputation. Bourdieu elaborates on the relation between *hurmah* and honor, suggesting that "*hurmah* in the sense of the sacred (*haram*), *nif,* and *hurma* in the sense of respectability, are inseparable." As he explains, the terms *hurmah* and *haram* have the meaning of taboo (1977, 61). In this sense, the term *hurmah* is reminiscent of the Polynesian term *tapu* from which the English term *taboo* derives. *Tapu* means "reserved" or "prohibited," as when persons are not to be interfered with. Polynesian women who are married are generally in a state of *tapu* (Firth 1963, 122; 1965, 201). A Yemeni woman is at once taboo to certain categories of men, and she must herself observe a number

---

[18] The active ingredient of *qat* is d-norpseudoephedrin (cathin).

[19] On this subject, see Abu-Lughod 1986, chap. 4.

of taboos. Here my analysis differs from that of Lambek, who, along with other writers on the subject, conceives of taboo observance as a subject-object relationship. The Yemeni woman, being the tabooed object, is herself responsible for not violating the taboos. She will be blamed for any indiscretion, but it will also detrimentally affect her husband and her agnates. For example, talking to an unrelated man in the street might lead to the suspicion of a liaison; a woman's repeated encounters with somebody who is not her *mahram* might expose her to malicious gossip. In such cases, her brothers might face difficulties in contracting marriages with women of equal status, and she might be repudiated by her husband.

By examining taboo observance, I refer to taboos as acts that represent the negative, denying aspect of the person. As Alfred Gell (1979) and Lambek (1992) have argued, in some respects the person is constituted through a relationship of negation (e.g., *not* speaking to, and so forth) he or she establishes with the social world. Performing these acts allows for both self-identification and resistance to the cultural symbols that define womanhood. The taboos I examine are still practiced by most women of the old elite. Education, the unification of the former Yemeni states in 1990, the media, and travel and studies, both in Yemen and abroad, produce a degree of variability in the strictness of observance. One must also bear in mind that the ideological pluralism characteristic of Zaydi Islam has always accommodated a variety of practices. People who wish to act in conformity with orthodoxy adhere to the judgments of the religious authorities of their choice. Both men and women consult scholars for their advice on matters that concern them. In the following analysis of taboo practices, women are defined in terms of what they refrain from doing. These practices are informed by the knowledge of social distinctions "acquired" by the body in the process of gendering (see Bourdieu 1977, 90).

Disguising the body

On attaining physical maturity, a woman is said to be '*aurah,* literally, "that which is indecent to reveal." According to Zaydi law, a woman's whole body is '*aurah.* In other words, no part of the female body is given a neutral status. One of the guiding principles of learning to be female is to conceal one facet of identity—the surface of the body—from non-*mahram* both at home and in the street.

Women's outdoor garments are the black *sharshaf* and the *sitarah,* a colored printed cloak that is worn only by a few elderly women. Professional women tend to expose their faces while at work, but some cover them with the exception of the eyes. Some students and professionals have adopted the *baltu,* an overcoat that is worn with a headscarf. Underneath the *shar-*

shaf, the head is covered by the *lithmah,* a rectangular piece of cloth (mostly silk georgette) wrapped ingeniously so as to cover the forehead, nose, and mouth. The concealment of the body is aimed at preventing the sexual interest of non-*mahram* and to give women freedom of movement. A "good woman" conceals her body; failing to do so signifies, as one man put it, that "she wants something from men." A woman who wears the *sharshaf* can be identified by those who know her only by the way she walks and by her shoes and handbag. Ianthe Maclagan (1993, 134), writing about a rural town in Yemen, says that women recognize others through their coverings: "Women instantly recognised and pointed out minute veiled women in photographs I had taken of the town, tiny women on their rooftops whom I had not even noticed and was dismayed to find in the picture."

Veiling is not tied to Yemeni women's reproductive cycles. Girls start to cover their faces before or after the onset of menstruation. Unlike Egyptian Awlad 'Ali women, for example, Yemeni women continue to veil until the end of their lives. Awlad 'Ali who are widowed, divorced, or postmenopausal do not veil at all or do so less than married women (Abu-Lughod 1986, 161). Small Yemeni girls are aware that veiling plays an important part in achieving adulthood. They take great pleasure in trying on parts of their mothers' *sharshaf,* presenting themselves proudly and shyly. By the age of three or four, children have clear notions of the divisions of sociomoral space. For example, whenever a female friend's small boy got tired of us chatting indoors for hours and wanted to go out, he brought her *sharshaf* and threw it to her impatiently.

The *sharshaf* was introduced by the Ottomans at the turn of the century; however, women have been required to cover their faces since the ninth century when the Imamate was founded (Mundy 1983, 535). In past centuries, the *'ulama* have debated under which circumstances non-*mahram* were allowed to see a woman's face. This legal debate suggests a hierarchy of parts of the body according to their function as erotic stimuli. In this hierarchy, a woman's face and hair are assigned a prominent place. One of the scholars who illuminated for me the opinions of his predecessors explained that a woman's face was the most beautiful part of her body. It had to be concealed because "catching someone's eye paves the way to illicit encounters" (*Al-nazar barid ila'l-zinah*).[20] Within Zaydi orthodoxy, three different views are taken by the *'ulama* concerning the legality of a man's sight of a woman's face. According to one verdict, from the onset of

[20] According to Mernissi 1975, 141, the eleventh-century writer al-Ghazali considered a woman's eye an "erogenous zone."

puberty a man must not see a woman's face except that of a slave. Other scholars claimed either that a man's sight of a woman's face was lawful even if she attracted him or that he was permitted to see her if he did not approach her with desire. All scholars agreed that apart from men who can communicate freely with a woman (*mahram*), a woman can be seen by a witness, a doctor, a judge, an executioner, a rescuer, and men who intend to marry her.[21] One of the younger scholars with whom I discussed this subject argued that since women did not cover their faces during the pilgrimage to Mecca, there was no reason to require them to do so at other times.

Women do their utmost to guard their faces against intruding glimpses. Once when I accompanied a woman to her house, which had only one entrance, she lifted her veil while entering without realizing that one of her husband's male guests was about to leave. She slipped sideways to the ground, keeping to the wall, and thus successfully managed to conceal her face. As noted, because of the fear of the consequences of exposing their bodies to non-*mahram*, women are constantly preoccupied with guarding the very movements that in part define them as female subjects. A woman's moral education is founded on the logic of body politics according to which her face — a central erotic part of the female body — must never be uncovered in the presence of non-*mahram*. A man humiliates another man of equal or higher status by seeing his wife's naked face, provided that the husband did not give the other man permission to do so. A man's intruding gaze is a symbolic conquest of another man's most intimate "symbolic capital." The example illustrates Bourdieu's (1990, 71) observation that early learning processes inculcate "a sense of the equivalences between physical space and social space and between movements (rising, falling, etc.) in the two spaces and thereby roots the most fundamental structures of the group in the primary experiences of the body."

Both a man's first sight of his bride's face and first intercourse are part of the consummation of marriage. Although according to Zaydi law a suitor is allowed to see the woman he is interested in marrying, marriages are usually arranged and couples do not see each other before the wedding night. A marriage cannot be contracted without the man's payment of the *mahr* (indirect dowry), nor will the bride's face be revealed to him before he has remunerated her assistant (*shari'ah*) charged with lifting the bride's veil on his behalf.[22] Both seeing the bride's face and having intercourse with her involve financial transactions.

---

[21] Al-Murtada 1975, vol. 4, 8.

[22] The *mahr* is a fixed sum given to the bride by the groom (or his family). Without the *mahr*, the marriage is invalid.

During the decades preceding the 1962 revolution, the ideal of eminent families was that non-*mahram* would hold merely elusive notions of their women's existence as embodied subjects. In the religious enclaves in the countryside (*hijar*), these women were to be invisible to the extent that their bodies, even if entirely covered, would not be exposed to the gaze of non-*mahram*. The women were supposed to spend most of their time at home and be visited by others. If they had to attend life-crisis rituals performed in the houses of relatives and friends, they left after dusk in the company of their husbands or a guard. A niece of Imam Ahmad (1948–62) recalled that when darkness fell, she went out in a group of three or four other women, a soldier walking ahead, holding a lamp.[23]

Depending on such factors as closeness and trust between male kin and spouse, and age difference, the taboo on communication between non-*mahram* is practiced less rigidly. As Karin Ask (1994, 66) observes, following Bourdieu, part of the knowledge of being in charge of one's body is submerged in the body and is not reflected on. However, the minutiae of taboo practice never become completely internalized because every context requires spontaneous judgment and decisions as to the manner in which different parts of the body must be covered, one's voice must be used, and so forth. This is demonstrated by the following example of 'Abdullah.

'Abdullah, who set up his own household when he got married, goes to visit his mother and unmarried sister in the morning. He finds only the female members of the household and their visitors and children at home. (Those who are resident are his father, his brother and his family, his paternal grandmother, his mother and her cowife, and his younger siblings.) Several relatives have come to discuss his sister's forthcoming wedding. After he has knocked at the door, a voice from behind the door or upstairs asks, "*Man?*" (Who is it?). After one of the women has identified his voice, the door is opened by a string that is pulled from upstairs or by one of his *mahram*. She stands behind the door wearing her *lithmah*, opening the door only slightly so that he can slip in. He says with a loud voice "Allah, Allah" so that everybody is aware that a man has arrived. (He also does so whenever he moves about in the house.) While he enjoys a cup of coffee with his sister and his mother, they are joined by his maternal and paternal cousins, his mother and her cowife, his brother's wife, and his paternal aunt. He can see and talk to his paternal cousin because she is twelve years older than him. His maternal cousins do not veil from him because they are his milk-sisters and are thus allowed to chat and joke with him like his sister.[24] Because he and his brother are very close to each other, his sister-

---

[23] See Hugh Scott's (1942, 130) report from the 1930s.

[24] His maternal cousins are his *mahram* because they have been nurtured by his mother.

in-law does not conceal her face in front of him. His paternal cousin's wife speaks to him wearing a *lithmah;* his mother's cowife's sister remains out of sight, talking to him from behind the door.

'Abdullah's father and brother have returned for lunch. Everybody gathers to sit in a circle on the floor sharing a few dishes. A few years ago, the men would have eaten before the women because of the presence of non-*mahram*.[25] On this day, women who veil from the men present sit slightly remote from them, holding their veils in such a way as to hide their faces while eating. While the act of picking up food from the same plates inevitably produces physical proximity, the veil maintains sociomoral space between non-*mahram*.

Names

The restriction on self-naming underscores a woman's being *hurmah*. Women's first names must not be used by, or in the presence of, non-*mahram*.[26] When one meets a woman for the first time, she usually identifies herself as "wife of so-and-so," or "from *bayt* so-and-so" (the house of . . .). Young professionals are more likely to use their first names. In her study of a rural community near San'a, Martha Mundy (1979, 172) notes that land owned by women is listed in their father's name or as "so-and-so and his sister or wife."[27] At places such as laundries and physicians' offices, women register their husband's name. Prior to the revolution, elite women were given male names and titles by their kin or spouses. For example, they were called *sidi* 'Abd al-Wali (my master 'Abd al-Wali) or Wajih al-din ("the one who excels in religion," an honorific for men whose names begin with the prefix 'Abd). These titles were most commonly used by the Imam's female kin who were the center of public attention. The use of male names made it possible to talk about them without invading their privacy. Furthermore, messages were conveyed to women of the royal household who were known to have influence on the Imam.

Families that have recruited rulers, governors, and scholars possess documented histories, some of which range over a millennium. Genealogies and documents relating other important events such as official appointments or periods of study in places around the country or abroad have been recorded and are being updated. Women's names hardly ever appear

---

[25] In the religious enclaves of the northern province of Sa'dah, household members who are not *mahram* to each other—either through consanguinity or affinity—do not share meals together.

[26] See Bourdieu 1965, 224.

[27] A study of seven banks in San'a revealed that about 5 percent of the accounts are held in women's names. All accounts were rial and dollar deposits (Glander 1994, 115).

on genealogical charts. However, women poets and teachers and women who have initiated endowments are referred to in the documents. Women, just as men, are focused on as members of patrilines, but they are also seen in their own right as teachers. While the names of deceased women may be mentioned, references to living wives and mothers, for instance, in poetry, have been rare in the nineteenth and twentieth centuries.[28] Some men have written their mothers' and daughters' biographies.[29] Those that are unpublished are not available to visitors who would otherwise be welcome to read or borrow any book they like. Instead, they are stored away from other books, sometimes hidden under a cushion next to the seat taken by their authors.[30]

Writing

Before the 1960s, some women were also subjected to the repression of nonsensory modes of communication such as writing. Elite women were taught how to pray and to read the Qur'an, but not all learned how to write for fear they would exchange letters with men. Whereas male literacy was highly valued, in a woman's hand the pen was seen as a potential instrument for initiating illicit encounters. In one case, an elderly woman reported that her father asked that his children's homework be shown to him every night. One day he came across a particularly fine piece of writing. On learning that it was his daughter's, he asked her teacher to stop instructing her. He was worried that she might not find a husband.[31]

The context of writing reveals that in certain circumstances transgressing taboos can be an expression of personal affection and evidence of close male-female relationships. Women's agnates had reservations about their sending letters to their husbands while they were traveling or jailed. After an uprising in 1948 seeking to establish a constitution, many intellectuals and politicians were imprisoned. In one case, a woman who wrote a letter to her husband in jail was told by her father that she should ask only about his health and inform him that they were all well. He discouraged her from expressions of intimacy for fear that her letter might fall into the

---

[28] See, e.g., Al-Shami 1986, 292, 455, 487, 532.

[29] Al-Wazir 1992.

[30] Because I was a female researcher, these works were shown to me with pride, and passages were read aloud to me and commented on.

[31] Ende 1994, 55–56, quotes Ibn Hajar, a sixteenth-century Meccan scholar, as saying that men would find it much easier to approach women who could read and write by sending written messages to them rather than involving messengers. Yemeni middle-aged men who collected the letters they had received from women consider them part of their dearest reminiscences. See also Baron 1991, 280.

wrong hands. The woman ignored her father's advice and even enclosed her photograph in the letter. According to her husband, her picture inspired him to compose poetry about her in prison (Al-Shami 1986, 362). Another wife of one of the imprisoned men recalled that her being unable to correspond with him because she had not been allowed to learn to write contributed to her suffering. She was moved to tears remembering that she had to dictate her letters to male relatives, feeling ashamed to use intimate language.

Voices and odors

While in the surroundings of non-*mahram,* women must refrain from aural and olfactory transmission. Decorated bodies can be disguised, but perfumes are neither destined to remain with their wearers nor can they be prevented from enchanting those who detect them. Therefore women who attend the regular female afternoon gatherings, which I discuss below, use perfume only on arrival unless they are driven to the gatherings by their *mahram.*

In theory, a woman's voice is part of her *'aurah.* There is little objection to women's talking to shopkeepers and relatives, as the example of 'Abdullah demonstrates. Women feel more at ease talking to and joking with men of lower status such as taxi drivers, and some do not veil from men who provide services for their families.[32] If a woman wishes to speak to her husband while he is in the company of men who are not her *mahram,* she either claps her hands or sends a child with a message. A middle-aged man recalled that his mother used to put a finger into her mouth in order to disguise her voice when speaking to a servant boy (*duwaydar*).[33]

While I was doing fieldwork in a village in Sa'dah province, which is predominantly inhabited by people devoted to religious learning, the men debated whether it was lawful (*halal*) for them to have conversations with me. It was easy to conceal my face on request, but I was disinclined to gain information from men only by way of questionnaires. In the end they decided that listening to my voice was a concession that was justified by my quest for knowledge. The village was referred to as *bilad al-din* (religious community). All sounds regarded as arousing—for example, women's voices and singing—were outlawed. Apart from the walls by which most houses were surrounded, the silence of the village was one of its most remarkable features. Music was said to be from the devil, and one could

---

[32] See Abu-Lughod 1985, 640; 1986, 162; Lutfi 1991, 104; vom Bruck 1996, 153–54.

[33] A *duwaydar* served in the women's quarters until he had reached puberty. He is referred to as *khadim al-dar* (servant of the house).

easily walk around the village all day without ever hearing a woman's voice. (By contrast, in surrounding villages whose inhabitants define themselves as members of a *qabilah*, or "tribe," women shouted each other's names from the rooftops.) Women were asked to watch only religious programs on television. The women of my household used to quarrel about what we ought neither to watch nor to hear. All of them seemed quite keen to watch Egyptian and Syrian films, but the older women felt obliged to prevent the others from listening to the film music. The young women were supposed to jump from their seats and switch off the television whenever a scene was accompanied by music. One woman infuriated her aunt by watching an Egyptian singer after the nightly religious program had finished. Her niece's disobedience upset the old woman, who was worried that the men might find out and punish them by getting rid of the television.

Compliance and defiance: Marriage and self-enhancement

In the presence of non-*mahram,* taboos on body exposure, which include the use of personal names and perfumes, must be observed by women collectively. Other taboos that center on dress styles and cosmetics are instrumental in differentiating women from each other. The unmarried must not participate in the daily afternoon gatherings (sing. *tafritah*) where married women display their attire, which symbolizes the achievement of fully gendered adulthood. The gatherings take place daily in women's houses and are held in the main sitting room. There are no formal invitations. The social composition of the meetings tends to be varied. Some are attended only by women of equal standing; others by neighbors of lower status and servants. News is exchanged, personal problems are discussed, and *qat* and coffee are consumed.[34]

Because of the "public" nature of these gatherings, the Yemeni house cannot be identified with "domestic" space (vom Bruck 1997, 152). The house is not a "sanctuary of intimacy" and an "enclosure of feminity" as Bourdieu (1979, 142) and Joëlle Bahloul (1996, 30) have suggested in the context of Algeria. For example, in an extended Yemeni family, which includes the husband's married brothers, a woman must always beware of the gaze of her brother-in-law, who must not see her hair or her adorned face. When women's gatherings take place, men must leave the house or stay in a room or on a floor of the house not entered by the women. The

---

[34] On the *tafritah,* see Makhlouf 1979, 22, 26; Mundy 1983, 535; Champault 1985, 207; Naïm-Sanbar 1987, 98. Among those of low status, the *akhdam* (sweepers) never attend.

men must avoid encountering an unveiled guest. Toddlers who have been brought along by their mothers play in the courtyard. The unmarried girls who are too old to join them spend time in another room because they are to be excluded from discussions of marital problems and sexual joking. Hence, women do not collectively maintain the boundaries of "female space." In some villages north of San'a, the unmarried join the *tafritah*, but they wear the *lithmah* across the nose and mouth.[35]

Unmarried women

Divisions between married and unmarried women are marked by different taboo practice and terms of address. In light of the taboos they all observe and their classification as *banat*, the unmarried form a distinct category, and they have a common status. The following example shows that women themselves clearly conceive of married and unmarried women as two separate categories. I spent the afternoon at a house where a wedding was to take place a few days later. The bride's aunt was about to finish sewing the girl's dress. Recalling the last few weddings they had attended, the women of the household and a couple of their friends were discussing the skills of the hairdresser and the bridal dresser who were to enhance the girl's beauty.[36] In anticipation of the wedding night, the bride was looking rather anxious. When one of the women noticed her apprehension, she tried to calm her by saying, "Don't worry. You are already one of us."

In her study of Beirut, Suad Joseph (1994, 51) refers to a man who repeatedly encouraged his twelve-year-old unmarried sister to dress attractively. As a girl approaches puberty, she is expected to embellish herself. Among the old elite of San'a, a girl's dressing up — irrespective of the social categories with which she is interacting — is considered immodest and frivolous. Lila Abu-Lughod (1993, 78) quotes an Awlad 'Ali woman telling her great-granddaughter: "It's shameful for girls to wear hairclips. Why do you want a hairclip? Are you looking for a husband?"

The unmarried must wear plain outfits, very little jewelry, and no makeup, but they are allowed to use *naqsh* (literally, drawing, inscription) on their hands.[37] *Naqsh*, which has a gall-ink (*khidhab*) base, is an ornamen-

---

[35] While there is evidence of Muslim men who veil from each other (Casajus 1985), women do not usually do so (see Abu-Lughod 1986, 161).

[36] The term *coiffeur* has now entered Yemeni vocabulary. Previously, a *muzayyinah*, who sings at weddings and dresses and decorates the bride, would also style her hair.

[37] When outdoors, the unmarried cannot be distinguished from the married. For a contrasting picture, see Abu-Lughod 1986, 17, 134–37. In Jiddah, in shopping areas only the unmarried cover their faces (Altorki 1986, 38).

tal pattern that resembles tattoos, but it does not last longer than about a fortnight.[38] During religious holidays, girls are allowed to apply *naqsh* on their hands, but not on other parts of the body such as the face. A member of the former royal dynasty recalled that in defiance of the prohibition against the use of makeup, she and her sisters secretly beautified their lips and cheeks with the red powder (*turbat khumrah*) used by the Imam to dry the ink of his stamps.[39] In the company of married women, an unmarried girl can be easily identified. For example, a girlfriend of mine was looking for a suitable spouse for her brother who had recently been divorced and was desperately wanting to remarry. I had just returned from Sa'dah, and I was going to visit one of the families who occasionally spend time in the capital. My friend asked me to introduce her to these families because her brother was looking for a pious wife. I took her to the house of a girl I knew was eager to live in San'a. At the house there were only members of the extended family, and there was no need for me to point out to my friend which woman I had in mind. After we left the house, she said to me: "I immediately knew who she was. She wasn't wearing any lipstick."

The unmarried realize that indulgence in self-beautification is contingent on conjugal relationships. I heard a girl moan ruefully while watching her mother getting ready for the *tafritah:* "If we don't get married, we can never wear any makeup." Her statement expressed her desire to dress up like a married woman, but it also revealed her awareness that decorative cosmetics are markers of female adulthood. Women hold the view that, particularly in the past, girls would readily agree to a proposed marriage because their lives were intolerably circumscribed. One of the few occasions when unmarried girls were allowed to wear makeup was during the celebration taking place after children between the ages of seven and twelve had finished reading the Qur'an. One of the women who had the ritual performed for her at the age of nine recalled that she enjoyed wearing makeup so much that she wanted to get married only to be allowed to put it on. On the day of the celebration she was reluctant to remove it and did so only superficially after her mother urged her (vom Bruck 1994, 167). Adornment is one of the things women value about marriage; it is appreciated aesthetically beyond what it signifies for sexual relationships between

[38] *Khidhab* contains 'afs (gall of the oak tree *Quercus infectoria*) and *sikkah* (copper [I]-oxyd) (see Schönig 1995, 22).

[39] Before the revolution, women used kohl and white face powder and lipstick brought by local traders from British-governed Aden.

men and women. To this young girl, who was not yet concerned about sex and reproduction, marriage seemed desirable because it would transform her body into that of a fully adorned grown-up.

It is important for unmarried women to communicate moral restraint particularly to other women because they act as chief marriage brokers. Since marriages are often arranged, women look for suitable spouses for their sons and brothers. Although the great majority of women are anxious to find spouses, they must pretend that they are not eager to get married quickly in order to avoid suspicion of concealing physical or character defects.[40] Women argue that girls who do not exercise restraint while they are still virgins might not be chaste and obedient wives; a virtuous girl would receive marriage proposals anyway without advertising her charms.[41]

Women who seek brides for their sons assess the daughters of their friends and relatives, but there are obstacles to taking a closer look at girls whose families they do not know well. Girls are expected to hide from these women. Mothers encourage their daughters to leave the house as soon as they suspect that visitors have come to inspect them. One woman explained to me that her daughter was not a marketable asset; "After all she is not for sale — I don't want people to come and decide whether they want her or not." Usually a woman has to come a few times under a pretext before she will be able to see the would-be bride. If the girl is not interested in the match, she goes on hiding or her family spreads rumors that she is already engaged to someone else. Her hiding is an act of symbolic veiling, like body concealment, which must be practiced in cross-gender relationships between non-*mahram*. A girl hides or veils from women whose gaze is represented as male. Women who scrutinize other women's bodies on behalf of men are attributed masculine qualities. Indeed the imagery women use to describe potential brides to their sons and brothers resembles that of male love poetry. Some women also veil from women who produce videotapes at weddings. They are worried that the tapes might fall into the hands of unrelated men. Most do not object to being filmed by close relatives or friends whom they feel they can trust. Usually members of the bride's family videotape the celebration, and they retain control of the tapes.

[40] Similar points have been made by Abu-Lughod 1986, 153; and Altorki 1986, 129, 135.

[41] In Jiddah, "showing off" one's daughter is stigmatized only in cross-gender gatherings. The girls' families would be suspected of "exhibit[ing] their women to the men in order to secure husbands for them" (Altorki 1986, quote on 15, 39). By contrast, at Moroccan weddings, unmarried girls "who are still finding their position 'in the market'" are not expected to be shy and reserved (Kapchan 1996, quote on 172, 199).

Some of the taboos the unmarried practice apply to both males and females, but adults are more lenient regarding how far their sons must adhere to taboos. Until recently, children and adolescents were asked to avoid stimuli such as *qishr*, a hot drink prepared from coffee husks. *Qishr* is prepared with ginger, which is considered an aphrodisiac (see Schopen 1983, 74, 143). Children were discouraged from drinking *qishr* because of this effect and for fear that they might wet their beds. Whereas adolescent boys' consumption of *qishr* received little comment, girls, until they were married, were asked to refrain from drinking it by being told that it would break their hymen or cause a dark complexion.[42] Unmarried girls must also neither chew *qat*, which has a sensualizing effect, nor smoke the water pipe.[43]

Maintaining good marital relations
With the beginning of the marriage ritual, previously stigmatized self-adornment is transformed into socially appropriate behavior. Body decoration acts as a signifier of both marital status and fully gendered personhood. Because bodily adornment and marital status are inextricably linked, marriage legitimates bodily enhancement. Enhancement of the self is an expression of deference toward a husband and of fulfillment of wifely duties.

On the occasion of her wedding the bride is allowed to attend the *tafritah* for the first time. Her appearance signifies her ambiguous status. Prior to consummation of the marriage, she belongs neither to the unmarried nor the married. On the first day, she spends only a short time among the married women while her whole body remains disguised. She is then taken back to the room of the unmarried where she continues to cover her face with the exception of the eyes. On the second day, her attendant applies *naqsh* to her little finger. Before she is taken to the groom's house by her agnates on the following day she is presented to all female guests at her father's house. On her wedding night *naqsh* is applied to parts of her body

---

[42] Fair skin is considered ideal beauty. Prescriptions about the appropriate comportment and attire of males are linked to physical maturity rather than conjugality. A man who has reached puberty is allowed to attend the male gatherings (sing. *madka*, *maqyal*), chew *qat*, and smoke in front of his parents and elder relatives. He may wear precious decorative artifacts such as daggers, use perfume, and apply kohl around his eyes during the month of Ramadhan. This is encouraged because the Prophet is reported to have done so.

[43] In accordance with the notion of the greater sensuous qualities inherent in women's bodies, the kind of *qat* that is regarded most stimulating and numbing is called *qat nisa'i* (female *qat*) (see Schopen 1981, 498). *Qat* serves as an erotic stimulant for both men and women, but it causes temporary impotence in some men.

such as her hands, arms, face, feet, and chest.[44] She wears a white dress and coral and gold jewelry.

At the *tafritah* the majority of women wear ankle-length dresses made of shiny polyester or silk imported from Japan, Korea, or India. Prêt-à-porter from Europe is available at high prices. Part of a woman's outfit is a headband (*al-masar al-tal'i*) consisting of cardboard wrapped with a piece of patterned silk worn over a scarf. (The unmarried must not wear the headband.) Women dance singly or in pairs. A dance called *San'ani* is danced by pairs of women, but Egyptian-style dance is performed only by individual women. Dancing used to be the prerogative of married women. Today, it is not unusual to find a group of girls dancing to the sounds of Michael Jackson or Kuwaiti music at weddings. Older women are scandalized by young girls' dancing. A friend visiting Yemen for the first time since the revolution expressed to me her indignation at what she saw.

Most men and women consider a woman's bodily enhancement to be a necessary means by which marriage is sustained. Women often remark: "Don't we have to look after ourselves? After all our husbands can't take pleasure in other women because they are veiled [*muhajjabah*]. If you don't take care of your looks, your husband will start thinking about another woman." One aspect of body concealment women appreciate is that it prevents men from seeing other women in the flesh, which might tempt them to think of another wife. Both divorce and her husband's taking another wife would lower a woman's personal status. A friend of mine who was returning to Yemen after studies in Britain was looking forward to wearing the *sharshaf*. She argued that since "in the West" women had fewer children and had access to fitness clubs, they could take better care of their bodies, but their display in space shared by men would only cause other women's apprehension.

Jealousy and resentment of one's husband's admiration of other women's appearance are expected behavior that demonstrates a woman's appreciation of her husband. While I was watching a Syrian feature film with a female friend and her mother-in-law, my friend pointed to the main actress and said, "This is Muhammad's [her husband] favorite." The composure of her voice caused her mother-in-law's indignation. It was apparent that her mother-in-law expected my friend to talk about this subject with apprehension; it was clear that the mother-in-law also disapproved of her son's insensitive remarks in front of his wife.

---

[44] The wedding night precedes further celebrations taking place during the following months. Some women who go on honeymoon to Europe avoid *naqsh* because they fear it will attract unnecessary attention.

When at a *tafritah* I drew a friend's attention to the glamorous outfit of a woman who had married a few days previously, she commented: "In Yemen, marriage is not just one night." She meant that women not only had to do their utmost to highlight their beauty when they met their husbands for the first time, but they ought to do so throughout their marital lives as well. The newly wed woman is expected to present herself as self-assured of her seductive power. Her husband's attraction to her is considered vital especially during the early months of their marriage. At this stage the couple have yet to establish intimacy and the woman's position in the patrilocal household has not yet been consolidated.

A woman's adornment communicates her success in marriage, deference to her husband, and prosperity, but its vocabulary is that of sexuality. When ʿAbdullah's wife returned home from the *tafritah* and did not find her children in bed, she took off her makeup and even put on a simple dress. Her husband, who enjoyed seeing her adorned, asked, "Why do you put on makeup for your [female] friends and not for me?" His wife was embarrassed in front of her teenage children, thinking that they would assume that she was going to have sex that night because she was all dressed up. Abu-Lughod (1986, 161) has argued that the veil covers sexual shame; in this context, fancy dress signifies this shame. Some women change their dress after returning from the *tafritah* and put on another fancy one in order to look fresh and appealing during the evening hours (*samrah*) spent with their husbands.[45]

As Abu-Lughod (1986, 153, 156) notes, good women deny interest in sexual matters except in the company of their peers. The *tafritah* is a celebration of the sensuality and fertility ideally associated with marriage. Most women enjoy dressing up, and they take great pleasure and appreciation in their own and other women's glamour. At the *tafritah,* a woman communicates her ability to attract a man and to secure his ongoing attention to her through the media of dress, dance, and cosmetics. At the gatherings, stimuli such as *qat* that can be directed toward libidinal recharging are consumed. Ideally, the bodies displayed at the *tafritah* tell moral success stories; the small children who are brought along are part of these stories. In Sanʿa, babies are usually nursed in another room, but in Saʿdah, they are given constant attention by their mothers and other women. They are shown off and passed round and fondled by everyone.

---

[45] *Samrah* comes from *samar* (pl. *asmar*), evening or nightly conversations. Note in this context that the fourteenth-century Egyptian scholar Ibn al-Hajj suggested that a wife's desire can be sensed from her adornment (Lutfi 1991, 107). ʿAbdullah was concerned about his wife's conduct because he began asking himself whether he should interpret her lack of adornment as a sign of her declining desire for him.

Embellishment also serves as a medium through which both competition and hierarchy among married women is enacted. A woman's jewelry, dress, the kind of *qat* she chews, and, though rarely, a servant who carries the *qat* all indicate her worth, her seductive potential, and her husband's affection and respect for her. She invests her *mahr* in gold jewelry, and on her wedding she receives jewelry and clothing from her family. Her husband and her agnates are also expected to present such gifts at the birth of each child.[46] For women, jewelry is an important investment in movable property — the more they possess, the more secure they feel. Jewelry also demonstrates male prosperity and achievement, and it is used as a means of compensation. Men present gifts to their wives when they wish to apologize for wrongdoing, or when they take another wife. A woman who does not chew *qat* is entitled to objects she values. The material and aesthetic value of jewelry and clothes rather than their suitability for their wearers excites admiration. If a woman cherishes another's special piece, the wearer informs her about its price and other more valuable ones that she possesses. Her attire indicates how much her relatives and her husband value her. Women also inquire about the costs of dresses and the tailors who produced them.[47] Although men tend to judge women's beautiful outfits as their appreciation for them, they also resent their demands for new clothes. A man complained to me that his wife asked him to buy new dresses while there were some she had not even worn yet. "I told her to wear these first and that I would buy her new ones when the others were worn out. But she wouldn't listen. She accumulates and accumulates."[48] One man explained the origin of gender inequality in terms of women's desire for gold and cosmetics. When a few millennia ago they started to

---

[46] On this issue, see Mundy 1983, 537; Marcus 1992, 101; Maclagan 1993, 128, 136, 142; Glander 1994, 144. In parts of eastern Yemen, a man is supposed to place jewelry or money under his wife's pillow after he has had sex with her for the first time, thus confirming her new status and expressing his appreciation.

[47] The competition that is acted out in the sphere of aesthetics causes marital problems and leads adolescent girls to despair. Two cousins, one of whom was wealthier than the other, were going to have a joint wedding. When the poorer girl heard that her cousin's dowry was composed of thirty pairs of shoes and an equal number of handbags to match them, she refused food for two days.

[48] According to Wikan 1977, 317, "The husband . . . has to discipline himself and perform acts which may be inconveniences or hardships, but serve *her* needs — as when working to provide her with ornaments literally by the sweat of his brow in the fierce heat of an Omani summer's day." A Yemeni story demonstrates the tensions women's quest for attire causes to marriages (see appendix). The story implicitly puts the blame on women, who are portrayed as being unreasonably greedy.

compete with each other and demanded more and more attire, he said, they became dependent on men, who had to provide it.

In some contexts, taboos that are reminiscent of the premarital life phase must be observed. During the forty-day period after childbirth when the couple are to abstain from sexual intercourse, women must not use makeup and must wear a black scarf over their headband. Fully adorned divorcees and widows would be looked at with suspicion. However, as older women who have never married do, divorcees and widows might chew *qat* and smoke.

In Sa'dah province, the use of henna—which Fatima, the Prophet's daughter, was said to have used on the day she was married to 'Ali—was highly approved of. Indeed women argued that a Zaydi woman's prayer was incomplete without it. In contrast, when a woman brought nail varnish from San'a, the elder women decided that their prayers were invalid unless the varnish were removed. In compliance with their decision, the younger women used the varnish only during menstruation when they must not pray. Women are concerned that their interference with God's creation—implied by the modifications of their bodies—is compatible with religious precepts. In another case, a woman intended to dye her hair during her forthcoming trip to England. The scholar with whom she raised this question replied that to do so was lawful as long as no man other than her husband would see her hair.

Adornment and resistance

Because adornment is so closely associated with femininity, married women defend and justify both the right and obligation to decorate themselves. However, as with failing to cover central parts of the '*aurah*,[49] in certain contexts married women's abstention from bodily adornment is a means of resistance and defiance. In the eyes of other women, those who do not dress up, and thus present themselves as if they were still unmarried, lack respect for their husbands as well as for their (women) friends and relatives. To other women, unadorned women appear defiant, as if they resented the duties and obligations marriage entails. They violate the exchange relationship established between spouses. Perhaps the superciliousness that is attributed to a woman who neglects herself derives from her display of a sense of superiority over other women, which they resent. She presents herself as self-assured and certain of her husband's affection

---

[49] For example, Altorki 1986, 54, notes that women fail to veil from male servants during their husbands' absence. See also Badran 1991, 203.

without having to enchant him through modifying her appearance. The act of abstention from conjugal duty might be interpreted as an assertion of independence that other women consider to be illusory.

In one case, a woman expressed her resentment at her forthcoming wedding by refusing to use *naqsh,* the classical technique used to beautify the bride. She had been persuaded by her father to marry the son of her mother's cowife, who had been previously married. The man had insisted on marrying the girl, and his mother had urged her husband to convince her that this would be a good match. To the girl, he had always been a brother, and she argued that she could never feel differently about him. On her wedding day, she was sad and lethargic; she let her attendant do her hair and put on some makeup, but she refused to have *naqsh* applied to any part of her body. Her defiant behavior thus subverted the notion that a woman must adorn herself for the husband's delight.

Women who are disinclined to adorn themselves are blamed if their marriages fail or their husbands take another wife. I learned of a man who had often commented on his wife's off-putting appearance; finally he married another woman. Both her relatives and other women held his first wife responsible for her misfortune, accusing her of neglecting her looks.[50] On one occasion I took a Yemeni friend to a celebration on the day after a wedding. She had never seen the bride and was unable to spot her; when I pointed her out, she was surprised that the bride was wearing a very plain European-style dress and commented: "She will be divorced very soon." The bride was the daughter of a diplomat and had spent many years in Europe where she had obtained a degree from Oxford.[51] She disliked fancy clothes, but she had her husband's approval. He had been brought up in an area close to the Aden Protectorate and had also studied abroad. He explained to me that he wanted an educated wife who was not always going to talk to him about other women's outfits when he returned home at night. This woman refused to conceive of her adorned body as one of the major sources of her self-esteem and self-valuation. Her case, and that of the bride who refused to wear *naqsh,* substantiate Butler's (1990, 141;

---

[50] Elite women of Jiddah have formed (same-gender) study groups during which they analyze religious sources. At the gatherings, they refrain from wearing bright colors and makeup, arguing that bodily decoration was the work of the devil and associated with "Western" moral corruption. Those who do not even use makeup while spending time with their husbands are warned by other women that they are going "to ruin their marriages" (Yamani 1994).

[51] This woman does not belong to the old elite; her father made his career in the army after the revolution.

1993, 231) claim that performing "gender norms" is never wholly conclusive. Women may resist the dictates of specific aesthetic regimes.

The above examples demonstrate both the strength and the limitations of Bourdieu's theory of symbolic violence (see vom Bruck 1997, 161–62). According to Bourdieu (in Bourdieu and Wacquant 1992), certain systems of meanings are imposed on social groups (esp. women) in such a way that they are experienced as natural and legitimate. By taking these meanings for granted, women themselves contribute to the systematic reproduction of the relations of domination (167–74). For Bourdieu, women's self-adornment confirms women's complicity with this form of violence. He argues that because women are "*objects*" of the symbolic exchanges carried out by men, they "are forced continually to work to preserve their symbolic value by conforming to the male ideal of feminine virtue defined as chastity and candor, and by endowing themselves with all the bodily and cosmetic attributes liable to increase their physical value and attractiveness" (173). Yet, as in the case of the bride who disapproved of fancy dress, women do not always comply with the dominant cultural ideology. Bourdieu additionally overlooks that, even though self-adornment indicates wifely deference through the demand for and display of decoration at their gatherings, women thus also reassert their social and moral worth as wives and mothers. This must be stressed because as wives and mothers, they are able to gain "symbolic value" in their own right (173). The case of the woman who was blamed for the breakdown of her marriage confirms Bourdieu's ideas. He explains that women "collude with and even actively defend or justify forms of aggression which victimize them" (172, n. 126). Surely the instability of this couple's marriage had several causes, but the women rationalized its breakdown in terms of the wife neglecting her appearance. The women's discourse reflected a notion of womanhood that centers on beauty, a female attribute men value in a wife. It also revealed their awareness of women's dependency on men. Women argue that a woman should not "cut the hand that feeds her" by failing to please her husband. Rather than blame the woman's husband for taking another wife, they denigrated his first wife for failing to "be a real woman." This example shows that adornment is a medium through which women play out their rivalries and seek control over each other by defining images of virtuous women.

"Women's worlds," gender, and autonomy

Having considered how performance at the *tafritah* articulates to a woman's life cycle, I turn to the question of whether the *tafritah* forms part of

Yemeni women's "own worlds" or "societies" that constitute autonomous moral spheres. It has often been argued in respect to both the Muslim and non-Muslim world that women's gatherings remove them from men's control. They are said to help women to produce shared alternative views of reality and to mitigate their experience of subordination and dependency.[52] According to Abu-Lughod (1985, 644), the women's "community regulates its internal affairs free from the interference and often the knowledge of men. Sexual segregation is also a source of personal autonomy for women."

It should be noted that in spite of the disguise of their bodies and the organization of same-gender gatherings, Yemeni women do not exist merely as disembodied figments of men's imagination. Men retain their childhood memories of women's faces, which they describe with remarkable clarity. Old men admitted that when they still accompanied their mothers to the *hammam* (public bath) and mixed freely with their women friends, they were traumatized by the prospect of never seeing these women's faces again. They follow up the women's life stories through the information transmitted to them by their female kin. Unlike Awlad 'Ali women, who do not share information with men, Yemeni men participate in the joys, worries, and conundrums of women they have never seen or spoken to. This is highlighted by the fact that men compose death poetry about women whom they have never met (see, e.g., Al-Shami 1981, 66).

The *tafritah* has multiple functional resonances. It constitutes an all-female sphere within the house, but like the house, it is not a "retreat of *haram*" (Bourdieu 1977, 89) free from the constraints usually experienced by women. At the *tafritah,* women find support, but it is also the place where rivalry and competition are acted out and the pool from which a woman's cowives are recruited. Rather than be aloof from male control and create spheres for autonomous action, at the *tafritah* women are subjected to the moral scrutiny of other women who partly act on behalf of men. Women criticize others for failing to live up to the standards of "aesthetic propriety" (Boddy 1982, 694) or for negligence in not looking after their husbands because they spend time studying or working. It is they who encourage men either to divorce their wives or to take another. In doing so, women both exercise control over other women and reaffirm their own status as dutiful and conscientious wives. At the gatherings, women are also made to suffer the consequences of actions taken by their

[52] See Rosaldo 1974, 27, 39; Messick 1978, 218, 221; Makhlouf 1979, 29; Wikan 1982, 109, 113; Abu-Lughod 1985, 647; 1989, 291; 1990, 49; Marcus 1992, 94; Sered 1992, 17. The implicit assumption that men are generally autonomous is also problematic.

male kin. The 1948 uprising against the ruling Imam was organized by members of leading scholarly families. After the ruling Imam's son regained power, the men who led the uprising were imprisoned and executed and their property confiscated. Whereas the female relatives of the leaders of the revolt had previously been the focus of attention at the *tafritah,* in the aftermath of the uprising they suffered tremendous hardship, being passed by other women at the *tafritah* without a word of greeting.

Through victimizing other women, women reproduce their own subordination, but they also construct themselves as victims. They spend much time at the *tafritah* discussing the distress of women whose spouses took other wives or divorced them for no convincing reason, labeling these men *harami* (wrongdoer, thief). In some contexts, they advise men to marry a second wife, and, in others, they persuade their husbands to turn down proposals to their daughters by men who already have other wives.

Women, like men, engage in multiple and often contradictory discourses. Both at once reproduce and challenge the aesthetic regime I have described. For example, a bridegroom who wonders whether the bride is attractive is told by his female kin that "beauty is to be found in the manners" (*al-jamal fi'l khuluq*). Occasionally men also express their indignation about those who divorce their wives in order to marry young girls, arguing that their wives had been their loyal companions for many years.

The Yemeni aesthetic regime, rather than merely enforce women's subordination, constrains both men and women. It leaves vulnerable those women who refuse, or are unable, to comply. However, it also poses challenges to the masculinity of less prosperous men who are confronted with their wives' detailed descriptions of their peers' outfits and their laments about being inadequately dressed. Demands for aesthetic propriety offer women the opportunity to manipulate relations of domination. They claim they cannot attend the *tafritah* because they have been seen too often in their old outfits, thus putting shame on men. On these grounds it would be difficult to argue that women either entirely subscribe to male values or develop a discourse that exists separately from a dominant male ideology.

Conclusion

In drawing on data from Yemen, I show that in accordance with definitions of "woman" as either virgin/sister or wife/mother, women's bodily practices are discontinuous. Female gender identity is enacted over time through appropriate performance that, although not entirely determining, is a "reiterative" process (Butler 1993, 2). I have argued elsewhere that until adolescence, gender difference between Yemeni males and females is not expressed in radically distinct types of behavior (vom Bruck 1994). For females, the practice of specific taboos and self-adornment form part of the process of feminizing the body. In addition, adornment is crucial to the moral construction of the female gender identity. An unmarried woman must refrain from embellished self-presentation lest she jeopardize her marriage chances. In marriage, as long as the adorned body is not exposed to non-*mahram,* self-decoration is encouraged. It is regarded as a fulfillment of a woman's marital duty and an expression of her affection and respect for her husband and her feeling of her own value. For her, it is no longer only body concealment, but its inversion, embellished exposure, that marks her status as wife and mother.

Thus, on marriage, gender becomes more central to a woman's identity, and it is fully substantiated when she starts engaging in reproductive sexuality. Older women play a significant role in authorizing specific social and sexual relations, and they construct other women as fully gendered persons. They select partners for their sons and brothers, they have the power either to grant or to deny other women access to their gatherings where all matters vital to women's lives are discussed, and they shape appropriate images of women as female persons in their discourse.

Wives are socially and morally superior to unmarried women, and mothers are superior to wives. A woman is most fully gendered and enjoys most authority in her household from about the time she has given birth to her first child until her own children's maturation. In his study on the place of virgin marriage in the definition of Mayotte womanhood, Lambek (1983, 274) holds that defloration marks the transformation from childhood to adulthood. The Yemeni data suggest that this transformation is achieved only when a woman produces a child. Until then, a married woman is still referred to as a bride, and if she should prove infertile, she is regarded as almost as incomplete as an unmarried woman.[53] Because biological females become properly feminized through motherhood, the definition of "woman" is critically contingent on the concept of "mother." Women realize both their full gender potential and social adulthood once their sexuality and fertility are affirmed and celebrated at the daily gatherings.

While exploring how appropriate performance constitutes female personhood and gender identity, I have given special consideration to a woman's status as unmarried sister or wife. My argument that unmarried sisters are less gendered than wives and mothers accords with Ortner's observa-

---

[53] Here I refer to social adulthood. A woman is legally an adult once she has reached puberty.

tion that in her role as a generic kinsperson a woman's feminine capacity is played down. Ortner (1981, 399–401) argues that in Polynesia kinship takes priority over affinity, and a woman's personal status is defined more in terms of kinship than conjugality. Emphasis is placed on women as co-members of their status groups, and only secondarily on their being females. In his work on Samoa, Serge Tcherkezoff (1993) goes further than Ortner by proposing that brothers and sisters are *not* men and women because they are linked through social continuity rather than sexual reproduction. A woman is responsible for the ritual perpetuation of the family title of which her brother is the "trustee." Ortner's and Tcherkezoff's interpretations, which focus on the way gender enters into the brother-sister relationship, merit comparison with the Yemeni pattern.

From the point of view of a Yemeni man, his sister belongs to his house and, moreover, is "from the same womb" (*'asaba*); like him, she cannot be denied the rights to permanent membership of the house in which she was born and to carry the family name. He refers to her as *karimati* ("what is precious to me") rather than *ukhti* (my sister). Yet he also looks at her as the future wife of another man whose *sharaf* she will "become." Thus in the Yemeni brother-sister relationship, gender is at once glossed over and highlighted. In one important respect, the unmarried sister is a woman, or rather a potential wife and childbearer; therefore, her deportment is meticulously scrutinized by her brother and other close relatives. The Samoan data also lead to the conclusion that, on one level at least, gender comes into play in the brother-sister relationship because brothers are as much concerned with their sister's chastity as are Yemeni men (Ortner 1981, 375; Shore 1981, 199–201).

On marriage, a Yemeni woman's membership of her house ceases to be the primary defining criterion of her personal status, and her husband gains primary authority over her. However, once she becomes fully engaged in her reproductive roles and thus more gendered than an unmarried woman, the brother-sister relationship remains vital. The gifts a married woman continues to receive from her kin on ritual occasions symbolize both a recognition of her fully gendered status and the enduring bond of the *'asaba*. They reassure her of their commitment to support her in times of crisis, but they also remind her that their loyalty depends on her propriety.

Although in both the sister-brother and wife-husband relationships gender is central, because it is bound up with either the potential for procreation or its actualization, wives are more gendered than unmarried sisters. Here I have examined different performative acts that articulate processes of gendering. In focusing on the acquisition of feminine identity, I do not adopt a radical, social-constructionist view of the body as a tabula rasa that is merely the product of discursive and bodily practices. Indeed, such an analysis would deviate from the notions of "woman" held by those who provided the raw material for this article. Yemenis distinguish between individuals according to anatomical features. However, as the classification of unmarried women as "incomplete" shows, those born female are not automatically fully gendered.[54] Thus, Yemenis themselves argue that femininity is achieved rather than given.

Feminist critiques of the unitary category "woman" place emphasis on differences within that category on the basis of race, class, sexuality, and so forth (McNay 1992, 37; Moore 1993, 195; 1994, 25). Since those writing about the Middle East criticized ahistorical notions of "Muslim women," studies have appeared that demonstrate that the status and self-representation of these women were informed and shaped by factors such as age, class, and the salience of local ideologies (Kandiyoti 1996, 9–12). Some of these studies identify dominant and subordinate forms of masculinity and femininity in relation to class variations (Messick 1978; Kandiyoti 1994). Rather than relate women's different bodily practices to their occupation of different status positions, I have shown how women who belong to the same status category achieve feminine identities. They are not equally gendered, and they exhibit and experience their bodies in different ways.

London School of Economics and Political Science

Appendix

A rural woman who had married a man from San'a was happy until one day a neighbor came to visit. She was wearing fine clothes and jewelry. On the question, "Why all this?" she answered: "From my husband." "What do you say to him?" "I tell him I want this and that, and he never returns home without it." The other woman became very thoughtful, and at night she did not prepare any food. Returning from work, her husband asked, "Where is the coffee, where is my dinner?" "I don't know." "What's the matter with you?" "I don't know." "Shall I wait until you make some coffee for me?" "No." He prepared his coffee and dinner himself. When he woke up in the morning, he found his wife asleep. He left the house without taking his breakfast. At lunchtime, he found her in the same mood, and the meal was not ready. She had baked only two pieces of bread for herself. In the afternoon, her neighbor came to visit her again, telling her about the food her family was eating, and how well off she was. At night, the

---

[54] There is, however, a category of men who are anatomically male but disposed to act socially as females (vom Bruck 1996).

woman's husband asked her to tell him what was bothering her. "What can I tell you about my disappointment?" "What disappointment? There is nothing wrong with you, you wake up in the morning and your face looks like the moon." "It's not enough." "What's missing? I shall give you from my eyes [all you want]." "Jewelry. I want jewelry; necklaces, bracelets, and rings just like other women have them. Why should I be different?" "You deserve everything, you are the dearest person to me, and nothing will come before you. I shall buy you all you want when God will give us." "When will God give us?" "When God gives it to us." He went to bed with an empty stomach. After he finished work the next day, he went to visit his father-in-law in the countryside and told him what happened. He explained to him that his wife had suddenly turned against him. His father-in-law advised him to return home and to tell her that her father's house was ready for her if she was not content with her husband. When he arrived home, he found his wife sobbing as if she had lost one of her children. "You don't seem to feel comfortable in this house any longer." "I am not, and I don't expect happiness ever to come." "Your father's house is close to your heart, go and stay there for a few days or months." He took her to her father's house. She had offered her husband the "black breast" (black is associated with death and impurity). Her father welcomed her, but he did not mention the subject before the next morning. He woke her up at prayer time and told her to get ready to work with him in the fields. As the days went by, the sun darkened her skin, and her hands became chapped and swollen. She lost her looks and began to resent her life in the country. One day her husband came to have lunch with them. As he got ready to leave, his father-in-law urged him to stay. His wife said to her father, "No, father, let us go back, there's nobody at home." She no longer desired any gold, and she took pride in her family. She was "like a rose," and her husband kept her happy.

References

Abadan-Unat, N., ed. 1981. *Women in Turkish Society*. Leiden: Brill.

Abu-Lughod, L. 1985. "A Community of Secrets: The Separate World of Bedouin Women." *Signs: Journal of Women in Culture and Society* 10(4):637–57.

———. 1986. *Veiled Sentiments: Honor and Poetry in a Bedouin Society*. Berkeley and Los Angeles: University of California Press.

———. 1987. "Bedouin Blues." *Natural History* 96:24–33.

———. 1989. "Zones of Theory in the Anthropology of the Arab World." *Annual Review of Anthropology* 18:267–306.

———. 1990. "The Romance of Resistance: Tracing Transformations of Power through Bedouin Women." *American Ethnologist* 17(1):41–55.

———. 1993. *Writing Women's Worlds*. Berkeley and Los Angeles: University of California Press.

Ahmad, L. 1992. *Women and Gender in Islam*. New Haven, Conn., and London: Yale University Press.

Altorki, S. 1986. *Women in Saudi Arabia: Ideology and Behavior among the Elite*. New York: Columbia University Press.

Ask, K. 1994. "Veiled Experiences: Exploring Female Practices of Seclusion." In *Social Experience and Anthropological Knowledge*, ed. K. Hastrup and P. Hervik, 65–77. London: Routledge.

Badran, M. 1991. "Competing Agenda: Feminists, Islam and the State in Nineteenth- and Twentieth-Century Egypt. In Kandiyoti 1991, 201–36.

———. 1995. *Feminists, Islam, and Nation: Gender and the Making of Modern Egypt*. Princeton, N.J.: Princeton University Press.

Bahloul, J. 1996. *The Architecture of Memory*. Cambridge: Cambridge University Press.

Baron, B. 1991. "The Making and Breaking of Marital Bonds in Modern Egypt." In *Women in Middle Eastern History*, ed. N. Keddie and B. Baron, 275–91. New Haven, Conn.: Yale University Press.

Boddy, J. 1982. "Womb as Oasis: The Symbolic Context of Pharaonic Circumcision in Rural Northern Sudan." *American Ethnologist* 9(4):682–98.

———. 1989. *Wombs and Alien Spirits*. Madison: University of Wisconsin Press.

Bourdieu, P. 1965. "The Sentiment of Honour in Kabyle Society." In *Honour and Shame: The Values of Mediterranean Society*, ed. J. Peristiany, 191–241. London: Weidenfeld & Nicolson.

———. 1977. *Outline of a Theory of Practice*. Cambridge: Cambridge University Press.

———. 1979. *Algeria 1960*. Cambridge: Cambridge University Press.

———. 1986. *Distinction*. London: Routledge.

———. 1990. *The Logic of Practice*. Oxford: Polity.

Bourdieu, P., and L. Wacquant. 1992. *An Invitation to Reflexive Sociology*. Oxford: Polity.

Buckley, T., and A. Gottlieb. 1988. *Blood Magic*. Berkeley and Los Angeles: University of California Press.

Butler, J. 1990. *Gender Trouble: Feminism and the Subversion of Identity*. London: Routledge.

———. 1993. *Bodies That Matter: On the Discursive Limits of "Sex."* London: Routledge.

Casajus, D. 1985. "Why Do the Tuareg Veil Their Faces?" In *Contexts and Levels: Anthropological Essays on Hierarchy*, ed. R. Barnes, D. de Coppet, and R. Parkin, 68–77. Oxford: Journal of the Anthropological Society of Oxford.

Champault, D. 1985. "Espaces et matériels de la vie feminine sur les hauts plateaux du Yemen." In *L'Arabie du sud*, ed. J. Chelhod, 3:185–230. Paris: Editions G.-P. Maisonneuve & Larose.

Comaroff, J., and J. Comaroff. 1992. *Ethnography and the Historical Imagination*. Boulder, Colo.: Westview.

Cornwall, A., and N. Lindisfarne, eds. 1994. *Dislocating Masculinity.* London: Routledge.

———. 1995. "Feminist Anthropologists and Questions of Masculinity." In *The Future of Anthropology,* ed. A. Ahmed and C. Shore, 134–57. London: Athlone.

Delaney, C. 1991. *The Seed and the Soil.* Berkeley and Los Angeles: University of California Press.

Eickelman, D. 1989. *The Middle East: An Anthropological Approach.* Englewood Cliffs, N.J.: Prentice-Hall.

El-Solh, C., and J. Mabro. 1994. "Introduction: Islam and Muslim Women." In *Muslim Women's Choices,* ed. C. El-Solh and J. Mabro, 1–32. Oxford: Berg.

Ende, W. 1994. "Sollen Frauen schreiben lernen?" *Gedenkschrift Wolfgang Reuschel.* Stuttgart: Franz Steiner.

Errington, S. 1990. "Recasting Sex, Gender, and Power: A Theoretical and Regional Overview." In *Power and Difference: Gender in Island Southeast Asia,* ed. J. Atkinson and S. Errington, 1–58. Stanford, Calif.: Stanford University Press.

Firth, R. 1963. *We, the Tikopia.* Boston: Beacon.

———. 1965. *Primitive Polynesian Economy.* London: Routledge.

Gell, A. 1979. "Reflections on a Cut Finger: Taboo in the Umeda Conception of the Self." In *Fantasy and Symbol,* ed. R. Hook, 133–48. London: Academic Press.

———. 1993. *Wrapping in Images.* Oxford: Clarendon.

Gilmore, D. 1982. "Anthropology of the Mediterranean Area." *Annual Review of Anthropology* 11:175–205.

Gilsenan, M. 1996. *Lords of the Lebanese Marches.* London: I. B. Tauris.

Glander, A. 1994. "Inheritance in Islam. A Study on Women's Inheritance in San'a (Republic of Yemen): Law, Religion, and Reality." M.A. dissertation, University of Vienna.

Haeri, S. 1994. "Temporary Marriage: An Islamic Discourse on Female Sexuality in Iran." In *In the Eye of the Storm: Women in Post-Revolutionary Iran,* ed. M. Afkhami and E. Friedl, 98–114. London: I. B. Tauris.

Hendrickson, H., ed. 1996. *Clothing and Difference: Embodied Identities in Colonial and Post-Colonial Africa.* London: Duke University Press.

Hessini, L. 1994. "Wearing the Hijab in Contemporary Morocco: Choice and Identity." In *Reconstructing Gender in the Middle East: Tradition, Identity, and Power,* ed. F. Müge Göçek and S. Balaghi, 40–56. New York: Columbia University Press.

Hoodfar, H. 1995. "The Veil in Their Minds and on Our Heads: The Persistence of Colonial Images of Muslim Women." *Resources for Feminist Research* 22(3–4):5–18.

Jenkins, R. 1992. *Pierre Bourdieu.* London: Routledge.

Joseph, S. 1994. "Brother/Sister Relationships: Connectivity, Love, and Power in the Reproduction of Patriarchy in Lebanon." *American Ethnologist* 21(1):50–73.

Kanafani, A. 1983. *Aesthetics and Ritual in the United Arab Emirates: The Anthropology of Food and Personal Adornment among Arabian Women.* Beirut: American University of Beirut.

Kandiyoti, D. 1988. "Bargaining with Patriarchy." *Gender and Society* 2:274–90.

———, ed. 1991. *Women, Islam and the State.* London: Macmillan.

———. 1994. "The Paradoxes of Masculinity: Some Thoughts on Segregated Societies." In Cornwall and Lindisfarne 1994, 197–213.

———. 1996. "Contemporary Feminist Scholarship and Middle East Studies." In *Gendering the Middle East,* ed. D. Kandiyoti, 1–27. London: I. B. Tauris.

Kapchan, D. 1996. *Gender on the Market: Moroccan Women and the Revoicing of Tradition.* Philadelphia: University of Pennsylvania Press.

Al-Khu'i, A. 1985. *Articles of Islamic Acts.* London: Al-Khu'i Foundation.

Knauft, B. 1989. "Bodily Images in Melanesia: Cultural Substances and Natural Metaphors." In *Fragments for a History of the Human Body,* ed. M. Feher, 198–279. New York: Zone.

Lambek, M. 1983. "Virgin Marriage and the Autonomy of Women in Mayotte." *Signs* 9(2):264–81.

———. 1992. "Taboo as Cultural Practice among Malagasy Speakers." *Man* 27(2):245–66.

Launay, R. 1995. "The Power of Names: Illegitimacy in a Muslim Community in Côte d'Ivoire." In *Situating Fertility,* ed. S. Greenhalgh, 108–29. Cambridge: Cambridge University Press.

Lindisfarne, N. 1994. "Variant Masculinities, Variant Virginities: Rethinking 'Honour and Shame.'" In Cornwall and Lindisfarne 1994, 82–96.

Lutfi, H. 1991. "Manners and Customs of Fourteenth-Century Cairene Women: Female Anarchy versus Male Shar'i Order in Muslim Prescriptive Treatises." In *Women in Middle Eastern History,* ed. N. Keddie and B. Baron, 99–121. New Haven, Conn.: Yale University Press.

Maclagan, I. 1993. "Freedom and Constraints: The World of Women in a Small Town in Yemen." Ph.D. dissertation, University of London.

Macleod, A. 1996. *Accommodating Protest: Working Women, the New Veiling, and Change in Cairo.* New York: Columbia University Press.

Makhlouf, C. 1979. *Changing Veils: Women and Modernization in North Yemen.* London: Croom Helm.

Marcus, J. 1992. *A World of Difference: Islam and Gender Hierarchy in Turkey.* London: Allen & Unwin.

Marsot, A. 1978. "The Revolutionary Gentlewoman in Egypt." In *Women in the Muslim World,* ed. L. Beck and N. Keddie, 261–76. Cambridge, Mass.: Harvard University Press.

Mauss, M. 1979. "The Notion of Body Techniques." In his *Sociology and Psychology: Essays,* trans. Ben Brewster, 97–119. London: Routledge & Kegan Paul.

Maynard, M. 1994. *Fashioned from Penury: Dress as Cultural Practice in Colonial Australia.* Cambridge: Cambridge University Press.

McNay, L. 1992. *Foucault and Feminism.* Oxford: Polity.

Meriwether, M. 1993. "Women and Economic Change in Nineteenth-Century Syria." In *Arab Women: Old Boundaries, New Frontiers,* ed. J. Tucker, 65–83. Bloomington and Indianapolis: Indiana University Press.

Mernissi, F. 1975. *Beyond the Veil: Male-Female Dynamics in Muslim Society*. London: Saqi Books.

Messick, B. 1978. "Subordinate Discourse: Women, Weaving, and Gender Relations in North Africa." *American Ethnologist* 14(2):210–25.

Mir-Hosseini, Z. 1996. "Women and Politics in Post-Khomeini Iran: Divorce, Veiling and Emerging Feminist Voices." In *Women and Politics in the Third World*, ed. H. Afshar, 142–70. London: Routledge.

Moore, H. 1988. *Feminism and Anthropology*. Oxford: Polity.

———. 1993. "The Differences Within and the Differences Between." In *Gendered Anthropology*, ed. T. del Valle, 193–204. London: Routledge.

———. 1994. *A Passion for Difference*. Oxford: Polity.

Mundy, M. 1979. "Women's Inheritance of Land in Highland Yemen." *Arabian Studies* 5:161–87.

———. 1983. "San'a Dress, 1920–75." In *San'a: An Arabian Islamic City*, ed. R. Serjeant and R. Lewcock, 529–41. London: World of Islam Festival Trust.

Al-Murtada, A. 1975. *Al-Bahr al-zakhar*. Vols. 1–5. Beirut: Al-Risalah.

Musallam, B. 1983. *Sex and Society in Islam*. Cambridge: Cambridge University Press.

Naïm-Sanbar, S. 1987. "Tufrutah: Une réunion de femmes." In *Sanaa: Parcours d'une cité d'arabie: Sous la direction de Pascal Marechaux*, 98–99. Paris: Institut du Monde Arabe.

Nicholson, L. 1994. "Interpreting Gender." *Signs* 20(1):79–105.

O'Hanlon, M. 1989. *Reading the Skin: Adornment, Display and Society among the Wahgi*. London: British Museum.

Ortner, S. 1981. "Gender and Sexuality in Hierarchical Societies: The Case of Polynesia and Some Comparative Implications." In *Sexual Meanings*, ed. S. Ortner and H. Whitehead, 359–409. Cambridge: Cambridge University Press.

Rosaldo, M. 1974. "Woman, Culture, and Society: A Theoretical Overview." In *Woman, Culture, and Society*, ed. M. Rosaldo and L. Lamphere, 17–42. Stanford, Calif.: Stanford University Press.

Sanders, P. 1991. "Gendering the Ungendered Body: Hermaphrodites in Medieval Islamic Law." In *Women in Middle Eastern History*, ed. N. Keddie and B. Baron, 74–95. New Haven, Conn.: Yale University Press.

Schönig, H. 1995. "Traditionelle Schönheitsmittel der Jemenitinnen." *Jemen-Report* 26:22–24.

Schopen, A. 1981. "Das Qat in Jemen." In *Rausch und Realität*, ed. G. Völger, 496–99. Köln: Rautenstrauch-Joest-Museum.

———. 1983. *Traditionelle Heilmittel im Jemen*. Wiesbaden: Steiner.

Scott, H. 1942. *In the High Yemen*. London: John Murray.

Sered, S. 1992. *Women as Ritual Experts*. Oxford: Oxford University Press.

Al-Shami, A. 1981. *Atyaf*. London: Ithaca.

———. 1986. *Diwan al-Shami*. Cairo: Dar al-ma'arif.

Shilling, C. 1993. *The Body and Social Theory*. London: Sage.

Shore, B. 1981. "Sexuality and Gender in Samoa: Conceptions and Missed Conceptions." In *Sexual Meanings*, ed. S. Ortner and H. Whitehead, 192–215. Cambridge: Cambridge University Press.

Strathern, M. 1979. "The Self in Self-Decoration." *Oceania* 49:241–57.

Strathern, M., and A. Strathern. 1971. *Self-Decoration in Mount Hagen*. London: Duckworth.

Tapper, N. 1983. "Gender and Religion in a Turkish Town: A Comparison of Two Types of Formal Women's Gatherings." In *Women's Religious Experience*, ed. P. Holden, 71–88. London: Croom Helm.

———. 1991. *Bartered Brides*. Cambridge: Cambridge University Press.

Tarlo, E. 1996. *Clothing Matters: Dress and Identity in India*. London: Hurst.

Tcherkezoff, S. 1993. "The Illusion of Dualism in Samoa: 'Brothers-and-Sisters' Are Not 'Men-and-Women.'" In *Gendered Anthropology*, ed. T. del Valle, 54–87. London: Routledge.

Turner, T. 1969. "Tchikrin: A Central Brazilian Tribe and Its Symbolic Language of Bodily Adornment." *Natural History* 78:50–60.

———. 1980. "The Social Skin." In *Not Work Alone*, ed. J. Cherfas and R. Lewin, 112–40. Beverly Hills, Calif.: Sage.

Uberoi, J. 1967. "On Being Unshorn." *Transactions of the Indian Institute of Advanced Study* 4:87–100.

vom Bruck, G. 1991. "Descent and Religious Knowledge: 'Houses of Learning' in Modern San'a, Yemen Arab Republic." Ph.D. dissertation, London School of Economics.

———. 1993. "Réconciliation ambiguë: Une perspective anthropologique sur le concept de la violence légitime dans l'Imamat du Yémen." In *La violence et l'état*, ed. E. Le Roy and T. von Trotha, 85–103. Paris: L'Harmattan.

———. 1994. "Down-Playing Gender: Ḥatm Rituals in San'a." *Quaderni di studi Arabi* 12:161–82.

———. 1996. "Being Worthy of Protection: The Dialectics of Gender Attributes in Yemen." *Social Anthropology* 4(2):145–62.

———. 1997. "A House Turned Inside Out: Inhabiting Space in a Yemeni City." *Journal of Material Culture* 2(2):139–72.

Al-Wazir, I. 1992. "Ummun fi ghimari thawrah." *Al-Shura*, March 5–August 6, nos. 42–57.

Weir, S. 1989. *Palestinian Costume*. London: British Museum.

Wikan, U. 1977. "Man Becomes Woman: Transsexualism in Oman as a Key to Gender Roles." *Man* 12:304–19.

———. 1982. *Behind the Veil in Arabia: Women in Oman*. Baltimore: Johns Hopkins University Press.

———. 1984. "Shame and Honour: A Contestable Pair." *Man* 19:635–52.

Yamani, M. 1994. "Feminism behind the Veil." Paper presented at the School of Oriental and African Studies, Islam and Feminism Series, London, October 4.

Yanagisako, S. 1979. "Family and Household: The Analysis of Domestic Groups." *Annual Review of Anthropology* 8:161–205.

Elora Shehabuddin

Contesting the Illicit: Gender and the
Politics of Fatwas in Bangladesh

On January 10, 1993, in the northeastern district of Sylhet in Bangladesh, a twenty-two-year-old woman called Nurjahan was dragged out of her home by her hair to be punished for adultery.
Nurjahan's first marriage had ended in divorce some time ago and she had recently married Mutalib. After having confirmed that Nurjahan was indeed divorced from her first husband and thus free to marry Mutalib, the local imam, Maulana Mannan, had performed the marriage ceremony.[1] As is common in rural Bangladesh, neither the divorce nor the marriages were formally registered; consequently, there was no documented proof of either action. Not long after, some people in the village began to protest that Nurjahan had not obtained a proper divorce from her first husband and therefore could not be married to Mutalib; they accused the couple of living in sin. A *salish,* convened under the leadership of Mannan himself and comprising several members of the local elite, pronounced that Nurjahan's marriage to Mutalib was not in accordance with Islamic law and hence invalid.[2] The *salish* issued a fatwa declaring that Nurjahan and Mutalib should both be punished for engaging in unlawful sex.

On that cold morning, Nurjahan and her husband were forced to stand in a waist-deep pit in the ground and then each was pelted with 101 stones;

I gratefully acknowledge the support of the Social Science Research Council, the Council for Regional Studies, and the Center for International Studies/World Order Studies at Princeton University, and Ain-o-Salish Kendra (Law and Mediation Center), Dhaka, during the research on which this project is based. I am also grateful for an Andrew W. Mellon Post-Enrollment Grant, Princeton University, and a Woodrow Wilson Dissertation Grant in Women's Studies at the time of writing. A version of this article was presented at the Conference on South Asia at the University of Wisconsin, Madison, on October 18, 1997. I wish to thank Ussama Makdisi, Anne Waters, and the anonymous reviewers for *Signs* for their insightful comments.

[1] Literally, *imam* means leader; the term is commonly used for the man who leads congregational prayers in a mosque. *Maulana* is a term of address for one known or believed to be learned in religious matters.

[2] A *salish* is a traditional village arbitration council, usually presided over by local social and religious notables.

[*Signs: Journal of Women in Culture and Society* 1999, vol. 24, no. 4]

Nurjahan's elderly parents were given fifty lashes each. Later that day, Nurjahan killed herself by drinking agricultural pesticide.[3]

I   I   I

The term *fatwa,* which in Islamic legal parlance refers to a clarification of an ambiguous judicial point or an opinion by a jurist trained in Islamic law, gained worldwide notoriety following Ayatollah Khomeini's fatwa against the British author Salman Rushdie in 1988. Bangladesh, for so long of interest only to economists, disaster relief workers, and development agencies, has recently attracted a new sort of international attention. In September 1993, a small group by the name of "Soldiers of Islam" announced a prize of fifty thousand takas (US$1,250) for the execution of writer Taslima Nasrin on the grounds that her works were insulting to Islam. suddenly, Bangladesh was pinpointed on the map as a center of resurgent Islamic fundamentalism, a place where death threats could be issued against an author for challenging established religion. High-profile figures, however, are not the only targets of fatwas. Between January 1993 and December 1996, more than sixty incidents of fatwa-instigated violence, directed mostly against impoverished rural women, were reported in Bangladesh (Begum 1994; Ain-o-Salish Kendra 1997). Members of the rural elite had charged the women with adultery and issued fatwas that they be whipped, stoned, or, in one instance, burned at the stake. In addition, after fatwas were issued by several local and national religious leaders accusing nongovernmental organizations (NGOs) of converting girls and women to Christianity, villagers in various parts of the country set fire to NGO schools imparting basic literacy skills to women and chopped down mulberry trees planted by women with the assistance of NGOs. In certain districts, women were prevented from going to the polls in several recent elections following fatwas declaring that it was inappropriate for women to vote. The incidents have a number of factors in common: the targets are predominantly women from the poorest stratum of rural society; the fatwa-issuers are the elite men of their villages, often local landowners or religious leaders; and the state has been slow to take action and has done so only following the intervention of women's and human rights groups.

At the same time, indigenous institutions such as the Grameen or Rural

---

[3] Given the extensive coverage of this incident in both the Bengali and English presses in Bangladesh, I have been able to refer to a large number of reports that appeared between January 1993, when the incident occurred, and February 1994, when the men responsible were finally sentenced to seven years imprisonment. I list only a few of the reports here: Begum 1993; Khan 1993; *Ittefaq* 1994; Kamal 1995; Ain-o-Salish Kendra n.d. All translations from Bengali in this article are my own.

Bank have achieved worldwide acclaim for their programs for impoverished rural women. Bangladesh is also in the remarkable position of having had two consecutive women prime ministers — Begum Khaleda Zia of the Bangladesh Nationalist Party (1991–96) and Sheikh Hasina Wajed (since 1996).[4] These seemingly contradictory trends in Bangladeshi society and politics are also evident in the increased polarization of national political discourse between secularist and Islamist positions, not only in matters pertaining to women but also in blueprints outlining the future direction of the nation. In recent years, major political parties, members of the rural socioeconomic and religious elites, and various NGOs have increasingly used the language of secularism or Islam to regulate — and even legislate — various aspects of women's lives. The state, for its part, has found itself confronted with contradictory prescriptions regarding gender and development from donors with very different agendas, for instance, the United Nations on the one hand, and Saudi Arabia on the other; this is reflected in the state's policies regarding women.

In this article, I investigate the polarization in the national and almost wholly urban-based debates about fatwa incidents and also examine the concerns and interests of those at the lowest levels of all social, political, and economic hierarchies — impoverished rural women.[5] At first, the fatwa incidents appear to buttress widely prevalent notions of Islam as fundamentally incompatible with women's rights. While secularist groups in Bangladesh attribute these attacks to the increasing Islamization of society, Islamist forces such as the Jama'at-i Islami (Party of Islam) believe that it is the very absence of Islam in the public sphere that has permitted "unqualified" men to abuse religion in this manner. I contend that the distinctions between secularists and Islamists become less clear — and the role of Islam less significant — in the realm of popular politics, among the poorer strata of society, and among landless women in particular, who are pulled by competing interpretations of modernity, development, Islam, and feminism. At the same time, their lives and behavior are governed by the multiple constraints of poverty, the laws of the land, the customs and traditions of their particular community, and the power of local elites.

---

[4] Zia is the widow of Bangladesh's first military ruler, Ziaur Rahman, who was assassinated in 1981. Wajed is the daughter of Sheikh Mujibur Rahman, who led the independence movement for Bangladesh and, along with most of his family, was gunned down in 1975.

[5] I focus on the poorest of the poor — the landless families of rural Bangladesh; traditionally, they have supported themselves through daily labor, usually in the fields for men and in wealthier households for women. Also, although there are instances of fatwas issued against Hindu women, I focus on the majority Muslim population; since fatwa is an Islamic term, I expect that it holds greater meaning for Muslims than for members of other communities.

On the basis of extensive research in rural Bangladesh, I argue that, despite much-publicized differences, both secularist and Islamist perspectives represent elitist visions of society and of the role of the rural poor within it.[6] While their analyses of the phenomenon of rural fatwas differ, both groups assume that the rural poor are ignorant and easily duped by the ideology of the *other* group. Yet, confounding such urban elite expectations, most impoverished, illiterate, and pious Muslim women have not blindly followed either the Islamists or the secularists. I posit that while there may indeed be a great deal of ignorance in rural Bangladesh, it is actually knowledge — that is, the knowledge, grounded in experience, that the state is weak and incapable of enforcing its own rules and helping them to improve their lives — that compels the rural poor to comply with Islamist notions at certain times, with secularist notions at others.

In this article I argue for the need to move beyond seeing impoverished men and women as either passive victims or heroic resisters. While I concede that revolutions in the traditional sense are rare, rural society in Bangladesh today is undergoing profound changes catalyzed by the introduction of new ideas and material resources, among them increased questioning of the status quo and, perhaps more important, increased access to the means of challenging the status quo. Changing conditions, therefore, are enabling certain members of impoverished groups to recognize that hidden resistance cannot bring about significant change in their lives. Even landless women in rural Bangladesh, subject to stricter cultural codes of conduct and greater material deprivation than their male kin, actively engage in efforts to ameliorate their own lives and those of their families.

The current debates about tradition versus modernity are strikingly reminiscent of nineteenth-century reform movements against child marriage, for example, when local elites and British colonial authorities concurred on the barbarity of various local practices and sought to pass prohibitive laws over the opposition of religious leaders. Today, however, the "ignorant rural masses" need no longer be silent observers in deliberations regarding their lives and practices. Through an examination of the voices,

[6] This article is based on prolonged fieldwork conducted in Bangladesh in 1995–97, during which I interviewed local scholars, political leaders, NGO activists, and rural men and women. I also draw on the findings from a research project at Ain-o-Salish Kendra (Law and Mediation Center), Dhaka, that I designed and supervised, in the course of which a team of research assistants and I traveled to various parts of rural Bangladesh in June–August 1996 and spoke with approximately nine hundred people (about two-thirds were women; the rest were landless men, usually relatives of the women we interviewed, or elite men of the villages) primarily about their views on gender relations, religion, national and local politics, and NGOs. Most of the questions were open ended, while some required simple yes or no responses. Unless otherwise specified, the discussion of rural men's and women's views presented in this article draws on the interviews from the Ain-o-Salish Kendra research project.

concerns, and perspectives of the primary targets of fatwas — impoverished rural women — I seek to offer an alternative analysis of the fatwa problem to that proposed by the present generation of secularist and Islamist elites.

I unfold the argument below in four parts. Following a brief discussion of the position of Islam and fatwas in Bangladesh's legal system, I examine a variety of fatwas issued in recent years to regulate the social, economic, and political behavior of rural women. In the third section, I present current explanations for the fatwa problem, dividing them broadly into secularist and Islamist perspectives but maintaining that, while this classification holds at the elite level, it obscures more than it reveals about the variety of views among the rural poor themselves. I end with a discussion of poor rural women's responses to the different fatwas and their endeavors to better their lives.

Islam, fatwas and the law in Bangladesh

In Bangladesh, established in 1971 as a secular republic, fatwas carry no legal weight. The 1972 constitution defined secularism as equal respect for all faiths and prohibited the political use of any religion; consequently, all religion-based parties such as the Jama'at-i Islami and the Muslim League were banned from political activity. With the advent of military rule in 1977 under Ziaur Rahman, the term *secularism* was replaced in the constitution with "absolute faith in Allah" and formerly banned religion-based parties were rehabilitated in the political arena. In 1988, a second military government led by Hussain M. Ershad formally declared Islam the state religion, although no substantive changes were made in the laws of the land.

The civil laws, which cover matters such as constitutional rights, the civil and criminal procedure codes, and the penal code, are generally secular, many dating back to British colonial rule. In the matter of personal laws (e.g., marriage, divorce, inheritance, custody, and guardianship), however, an individual is governed by the laws of "the community into which one is born irrespective of one's actual religious belief," whether Muslim, Hindu, or Christian (Sobhan 1978, 3–4, 19).[7]

In Islamic jurisprudence, a fatwa is "an opinion on a point of law rendered by a *mufti* [legal consultant] in response to a question submitted to him by a private individual or by a *qadi* [religious judge, magistrate]." Since it is a clarification or opinion, a fatwa is not legally binding, although a *qadi* may take fatwas into consideration when making a legal decision (Esposito 1982, 128). Thus, while an individual may seek a fatwa for clarification of

---

[7] For a historical discussion of the actual codification and subsequent reforms of family laws in British India and then Pakistan, see Anderson 1976 and Esposito 1982.

a complicated legal issue, he or she is not in any way bound to accept it and, as with medical matters, is free to seek a second opinion. James Piscatori cites the opinion of the Muslim Tunisian writer Moncef Marzouki, who, like many Muslims, was outraged at the Rushdie affair because he believed that Khomeini lacked the authority to issue such a fatwa: "[Khomeini] made this sentence in the name of Islam and all Muslims, that is, also in my name. I deny him this right for all sorts of reasons. First of all, there is no papacy in Islam and even less is there infallibility. . . . Khomeini claims himself to be the spokesman of God. But this God is bereft of His two principal attributes [leniency and mercy]" (quoted in Piscatori 1990, 777).

While physical punishment for adultery is specified in the Quran, under Bangladesh's penal code adultery is not a criminal offense; at most, it is a crime against the husband of the adulterous wife, and he may pursue charges against the man with whom his wife is having an affair.[8] Salma Sobhan, a prominent lawyer and human rights activist in Bangladesh, challenges this ruling, arguing that "adultery, if it is an offence, is surely between the man and woman who are married where one or the other has been unfaithful, and not an offence against the man whose wife has been seduced unless the wife is regarded as a piece of property. There is an unmistakable hint of indignation at the violation of property rights rather than for the breach of any code of morals or honour — 'You have used my car without my permission' " (Sobhan 1978, 14). In any case, in many of the incidents reported in the press in recent years, the problem was not one of adultery as it is normally understood, that is, as a sexual relationship between a married person and someone other than his or her legal spouse. In the case of Nurjahan, for example, Nurjahan, Mutalib, and her parents believed Nurjahan was married to Mutalib. She was charged with living in sin with a man whom she knew as her lawful husband. Furthermore, neither *salishes* nor local elites have any legal authority to sentence and punish.

Defining the illicit

Women as sexual transgressors

Scholars, novelists, and ordinary villagers bear ample witness to the traditional use of the institution of *salish* to judge a woman who is consid-

---

[8] Bangladesh Penal Code, S. 497–98 (1860). The Quran calls for flogging as the punishment for adultery (24:2); however, during the reign of the second caliph 'Umar (634–44), stoning rather than flogging became codified (Ahmed 1992, 60) on the basis of certain hadith (sayings and traditions of the Prophet — after the Quran, the most important source in Islamic jurisprudence) in favor of stoning.

ered to be behaving inappropriately. The punishment given to a woman deemed guilty of "illicit" sexual relations has varied over time and from place to place. Priyam Singh's analysis of nineteenth-century documents and journalistic accounts reveals that under Hindu law adultery was one of only two offenses that merited capital punishment: an adulterous woman was to be "devoured by dogs" and a man "burned on an iron bed." Generally, *panchayats* (village councils traditionally comprising five [*panch*] members of the local elite) were responsible for dealing with such matters even during much of colonial rule; punishments handed out to upper-caste women included mutilation and excommunication (Singh 1996, 28–29). Shahidullah Kaiser's celebrated novel *Shangshaptak,* for example, opens with a detailed description of a village *salish* involving a woman called Hurmoti. Charged with adultery, she is branded on the forehead with hot copper — more specifically, with a coin bearing the image of King George V of England (Kaiser 1993, 13). There is nothing new, then, in either village councils' — whether *panchayats* or *salishes* — regulation of the morality of villagers, especially women, Hindu and Muslim alike, or in religious leaders' participation in these tribunals. Indeed, my research reveals that such regulation is very much a part of village life and far more widespread than press reports indicate.

The novelty of the more recent incidents lies perhaps in their use of the term *fatwa*. Historically, prominent religious leaders in South Asia issued fatwas to justify different positions vis-à-vis British colonial authority, Western education, or "modernity." In contrast, recent fatwas have been used to evoke Islamic law and the authority to regulate the social, economic, and political behavior of poor village women specifically. Moreover, they often have been issued by men who, by the standards of Islamic jurisprudence, are not qualified to do so and who, as far as the state is concerned, lack the authority to mete out such judgments and sentences.

In rural Bangladesh, a variety of punishments have been imposed on women charged with adultery: Nurjahan was stoned 101 times; a few months later, a second Nurjahan was tied to a stake, doused with kerosene, and burned to death; later that year, a woman named Firoza was given 101 lashes for her involvement with a Hindu man and then committed suicide; in June 1994, a fatwa was issued in a Rajshahi village to expel a young Hindu woman, Anjali Karmakar, from the community for engaging in the immoral activity of talking to a Muslim man (Ain-o-Salish Kendra 1997). Another particularly shocking incident is the 1994 *salish* case of Rokeya in the southeastern district of Feni. After her husband's death, she moved back to her parents' home with her two young children. With assurances of marriage, her neighbor Dulal initiated intimate relations with her and she became pregnant. When he refused to marry her, she filed a case against him but then dropped charges under pressure from him and more powerful villagers. Shortly thereafter, Dulal came into her house and raped her. The following day, he dragged her out of the house naked and beat her up in public; he then took her back inside and kept her locked up for several days. In accordance with a fatwa from a local *salish,* which had found her guilty of *zina* — she was, after all, a pregnant widow — she was dragged, half-naked, to an open field near the village school and tied to a large tree.[9] In front of a few hundred people, her hair was cut short, and her face and breasts were smeared with soot.[10] At that point, local elected officials arrived at the scene, untied her, and proposed what they considered a more humane punishment: she was made to wear a garland of shoes and parade, in her half-naked state, around the village (Khan 1996, 28).

In interviews throughout Bangladesh, rural men and women cited a variety of ways *salishes* deal with adultery. They pointed out, for example, that the first time an extramarital affair is brought to the attention of a *salish,* very often the committee simply issues a warning to the "adulterous" couple; only if they do not desist from their "unlawful" activity are further measures necessitated. The next step may be a fine. Several respondents concurred that the punishment for a married woman who commits adultery is generally harsher than that for a married man. When a married man is discovered having an affair, the *salish* usually recommends that he marry the woman; if he does not wish to divorce his first wife, he may simply take his mistress as a second wife. In the case of a married woman having an affair, matters are more complicated, since it is far more difficult for her to obtain a divorce, and she may not take on a second husband. Ideally, her husband grants her a divorce, and she marries the other man. As Akhlima Khatun, a twenty-six-year-old woman in Jessore, put it, "If the woman no longer wants to eat her husband's rice and if the other man's family consents, then they get married. Usually, however, they don't. Instead, they are flogged and fined." Abdul Aziz of Dinajpur remarked that punishment varied with gender and class: "An adulterous couple is usually beaten with shoes. But, sometimes, when the man is well-off but the woman isn't, only the woman gets punished." According to Samiyara, a landless woman in Rajshahi, common punishments for *zina* in her community are public flogging and being paraded around the village wearing a garland of shoes.

The reasons for fatwas, however, have not been restricted to women's

---

[9] In Islamic jurisprudence, *zina* generally refers to any sexual activity other than between husband and wife, e.g., adultery and (nonmarital) rape.

[10] In a culture where long thick hair is considered a highly prized asset for any woman, the humiliation implicit in cutting Rokeya's hair in this manner would not be lost on the spectators.

behavior in the privacy of their bedrooms and homes. As I show below, fatwas have also been used to express local objections to women's increasing access to credit, employment, and educational opportunities outside the home.

Women as NGO beneficiaries

In recent years, particularly since the mid-1970s and the onset of the United Nations International Decade for Women, NGOs and, to a certain extent, the Bangladeshi government, have played an important role in targeting rural women as recipients of education, credit, employment opportunities, and health care. They have exalted rural women for their ability to attract foreign aid, to contribute to the nation's gross domestic product, to help control the country's population growth, to present positive images of Bangladesh on foreign television and at international meetings on women's rights and poverty alleviation — that is, something other than the usual images of floods and famine — and even to inspire a 1995 visit by the U.S. First Lady to observe them at work.[11] This does not mean, however, that rural women have been recognized as social actors in their own right or that NGOs have been unconditionally welcomed throughout the country. Nonetheless, while some local suspicion is inevitable whenever outsiders — be they from Dhaka, Washington, D.C., or Oslo — arrive in a new area and try to initiate change, the widespread violent outburst against NGOs in the early 1990s was unprecedented and, as I show below, stems directly from objections to the increasing visibility of rural women.

One of the most profitable projects of the Bangladesh Rural Advancement Committee (BRAC), the largest NGO in the country, is sericulture. Local women are involved at various stages of the production process, including growing the mulberry trees needed to sustain silkworms. In 1994, Nojimon Begum, then thirty-seven years old, was working for BRAC as a guard on a road in Bogra where six hundred trees had been planted. In exchange, she received three kilograms (about six and a half pounds) of wheat a day. She describes how, one day, Ansar, her husband of eighteen years, came to see her while she was working and informed her that he was divorcing her: "[He] said to me, 'You've gone onto the road. You greet everyone. You spend the whole day there. You have no honour. You take loans from them, you go and chat with them. You have no need of a

---

[11] In 1990–91, e.g., the Grameen Bank's work with women was the subject of the U.S. news program *60 Minutes* and of an episode of the WGBH (Boston) television series *Local Heroes, Global Change*. NGOs targeting rural women in Bangladesh were also featured prominently at the United Nations Social Summit in Copenhagen and the Beijing Conference on Women, both in 1995, as well as at the International Micro-Credit Summit in Washington, D.C., in 1996.

husband.' . . . And then one day, he was gone" (quoted in Khan 1996, 25). Because Nojimon worked on the main road, local mullahs had issued a fatwa that Ansar should divorce her (25–26).[12] According to one newspaper report, ten women in that area were informed that simply because of their involvement with NGOs—just by accepting a loan—they had become "automatically" divorced from their husbands. Maulana Idris Ali of Nondigram explained, "[NGOs] are bringing women out of the homes and making them go without purdah."[13] Miarul, a local NGO worker, points out that performing marriage ceremonies is an important source of income for the mullahs. Not surprisingly, many of these "suddenly divorced" couples come to them seeking to be remarried, and an imam earns about fifty takas (US$1.25) per ceremony.[14] Journalist Mizanur Rahman Khan found that about fifty such marriages had been performed over a few months and that before each such ceremony, the wife was caned several times and then "reconverted" into a Muslim (Khan 1996, 31–32).

After a fatwa declaring that mulberry trees were anti-Islamic and that the village women who looked after them were no longer Muslims, local mullahs and other village men in Nandail chopped down hundreds of thousands of takas worth of trees in early 1994.[15] The BRAC estimates that approximately 180,000 mulberry trees were destroyed nationwide in accordance with such fatwas, affecting the livelihood of seven hundred female guards like Nojimon (Khan 1996, 31).

In another example, Majeda, then twenty-two years old and pregnant for the first time, had signed up for prenatal care at a BRAC clinic. One day, her husband, Kalimuddin, came home and, not finding her there, marched off to the clinic to fetch her. He dragged her home immediately, beating her along the way. Her child was born two months premature and died two days later. Local mullahs had issued a fatwa declaring that pregnancy should not be on public display—that it is a woman's personal matter and that it is inappropriate for strangers such as workers at a clinic to be aware of a woman's pregnancy. Moreover, the mullahs had argued, for a woman even to travel to the clinic is a clear breach of purdah (Rahman

---

[12] *Mullah* is a largely pejorative term used to refer to the local religious zealot and self-proclaimed authority on Islam; *mullah* is to be distinguished from the term *ulama* [scholar]. I use *mullah* in this article only when the women themselves used it in their accounts.

[13] *Purdah*, literally "curtain," refers to a range of behaviors designed to maintain a barrier between women and all men other than close kin. It may involve covering one's body, head, and face; never leaving one's home; or simply walking only on paths not frequented by men.

[14] Of course, once "divorced," a couple who live together without undergoing such a ceremony risk being charged with adultery, as was Nurjahan of Sylhet.

[15] As far as I have been able to ascertain, the only discussion of silk in Islamic law is a prohibition on men wearing silk when praying.

1995, 72; Khan 1996, 32). They also announced that a child born under the care of NGO doctors and health workers would be born Christian. Such fatwas prevented about one hundred pregnant women from seeking medical treatment from BRAC in March 1994 alone (Begum 1994).

Local religious leaders also made known their objections to the monitoring of children's height and weight at NGO clinics, claiming that it was a "Christian" idea and that Muslims need to be weighed only once ever — on the Last Day, when the balance of good and evil in a person would be ascertained. The effectiveness of this fatwa may lie in part in the rumor that NGO workers had placed a small Quran under the weighing scales; thus, if one stood on the scales, one was effectively standing on the Quran and thereby jeopardizing one's faith and salvation. When the villagers were asked whether they had actually seen this happen, many responded, "No, I haven't seen it with my own eyes. The *huzurs* told us about this. And the *huzurs* don't lie!" (Khan 1996, 34).[16]

The *huzurs* have also convinced many families not to have their infants vaccinated by suggesting that the vaccines come from "Christian lands" and contain extracts from pigs and dogs, two animals considered unclean in Islam and prohibited for consumption (Khan 1996, 34). In February 1994, following similar arguments about tuberculosis medication, twenty-six tuberculosis patients were prevented from seeking medical care from BRAC (Begum 1994, 5). At least three died as a result. Mariam, about seventy years of age, explained why she stopped treatment for tuberculosis: "I'm not going to live much longer. I don't want to take this medicine and then die a Christian." As her situation deteriorated, however, Mariam approached the health workers secretly and asked for the medication (Khan 1996, 35).

Schools run by NGOs for children and adults have not been spared the brunt of the mullahs' offensive. They issued a fatwa declaring that these schools were inculcating rural Muslim children with Christian values and ideas, and they expressed particular objections to the education of girls at such schools, claiming that it made them shameless, too knowledgeable about their own bodies, too informed of "un-Islamic" legal rights, and irreverent toward religious authority.[17] Following the fatwa, about twenty-five BRAC schools were set on fire, and many parents withdrew their children, especially daughters, from the schools (Begum 1994, 5).

Mullahs have also attacked rural women involved with NGOs by

---

[16] *Huzur* means literally "sir or master"; today the term is reserved for religious leaders.

[17] Regarding "un-Islamic" legal rights, the 1961 Muslim Family Code, e.g., requires that a man must have the permission of his first wife if he wishes to take a second wife; many consider this stipulation to be contrary to Islamic law.

declaring them and their families social outcasts. About sixty families in Bogra suffered this fate. Many of them found that a high bamboo fence had been erected around their homes as an indication that other villagers were not to interact with them. Religious leaders have also refused to officiate at naming ceremonies, weddings, and funerals in these families. For example, when Rumena Begum's husband died, the local imam refused to perform the *janaza* (funeral) until she had "repented" her work as a midwife with a local NGO and promised never to work there again (Khan 1996, 38).

Charges have been hurled against NGOs from the national pulpits as well. Various Islamist organizations came together to form the Shommilito Shangram Parishad (United Action Council [UAC]), whose stated goals included shutting down all NGOs (Rashiduzzaman 1994, 983). Even a "powerful Bangladeshi politician" cited in *Newsweek* explains, "These NGOs have challenged the most basic traditions of Islam. They have challenged the authority of the husband" (Klein 1995, 56). In his address to an anti-NGO rally, an important leader of the UAC exhorted nationwide resistance to NGO schemes targeting women: "[NGOs want] to destroy our social system . . . and to create Taslima Nasreens and Farida Rahmans.[18] The primary targets of NGOs are our mothers and sisters. It is to socially ruin them that NGOs are enticing them out of their homes with money and inciting them against their husbands. . . . The laws laid down by Islam 1,400 years ago will be valid until the Day of Judgment. And in no way does Islamic law infringe on women's rights. Islam has given women rights that no other religion has" (*Inqilab* 1995). An article in *Sangram* a few months later again decried women's involvement in NGOs, arguing that it was ruining the "traditional" family structure and values of the country:

> [NGOs] cannot tolerate Bangladesh's traditional marriage system. With the goal of establishing a society without marriage and responsibilities, they are dragging in the Western world. Even though there are 20 million educated unemployed young men in the country today, NGOs are giving ninety percent of their jobs to beautiful young women. Then [the women] . . . are sent off to places where they have no relatives, only unmarried young men for company. Men and women sleep in the same room. Illicit mixing of the sexes is just one of the training courses for the job. By pitting these wanton women against unemployed men, having them "work" at all hours of the

[18] At the time, Rahman was a member of parliament of the Bangladesh Nationalist Party. In 1993, she had presented a bill in parliament proposing changes in the law on polygamy in the Muslim family code.

night, the NGOs are shredding families, especially in the villages, into little pieces. . . . Even though some of the male workers may lose their jobs from time to time, the "smart women" never do. (Salim 1995)

Abdur Rahman Siddiqi too makes clear his great cynicism about the expressed motivations of NGOs and international donors interested in Bangladesh and Bangladeshi women. He writes,

> The proclaimed goals of these NGOs are to develop our backward society, help the destitute, protect human rights, to enrich the downtrodden, to liberate women, to improve the nation, etc. They get their money from the wealthy nations of the West.
>
> Here it is necessary for us to keep in mind a very important truth: the people of these donor countries or societies do not let go of a single penny without some thought of future profit—why would they send millions of dollars to the impoverished and famine-stricken people of this small region? Are the hearts of the world-pillaging people of the Western world suddenly overflowing with sympathy for our sorrows? Has a concern with humanity flooded their souls?
>
> In that case why do they do nothing for their own neighbours?
>
> In front of their very eyes, on the streets of Rome, thousands of desperate young girls sell their bodies. Under their very noses, in London, New York, Paris, thousands of homeless people spend their lives on the streets and are utterly ruined there. In Western countries, the honour of women is bought and sold every day in casinos and through pornography. Where do these great champions of women's honour and human rights hide then? Why do they forget about their own countries and demonstrate such sympathy for foreigners? Those who are running all over this country with the pretext of alleviating the plight of the destitute and downtrodden—why do they not go to Bosnia? Why do they not pick up the young women lying on the streets of Rome, a stone's throw from the Vatican? (Siddiqi 1995)

According to Siddiqi, national development and social care are not the true objectives of the NGOs. Rather, he argues, the NGOs are no more than a Trojan horse left inside the country by Western imperialists to attack "our education, culture, religion in the homes of the weakest members of our society" (Siddiqi 1995).

Fatwas have been issued to clamp down not only on "immoral" women and "alien" NGOs, but also, as I describe below, on ordinary female citizens seeking to assert their democratic right to vote.

Women as citizens and voters

Universal adult suffrage, established in East Pakistan in 1947, was re-affirmed in Bangladesh's constitution in 1972; however, because of extended periods of military rule both before and since Bangladesh gained independence, most citizens' experience of democracy has been rather limited. Finally, the 1991 elections were accepted by domestic and international observers alike as largely free and fair, as were the 1996 elections. Unfortunately, this seal of approval obscures the fact that many people who wished to vote were not permitted to do so. Furthermore, many who did were not allowed to vote for the party that they personally favored. Women and minorities, particularly Hindus, figure prominently in both of these voter categories; however, I limit my discussion here to women voters.

In the union (a subdivision of a district) of Kalikapur, in the Madaripur district in southwestern Bangladesh, women have not been permitted to vote for thirty years.[19] Many local villagers insist that it is simply the *rewaz* (custom) in the area that women do not vote. On investigation, however, *Bhorer Kagoj* journalists learned that before every election, the elite men of the village met to discuss whether women should be allowed to vote. To date, they have decided against it every time, with the rationale that it is un-Islamic for women to vote. Consequently, at every election, women stayed away from the polls. Halani Begum of the Kalikapur union considers herself fortunate that at least she has voted once in her life — although it was thirty years ago — while many women in her village have never been able to vote for fear of the wrath of the community's leaders. Forty-year-old Shonabhan Bibi laments, "Women don't run the community. Even though women run the country, it is men who are in charge in the community." When asked why women were not permitted to vote in Kalikapur, a village elder, Makbul Hossain Khan, age sixty-five, cited religion as the main reason. When it was pointed out to him that women in the neighboring unions vote, he responded angrily, "Let them. They don't [vote] in this union and never will" (*Bhorer Kagoj* 1996).

Not all of the women in the village, however, feel deprived of a valuable opportunity. Haju Bibi, for example, is content with the present situation and demands, "Why should women vote? Shall we not have to die one day?[20] Do we go around like men with our heads uncovered that we should

---

[19] As mentioned earlier, East Pakistan/Bangladesh has undergone long periods of military rule; therefore, these thirty years have not seen as many elections as they might have if democracy had prevailed.

[20] She is concerned that, on dying, she would be called on to explain to God why she committed the sinful act of voting.

go vote [like them]?" Similarly, Joynab Bibi tells a newspaper reporter, "You may think that women should vote, but I do not. . . . I do not take a single step without my husband's permission" (*Bhorer Kagoj* 1996).

In the union of Mohamaya in Feni, in the southeastern part of the country, women have not voted in parliamentary elections in over forty years because everyone is terrified that if they do, disaster may descend on the village (Nagorik Uddyog n.d.). Before local elections in March 1994, the principal of a nearby *madrassah* (religious school) issued a fatwa declaring that it would be un-Islamic and a breach of purdah for women to go to the polling centers; local candidates, informed of this decision, did not even seek votes from women. This fatwa was bolstered by a local legend: that an important *pir* (holy man) who has a shrine in the area was deeply opposed to women voting. Consequently, not one of the 6,436 eligible women in the area voted (Falguni 1996, 13).

Women also have not been permitted to vote for many years in the Alampur union in the northern district of Rangpur. Once again, it appears that members of the local elite "persuaded" the women's "guardians"—that is, male relatives—that it is inappropriate for women to go to voting centers (*Sangbad* 1996). One election officer reported that, on June 12, 1996, he waited at his women-only voting center in the southern district of Barisal all day and not one woman came to cast her vote; he had to turn in an empty ballot box at the end of the day. Apparently such poor turnout had been the case in all recent elections—parliamentary and local—at that particular center as well as in some neighboring centers (*Ittefaq* 1996).

A difference in opinion?

Urban elites contend that fatwas such as those discussed above represent a backlash by the traditional power-holders against rural women's attempts to carve out new roles for themselves. I maintain, however, that this explanation tells only part of the story.

It is true that attitudes and power relations in the countryside are being transformed by the incursion of "alien" ideas through NGOs seeking to inform rural women, by government initiatives to improve female literacy through tuition remission and a food-for-education program, by satellite stations broadcasting risqué films from Bombay, by urban-based export-oriented factories seeking cheap female labor, and by an improved infrastructure that brings in more visitors than ever before. Whatever the actual impact of NGO and government efforts on women's living standards, the very focus of domestic and international programs on poor women is seen by many Bangladeshis as a threat to the traditional class system and to gender relations within the family and community. The village elite constantly bemoan the increasing difficulty of "finding good help" as young women from families who have supplied domestic servants for the local landowner for generations are now taking advantage of self-employment opportunities provided by various NGOs; those who do not join NGOs are at least aware that they can now charge higher wages. Mullahs are suffering from a decline in the female clientele who used to beat a path to their door to purchase special prayers and amulets for sick children or ailing animals, since today most of these women can obtain the information and assistance they need for a smaller fee or even for free from a local NGO.

The notion of a backlash thus helps to explain why members of the rural elite are attacking poor rural women. It does not explain, however, why fatwas are their chosen weapon in this struggle or how the poor themselves are responding to such fatwas. To better understand the fatwa phenomenon, both the material and ideological factors affecting the responses of impoverished rural women need to be explored.

For the purposes of this article, I divide public opinion on fatwas into secularist and Islamist perspectives, which correspond to Rashiduzzaman's characterization of "liberals" and the "religious right," whom he identifies as separated by "a formidable cultural divide" (1994, 974). The liberals "support freedom of speech, secularism, individualism, and enhancement of women's rights," whereas the religious right comprises "conservative Islamists and a variety of other like-minded groups and individuals who articulate the importance of Islam and a Muslim identity in Bangladesh" (975). The first perspective is most widely disseminated through English dailies such as the *Daily Star* and Bengali newspapers such as *Janokantho* (Voice of the people), *Bhorer Kagoj* (Morning paper), and *Ajker Kagoj* (Today's paper) and the second through the dailies *Sangram* (Struggle) and *Inqilab* (Upheaval). While I find this classification useful for understanding the debates at the national level, I argue that this differentiation does not extend to the vast majority of the country's population, the impoverished rural men and women of Bangladesh.

According to the secularist intelligentsia, foreign-funded NGOs, prominent cultural figures, and professionals, perhaps the greatest obstacle to (their vision of) development, progress, and the secular Bengali nation is fundamentalism or the religious right; for them, the phenomenon of the fatwa is part of a larger trend of the increasing Islamization of Bangladeshi state and society. Generally speaking, secularists want rural women to cast off the shackles of tradition and purdah and embrace their vision of modernity; they believe, however, that women's attempts to do so have ignited a fundamentalist backlash. Paradoxically, they regard poor rural women and NGOs as the primary targets of a "medieval," "barbaric" Islamic backlash in the countryside but at the same time hold the gullible "innocent rural masses" responsible for the reach of fundamentalism in rural Bangladesh (Kabir 1995a, 5).

The prominent liberal intellectual Kabir Chowdhury attributes the recent rise in Bangladesh of what he terms "fundamentalism" to its "particular appeal to the frustrated, the poor, the hungry and the uneducated" and, paraphrasing Marx, to fundamentalists' "clever motivated use of religion among the vast illiterate and poor people of this region as a kind of opium" (K. Chowdhury 1995, 15–16). According to Saira Rahman, a lawyer and human rights activist, the village elite have been able to use fatwas to suppress the poor because

> villagers, illiterate and simple, put their full trust in the conniving village clergy and believe that whatever they preach, in the name of Islam, is true. . . .
>
> About ninety percent of the people in the villages are illiterate, and that, combined with blind faith, is a deadly weapon in the hands of the Imam and the village clergy, who take advantage of the followers by instilling the fear of hellfire and grave punishment in the afterlife to such an extent by religious misinterpretations, that the poor people are incapable of thinking otherwise. (Rahman 1995, 73)

Because religion is susceptible to misinterpretation and misuse, members of the liberal elite advocate the total abolition of Islam from the public sphere, from politics, and from the nation's legal framework. They associate religion-based politics with West Pakistani rule and exploitation of East Pakistan, now Bangladesh, in the name of a common religion, and many of them support the National Coordinating Committee for the Implementation of the Values of the Bangladesh Liberation War and the Extermination of the Killers and Collaborators of 1971. Established in 1992, the Nirmul Committee, as it is popularly known, is one of the most vociferous opponents of the public use of religion. Its main objective is to bring to trial war criminals of the 1971 war and ban all religion-based political parties (Kabir 1995a). Its members identify secularism, one of the four pillars of Bangladesh's 1972 constitution, as one of the most important values of the Bangladesh Liberation War and warn that it is in grave danger of being eroded by the growing presence of fundamentalist forces in the country.[21]

---

[21] Originally, the four pillars were secularism, nationalism, democracy, and socialism. Over the years, the principle of socialism has given way to increasing privatization and liberalization, while Bengali nationalism has been replaced by Bangladeshi nationalism in order to distinguish the citizens of Bangladesh from the predominantly Hindu Bengalis of West Bengal, India.

The fundamentalist parties continue to be a violent threat today; we are specifically alarmed at the violence directed towards the members of progressive political parties, the NGOs whose programmes have been raided and disrupted, towards women who are the victims of *fatwas* (religious decrees) simply because they do not conform to the religious norms as defined by the fundamentalists. . . .

Under these circumstances, now that it is clear that the Jama'at and Shibir [the Jama'at's student wing] intends to turn history back and reimpose the religious communalism which the nation fought against in the 1971 war, we the Nirmul Committee stand in defence of the secular tradition inherent in our Bangladeshi nationhood. (Kabir 1995a, 95)

A common theme underlying the writings of many (urban) liberals is that fatwa incidents reflect the "backwardness" and "darkness" of *rural* Bangladesh. A former supreme court justice, for example, compares the Bangladeshi village *salish* to the inquisitions of medieval Europe, lamenting, "What was discarded by Europe in the 17th century is being adopted by the Bangladeshi villages in the wake of the 21st century" (Subhan 1993). Similarly, an anonymous columnist in one of the national Bengali dailies inquires,

Can somebody tell me where we are right now? In which country, at which time? No, one cannot say for sure. One might say that we are in the eighteenth century when Hindu women in this country performed *sati* on their husbands' funeral pyres. . . . The fire outside can be seen, but the fire in the mind — the fire of oppression, torture, disgrace, humiliation, insult — cannot be seen. Many puff out their chests and say, such things may exist in Hindu society, but not in Muslim society — women have been given full rights in Islam. True, they have indeed. That has been done in pen and paper. In practice, in the matter of women's oppression, there is no difference between Hindus and Muslims. (*Banglar Bani* 1993)

Clearly, for this group, part of the blame for the fatwas falls squarely on the shoulders of the poor. According to secularists, it is the ignorance of the rural poor, especially women, about the laws of the land that allows unscrupulous forces to exploit them in the name of religion. As Sigma Huda, a prominent women's and human rights lawyer, points out, Nurjahan was "ignorant and that is why she was wrong in not going to the court for an official divorce. This is only because of illiteracy" (Fahmida 1993).

There are, however, several rifts among secular elites themselves, with perhaps the most important division occurring over the issue of NGOs. While secularists have all called for a cessation of violence against NGOs, some profess to understand the resentment against them. Among their main grievances are the lack of financial accountability of NGOs to anyone other than their foreign donors and the lack of coordination among NGOs. Other secularist critics complain that many of these organizations have no deep attachment to the issues on which they work; rather, they switch focus in accordance with donor interests and priorities, a practice that

> can be referred to as the "flavour of the month" approach to development. What it basically means is that whichever buzzword or term is in common use to reflect the priorities being assigned by the funding agencies is then blindly recited by all the fund-hungry NGOs in the hope of obtaining more foreign funding. . . .
>
> Over the last ten years, it has covered a variety of subjects. These have included women's rights (a longtime favourite, this one — a tired and overused term to describe just about any programme which can in any way be linked to women as beneficiaries, no matter how tenuous the link) and family planning (another old favourite reflecting the western obsession with how to keep the third world population — also known as "them" — in check) as well as more recent innovations, such as the flood action plan (FAP), the environment and children's rights. (N. Chowdhury 1995)

The Islamist perspective, most articulately voiced by the Jama'at-i Islami, is similarly divided on the issues of NGOs and women's rights. While many Islamists have openly supported the attacks on NGOs, they generally condemn fatwas against individual women. There is, nonetheless, a general consensus among Islamists that the fatwa-related violence against women has been possible precisely because Bangladesh is not under Islamic rule. Although they are not necessarily opposed to physical punishment for adultery, Islamists argue that proper Islamic procedures were not followed in the fatwa incidents reported in the press — that is, unqualified men issued the fatwas and the correct number of witnesses were not summoned to establish guilt — but because of their ignorance, the poor had no alternative but to accept these specious verdicts.

In interviews and articles in *Sangram* and *Inqilab,* several prominent Islamic figures have denounced the rural fatwas, arguing that they are a gross misuse of a very important aspect of Islamic jurisprudence. As Maulana Ubaid ul-Huq, the *khatib* (preacher; one who gives the Friday sermon) of the National Mosque Baitul Mukarram, explains, "Only somebody who is properly trained in the Quran, *hadith* [the Prophet's traditions], and *fiqh*

[law] as well as knowledgeable about modern society and its needs is qualified to issue a fatwa" (*Sangram* 1995a). He insists that there is a genuine need in society for fatwas to clarify ambiguity in the laws; however, special arrangements are necessary. He elaborates: "From the earliest days of Islam until the end of Muslim rule, the Islamic state would appoint the individual responsible for issuing fatwas. Today, because we don't have this arrangement, it is possible for random, illiterate men to issue fatwas and deceive people. If the state appointed qualified people to issue fatwas throughout the country, there would be no opportunity for such deceptions and no-one would even dare speak ill of genuine fatwas" (*Sangram* 1995a). Ubaid ul-Huq and other Islamic leaders express outrage at liberals' coinage of the word *fatwabaz,* a derogatory term for one who issues fatwas, and the immediate adoption of the term on television and radio (*Inqilab* 1994). One woman writes, "Those who have no knowledge of religion, in particular those who are ignorant and illiterate about Islam and indeed present themselves as the enemies of Islam—they have no authority to speak about religion or fatwas. This is the height of arrogance on their part" (Khatun 1993). In an interview, Razia Fayez, a former minister, also warns against the dangers of too readily accepting just anybody's opinion as a fatwa: "Just as a court or trial that suddenly springs up on the side of the road is not really a court or trial, similarly just because a few random people get together and issue a fatwa, that does not automatically become a fatwa—it simply adds to misinterpretations of the law." She points out the need for fatwas or learned opinions in other religions, for example, in Catholicism, when the Pope is asked to give his opinion about abortion (*Sangram* 1995c).

Others feel that "liberals" have unjustifiably conflated Islam, religion-based politics, and a few isolated incidents in rural Bangladesh, as described in an article that appeared not long after the 1993 incident involving Nurjahan and Mutalib:

> A photograph appeared in Britain's renowned paper *The Guardian* on January 26, 1993. The photograph was of a meeting on women's rights convened by the leaders of the Mahila Parishad.[22] Two placards are visible in this photograph. One says, "We demand the trial of Maulana Mannan, responsible for the death of Nurjahan"; the second, "We demand a ban on communal politics." Such a picture did not end up in the pages of a well-reputed foreign newspaper by pure accident. The intention is to convey the impression that it has become quite commonplace for women in Bangladesh to be stoned to

[22] The Mahila Parishad is the largest women's organization in the country, with over thirty thousand members (Jahan 1995, 93).

death and, furthermore, that the politics of a particular community are connected to such incidents. Thus the women of Bangladesh are conflating the punishment by stoning of adulterous women with religion-based politics. (Samad 1993)

Another observer detects a conspiracy of "progressives" and NGOs out to taint the name of Islam with this furor over fatwas: "Fatwa is a very important and integral part of *shari'a* or Islamic law . . . yet recently, a familiar group hostile to Islam has been making up and spreading various tantalizing stories about 'fatwa.' Their objective is to please and fill the pockets of the enemies of Islam, both here and abroad. They have taken a few isolated incidents in the rural areas and woven intricate tales around them." The primary objective of these conspirators, he goes on to argue, is "to oppose Islam in the name of opposing 'fundamentalism,' to be constantly involved in opposing Muslim interests, to destroy religious and social values" (Khasru 1995).

Maimul Ahsan Khan, a professor of law at Dhaka University, explains that it is easy for untrained people to mete out fatwas and be taken seriously because, basically, people are always in need of advice. Most people in Bangladesh are Muslim and they naturally turn to those they believe to be knowledgeable about religious injunctions: "There are nearly 200,000 mosques and as many *madrassahs* in the country. . . . Ordinary Muslims approach the members of these organizations with various family and social problems — because the nation's legal system constantly fails to satisfactorily resolve their problems. In addition, the present laws of the land were created by the foreign imperial masters. And from their successor Pakistani state, we have inherited some decrepit, westernized and inhuman laws and regulation which combine to form our inefficient and corrupt police and legal structure. That is why this is now a haven for fatwas" (*Sangram* 1995b).

According to a senior Jama'at-i Islami leader whom I interviewed, the fatwa incidents can be attributed directly to the gullibility of the rural poor: "Those crimes are being committed by people who don't know everything that they need to about Islam. A man puts on an *alkhella* [long shirt, usually worn by an imam] and people start calling him *huzur*. The only way to stop this is by spreading knowledge of Islam."[23] For Khasru, this reverence of ordinary people for anybody who looks sufficiently "religious" makes them perfect victims of NGO conspiracies to tarnish Islam: "Some thoughtful observers who have analyzed the various fatwa-related falsehoods even suspect that the NGOs sought out some of these half-literate *imam-muezzin* of village mosques and *madrassah* teachers, who

---

[23] Interview by author, Chittagong, March 16, 1996.

wear Islamic dress like the prayer cap and sport a beard and influenced them to produce this fatwa drama" (Khasru 1995).

It is of no political significance, according to secularists, that about 86 percent of the country's population is Muslim. Their solution to the recent fatwas is the total abolition of Islam from the public sphere. More specifically, since Islam is formally present in the legal structure in matters of family law, they would like to see the enactment of a secular civil code applicable to all citizens regardless of religious background. Islamists, by contrast, believe that in a Muslim majority state it is only natural that Islam be recognized as an important determinant of both cultural identity and formal politics. For them, the solution to the misuse of religion lies in the establishment of an Islamic state, in which law, politics, and society would be governed by Islamic principles.

Between acquiescence and heroism

My extensive fieldwork in rural Bangladesh suggests that the solution to the oppression of poor rural women in the name of religion lies neither in a completely secular society nor in the Jama'at's interpretation of an Islamic state. Despite all their differences, the secularists and Islamists ultimately share a number of primary assumptions: that the "masses" are a homogeneous group, that the role and conduct of women are of great importance in the future development of society, and that it is the rural poor's ignorance of state and Islamic laws that renders them susceptible to exploitation in the name of religion and to being led "astray" by the other group. In this section, through a series of examples from rural Bangladesh, I demonstrate the fallacy in positing the fatwa phenomenon as a fight at the grassroots level between secularism and Islamism and argue instead that this polarization arises directly from attributing the decisions and conduct of the rural poor, particularly women, to narrow concerns about either one's stomach or one's soul. I propose that neither the secularists nor the Islamists are likely to win the battle for the loyalty of poor rural women in Bangladesh; rather, the women choose elements of both views according to their needs and interests. Because neither group adequately represents their concerns, the women embrace neither wholeheartedly. As the examples below indicate, every blow against the Islamists by rural women is not a vote — figuratively or literally — for the secularists and vice versa. Rather, poor rural women's actions are motivated by different and often contradictory concerns at different times, and it is nearly impossible to classify any one person as either pro-secularist or pro-Islamist, as either a victim or a resister.

I concur with the general assessment that the traditional elite is engaged in a backlash against impoverished rural women and that fatwas represent an important tool in this assault. I disagree, however, that fatwas work as a weapon because the rural poor are gullible and believe anything that is said in the name of religion—an argument made by secularists and Islamists alike. In contradistinction, I argue that the poor do not always submit to fatwas and that when they do, it is not necessarily because they believe that they are following the word of God but because to disobey would incur the wrath of the local elite. Thus, while it is true that there is much ignorance in rural Bangladesh, there is also much deliberate evasion of the law. I suggest that not only ignorance of the laws but also knowledge that the state lacks the will and ability to enforce its laws and protect its citizens influence the decision making of the rural poor. For the ordinary poor villager, it is often more important to maintain good relations with the local elite than to follow the rules of a state that neither enforces its own laws nor is likely to defend the villager against wealthier neighbors. To illustrate that the poor do not always submit to fatwas, I present a second example of a case of "illicit sexual relations"—one with less tragic consequences than that of Nurjahan and Mutalib but perhaps more accurately representative of rural Bangladesh. By coincidence, this case also involves a young woman called Nurjahan.

This Nurjahan lives in Savar, not far from the capital city, Dhaka, and she too was accused of living in sin with a man she knew to be her husband. The following is her husband's, Fazlu's, account of the incident that sparked the controversy: "I came home from the fields one afternoon. I asked Nurjahan to fetch the water for my bath. We started arguing over something. At some point she locked the door. I knocked for a little while. Because I couldn't hit her, I angrily said, 'I divorce you.' Then people rushed over and stopped the argument" (quoted in Khan 1996, 54). Nurjahan claimed that she could not hear what he was saying from the other side of the door. After they stopped fighting, she came out and life continued as usual—that is, until a few days later, when the local imam and some villagers issued a fatwa that they could no longer live together, that they should each be whipped or stoned 101 times in order to purify themselves, and that they should perform *hilla* if they wished to remarry.[24]

Fazlu explained to the local imam that he had said "I divorce you" in

---

[24] Under some schools of Islamic law, a divorced couple who wish to remarry one another must undergo *hilla*—that is, the wife must marry and divorce a second husband before she can remarry her first husband. Many religious scholars believe that this intervening marriage is required precisely in order to deter husbands from divorcing their wives on a whim.

a flash of anger and not really meant it. He had also already sought the advice of religious experts in Dhaka, who had informed him that, according to Islamic law, the man must say "I divorce you" three times over the course of three months, giving the matter much thought between each pronouncement, for the divorce to be final. Fazlu and Nurjahan had also found out that, under the Family Law Ordinance of 1961, they were not considered divorced, and, in any case, even divorced couples wishing to remarry were no longer required to perform *hilla*. Thus reassured, Fazlu and Nurjahan refused to go through *hilla* and resumed conjugal life. The elders and religious leaders of the village, however, declared these opinions from Dhaka completely invalid, arguing, "This was passed by the government. It has nothing to do with Islam — because it was not passed by an Islamic government. Even if it means going against the government's law, we stand by our fatwa" (quoted in Khan 1996, 64). They sought a fatwa from another source in Dhaka, which confirmed that Fazlu had indeed divorced his wife and that the couple must perform *hilla* if they wished to remarry. After local government officials were brought in, the imam lost his job. Nurjahan and her husband now live together again.

Central to both Nurjahan stories is the legality of certain procedures for marriage and divorce. Various groups — within both the poor and the elite — have different ways of ascertaining whether or not a couple is cohabiting legally and have different perspectives on a community's right to take action against what it considers to be illicit or immoral activity. As this second story so aptly demonstrates, a number of legal codes coexist — albeit in great tension — in Bangladesh: the state's own reformed Muslim Family Code, which is derived from Islamic law; the state's secular criminal code; Islamic laws, which tend to be interpreted very differently by the urban-based Jama'at and rural religious leaders; and a more international human rights perspective as espoused by the different secularist development organizations. What is of interest is how and when rural men and women select from these different codes — or choose to disregard them altogether.

Despite the growing prominence of rural women in recent years, the discussions regarding the problem of fatwas have remained elitist, with both secularists and Islamists looking down at the rural poor as naive and ignorant. If only we had secular laws, argue the secularists, these mullahs could be locked up for good. Or, if only we had true Islamic rule, argues the Jama'at, only properly trained religious leaders would be permitted to issue fatwas and there would be no abuse of religion. I argue, however, that the main problem is not ignorance of the law but deliberate evasion of it, by both the rural poor and the rural elite. Even those who do know the law often choose to ignore or break it, for a number of reasons. First, they may simply believe that they can "get away with it." Time and again, interviewees express little faith in the ability of the state to protect the weak and vulnerable or to punish wrongdoers, because the state itself is weak, corrupt, and inefficient. Second, they find that existing laws do not suit their social and economic concerns—for example, in the matters of child marriage or dowry.

The first Nurjahan story provides a vivid example of the consequences of a weak state and an inaccessible legal system: the very absence of the state, police, and law courts at Nurjahan's marriage, divorce, "trial," and death makes them conspicuous. The ordinary villager may often be unaware of the differences between the laws of the land and what the local elite claim is true Islamic law but choose to follow the latter because, from his perspective, he has to answer to God and to the local elite for his actions, while he may go through life without ever directly encountering any branch of the state. In the case of the first Nurjahan, her father himself later admitted that, as the elite men of the *salish* demanded that his daughter step into the pit, he urged her forward, telling her, "Daughter, do as they tell you." In contrast, Nurjahan and Fazlu tried to bypass the local elite by obtaining a written fatwa from a religious center in Dhaka, but they did not seek the assistance of the local police. An unscrupulous elite is not about to rush to reform a corrupt law-and-order system; as the first Nurjahan protested the fatwa against her—even as she was being dragged into the pit—the *salish* committee kept repeating, "The law is in our hands. Do as we tell you" (Ain-o-Salish Kendra 1994).

Secularists express concern as well that the rural poor, through their support of religion, may well destroy the secular foundations of the country. Although many poor rural women who identify themselves as Muslim are pious, they have been known, nonetheless, to resist local religious decrees when they seem contrary to their own interests, to what they perceive to be the "true spirit" of Islam, or to the law of the land. For example, despite a nationwide Islamist campaign declaring that foreign- and/or Christian-funded NGOs are secretly turning Muslim women away from their faith, millions of women remain NGO members. Many women we interviewed described the objections they encountered when they first joined an NGO program:

My husband told me that NGOs are alien to us. (Ayesha, age forty-two, Jessore)

Local people told me I'd lose my religion, that I'd become Christian. (Morjina, age twenty-five, Jessore)

The village *munshis* [scribes, teachers], my husband, everyone said that women were going to sell the country [to the foreigners]; why do women need to work? They are now without *hadith*. (Omisa, age thirty, Dinajpur)

The women, however, did not sit back and accept these obstacles meekly. Values among the rural poor have changed over time: what would have been unthinkable and warranted much malicious gossip even a few decades ago—such as women leaving their homesteads to attend NGO meetings—today only raises a few eyebrows at most. These changes are tolerated, I argue, largely because the poor recognize that social and economic transformations are necessary. Ayesha, for example, patiently explained to her husband what the NGOs wanted to accomplish and then, over time, showed him what could be done with an NGO loan. "Now," she says proudly, "along with my husband, I am raising poultry, fish, and a cow to meet household expenses." Similarly, Omisa describes how, despite criticism, she bravely went ahead with her dealings with an NGO: "I explained to everyone what I was really doing. I've been able to do something for my village. I now have a business that I started with a loan. [Our village] has received sanitary latrines and violence against women has gone down." Morjina also refused to pay attention to the objections that people raised because, she says, "I wanted to become independent." Somirunnessa explained that she had to ignore local statements of disapproval because "I had to think of my stomach. . . . [Since joining,] I've formed a *samity* [committee or cooperative] and am earning a living from sewing and embroidery." Fatima, too, was glad that she had paid no attention to detractors; through NGO involvement, she was able to buy a cow and some land and even build a small house. Miles away, in the district of Chittagong, Farida had been subjected to similar objections and was furious: "People said a lot of things when we first took money from the Grameen Bank—that we were becoming Christian, that we were losing our religion. If we are, then we must. When have *they* ever lent us 10 takas? We must do what we can to survive. Sometimes they say these things because they are afraid that the poor will become rich!"[25] Although Nojimon and the other women guarding the mulberry trees were physically unable to prevent the mullahs from chopping down the trees, they did question the mullahs' rationale for doing so. One woman lamented, "This isn't just cutting down a tree. It is actually like demolishing a mosque. It is like kicking someone in the belly. If we don't work, we'll starve." Another woman pointed out that the trees had not harmed anyone, that they had been

[25] Interview by author, Chittagong, February 24, 1996.

planted not on anybody's private property but alongside "government" (i.e., public) roads (Ain-o-Salish Kendra 1994).

A great many destitute women throughout Bangladesh have not joined NGO programs; my research suggests that their decision was influenced less by local or national fatwas against NGO involvement than by fear of taking on the responsibility of loans or by opposition from family members. Although many lending organizations such as the Grameen Bank target the "poorest of the poor," they are not always successful. I have found that very often the poorest are afraid to take out loans because they may be unable to repay them—unlike a slightly better-off neighbor who can use funds from an additional source of income or from another working member of the family to make regular payments on the loan. Borrowers who had at least one relative with a regular income were better able to raise the money for the weekly payment. As Asya explains, "I have no husband, no son. On whose strength can I take a loan?"[26] Clearly the poorest women in the village are not the ones taking advantage of the credit opportunities provided by NGOs.

What support there is for Islamist critiques of NGOs was voiced not by the poorest women of the village but by those who were financially better off and could afford to observe purdah—either by never venturing outside their homestead or by wearing a *burqa* when they did go out.[27] Halima explains the position she took when the Grameen Bank first began work in her village: "I have not fallen so low that I would degrade myself by parading in front of strangers from other districts, doing physical drills, and loudly chanting slogans about the Grameen Bank" (Shehabuddin 1992, 131). Interestingly, very few rural women see themselves as not observing purdah—comments and criticisms from neighbors and the village elite notwithstanding. For many women, purdah is a matter of personal feeling; for others, it entails adhering to strict behavioral codes such as not being seen by male strangers, covering one's head with the end of a saree, and wearing a *burqa* when out in public. The *burqa*, so favored by Islamists and wealthier women, is simply beyond the financial reach of most poor women and was cited by few as an accurate indication of purdah. In her fascinating study of a village in Sylhet—the same district where the first Nurjahan was stoned—Katy Gardner (1998) finds that those families with members in England or the Middle East tend to espouse more purist interpretations of Islam; foreign remittances enable them to engage in

---

[26] Interview by author, Chittagong, February 19, 1996.

[27] A *burqa* is a long, coatlike garment that conceals the entire body, head, and, if wished, face.

"higher-status activities," such as performing hajj and offering sacrifices on religious occasions, and the money absolves the women from having to go out in search of employment.[28]

Fatwas issued against NGO-provided health care, although not initially preventing most pregnant women from receiving prenatal treatment, led several resourceful women to seek out an alternative fatwa — as one might a second medical opinion — stating the treatment provided by NGO-run clinics was not contrary to Islam. Thus armed, they clandestinely resumed their treatment (Khan 1996, 34).

Although fatwas against women voting have been more strictly enforced in some regions than in others, women throughout Bangladesh have been told, at various times, that going to a polling center to vote is a breach of purdah. Yet, from a national perspective, not only have women voted in increasing numbers in recent elections, but they have also tried to use the "system" in innovative ways for personal benefit. Rashida, for example, describes how village women have turned the local insistence on observing purdah to their own advantage in recent elections. In exchange for a small sum of money from one of the local candidates, she arranged for a group of women voters to cast multiple votes in favor of that particular candidate. The only way for a polling center official to verify whether someone has already voted is to look at the person's face and to check the person's thumb for the ink stain that signals that a vote has been cast. These women avoided detection by vigorously rubbing their thumbs with a local plant secretion and by donning a different *burqa* every time they entered the polling station. They kept their faces covered, knowing that no polling officer, for fear of violating purdah and causing offense, would insist that they uncover them. This tactic — combined with an unstained thumb — allowed the same women to return to the polls multiple times.[29]

In the days preceding the June 1996 election, some women decided to take advantage of the situation by promising to vote for whichever party gave them "presents," such as sarees: "Since we never hear from any of the parties once they get into office, I decided I might as well go with whichever one is most generous before the elections! Maybe I'll get a new saree before the next elections too!"[30] Yet, when asked why they voted, the overwhelming majority of women said it was their duty to do so, while others said it was important to show support for one's party or candidate. Despite

---

[28] *Hajj* is the pilgrimage to Mecca prescribed as a religious duty for all Muslims who can afford to undertake it.

[29] Interview by author, Chittagong, February 20, 1996.

[30] Interview by author, Jessore, June 12, 1996 (election day).

this public expression of democratic duty, most women seem resigned to the notion that the state, or *sarkar*—secular or otherwise—is of little relevance to their daily life. This outlook is primarily a result of the state's perceived failure to provide essential resources such as education, health care, employment, and security. As one woman lamented, "So many governments have come and gone and nothing has changed in my life. The people in Dhaka must be terribly busy with other things" (Shehabuddin 1999, 157).

Nonetheless, many women did vote in the 1996 parliamentary elections and did carefully study the various parties and candidates. Assurances by the interim "caretaker" government that there would be no violence on election day helped to encourage women's participation. As a result, they and their male guardians were less hesitant about their traveling to voting centers. A small number of the women interviewed admitted that they had voted only because it was their husband's wish and that they had voted as he had instructed. For others, the elections provided an ideal opportunity to express their displeasure with those who, they believed, sought to curtail their NGO activities—the Islamist party, Jama'at-i Islami. After the elections, some of these women explained that they had not voted for the Jama'at precisely on the grounds that "if the Jama'at comes to power, they'll say that I can't leave the house anymore to earn a living. Who's going to feed me and my children then?" (Shehabuddin 1999, 158).

At the same time, it would be difficult to argue that the rural poor are firmly planted in the secularist camp. Opinions among them vary. The example of Nurjahan and Fazlu demonstrates that some may be willing to privilege the 1961 Muslim Family Code, which is basically reformed Islamic law, over traditional interpretations of Islamic law. The couple insisted that because Fazlu had said "I divorce you" in a fit of rage and because his declaration had not been registered with local officials, he had not actually divorced Nurjahan. However, not all of their fellow villagers agreed with that interpretation of the situation. Although Nurjahan and Fazlu have resumed conjugal life with state sanction, the villagers are not sure how to react. Many still believe that they are divorced in the eyes of God and are therefore sinning by living as a married couple. The result has been a social boycott of the couple and many of their relatives.

Rural men and women interviewees repeatedly stated that they do not believe that the state can protect them and therefore that "state laws," as distinct from "God's laws," may not be worth following. Consequently, a marriage that is not legally recognized may still be socially acceptable, or, as in the case of Nurjahan and Fazlu, a divorce that is not recognized by the state may seem perfectly valid to some members of the local community.

Very often, a man and woman are considered married if the local imam has said the necessary prayers and declared them married; indeed, the woman need not even be present at her own marriage. According to state law, however, all marriages must be registered with the local *qadi*. Another area of gross disparity between law and practice is that of underage marriages. The legal minimum age for marriage is eighteen years for women and twenty-one for men; yet, underage marriages persist. The reasons often given for the practice range from concerns about the chastity of unmarried young daughters and the economic burden they place on their families to the auspicious appearance of a prospective groom who does not demand dowry if the bride is sufficiently young or beautiful. Similarly, it is a criminal offense to give or take dowry, but most rural parents simply shrug their shoulders and admit that if they do not give dowry, their daughters will remain unmarried.

The rural poor's lack of faith in the state and its various branches is manifest in and reaffirmed by their everyday experience with institutions such as local government and government-affiliated medical centers, schools, and the police. One woman I spoke with in Tangail was quite scornful of the state's laws on dowry: "If someone from the *sarkar* [state, government] comes and charges me with [taking dowry at my son's wedding], I'd simply turn around and say, 'Why do *you* take bribes?' You know, we're both just trying to supplement our incomes."[31] In Chittagong, Rizia complained that the local government doctor charges for medicine that he is supposed to dispense for free (or for only a nominal fee): "One day, just before [the medications] were all about to expire, he told us to come and help ourselves to whatever we wanted. Another time, he threw all his medications into a village pond because he hadn't been able to give them away before they expired."[32] Several mothers accused teachers at the local government school of sitting around gossiping all day instead of teaching; however, as Shamsu describes, "When they expect a visit from the government inspector, the school officials run around the village rounding up children who don't even attend the school, have them dress nicely and sit in the classroom. That's how they make the school look full."[33] Asked what they thought are the duties of the police, many of the women we spoke with suggested the maintenance of law and order and catching criminals. Yet very few poor men, and even fewer poor women, had ever gone to the police for help. Banu said it was because the police always insist on "a little

---

[31] Interview by author, Ayeshakhandha, Tangail, June 20, 1996.
[32] Interview by author, Chittagong, February 25, 1996.
[33] Interview by author, Chittagong, February 25, 1996.

money for tea" — in other words, a bribe.[34] Similarly, Morjina's complaint that "the police don't help the poor without taking money from them" was echoed by large numbers of women in other parts of the country.

That the Bangladeshi state has had a limited effect on the poorest of the country's citizens is disputed by few. Ambitious schemes have been proposed at the center (Government of Bangladesh 1995); the problem, however, lies with the poor implementation of government policies. In the end, the state has consistently failed to deliver on its promises, such as the lofty goals outlined in Article 14 of the 1972 constitution: "It shall be a fundamental responsibility of the State to emancipate the toiling masses — the peasants and workers — and backward sections of the people from all forms of exploitation" (Government of Bangladesh 1994). In the subsequent Article, the state assumes responsibility for providing the "basic necessities of life, including food, clothing, shelter, education and medical care."

According to Rehman Sobhan, much of the problem lies in successive governments' lack of accountability, which "has diverted politics and development towards the enrichment of a narrow class of beneficiaries. External dependence sustained this system since the state did not have to raise resources from the people preferring to rely on donors to underwrite the development process. . . . The outcome of the Paris aid consortium meeting was thus always more central to the concerns of the GOB [Government of Bangladesh] than the passage of the national budget by parliament" (Sobhan 1993, 263).[35] In effect confirming the experiences of the rural women we interviewed, Sobhan bemoans the increasing "privatisation of the state," whereby private interests inform all decisions: "If someone wants a gas connection, a telephone repaired, guaranteed delivery of mail or to have a complaint registered at the police station this must be treated as a privately marketed service. It may be secured either through a personal nexus usually reinforced by a material exchange or by exercise of power and influence" (266). Since impoverished rural women and men lack both money and powerful influence, it is easy to see why they, as individuals, do not seek out government assistance in times of trouble.

In this article, I have tried to demonstrate that, contrary to secularist and Islamist dismissals of the rural poor as ignorant and gullible, it is in fact the ineffectiveness of the state that has compelled them to fend for themselves as best they can and that has permitted certain members of the

---

[34] Interview by author, Chittagong, March 2, 1996.

[35] Every year, major international donors and representatives of the Bangladesh government meet to discuss Bangladesh's use of past aid and determine the size of future aid packages. For many years, this meeting took place in Paris; the venue only recently shifted to Dhaka.

elite to commit excesses without fear of reprisal. When the poor "accept" a local fatwa, they are not automatically accepting all aspects of religion in the public sphere; similarly, when they decide to join an NGO despite fatwas against it, they are not necessarily rejecting religion. The failure of urban-based elites in Bangladesh, secular and Islamist, to incorporate the real life concerns and attitudes of the rural poor into their elaborate blueprints for the future ultimately belies their claim to represent the nation. Poor rural women, in the meantime, devise their own strategies to improve their condition, many of which entail very public acts such as joining NGOs and thus fall outside the realm of hidden resistance. In the process—though not always consciously—these women are able to challenge concepts such as democracy, modernity, feminism, and Islam that for so long have been controlled by the nation's elites. While secularist and Islamist elites squabble over their differences, impoverished rural women create their own fusion of Islam, democracy, feminism, and modernity and, in doing so, bring about further democratization of social, economic, and cultural power. In the end, the women are simply choosing the course of action that they believe best serves their interests.

Department of Politics
Princeton University

References

Ahmed, Leila. 1992. *Women and Gender in Islam: Historical Roots of a Modern Debate.* New Haven, Conn.: Yale University Press.

Ain-o-Salish Kendra (Law and Mediation Center). 1994. *Eclipse,* video recording produced by Ain-o-Salish Kendra, Dhaka (in Bengali and English).

———. 1997. "Oppression against Women in Bangladesh through Fatwas and Salishes, 1993–96." Unpublished manuscript, Ain-o-Salish Kendra, Dhaka.

———. N.d. "Protest against Imam for Indicting a Woman in a Village Salish for Adultery, Contrary to the Law of Bangladesh." Unpublished manuscript, Ain-o-Salish Kendra, Dhaka.

Anderson, Norman. 1976. *Law Reform in the Muslim World.* London: Athlone.

Banglar Bani. 1993. "A Hut of Bones, a Roof of Leather, Pieces Patched Together" (in Bengali). *Banglar Bani,* January 18.

Begum, Maleka. 1993. "By Her Death, Nurjahan Proved That the Rule of Law Has Not Yet Been Established" (in Bengali). *Bhorer Kagoj,* January 23.

Begum, Suraiya. 1994. "Fundamentalism and Women in Bangladesh: A Discussion" (in Bengali). *Shomaj Nirikkhon* 54:1–19.

Bhorer Kagoj. 1996. "Women Voters Unable to Vote!" (in Bengali). *Bhorer Kagoj,* May 29.

Chowdhury, Kabir. 1995. "Resisting Fundamentalists." In Kabir 1995b, 14–24.

Chowdhury, Nina. 1995. "What's the Flavour of the Month?" *Daily Star,* April 17.

Esposito, John. 1982. *Women in Muslim Family Law.* Syracuse, N.Y.: Syracuse University Press.

Fahmida, Rahat. 1993. "Barbaric Incident: In the Eyes of the Law." *Daily Star,* January 28.

Falguni, Aditi. 1996. "A Breach of Women's Right to Vote" (in Bengali). *Ain-o-Salish Kendra Bulletin* 3(6):13–14.

Gardner, Katy. 1998. "Women and Islamic Revivalism in a Bangladeshi Community." In *Appropriating Gender: Women's Activism and Politicized Religion in South Asia,* ed. Patricia Jeffery and Amrita Basu, 203–20. New York and London: Routledge.

Government of Bangladesh. 1994. *The Constitution of the People's Republic of Bangladesh.* Dhaka: Bangladesh Forms and Publishing Office.

———. 1995. "Women in Bangladesh: Equality, Development and Peace— National Report to the Fourth World Conference on Women, Beijing 1995." Dhaka: Ministry of Women and Children's Affairs.

Inqilab. 1994. "Strong Protest against Term 'Fatwabaz' " (in Bengali). *Inqilab,* November 18.

———. 1995. "If NGO and Qadiani Activities Are Not Shut Down within a Month, the God-Fearing Public Will Attack Their Strongholds" (in Bengali). *Inqilab,* April 1.

Ittefaq. 1994. "Nine Sentenced to Seven Years' Imprisonment with Hard Labor" (in Bengali). *Ittefaq,* February 23.

———. 1996. "A Voting Center without Voters!" (in Bengali). *Ittefaq,* June 15.

Jahan, Roushan. 1995. "Men in Seclusion, Women in Public: Rokeya's Dream and Women's Struggles in Bangladesh." In *The Challenge of Local Feminisms: Women's Movements in Global Perspective,* ed. Amrita Basu, 87–109. Boulder, Colo.: Westview.

Kabir, Shahriar. 1995a. Preface to Kabir 1995b, 5–8.

———. 1995b. *Resist Fundamentalism: Focus on Bangladesh.* Dhaka: Nirmul Committee.

Kaiser, Shahidullah. 1993. *Shangshaptak* (in Bengali). Dhaka: Pallab.

Kamal, Sultana. 1995. "Undermining Women's Rights." *Sanglap* 4 (August): 12–16.

Khan, Mizanur Rahman. 1996. *Fatwabaz* (in Bengali). Dhaka: Anupam Prokashoni.

Khan, Muhammad Musa. 1993. "We Are Mortified, We Are Concerned" (in Bengali). *Banglabazaar Patrika,* January 18.

Khasru, Amir. 1995. "Noteworthy" (in Bengali). *Sangram,* December 1.

Khatun, Hafeza Asma. 1993. "Who Are They to Demand that Fatwas Be Outlawed?" (in Bengali). *Sangram,* February 1.

Klein, Joe. 1995. "Mothers vs. Mullahs: A Program Favored by Hillary Clinton Meets Islamic Resistance." *Newsweek,* April 17, 56.

Nagorik Uddyog (Citizen Initiative). N.d. "Female Voter Education in Mahamaya and Kalikapur Unions." Unpublished manuscript, Nagorik Uddyog, Dhaka.

Piscatori, James. 1990. "The Rushdie Affair and the Politics of Ambiguity." *International Affairs* 66(4):767–89.

Rahman, Saira. 1995. "A Dangerous Ignorance." In Kabir 1995b, 68–78.

Rashiduzzaman, M. 1994. "The Liberals and the Religious Right in Bangladesh." *Asian Survey* 34(11):974–90.

Salim, Muhammad Abdus. 1995. "NGOs in Bangladesh and Some Related Matters." *Sangram*, August 8.

Samad, Ibne Golam. 1993. "Western Propaganda and the Women of This Country" (in Bengali). *Sangram*, February 16.

Sangbad. 1996. "4,500 Women in Pirganj *Thana* Wish to Vote, But . . . " (in Bengali). *Sangbad*, June 6.

Sangram. 1995a. "Exclusive Interview with the *Khatib* of Baitul Mukarram, Maulana Ubaid ul-Huq" (in Bengali). *Sangram*, December 1.

———. 1995b. "Exclusive Interview with Dr. Maimul Ahsan Khan" (in Bengali). *Sangram*, December 1.

———. 1995c. "Exclusive Interview with Razia Fayez" (in Bengali). *Sangram*, December 1.

Shehabuddin, Elora. 1992. *Empowering Rural Women: The Impact of Grameen Bank in Bangladesh*. Dhaka: Grameen Bank.

———. 1999. "Beware the Bed of Fire: Gender, Democracy, and the Jama'at-i Islami in Bangladesh." *Journal of Women's History* 10(4):148–71.

Siddiqi, Abdur Rahman. 1995. "If They Are Not Stopped Immediately, NGOs Will Gain Control of Both State and Society" (in Bengali). *Inqilab*, August 9.

Singh, Priyam. 1996. "Women, Law, and Criminal Justice in North India: A Historical View." *Bulletin of Concerned Asian Scholars* 28(1):27–38.

Sobhan, Rehman. 1993. *Bangladesh: Problems of Governance*. Dhaka: University Press Limited.

Sobhan, Salma. 1978. *Legal Status of Women in Bangladesh*. Dhaka: Bangladesh Institute of Law and International Affairs.

Subhan, K. M. 1993. "Bangladeshi Inquisition." *Dhaka Courier*, July 2.

Women in the Era of Modernity and Islamic
Fundamentalism: The Case of Taslima Nasrin of Bangladesh

In February 1993, a Bangladeshi woman writer, Taslima Nasrin, published a book titled *Lajja* (Shame). In the book, Nasrin presents a fictionalized form of an actual account of Bangladeshi Muslim men raping Hindu women in alleged retaliation for the 1992 destruction of the Babri mosque in Ayodha, India, by Hindu fundamentalists. Nasrin's book immediately sparked a controversy. Eventually, members of an obscure religious group from the northwestern town of Sylhet declared themselves the *Sahaba Sainik Parishad* (Council for Soldiers of Prophet's Companions) and issued a *fatwa* (religious decree) that accused Nasrin of blasphemy and conspiracy against Islam. At a rally in September 1993, the group put a price of about US$1,250 on Nasrin's head and demanded that the Khaleda Zia government arrest her and implement the verdict within fifteen days. Initially the principal fundamentalist party, the *Jamaat-e-Islam* (JI), had remained silent on Nasrin's writings and their allegedly blasphemous content. But in early 1994, the *Sirat Majlish*, widely known in Bangladesh as a front organization for the JI, declared that it would give US$2,500 to anyone who killed Nasrin. (The amount promised is a large sum in a country with a per capita gross national product of less than US$240.) While the Islamic fundamentalist parties demanded Nasrin's execution, the secular, progressive, and modernist intellectuals and writers were equally dismissive of her writings. Without demanding her death, they variously described Nasrin as "immature," "rather impulsive," "politically naive," "obsessed with sex," and an "antimale extremist." She was also identified by these intellectuals as a "female Salman Rushdie" in an attempt to associate her with Rushdie, the more widely known male writer who gained notoriety at the hands of

I am grateful to Dr. S. M. Nurul Alam, Samantha Maubach, Ed Versluis, and five anonymous readers of *Signs* for their critical readings of numerous earlier versions of this article. Any shortcomings of the article, however, are mine. A small grant from Southern Oregon University, during the summer and fall of 1995, allowed me to collect additional materials for this article. For that I thank then provost James Dean and Dan Rubenson, director, curricular affairs. While in Bangladesh, Sultan Ahmed helped me to locate relevant materials. My thanks to him as well.

[*Signs: Journal of Women in Culture and Society* 1998, vol. 23, no. 2]

Iranian mullahs for his book *The Satanic Verses,* which they considered blasphemous.

In this article, I put the entire Nasrin affair into a broad historical and political context. Furthermore, I seek to explain Nasrin's writings as a possible *gendered subaltern narrative* within the context of debate between Islamic fundamentalism and modernity.[1] More specifically, I argue that it would be a mistake both theoretically and methodologically to see the Nasrin case as a global confrontation between tradition (Islamic fundamentalism) and modernity. The former is considered a "backward" belief, and practices continue from a historically fixed set of traditions and cultures, whereas the latter is seen as a challenge to those beliefs. In actuality, such a duality closes itself off from the possibility of the gendered subaltern self-representation. From an analytical historical perspective, Bangladesh is a deeply segmented society with a long colonial history and a recent postcolonial nation-building process concerned with national identity and national consciousness. The result is not a homogenized or uniform cultural and political self-representation but rather a long dialectical tension between multilayered worldviews with political and ideological manifestations. This is not to say that tradition and modernity are wholly dichotomous. Rather, as Nasrin's case reveals, it is the continuity of the patriarchal relations in the context of both traditional and modernist discourse that creates the problem of gendered self-representation. My goal is to explore the relationship between Nasrin's writings and the fundamentalist response to them as contested rather than given.

This article consists of three sections. The first explains the position of women in the context of Islam and colonial modernity. The second deals with nationalist discourse as an outcome of colonial modernity and how it handles women's issues. I will argue that the nationalist discourse has subsumed women's separate space with its totalizing explanation of na-

---

[1] *Islamic fundamentalism* is a vague term, a catchphrase to denote the militant ideology of the contemporary Islamist movement. For lack of a better term, in the context of Bangladesh, I use the term *Islamic fundamentalism* to delineate a political movement whose intellectual and moral stand derives from an unchanging, divine Islamic text—the Quran and hadith. It calls for a reaffirmation of the fundamental elements of the Islamic faith and political mission. I use Islamic fundamentalism, then, in this article to imply the reaffirmation of foundational principles of Islam and the effort to reshape society in terms of those reaffirmed principles. At the same time, it needs to be kept in mind that fundamental differences—political, cultural, and historical—exist within the various Islamic fundamentalist movements throughout the world. The term *subaltern* has its origin in Gramsci's writings. To Gramsci, the subaltern categories include those social categories that lack hegemony or do not possess their own hegemonic positions and are subject to the hegemony of other social classes. See Gramsci 1971; and Alam 1993b.

tional independence and national liberation. The final section is an analysis of Nasrin's works. I will argue that Nasrin's writings represent the issue of gendered self-representation in an era when it has been denied by both Islamic fundamentalists and the modernizing nation-state.

Islam, colonial modernity, and women[2]

Since Iran's Islamic revolution in 1979, a new political discourse has entered the world political scene. This is Islamic fundamentalism's challenge to total Western economic, political, and cultural domination. From the Middle East to South Asia and the Far East, in many Muslim countries today a new mass movement has emerged that articulates Islamic religious traditions and practices. By rejecting Western modernity as false and alien discourse, Islamic fundamentalism has managed to posit the problem in terms of a historically sedimented antagonism—the modern West versus Islam. This antagonism, which Samuel Huntington (1993) incorrectly and in a highly orientalist tone describes as a "clash of civilization," has many layers that manifest themselves in various ways: reason versus dogma, democracy versus despotism, civilization versus barbarism, modernism versus tradition. In this section, I go beyond this dichotomy by locating this antagonism historically. The perceived antagonism between the modern West and Islamic fundamentalism is not the expression of an eternal conflict between two separate and irreconcilable worlds but, rather, is quite recent and must be seen as a contested terrain. More specifically, I hope to prove that, by historicizing the conflict in contemporary Bangladesh, the antagonism between modernity and Islam is displaced in the context of gendered self-representation. First, I will explain the historical growth of Islam in present-day Bangladesh. For this purpose, I use Sami Zubaida's (1989, 45) notion of *historical specificity*.

Historical specificity shows how, for any specific situation, a series of historical conjunctures leads to a distinctive configuration of a historical outcome. This historical specificity contrasts with the cultural essentialist position, which argues that inherent and continuous cultural elements need to be taken into account to specify a particular historical context. The other side of this cultural essentialist position is what Edward Said (1979) calls *orientalism*. An orientalist and essentialist position views the rise of Islamic fundamentalism as a historically sedimented antagonism between the West and Islam. This antagonism, however, is not the result of a clash of two distinct cultural essences but, rather, the result of various layers

---

[2] Various parts of this section appeared in Alam 1993a.

of historical and political logic configured to provide a distinct political discourse. In the context of contemporary Bangladesh, this configuration means that Islam is used for political and ideological purposes that emanate from a specific idea of Islam articulated in the context of contemporary Bangladesh.

Bengali Islam, as in many parts of the Muslim world, and as Clifford Geertz (1971) pointed out in the context of Indonesian Islam, has adopted numerous forms of many earlier religious traditions and has assimilated values and symbols not always in conformity with Quranic ideals and principles. The ideals of Islam in the context of Bengal underwent rapid transformation by the assimilation of the pre-Islamic past and gave birth to a set of popular beliefs and practices that became known as *Bengali Islam.* This assimilation, which Asim Roy (1983) calls *syncretistic tradition,* was challenged by the Islamic purist, which, in a way, appears to be a response to the idea of modernity imposed by colonialism and to the Hindu response to it.

This syncretistic tradition did not go unchallenged. Various fundamentalist reformist movements sprang up in Bengal to "purify the idolatrous heresy of the Muslims" (Ahmed 1981, 75). The reformist fundamentalist response to the syncretistic tradition in Bengali Islam was initiated primarily by two movements: the *Faraizi* movement, founded by Haji Shariatullah (1779–1840) of Faridpur in eastern Bengal, and the *Tariqui Mahummadiya* movement of Shah Sayyid Ahmed (1786–1831). They both belonged to the tradition of the *Waliullah* movement of Delhi and may have had some connection with the *Wahhabi* tradition of Saudi Arabia. The main thrust of their ideas was a renewed emphasis on *tauhid* (the unity of God); adherence to the right of the individual to interpret the Quran and hadith; opposition to all forms of polytheistic associations, including reference to the *pir* (Islamic holy man); and an earnest endeavor to remove all traces of animistic and Hindu beliefs and practices from Muslim society. This campaign of Islamization in the overall context of Bengali Islam led to a very limited imposition of the fundamentalist conception of the *Shariah* (Islamic principles) (Ahmed 1981, 75). It nonetheless provided a conflict of identity between the Bengali and the Muslim, which in Bengali political culture has often been formulated as two opposite poles. This identity quest of Bengali Muslims has been an oscillation between the two poles, which continues even now in Bangladesh. The British colonial invasion further complicated the identity of Bengali Muslims. Under British rule, there were three different scenarios: an all-India-based Islam, the uniqueness of Bengali Islam, and the nature of response to colonial modernity by the Muslims who called for a reinterpretation of Islam to accommodate colonial modernity. The response to colonial modernity transformed the entire Muslim community and was riddled with confrontation as well as accommodation.[3] The politics of Islamic fundamentalism and its relation to women's rights in contemporary Bangladesh should be understood in the context of these scenarios.

Most contemporary interpretations of women in Islamic societies argue two sides. First, conservatives and fundamentalists, by using the Quran, hadith, and life histories of Muslim women in early Islam, confirm and legitimize women's subordination and subjugation. Second, many feminists argue for gender equality under Islam, citing the egalitarianism of early Islam (Kandiyoti 1991, 10). This problem of interpretation is further complicated by the issue of heterogeneity within Islamic discourse, that is, the differences between Bengali Islam and the African tradition of Islam that have important interpretative implications for Islam and gender equality. In the context of contemporary Bangladesh, I will go beyond the two interpretations and focus instead on the issue of the *fatwa* that Islamic fundamentalist forces are using against women. By so doing, I hope to clarify the connection between Islamic fundamentalism and women in Bangladesh, because both fundamentalist and modernist traditions of Islam in Bangladesh are using the *fatwa* as a tool to subjugate and subordinate women.

According to the Islamic text, *fatwa* stands for a decree or a formal legal judgment based on the Quran and hadith (Netton 1992, 82). In other words, the main objective of a *fatwa* should be the interpretation of Islam and the identification of the rules and regulations on the basis of such interpretation that follows closely the textual source of Islam. "A fatwa normally takes the form of a *responsa,* a dispensation, a practical solution, a way out, addressed to the problems, paradoxes, anomalies and puzzles that life throws up constantly in the face of the faithful" (al-Azm 1993, 27). The person who can issue a *fatwa* is known as a mufti. A mufti constitutes a living bridge from a pure Islamic jurisprudence to everyday Islamic life. A mufti should be well versed in Islamic theology and jurisprudence. During the classical period of Islam, a mufti who could issue a *fatwa* was also a chief prosecutor appointed by the ruler. Here, a *fatwa* enjoys legitimacy.

In present-day Bangladesh, *fatwa* has become the most important tool for Islamic fundamentalism in politics. On June 5, 1994, the Bengali daily *Ajkar Kgoj* wrote that until mid-1994, five hundred cases of *fatwa* were reported and fifty women were killed as a result of these *fatwas. Dainik Janakanta,* another popular Bengali daily, reported additional cases of *fatwa* in September, November, and December 1995. In almost every case,

---

[3] For a detailed discussion, see Alam 1993a.

the *fatwa* was used exclusively against poor rural women who sought to obtain outside employment, to borrow money from banks to start small businesses, or to send their daughters to schools run by nongovernmental organizations (NGOs) — in other words, women who strove to be economically independent.

To illustrate the connection between antiwomen *fatwas* and Islamic fundamentalism in Bangladesh, I focus on one well-known case: that of Nurjahan Begum, daughter of a poor landless peasant from Jhatakjara village in the district of Sylthet, northeastern Bangladesh. In 1989, at the age of seventeen, she was married to a much older man. He was mentally unstable, chronically unemployed, and unable to support either himself or his wife. Eventually he left Nurjahan, and she moved home with her parents. A few months later, her father formally obtained a divorce from her husband, and she was married to Muthalab. After Nurjahan's second marriage, local mullahs who were involved in fundamentalist politics became interested in her case. They included the Imam (in this context, one who leads a prayer) of the local mosque, Maulana Mannan, and the local sirdar (chief), Munier. On January 10, 1993, they convened a *salish* (religious court) and issued a *fatwa* that Nurjahan's second marriage was *najayaj* (illegal), since she had not obtained a formal divorce from her first husband. The sexual union between Nurjahan and her second husband was "un-Islamic," and they were accused of committing adultery, thus violating the Islamic code of ethics. (It was later discovered that Maulana Mannan wanted to marry Nurjahan, but her father had rejected that proposal, and that Nurjahan's second husband, Muthalab, had a long feud with Munier.) During the *salish* procedure, when Nurjahan's second husband and her father produced the divorce document, Maulana Mannan and others called it a hoax. So the *fatwa* decreed that Nurjahan and Muthalab be buried waist deep and that 101 stones be thrown at them. Her parents also received fifty lashes each for their "sin." After the trial, the ashamed Nurjahan went home and committed suicide by drinking insecticide. Following her death, the Maulana issued yet another *fatwa* that said Nurjahan should not be given an Islamic burial since she had committed suicide. This case of *fatwa* was widely publicized in newspapers in Bangladesh, and eventually Maulana Mannan, Munier, and others were arrested and given jail sentences.

During this period, *fatwas* were being issued mostly against women.[4]

---

[4] *Fatwas* were issued against the various NGOs as well. Those organizations have been "accused" of educating women and helping them find alternative employment outside the home. It seems that the Islamic fundamentalist wrath against NGOs is precisely for this reason. See *Dainik Janakanta* 1994; and *Weekly Bichitra* 1994.

This particular fact warrants explanation because it is related to overall fundamentalist politics in Bangladesh. There are two broad levels on which Islam intersects with society that consequently affect gender relations in Bangladesh: first, the role of Islam in gender construction at the level of culture, and second, the role of the state wherein Islam could reinforce or thwart the Islam-based cultural construction of gender. These two domains are not separate but intersect on specific social and political conjunctures. In Bangladesh, at the level of culture, Islam informs the conception of sexuality, marriage, the family, the work site, and so on. From a fundamentalist point of view, these aspects of everyday life are self-evident and are always taken for granted; they are rarely subjected to challenge, negotiation, or transformation. That having been said, it needs to be mentioned that the cultural construction of gender relations is not homogenous. In Bangladesh, the modalities of the cultural construction of gender are constantly challenged and transformed by socioeconomic realities such as women's education, employment, political participation, and so on. In fundamentalist Islam, because of the strict adherence to the text, these socioeconomic realities do not permit any transformation of the modalities of the cultural construction of gender relations. For example, in Sathkira district, northwestern Bangladesh, a young woman committed suicide after she was given 101 lashes in public after a village mullah issued a *fatwa*. Her crime was that she had collected shrimp from the river and sold them in the market, thus violating sexual segregation. Hundreds of girls' schools were burned after mullahs issued *fatwas* to the effect that sending girls to school instead of to *madrasha* (religious schools) was an un-Islamic act. Delware Hussain Saidi, a top-ranking JI leader whose cassettes of speeches are readily available throughout rural Bangladesh, said in one of his speeches that when a woman works alongside her male colleagues, men will lose interest in her, because men are not interested in those women who are readily available (Begum 1994, 11). This particular argument by Saidi touches on another aspect of the Islam-based cultural construction of gender relations in Bangladesh: sexuality and sexual domination. The case of Nurjahan Begum, described above, is an example. Another such case is that of Bilkis of Dhamsar village in Brahamanbaria district, northeastern Bangladesh. Bilkis, twelve years old in 1993 and the daughter of a poor peasant, was raped and impregnated by Azizul, nineteen, from the same village. Initially Azizul confessed to the crime and agreed to marry Bilkis, but when the news of her pregnancy became public, Azizul retracted his confession. Since there was no witness to listen to Bilkis's plea, a *salish* was convened, and the *salish* judge, Maulana Fazlul Haq, issued a *fatwa* giving Bilkis 101 lashes for committing the un-Islamic act of premarital sex. (This story, however, has a happy ending. Hearing of Bilkis's plight, Bangladesh Mahila Parishad, a woman's advocacy group from Dhaka, became involved. Their representative discussed the matter with local law enforcement officials, and Bilkis was rescued three days before the lashing. *Dainik Janakanta* reported that on July 13, 1994, Bilkis became the mother of a boy and was living in a women's shelter in Dhaka.)

The second level, the relationship between the state and Islam, is more complicated and temporal. In Bangladesh, this relationship went through several distinct phases based on configurations of various political forces.[5] Without going through a detailed discussion, it could be argued that from 1971 to 1975, the ruling Awami League (AL) advocated the idea of secularism as state policy to make a separation between Islam and the state. During the two phases of military rule (1975–81 and 1981–90), Bangladesh was regarded as "the Islamic republic." The previous government of Khaleda Zia followed the military government's path regarding the relationship between Islam and the state. The present AL government of Hasina Wazed has not indicated, as yet, a return to its pre-1975 phase of secularism. In this contested relationship between the state and religion, Islam nonetheless played a crucial role in formulating state policy that directly affects women. One of these policy areas is Bangladesh family law. Inun Nahar (1993) argued that the Bangladesh family law is inherently discriminatory toward women. For example, marriage is essential in the Islamic family code, and it is the basis for the Bangladesh family code as well. According to this code, the legal age of marriage for women and men is eighteen and twenty-one, respectively. In practice, the age of marriageability for a woman is determined by age of puberty and first menstruation, which is typically at about age eleven or twelve years in Bangladesh. In rural Bangladesh, where most Bangladeshi live, this represents a contradiction.

Although women participate equally in economic activities, their work is systematically undervalued since that participation is mostly in food processing and domestic activities. Nahar (1993, 104) calls it a persistence of patriarchy that has direct bearing on the marriage age for young women. An unmarried woman is regarded in her father's family as a burden, and marrying her off as soon as possible is seen as a relief, economically and socially. This is further compounded by the idea of "body culture" in Bangladesh (Nahar 1993, 108). In folk culture, tales, stories, and fables, mostly in the oral tradition, always romanticize the physical purity of the female body. Numerous tales of heroic women killing themselves rather

[5] For a detailed account of these phases, see Alam 1993a, 1995.

than succumbing to sexual assault are very much a part of Bangladeshi folk culture. Thus, when a girl attains puberty, her parents immediately begin to suffer from a social anxiety about how to save their daughter's purity so that she can be regarded as a marriageable "good girl." This can be ensured by marrying daughters off as soon as possible.

Another case of state policy discriminating against women is the process of marriage registration. According to the 1974 Muslim Marriage and Divorce Code, unregistered marriages conducted only by a Maulana are regarded as valid. Because of the lack of adequate marriage registration offices (*kazi office*) and the marriage fees since mandated, many marriages in rural and poor households remain officially unregistered and are performed only by a Maulana. This practice discriminates against women because when there is a problem in the marriage and issues of divorce settlement (child support, alimony, and property sharing) arise, women are often denied equality. In many cases of *fatwa*, marriages and divorces have been declared illegal because they were not duly registered. Furthermore, as Nahar (1993, 109) points out, in many instances, because of distance and transportation problems in getting to the marriage office, many poor rural people have no other option than to seek a Maulana's help for religious approval of the marriage.

These two cases illustrate how a state policy formulated against the backdrop of religious cultural ethos has proved to be discriminatory against women of Bangladesh. This also occurs in the context in which the relationships between fundamentalist Islam and women in general, and between *fatwa* and individual women, could be understood. I turn now to the Islamist modernist interpretation of women.

As I have argued, Islamic modernism in South Asia was a response to British colonialism in the Islamic countries. Its goal was to find a way to accommodate traditional Islamic principles within Western modernity. Toward this end, Sir Sayyed Ahmad Khan, a modernist Muslim, in 1873 established the Anglo-Oriental College in Aligarh, an event that, to many, marks the beginning of Islamic modernism in India. Aligarh modernism influenced a group of Bengali Muslims, among them the landlord Nawab Abdul Latif (1828–95) and the first Muslim barrister, Sayed Amir Ali (1849–1929). They were from the Muslim aristocratic class of Bengal, the first to embrace Western modernity. Soon, a change in Bengal's rural economy allowed the cultivating peasants, known as *jotedars* (landholders), and other ordinary Bengali Muslims to send their sons for higher education (Mukherjee 1973, 404–5). This opportunity arose when the British colonial state, observing the difficulties that the zamindars (landlords) were experiencing in collecting rent from rebellious peasants, and intending to bring the rural economy of Bengal under the domain of British industrial capital, passed various land acts in 1859, 1868, and 1885 that recognized the rights of tenant cultivators (Turner 1984, 197). This legislation created a peasant cultivating class of *jotedars,* distinct from the zamindars created by the Permanent Settlement Act of 1773. About this time the demand for cash crops, especially jute, rose significantly, which improved the economic situation of the *jotedars,* who were largely Muslims, allowing them to send their sons to higher schools and to invest in urban businesses (Mukherjee 1973, 405). A large number of *jotedar* families forged links with the urban middle class. They became teachers, professors, lawyers, doctors, businessmen, civil officials, clerks, and so on (405).

The woman's position, however, did not change with this major societal transformation. Khan urged Indian Muslims to learn English and secure jobs in the colonial government, yet he remained adamantly opposed to women's education outside of the religious traditions. He believed that the colonial state had no business tinkering with the *Shariah,* particularly as it affected the structure of the family, and that education for women had to begin and end within the secure walls of the domestic arena. In 1882, Khan confessed, however, that the general state of female education in India was not good (Jalal 1991, 81). According to Khan, "there could be no satisfactory education . . . for Muhammadan females until a large number of Muhammadan males had received a sound education" (Khan, as quoted by Jalal 1991, 81). In other words, the education of young Muslim men should be the priority, and the education of women must be adjusted to the ratio and class distribution of educated men. Female education would be provided by well-supervised private schools rather than by government-run schools (Ahmed 1967, 74). These opinions were consistent with Khan's opposition to bringing women out of purdah (institutionalized seclusion), an integral feature of Muslim life. To Khan, purdah symbolized the Indian Muslim's identity and the integrity of the community as a whole. Limiting women's education to domestic chores and religious teachings insulated them from the corrupting influences of the public realm. It strengthened Muslim cultural resistance against both colonialism and Hinduism. Among these Muslim modernists, the idea of Muslim nationalism began to take root where a separate Bengali national identity, based on syncretistic tradition, was considered un-Islamic.

Nationalism and the woman question

The question of nationalism has always been a thorny political issue in Bangladesh. Indeed, the liberation war of 1971 was fought over the issue of Bengali national identity. This identity, however, is itself unclear and problematic because of historical, political, and ideological conjunctures that shape the very question of nationalism. During British colonial rule, the Bengali Muslim identity vacillated between purist Islamic and Bengali identity, where syncretistic tradition was given prominence. During Pakistani colonial rule (1947–71), this syncretistic tradition of Bengali identity was systematically undermined, since the Pakistani ruling forces used the universalistic idea of "unity under Islam" and "we are *all* Muslims" as a source of national integration in state formation endeavors. During this period, the modernist secular tradition of Bengali identity was considered counter to that of the Islamic Republic of Pakistan.

After the independence of Bangladesh in 1971, the AL became the ruling party, and its official discourse on nationalism was equated with the state-building process along with other modernist principles such as secularism, socialism, and democracy (Alam 1993a, 95). After the demise of the AL regime in 1975 and the ascendance of the military, Bengali identity was contrasted and defined in opposition to Bangladeshi nationalism to make a rupture from its secular syncretistic tradition, uphold the Islamic content of "Bengaliness," and distinguish it from Bengali Hindus in West Bengal, with whom Bengali Muslims share common linguistic, literary, and cultural heritage.

With all these turns and twists in the history of nationalism in Bangladesh, one pattern is quite apparent: a woman's identity is always subsumed within the idea of the *national,* meaning a gender neutrality in the construction of the concept of nation that emphasizes the collective national entity. In other words, a separate space for women was denied in the collectivist notion of national identity and national liberation. How could this be explained? The answer to this vital question lies in the common history of modernity and nationalism in post-Enlightenment Europe and its export to third world societies, especially in South Asia.

It is well known that the idea of national consciousness coincided with the emergence of European modernity (Chatterjee 1986). Nationalism shares the historical premises and promises of the Enlightenment, which include the idea of progress, democracy, and industrialization (15). Liberal-rationalist premises of modernity also underlie the idea of nationalism. Nationalism became attached to the bourgeois conception of knowledge established in the post-Enlightenment period of European intellectual history. Nationalism becomes viable when it agrees to be modern in its epistemic foundation. To understand this vitally important issue, the concept of modernity itself needs to be understood.

Without going through a detailed discussion of modernity, which is beyond the scope of this article, I use Jean Baudrillard's definition of modernity. "[Modernity] is a continual progress of the sciences and of techniques, the rational division of industrial work, [which] introduces into social life a dimension of permanent change, of destruction of customs and traditional culture" (Baudrillard 1987, 65). Thus, modernity is the epistemological project of elevating reason to an ontological status. In this way, modernity becomes synonymous with the civilizing process encompassing the entire globe. Here, *reason* is universalized as the basis for a model of industrial, cultural, and social progress. In short, totality, reason, and universality are the core constructs of modernity.

Partha Chatterjee argues that the realities of colonial power in India render the question of nationalism totally opposed to colonial rule or, conversely, affirm it with patriotic zeal. This leads to middle-class elitism, which ultimately restores the utopian and romantic version of nationalism that undercuts the existing political reality (Chatterjee 1993, 105). It is well known that Gandhi and his politics of nationalism were influenced by the writings of antimodern thinkers such as Ruskin and Tolstoy. Nehru, by contrast, adopted the idea of an "Indian state" and used it in the construction of the modern nation-state.

I have argued that nationalism in third world societies was a response to colonialism and that colonial rule was fashioned by the ideals of modernity. In South Asia, this relationship between modernity (read as colonial modernity), with its emphasis on totality, reason, and universality, and nationalism subsumed the question of women.

Chatterjee (1993) has argued that during the early and mid-eighteenth century, women's issues were at the forefront of modernizing social reform and were voiced by many nationalists. The campaigns against the practice of immolating widows, the legalization of widow marriage, and the abolition of child marriage were all seen as resulting from the forces of modernity and nationalism. But at the end of the nineteenth century, these concerns all but disappeared from social discourse. According to Chatterjee (1993, 117), this shift was the result of the nationalist leaders' ability to situate the woman question "in an inner domain of sovereignty, far removed from the arena of political contest with the colonial state." This inner domain of national culture was articulated by the discovery of tradition. Thus, Chatterjee (117) believes the nationalist discourse carries with it the material/spiritual split that corresponds to the ideological dichotomies of two social spaces—outer (*bahir*) and home (*ghar*). The outside world is conceived of as unimportant, external, and the domain of the material world governed by Western rationality. The inner world, by contrast, represents the true spiritual self, untouched by profane activities, with women as its true representatives (Chatterjee 1993, 120). This dichotomy as applied to the issue of women was not a rejection of modernity by the nationalist leaders but an attempt to make modernity consistent with the nationalist project. This dichotomy was also the central principle through which the nationalists resolved the woman question with nationalism's own historical project, making the social construction of the *new woman* central to nationalism's discourse. At the same time, this discourse attempts to reconcile the modernist ideals of equality and liberty by upholding the inherent superiority of the spiritual — that is, the inner — domain of Indian culture. This discourse was particularly relevant to women from the educated middle class, *bhadralok* (respectable men), an important social category of both late colonial and postcolonial South Asian societies. Enormous emphasis was given to the formal education of women. Education was regarded as a means of enhancing the social presence of Bengali women. Western education was seen as essential to the creation of a *bhadramahila* (respectable woman) (Borthwick 1984). Historically, it was Bengali Hindus who adopted English education, but eventually Muslim men, and later women, even from the conservative landed class, began to receive formal education.

One of the pioneers of formal education for Bengali Muslim women was Begum Rokeya Sakhawat Hossain (1880–1932). Born into a landed family in the Rangpur district of East Bengal, Begum Rokeya, as she was commonly known, argued that lack of education was the main cause of female degradation in Bengal. In order to promote education among Bengali Muslim women, she established the Sakhawat Memorial School in Calcutta in 1911 in the name of her deceased husband. Her call to educate Bengali Muslim women was wholeheartedly supported by men and women alike, even by the British colonial authority. However, this emphasis on education for women did not alter the assumption that women were to stay at home, an idea the modernist nationalist leaders were eager to maintain. Indeed, as Ghulam Murshid (1983, 56) explains, "The overwhelming majority of newly educated women, like their male counterparts, considered that the chief aims of female education were to get educated and well-placed bridegrooms and to produce better wives." Even Begum Rokeya argued that women's lack of education makes them unprepared for domestic activities and can make for an unhappy husband-wife relationship.

> Girls are not given such an education as will make them worthy companions of their husbands. Consequently, a highly educated husband has to live with a wife who has received only an elementary education.

In such cases, when the husband calculates the distance between a star and the sun, the wife measures the length and breadth of the pillow case (in order to sew it). While the husband, in his imagination, moves in the far-away solar system surrounded by innumerable heavenly bodies . . . and finds the motion of a comet, the wife moves in her kitchen, measures rice and lentils and watches the movements of the cook. Hello, Mr. Astronomer? Why isn't your wife by your side? Are you afraid that you might vanish in the intense heat of the Sun, if you want to approach it along with your wife? Is it because of this that you think she should stay in? (Begum Rokeya, as quoted by Murshid 1983, 56–57)

Thus, Western education (read modernity) for women was to make them good wives and mothers, to teach them to run their households (*ghar*) according to the new physical and economic conditions of the modern world. For this they also needed to have knowledge about the outside world. They might even be allowed into the outside world as long as it did not threaten their femininity and interfere with their womanly responsibilities. This nationalist construction of the *new woman* continues today in postcolonial Bangladesh.

Immediately after the physical withdrawal of the Pakistani colonial army in 1971, the state formation processes in Bangladesh started in earnest. The ideals through which the nationalist struggle was fought formally entered into the official hegemonic discourse, the constitution. Section 8, part 2, of the constitution, titled "Fundamental Principles of State Policy," argues the following: "The principles of nationalism, socialism, democracy and secularism . . . shall constitute the fundamental principles of State policy" (Government of Bangladesh 1972, 5). The idea of nationalism was defined in the constitution in the following way: "The unity and solidarity of the Bangalee nation, which, deriving its identity from its language and culture, attained a sovereign and independent Bangladesh through a united and determined struggle in the war of independence, shall be the basis of Bangalee nationalism" (5). On the issue of equality, the constitution argued that "it shall be a fundamental responsibility of the State to emancipate the toiling masses — the peasant and workers — and backward section of the people from all forms of exploitation" (5).

The issue of women appears in the constitution in part 3, "Fundamental Rights," subsection 2 of section 28: "Women shall have equal rights with men in all spheres of the State and of public life" (10). The constitution of 1972 was, not quite surprisingly, a modernist document. All the basic principles of liberal democracy, especially its British version, were very pronounced in the document. Part of the reason was that the main experts of the constitution-making process were trained in England, the most important of them being Kamal Hossain, a British-trained barrister, who later became the first foreign minister of Bangladesh.

One way to identify the subsumption of the woman issue within the totalistic discourse of nationalism, and the construction of the *new woman* in the early phase of postcolonial Bangladesh, was the social construction of *birangana* (courageous female warrior). This construction is related somewhat to the idea of the *new women* that Chatterjee (1993) discusses in the context of colonial Bengal. The *biranganas* are the thousands of women raped by the Pakistani colonial army during the civil war of 1971. In a country such as Bangladesh, where gender relations are organized through patriarchal relations, a woman who has been raped is seen as "damaged goods." Rape means dishonor and humiliation for the family and makes it virtually impossible for the victims to marry. Knowing very well the state's dilemma and inability to change the patriarchal stigma attached to rape, the postcolonial state of Bangladesh attempted to resolve the issue with nationalistic fervor. Identifying rape victims as *biranganas* supposedly gave them the same status as male *mukti bahini* (freedom fighters) in the official discourse. Sheikh Mujibur Rehaman, "the father of the nation" and the first prime minister, declared rape victims to be *biranganas* and encouraged young men to marry them. This idea, however, created much uproar and amusement when Bengali men began to demand that two adult sons of Sheikh Mujibur — Sheikh Kamal and Sheikh Jamal — should marry two *biranganas*.

After the overthrow of the AL regime by the military in 1975, a total reversal of the nationalist discourse in Bangladesh took place. Here the Islamic identity of "Bengaliness" was emphasized. Accordingly, two phases of military rule, the Zia regime and the Ershad regime, were unified in declaring Islam as the principal ideological discourse of the state.

However, the presence of Islam in nationalist projects became most visible during the military rule of General Ershad. Ershad, at a *Seerat* (Prophet Mohammad's way) conference in Dhaka on February 12, 1984, declared, "Islam is our ideal and it is the only way to our emancipation. The existence of the country will be at stake if we fail to establish Islam in Bangladesh. We the nine crore Muslim will certainly speak about Islam, think about Islam and dream about Islam. This is our only way for emancipation" (Ershad, as quoted by Osmani 1992, 130). In his speech at Sharshina, Barisal, in southern Bangladesh on March 13, 1988, Ershad declared that the head of state in Bangladesh is the Imam and he as the head of state is aware of his responsibilities as Imam (*South Asia Bulletin* 1988, 116). On June 10, 1988, Ershad argued that laws contrary to the Quran and Sunna (Prophet Mohammad's words) would not be enforced in Bangladesh.

In this spirit, on June 7, 1988, a constitutional amendment was drafted to declare Islam the state religion of Bangladesh (Kamaluddin 1988, 15). Commenting on this amendment, the general argued that after making Islam the state religion, the people had received a distinct identity in culture, language, geographical entity, independent sovereignty, and other spheres of nationalism (*South Asia Bulletin* 1988, 117).

The different trajectory of nationalism in postcolonial Bangladesh shares an important commonality: the integration of women into a postcolonial and modern nationhood, explainable in terms of citizens in a sovereign nation-state, differs from that of men. For example, in late 1988, after Ershad declared Bangladesh an Islamic republic, *Naripokho* (Women's Side), the pioneer feminist organization in Bangladesh, sued the state on behalf of a few individual women, saying that it discriminated against women and threatened the rights of women guaranteed by the constitution, because according to Islamic jurisprudence, women cannot become heads of state. In 1992, Bangladesh Nationalist Party (BNP) chief Khaleda Zia became the first female prime minister in Bangladesh. *Islamic Okiyo Jote*, an Islamic fundamentalist organization, reacted to her election by issuing a leaflet arguing that the head of an Islamic country is an Imam and enjoys similar status to one who leads a *namaj* (prayer). According to the *Shariah*, the title of Imamate — one who is an Imam — is unsuitable for women.

It is clear that the two trajectories of nationalism (secularized Bengali nationalism and "Islamized" Bangladeshi nationalism) do not view women outside the domain of nationalism, and women as agents are subsumed under the discourse of a modernizing nation-state. This is a homogenous and totalistic conception of nationalism that Homi Bhabha (1990) criticizes. Bhabha, by quoting Said and distancing himself from locating third world nationalism's all-inclusive totalistic discourse that failed to theorize women's oppression in a specific historical-cultural context, reads nation and nationalism in a way that has implications for Bangladesh: "[Nationalism is] an agency of ambivalent narration that holds culture at its most productive position, as a force for subordination, fracturing, diffusing, reproducing, as much as producing, creating, forcing, guiding" (Said, as quoted by Bhabha 1990, 4). An obvious question arises in this context. In a modernizing state where citizens' rights (women included) are constitutionally guaranteed, how is it that women's rights are being constantly violated and challenged? How is this contradictory situation to be explained?

In this context, B. S. Walby's (1990) distinction between private and public patriarchy and R. W. Connell's (1990) idea of *gender regime* are important constructs. According to Walby, patriarchy is multidimensional. Private patriarchy means the exclusion of women from public life, confining them to households and domestic jobs, whereas public patriarchy encourages and requires women to participate in employment outside the home, especially in government-sponsored developmental activities. Yet women are still subordinate within the male-dominated state structure. This dichotomy is problematic, because in many third world countries the private domain is in fact thoroughly penetrated and structured by the state, that is, the public domain. Following Connell (1990), this problem can be avoided by identifying the postcolonial state in terms of a *gender regime,* meaning that the state is centrally implicated in gender relations organized through the patriarchal ideology where women as agents are constantly subsumed by the discourse of nation and state. This subsumption is in no way complete and total; it is essentially a process of *contestation* that continually remakes itself. How can women in this process express their identities and political concerns outside the realm of the state? I turn now to this issue by arguing the case of Nasrin of Bangladesh.

Writing as subversion and gendered self-representation[6]

In early 1994, under pressure from Amnesty International, a human rights organization, and numerous well-known writers such as Allen Ginsberg, Gunter Grass, John Irving, Norman Mailer, Amy Tan, Mario Vargas Llosa, Milan Kundera, and, of course, Salman Rushdie, the Khaleda Zia government returned Nasrin's passport, which had been confiscated in early 1993 when *Lajja* was published.[7] While visiting Calcutta in May 1994, Nasrin was quoted by an Indian newspaper, the *Statesman,* as saying that the "Quran should be revised thoroughly." Nasrin immediately denied making such a statement, noting that she argued for change in the *Shariah,* not the

---

[6] Between 1989 and 1994, Nasrin published about nineteen books, including poems, short stories, novels, and newspaper columns that were eventually published as books. A list of Nasrin's books cited in this article appears in the reference list. For a complete list of Nasrin's works, see Riaz 1995, 22. Few of Nasrin's books have been translated into English. They include Wright et al.'s translation of *Shobo bibbaho* (Nasrin 1992c) and various of her poems published as *The Game in Reverse: Poems and Essays* (Nasrin 1995).

[7] In a speech given at the National Press Club in Washington, D.C., in January 1996, while promoting his latest book, *The Moor's Last Sigh,* Rushdie reiterated his support for Nasrin. He argued that the debate over whether Nasrin is a good or bad writer misses the real issue, which is that a *fatwa* against any writer is unacceptable.

Quran, and that the *Statesman* reporter had confused the two issues. "I [described] the Quran, the Vedas, and the Bible and all such religious texts determining the lives of their followers as 'out of place and out of time.' We crossed that social historical context in which these were written and therefore we should not be guided by their precepts; the question of revising thoroughly or otherwise is irrelevant. We have to move beyond these ancient texts if we want to progress. In order to respond to our spiritual needs let humanism be our new faith" (Nasrin, as quoted in Riaz 1995, 23).

In a letter to the speaker of the *Jatia Parishad* (National Assembly) in Parliament, Nasrin wrote, "I want a revised *Shariah* law, meaning a modern uniform civil code replacing the Muslim family law, in which the equality of rights of both sexes can be ensured" (Anderson 1994, 15). This denial produced very few results. A Muslim leader in Khulna, thirty miles southwest of Dhaka, offered US$2,500 cash for her assassination. The Khaleda Zia government intervened and on June 4, 1994, issued a warrant for her arrest, charging her with "deliberate and malicious intention of outraging the feelings of Muslims" (Weiner 1994, 6). Nasrin was warned by a friend before the warrant was issued and went into hiding. Meanwhile, German foreign minister Klaus Kinkel said on July 19, 1994, that European Union countries had instructed their ambassadors in Dhaka to make the necessary arrangements if Nasrin asked for protection and political asylum (Weiner 1994, 6). On August 3, one day before the expiration of her arrest warrant would have rendered her a fugitive, Nasrin appeared before the Dhaka High Court. She was immediately granted bail with freedom to travel. Finally, on August 9, as a guest of the PEN of Sweden, a writers' organization, she arrived in Stockholm to start her long exile.

Nasrin's case was well covered by the Western media. Almost every newspaper in Europe and America at one point or another published reports on her case. This is remarkable, because Bangladesh usually appears in the Western media only when there is a flood, a tornado, or mass starvation. Why such a change all of a sudden in covering Bangladesh? The answer to this question lies in the context of Islamic fundamentalism in general and Western response to it.

The rise of Islamic fundamentalism in the Muslim world is seen (incorrectly, as I argue here) as a conflict between democracy and totalitarianism, traditionalism, and modernism, and so on. Nasrin's case is seen as a resistance to the growing strength of Islamic fundamentalism in the Islamic world, and most important, this resistance is viewed automatically as an endorsement of Western liberal democracy and pluralism. This explains why not many attempts have been made to translate and analyze her works.

Often when her writings have been described, it has been in a manner of astonishingly simplistic caricature: "She advocates free sex and open marriage. A woman should be allowed to have as many as four husbands. . . . Religion is a great oppressor and should be abolished" (Anderson 1993, 3). Paul Gray described her in *Time* (1994, 26) as "Jane Austen she's not" and offered readers "Run Run," a rather weak poem by Nasrin, as a sample of all her writings: "When a dog is chasing you, be warned / That dog has rabies / When a man is chasing you, be warned / That man has syphilis."

I read Nasrin's text as a discourse of gendered self-representation, as an attempt by a woman to define herself. This representation, furthermore, involves subject constitution through subaltern narrative. More specifically, I view Nasrin's text as a critique of both nationalism/modernity and Islamic fundamentalism in Bangladesh vis-a-vis gendered self-representation.

Taken together, Nasrin's *Lajja* (Shame), published in February 1993, and *Fara* (Return) constitute a critique of nationalism and the postcolonial nation-state. *Lajja,* as mentioned earlier, depicts a fictionalized narrative of an actual rape and the torment of a Hindu minority family in Bangladesh after the destruction of the Babri mosque in Oudah, India, on December 6, 1992. The novel describes a Hindu family whose father, Sudhamoy Dutta, was a distinguished professor and physician. After the state of Pakistan was created on the basis of Islamic nationalism in 1947, Sudhamoy refused to go to India, where the majority are Hindus. The Pakistani non-Bengali ruling elite, through various state-building projects, tried to promote the idea of Pakistan as a state "for Muslims only." Sudhamoy, even in the wake of various *communal riots* (a South Asian term for riots between Muslims and Hindus), refused to go to India. Sudhamoy's son, Suranjan Dutta, an idealist like his father, was also influenced by the egalitarian thought of socialism. He too refused to accept the religion-based foundation of a nation-state. Using a variety of narrative events, Nasrin argues that the Dutta family, in their homeland, Bangladesh, remained *probashi*—alien. Suranjan was in love with Parveen, a Muslim woman, who, to avoid the social complications of marrying a Hindu man, married a Muslim. Then Suranjan dreamed of marrying a Hindu woman, Ratna. She too, for her own future security, ended up marrying a Muslim. Finally, in the wake of the anti-Hindu riots, Muslim fanatics kidnapped and raped Suranjan's only sister, Nilanjana. Suranjan tried unsuccessfully to get help from his Muslim friends to get his sister back. The following dialogue is between father and son:[8]

> Suranjan shouted, *"Baba* [Father], last night I wanted to tell you something. But I do not have the courage to say it. I know you will not keep it. But I am begging you. Leave, let us leave."
> "Where?" Sudhamoy inquired.
> "India."
> "India?" (Nasrin 1993b, 147)

Nasrin then describes the change in Sudhamoy:

> With great pain and sadness, Sudhamoy said, "Leave, Suranjan, let us leave!"
> Surprised, Suranjan asked, "Where, *baba?"*
> *Sudhamoy:* "India."
> Sudhamoy was ashamed, his voice trembled, as the mountain of commitments inside him crumbled. (150)

The night before the family left for India, Suranjan went to find a Muslim prostitute, Shamima Akthar; he brought her home and raped her. It was December 16, Victory Day, commemorating the day in 1971 when the Pakistani army surrendered and ushered in the creation of the state of Bangladesh. This event signifies the disintegration of the Islam-based state of Pakistan. Suranjan used to participate in these celebrations, but now Bangladesh was a foreign land to him and the act of raping a Bangladeshi Muslim woman indicated a rejection of all to which he had belonged.

Nasrin returns to the idea of dislocation created by the nation-state again in her book *Fara* (Return). She describes the friendship between two young women—Kalayni, a Hindu, and Sharifa, a Muslim. Kalayni was forced to leave East Pakistan (as Bangladesh was known between 1947 and 1971) for her own security and to go live with relatives in Calcutta, India. After twenty years, she returned to Mymensing, where she grew up, only to find a profound transformation. Islamic fundamentalism was in the hearts of small children, and people were rude to her because she was a Hindu. Kalayni could not find the place she left behind. This book, like *Lajja,* constitutes a powerful critique of nationalism in Bangladesh, in both colonial and postcolonial contexts. In *Fara,* Nasrin describes Kalayni's feelings in the following passage:

> Kalayni experienced all the anguish of partition. She understood why Harinaryan [Kalayni's father] had sighed. All the Urdu speakers were chased out of the land. The country is no longer a land for the Muslims, but for all Bengalis. Hindus had to leave with their bags packed. This country was created with the blood of three lakhs [three hundred thousand] Bengalis. Kalayni felt proud of the liberation war of

1971 that kicked out all the Pakistani, that made this country a Muslim homeland and made many people homeless, and proved that this country belongs to Bengalis not Muslims, here language is important, not religion. (Nasrin 1993a, 30–31)

The idea of Bengali nationalism is critiqued in the following terms:

In this country only the Razzakars [the Bengali paramilitia created by the Pakistani army during the liberation war of 1971] are doing well. Freedom fighters are starving to death. And those freedom fighters who are in good positions survived by compromising with the Razzakars. Fundamentalists are rising, who after the independence were hiding in holes, now they are coming out with the approval of various regimes. Now they are in the parliament. BNP won the election with their approval. Sheikh Mujib [Sheikh Mujibur Rehaman, the first prime minister] pardoned them and Zia [General Ziur Rehman], who put them in power, made them ministers. Sister, there is no difference between the present government [Khaleda Zia's government] and the *Jamaat*. (Nasrin 1993a, 66)

This theme of critique of nationalism is also apparent in Nasrin's nonfictional works. In her *Nirbachito column* (Selected column), she talks about the meaning of December 16, Victory Day, to her as a woman: "Everywhere there is celebration. The entire country danced with joy and happiness, a poor and wretched country of the Third World. On the cold and misty morning of December 16, I stand on the balcony and feel a cold snake crawling all over my body. . . . I burst into tears with the city's obscene celebration. Is there any one who can stop me and others like me, from crying? Where are the laws and reforms in this country? The war of liberation gave so many people so many things but what does it give women?" (Nasrin 1992a, 185).

For Nasrin, this feminist interrogation of nationalism in Bangladesh has a personal dimension. In 1971, when Nasrin was nine years old, the occupying Pakistani army destroyed her parent's home. Two of her uncles were killed, and her father, a physician, was tortured by Pakistani forces. After the liberation war everybody in her house and neighborhood was happy that it was finally over and that all the *mukti bahini* (freedom fighters) had returned. Nasrin recalled that her twenty-year-old aunt also returned home from the war without any fanfare or celebration. For the first time, Nasrin revealed in her *Nirbachito column* that her aunt had been raped in a *mukti bahini* camp for sixteen days by ten men. "Our society did not honor my aunt. All the big people talked with big words of the raped women in the newspaper and public meetings. They poked fun by calling them *biranganas* [brave female warriors]. Everybody accepts the inhuman torture, breaking, boots, bayonetings but never the incidents of rape. While political leaders shouted about the honor of mothers and sisters outside, my aunt hanged herself from the ceiling to save her honor from society, and the month was December" (Nasrin 1992a, 26).

In *Lajja* and *Fara*, Nasrin combines historical fiction with a subversive intent. Spivak argues this point while explaining Mahasweti Devi's fiction. "[Devi's] prose is beginning to blend into full-fledged 'historical fiction,' history imagined to fiction. The division between fact (historical event) and fiction (literary event) is operative in all these moves. Indeed, [Devi's] repeated claim to legitimacy is that she researches thoroughly everything she represents in fiction" (Spivak 1988, 244).

Seen from a counterhegemonic subaltern perspective, the imagination of an actual historical moment and happening becomes a work of both history and literature. "The writer (subaltern) acknowledges this by claiming to do research (my fiction is also historical). The historian might acknowledge this by looking at the mechanics of representation (my history is also fictive)" (Spivak 1988, 244). In an interview in a Calcutta newspaper, *Ajkal Kgoj* (1994), Nasrin said that in *Lajja* she had attempted to write a "factual novel" — that she got all the information about communal violence against Bangladeshi Hindus and Muslim men raping Hindu women from actual newspaper stories and then created the characters and fictionalized the narrative.[9] Nasrin describes the historical and fictional contents of *Lajja* in the following way:

> I saw the communal terrorism of December [1992] with my own eyes. *Lajja* is not a product of my sudden emotions, but the story of the defeat of all of us. *Lajja* is every one's sadness. . . . Human "Suranjan" became "Hindu Suranjan," human Haidar became "Muslim Haidar," to me these two are equally sad. *Lajja* protests religious conspiracy and fundamentalism. When religion becomes more important than humanity, then I feel responsibility to protest. In *Lajja*, Suranjan's swearing at Bangladesh means: the brave, honest, and secular Bangladesh that did *Bhasha Andolan* [language movement] and fought the freedom struggle is slowly becoming an Islamic and communal Bangladesh; Suranjan denounces this transformed Bangladesh. When democracy, Bengali nationalism, socialism, secularism are dropped from the state structure, every normal and conscious

---

[9] For a collective reaction to *Lajja* and for various interviews by Nasrin, see Yasmin 1994.

human being, whether Haidar (a Muslim) or Suranjan (a Hindu), must denounce Bangladesh. They denounce their country because they love it. They will build their country and watch it destroyed. . . . This is their land, it is from where they demand security and honor. [*Lajja*] is a protest, a protest of Suranjan's decadence, his failures and his rape. (Nasrin, as quoted in Yasmin 1994, 113)

In this powerful statement, Nasrin offers a critique of Bangladesh's "modernizing nation-state" and its gradual transformation into an Islamic fundamentalist state, a critique of Islamic fundamentalism itself, and finally a view of writing as a protest and a subversive act. This subversive act in many of Nasrin's works involves a genuine gendered self-representation where sexuality is seen as political as well as a matter of self-liberation.

In another of her novels, *Shoud* (Revenge) (1992d), Nasrin narrates a young woman's odyssey. Jumour is smart, educated, attractive, and a very good singer. Her future husband, Haroon, meets her at a musical festival. During their courtship, Haroon appears to be sensitive, attentive, and caring. After their marriage a total transformation of Jumour takes place. She no longer remains as her earlier self—educated, independent, and a singer. Now she becomes a wife, sister-in-law, and daughter-in-law. In other words, her identity becomes defined in relationship to Haroon, her husband. In a poem titled *Shobo bibbaho* (Happy marriage), Nasrin describes the transformation of a woman after marriage in the following way:

My life,
Like a sandbar, has been taken over by a monster of a man.
He wants my body under his control
so that if he wishes he can spit in my face,
slap me on the cheek,
and pinch my rear.
so that if he wishes he can rob my clothes
and take the naked beauty in his grip.
So that if he wishes he can pull out my eyes
so that if he wishes he can chain my feet
if he wishes, he can, with no qualms whatsoever,
use a whip on me
if he wishes, he can chop off my hands, my fingers.
If he wishes he can slash my thigh with a dagger,
so that if he wishes he can string me up and hang me
He wanted my heart under his control
so that I would love him:
in my lonely house at night

sleepless, full of anxiety,
clutching at the window grill
I would wait for him and sob.
My tears rolling down, I would bake homemade bread,
so that I would drink, as if they were ambrosia,
the filthy liquids of his polygamous body.
So that loving him, I would melt like wax,
not turning my eyes toward any other man,
I would give proof of my chastity all my life.
So that, loving him
on some moonlit night I would commit suicide
in a fit of ecstasy. (Nasrin 1992c)

In *Shoud*, after one and a half months of marriage, Jumour becomes pregnant. Her husband refuses to accept the fact that the baby is his and pressures Jumour to have an abortion. Jumour never forgives Haroon for this experience: "He purifies me by sucking the seed of suspicion from my ovary. A pure woman walks around, makes breakfast for her husband, makes different kinds of delicious food for all the relatives (of her husband's) of the house, then she goes to bed and engages in pure fun with her husband with her pure body" (Nasrin 1992d, 30). Jumour uses her sexuality to liberate herself from what appears to her to be a highly confining world. Sexuality becomes a tool of liberation and revenge, hence the title of the book. Jumour begins an affair with a neighborhood man who, to her, is everything that her husband is not: "Who is that boy? . . . Why do I like him to stare at me that much? . . . Is it true that consciousness of love with chains on its legs always longs to go outside, her attraction for an open field becomes intense, for the man in the open field? Or kneeling towards someone for shelter, when hurt by someone else?" (37). Jumour describes her desires for Afzal in the following terms: "When Afzal touches me, I feel like a Sitar, start playing different tunes with a simple touch. I am from a conservative family. . . . How is it possible that in spite of having an able and well off husband, I long for another man's touch. Where have all these restrictions gone? Restrictions that are in my blood, prepared me for a man for twenty four years, keeping me without a man's touch" (45).

The text continues: "He kissed me deeply. His two hands move down from my chin, my neck, to my chest. His hands stop on my chest briefly. Then they become restless again. I grab Afzal's hair. . . . Afzal takes away my sari. I close my eyes—he is not an unknown man, this is my dream man. The feeling is like taking a bath with our own water in a deep forest.

We are the world's only children. Nobody will ever bother us. . . . Afzal slowly takes my everything. I take him with my entire body" (48).

Jumour becomes pregnant by Afzal by calculating her fertile period and leaves him when he wants to be with her permanently. She does this in order to get back to her premarriage self—independence; she takes a teaching job and renews contact with her former college friends.

The themes of sexuality and the politics of personal liberation return in Nasrin's *Dukhaboti mayyee* (Sad girl) (1994), a collection of sketches, but at the same time "not quite short stories." In *"Din jai"* (Days go by), Nasrin describes the relationship between Mamta and her abusive husband. When her husband leaves her, Mamta becomes independent and liberated, sexually and socially. In *"Matritro"* (Motherhood), Nasrin deals with both religion and motherhood in a patriarchal social context. In these two stories Islam is seen as painfully and often hilariously antiwoman. In *"Matritro,"* one young woman is tormented by her husband for being *baza* (sterile), although a physical examination reveals that the wife could not get pregnant because of the husband's low sperm count. The husband forces her to see a *pir,* an Islamic holy man, who has the mysterious power to make sterile women pregnant; many women have benefited from this power. To receive maximum benefit, a potential mother must come and see the *pir* in the fertile period of her menstrual cycle. As it turns out, the *pir* rapes the women to get them pregnant. When the young wife tries to resist the *pir,* he identifies the rape as "revelations from Allah" (Nasrin 1994, 28).

Discussion of the female body may also be included within the theme of sexuality as a subversive act in Nasrin's writings. Nasrin does not view the body as a biological entity; rather, she attempts to unwrap the sociocultural meaning of the female body, especially the historical configurations of male-female power relations to which the female body in Bangladesh is subjected. "[Sexual difference between men and women] is a historically grounded complex ideological terrain across which are gathered a range of meanings directed toward notions of biological sex, social gender, gender identity, and sexual identification" (Riaz 1995, 25).

Riaz, furthermore, identifies this position with the Foucauldian view of sexuality. Foucault sees sex as a historical construct that deals with the "most internal element in a deployment of sexuality organized by power in its grip on bodies and their materiality, their forces, energies, sensations, and pleasures" (Foucault 1979, 145). This relationship between sexuality and power is most obvious in the description of the female body in Nasrin's writings. In Bangladesh, where the absence of discussion about the female is "a socially sanctioned silence," Nasrin attempts to break this silence by making it a power issue (Riaz 1995, 25). For example, when the Bangladesh government banned an issue of the Bengali feminist magazine *Shannanda,* published in Calcutta, Nasrin, in her *Nirbachito column,* sharply protested the banning (Nasrin 1992a, 36–38). This particular issue contained a very open discussion on women's bodies, health, and health-related anxieties. By pointing out that the government did not ban an earlier issue on men, Nasrin argued that a scientific discussion of the female body is essential: "If the discussion of the structure of a woman's body, different phases of development of the body, every stage, adolescence, menstruation, sexuality, conception, pregnancy, adulthood, menopause, postmenopause, illness and treatment, old age, exterior symptoms of old age and mental anxiety be banned, then medical science should be banned, women's living should be banned" (36).

Nasrin's writings constitute subversive politics. Can her politics be explained in terms of contemporary feminist theory, or, more specifically, gender relations? Following Inderpal Grewal and Caren Kaplan (1994, 20), Nasrin's text could be read as a displacement of both modernist and fundamentalist Islamist unitary subjects and concomitant multiple gendered subjectivity transfixed by international mobile capital. Grewal identifies this kind of feminist practice as "scattered hegemonies" (Grewal and Kaplan 1994, 7). In her poem *Progotier pristoshei* (On the back of progress), Nasrin attempts to displace the master narrative of Marxist class analysis by showing that women's subjugation indeed crosses class lines.

> That man sits in an air-conditioned room
> Who raped at least ten young women.
> Gets excited by staring
> at the belly of women at the cocktail party.
> He changes the taste of intercourse
> by sleeping with different women.
> At home he beats his wife
> For a clean handkerchief or
> for clean shirt collars.
>
> In the office he talks with people
> smokes cigarettes
> handles files.
> Calls through the calling bell
> and screams at his employees.
> Sips tea brought by the orderly.
> Writes character certificates for other people.
>
> . . . .

The orderly who brings tea
who keeps a lighter in his pocket
divorced his first wife for sterility
his second for giving birth to a girl
the third wife for not bringing any dowry.
Beats his fourth wife after returning home
for two hot green peppers or
for a handful of rice. (Nasrin 1992b, 23)

In this poem, the employer is one of the nouveau riche created by the international capital, or what Spivak calls *planetary capital,* that replaced the earlier space-based imperialism (Spivak 1990, 85). Nasrin shows that, although the employer and the employee have class differences, both practice gender discrimination and violence. In *Shoud,* Jumour's husband, Haroon, is also a nouveau riche, created by planetary capital. This juxtaposition of gendered subalternity and international capital is also an issue that critical postmodernity raises. Mary Layoun, echoing Fredric Jameson, argues that if postmodernity is the "cultural logic of capitalism," then postmodernity has had a significant analytical applicability in the postcolonial third world, especially since 1960 (Layoun 1994, 64). In the social and spatial geography of many third world megacities such as Sao Paulo, Mexico City, Bangkok, or Dhaka, futuristic and postmodern architectures are juxtaposed with open bazaars and manually driven carts. In Dhaka can be seen the *Jatia Sangshad Bhavan* (National Assembly building), a very postmodern design, which is not very far from the so-called floating population—a rural uprooted population in Dhaka living in slums hoping for a job and a better life. In posh residential areas of Dhaka, there are enclosed shopping malls for foreigners next to traditional open bazaars. In an essay in *Nirbachito column,* Nasrin describes an upper-class party scene in Dhaka (Nasrin 1992a, 105–8) where all the women speak fluent English, drink alcoholic beverages (a sure sign of modern living in a puritanical Muslim society), receive kisses on the chin from their husband's male friends, and flirt with them. This is a party for Dhaka's new rich, created by the flow of international capital. Although the women at the party seem modern and progressive, they still identify themselves as "Mrs. Ahmad," "Mrs. Chowdhury," and so on. In other words, their self-identity still derives from their husband's and they remain the sole caretaker of the house and the children.

If postmodernity stands for a critical rereading of modernity by offering us the chance to reconsider all that was "left unsaid" and to inject resistance with new meaning and political discourse (Richard 1987–88, 12), then the apparent postmodern juxtaposition is very clear in Nasrin's writings.

Thus, Nasrin's writings should be seen as an attempt to destabilize the humanist, modernist, and Islamic fundamentalist "grand narratives" by bringing them into the critical categories of gender, class, nationality, sexuality, and community (Hindu-Muslim relations). This border-crossing is at the heart of radical postmodernist politics. The recognition of common commitments serves as a springboard for solidarity and coalition. Nasrin's writings permanently galvanized and polarized political culture in Bangladesh. This political culture that Nasrin introduced through her writings is one of the freshest and most enduring aspects of her numerous contributions.

Conclusion: Toward a new politics of gender

After leaving Bangladesh and reaching Sweden, Nasrin, on various occasions, argued that her writings have nothing to do with religion but are all about politics. Indeed, her writings should be read as such. Her works appeared at a very tumultuous time for Bangladesh. Since independence in 1971, a quiet revolution has been taking place in Bangladesh, especially in the rural areas where most Bangladeshis live. Rural women are becoming politically organized and asserting themselves. Various NGOs are placing more importance on girls' education. Women are accepting family planning in greater numbers and lowering the birthrate, and women's contribution to the family income — a sign of independence — has increased. Rural Bangladesh, in particular, is going through a rapid social transformation where the Islam-based interpretation of gender relations is constantly being challenged. The Bangladeshi Islamic fundamentalists are responding violently to these challenges. Recently they demanded the abolition of the Western-funded NGO activities that establish schools for girls and issued numerous *fatwas* against those who do not send their children to *madrasha* (religious school), women who work outside the home, and women who bring their children to local health clinics (Baker 1994, 4; *Weekly Bichitra* 1994). Nasrin's works coincided with these and other numerous incidents of *fatwa*, especially the one against Nurjahan Begum, which received wide publicity in the media.

In an interview from exile in Sweden, Nasrin argued that her writings are part of a broad political movement against Islamic fundamentalists in their war against women (Weaver 1994, 58). In this case of the modernizing state and Islamic fundamentalism, how can the separate political space denied women be renegotiated and transformed? First, the three largest political parties in Bangladesh, judging by the number of seats in parliament — the ruling AL, the main opposition BNP, and the military dictator

General Ershad's Jatio Party—are unable or unwilling to negotiate a separate space for women in Bangladesh. It has been widely reported that an arrest warrant against Nasrin by the BNP government was meant to please and bring back the Islamic fundamentalist JI, which along with other opposition political parties boycotted the parliament and demanded a new election. The secular AL made a tactical alliance with the JI to bring down the BNP's Khaleda Zia government. In this situation, women's separate space must be reconstructed with a political organization that stands outside professional political parties and politicians.

This type of organizational work has a long history in Bangladesh. The activities of *Naripokho* (Women's Side) and the United Women's Forum, another prominent women's organization, are examples of such political work. These women's organizations have shown their political strength on quite a few occasions. In 1988, when the military regime of General Ershad passed an Eighth Amendment bill that established Islam as the state religion of Bangladesh, *Naripokho* and the United Women's Forum filed a petition before the Supreme Court challenging the validity of the amendment. The groups argued that the amendment discriminated against women since Islam does not approve of women as heads of state (Kamal 1990, 40; Chowdhury 1994, 106). Various women's organizations were also active on the issue of violence against women. In 1989, a young wife was murdered by her husband and his lover. The United Women's Forum and *Naripokho* staged demonstrations and marched to demand justice. The accused and his lover were sentenced to death by the trial court. In October 1991, an Islamic fundamentalist group calling itself the Un-Islamic Activities Resistance Committee (UARC) attempted to evict prostitutes from Dhaka's red-light district. Many women's organizations, including *Naripokho,* spoke with the prostitutes, and the prostitutes, after finding a leader of their own, began to mobilize public action and demanded the identification of clients and pimps. They created public awareness campaigns regarding the social and economic rehabilitation of prostitutes and the eradication of prostitution. Finally, the district administration defused the situation by forming a committee of local administrators and police, a journalist, and two members of the UARC to find a solution (Chowdhury 1994, 106).

A recent example of feminist political activism involved the case of the death of Yasmin. Yasmin, a fourteen-year-old from Dinajpur, northwestern Bangladesh, was waiting for a bus to go to visit her mother on the morning of August 24, 1995. She was picked up, raped, and killed by three uniformed policemen. The police and the home ministry tried in a press statement to portray Yasmin as a prostitute who jumped from the police van while being taken into custody (*Chinta* 1995, 12). Their attempt backfired, and the people of Dinajpur revolted; seven people were killed by police fire. Soon protest spread throughout the entire country. The *Sammilita Nari Samaj* (Women's Social Collective), a group of women's organizations, was a leader in the mobilization on the Yasmin case. Immediately after Yasmin's death, it adopted a two-pronged strategy: to protest the killing and demand prosecution of the criminals, and to draw public attention to the larger issue of violence against women and to politicize it. The *Samaj* organized demonstrations on September 4 and 12. On September 12, the demonstrators were attacked by police. During the demonstrations a number of demands were made (Ahmed 1995, 8; Akthar 1995; Khan 1995, 3). They included: proclaim August 24 (the day that Yasmin was killed) as a day of resistance, declare the seven people killed by police while protesting Yasmin's killing as *shahid* (martyrs for just/holy cause), punish those responsible for killing Yasmin and the seven other people, and stop police harassment of people all over the country. In larger political terms, these activities called for continuing and accelerating women's struggle against rape, murder, and *fatwas;* joining the movement of women workers, especially the garment workers fighting against repression; joining the movement of women in the slums in their demands for basic needs such as shelter, food, water, gas, education, and health facilities; helping women in the slums in their struggle against atrocities committed by local *mastans* (hooligans); and strengthening the struggle of women against police atrocities and other forms of social repression. Under pressure from the *Samaj* and other feminist organizations, the government took a number of actions, such as arresting the police responsible for the killing of Yasmin. This type of growing political activism in Bangladesh has had a profound impact on renegotiating a separate political space for women. If Islamic fundamentalists and secular/modernist political parties fail to address the issue of women's political space, the task will be entirely in the hands of women. The works of Taslima Nasrin have been a major contribution in this direction.

Department of Sociology and Anthropology
Southern Oregon University

References

Ahmed, Aziz. 1967. *Islamic Modernism in India and Pakistan*. London: Oxford University Press.
Ahmed, Natasha. 1995. "Shammilita Nari Samaj Presses for the Trial of Yasmen's Killers." *Holiday* 5 (November 3): 1, 8.

Ahmed, Rafiuddin. 1981. *The Bengal Muslims: 1871–1906.* Delhi: Oxford University Press.

Akthar, Farida. 1995. "Remember Yasmin, Every Month." *Daily Star,* September 24, 10.

Ajkar Kgoj. 1994. *Ajkar Kgoj,* June 5.

Alam, S. M. Shamsul. 1993a. "Islam, Ideology and the State in Bangladesh." *Journal of Asian and African Studies* 28(1–2):88–106.

———. 1993b. "When Will the Subaltern Speak? Central Issues of Historical Sociology of South Asia." *Asian Profile* 21(5):431–47.

———. 1995. *The State, Class Formation and Development in Bangladesh.* Lanham, Md.: University Press of America.

Anderson, John Ward. 1993. "Feminist with a Price on Her Head." *San Francisco Chronicle,* December 26, 6.

———. 1994. "Bangladeshi Militants Seek Writer's Death." *Guardian Weekly,* June 26, 15.

al-Azm, Sadik. 1993. "Is the 'Fatwa' a Fatwa?" *Middle East Report,* July–August, 27.

Baker, Deborah. 1994. "Exiled Feminist Writer Tells Her Own Story." *New York Times,* August 28, 4E.

Baudrillard, Jean. 1987. "Modernity." *Canadian Journal of Political and Social Theory* 11(3):63–72.

Begum, Soruya. 1994. "Bangladeshe moulobad abong nari." *Samaj narikkhon* 54:1–19.

Bhabha, Homi, ed. 1990. *Nation and Narration.* London: Routledge.

Borthwick, Meredith. 1984. *The Changing Role of Women in Bengal, 1849–1905.* Princeton, N.J.: Princeton University Press.

Chatterjee, Partha. 1986. *Nationalist Thought and the Colonial World: A Derivative Discourse.* London: Zed. Reprint, Minneapolis: University of Minnesota Press, 1993.

———. 1993. *The Nation and Its Fragments.* Princeton, N.J.: Princeton University Press.

Chinta. 1995. "Yasmin." *Chinta,* September 30.

Chowdhury, Najma. 1994. "Bangladesh: Gender Issues and Politics in a Patriarchy." In *Women and Politics Worldwide,* ed. Barbara J. Nelson and Najma Chowdhury, 94–113. New Haven, Conn.: Yale University Press.

Connell, R. W. 1990. "The State, Gender and Sexual Politics: Theory and Appraisal." *Theory and Society* 19(5):507–44.

Dainik Janakanta. 1994. *Dainik Janakanta,* April 8, July 13.

———. 1995. *Dainik Janakanta,* September 16.

Foucault, Michel. 1979. *The History of Sexuality.* Vol. 1, *An Introduction.* Trans. R. Hurley. New York: Vintage.

Geertz, Clifford. 1971. *Islam Observed: Religious Development in Morocco and Indonesia.* New Haven, Conn.: Yale University Press.

Government of Bangladesh. 1972. *Constitution of the People's Republic of Bangladesh.* Dhaka: Government of Bangladesh.

Gramsci, A. 1971. *Prison Notebooks.* New York: International Publishers.

Gray, Paul. 1994. "Jane Austen She Is Not." *Time,* August 15, 26.

Grewal, Inderpal, and Caren Kaplan, eds. 1994. *Scattered Hegemonies: Postmodernity and Transnational Feminist Practices.* Minneapolis: University of Minnesota Press.

Huntington, Samuel. 1993. "The Clash of Civilization." *Foreign Affairs,* Summer, 22–49.

Jalal, Ayesha. 1991. "The Convenience of Subservience: Women and the State of Pakistan." In *Women, Islam and the State,* ed. Deniz Kandiyoti, 77–114. Philadelphia: Temple University Press.

Kamal, Sultana. 1990. "Move Towards State Sponsored Islamization in Bangladesh." *South Asia Bulletin* 10(2):35.

Kamaluddin, S. 1988. "The Islamic Way." *Far Eastern Economic Review,* June 23, 14–17.

Kandiyoti, Deniz. 1991. "Women, Islam and the State." *Middle East Report* 21(6):9–14.

Khan, Naila. 1995. "Yasmeen Has Left Her Signature in Blood, for Her Own Kind to Redeem." *Holiday,* September 22.

Layoun, Mary. 1994. "The Female Body and 'Transnational' Reproduction; or, Rape by Any Other Name." In Grewal and Kaplan 1994, 63–75.

Mukherjee, R. K. 1973. "The Social Background of Bangladesh." In *Imperialism and Revolution in South Asia,* ed. K. Gough and H. Sharma, 399–418. New York: Monthly Review Press.

Murshid, Ghulam. 1983. *Reluctant Debutante: Response of Bengali Women to Modernization, 1849–1905.* Rajshahi, Bangladesh: Rajshahi University Press.

Nahar, Inun. 1993. "Muslim inier dristritay nari." *Samaj narikkan* 47:103–29.

Nasrin, Taslima. 1992a. *Nirbachito column.* Calcutta: Ananda Publisher's Private Limited.

———. 1992b. *Progotier pristoshei.* In *Nirbachito nari.* Dhaka: Afsar Brothers.

———. 1992c. *Shobo bibbaho,* trans. Carolyne Wright, Mohammed Nurul Huda, and Mary Ann Weaver. In Weaver 1994, 55.

———. 1992d. *Shoud.* Dhaka: Annanya.

———. 1993a. *Fara.* Dhaka: Yaan Kosh.

———. 1993b. *Lajja.* Dhaka: Pearl.

———. 1994. *Dukhaboti mayyee.* Dhaka: Mowla Brothers.

———. 1995. *The Game in Reverse: Poems and Essays.* New York: George Braziller.

Netton, Ian Richard. 1992. *A Popular Dictionary of Islam.* Atlantic Highlands, N.J.: Humanities Press International.

Osmani, Shireen Hasan. 1992. *Bangladeshi Nationalism: History of Dialectics and Dimensions.* Dhaka: University Press Limited.

Riaz, Ali. 1995. "Taslima Nasrin: Breaking the Structural Silence." *Bulletin of Concerned Asian Scholars* 27(1):21–27.

Richard, Nelly. 1987–88. "Postmodernism and Periphery." *Third Text,* no. 2, 6–12.

Roy, Asim. 1983. *The Islamic Syncretistic Tradition in Bengal.* Princeton, N.J.: Princeton University Press.

Said, Edward. 1979. *Orientalism.* New York: Pantheon.

South Asia Bulletin. 1988. *South Asia Bulletin* 8:116–18.

Spivak, Gayatri Chakravorty. 1988. *In Other Worlds: Essays in Cultural Politics.* New York and London: Routledge.

———. 1990. "Gayatri Spivak on the Politics of the Subaltern." Interview by Howard Winant. *Socialist Review* 20(3):116–18.

Statesman. 1994. *Statesman,* May 25.

Turner, Brian. 1984. *Capitalism and Class in the Middle East: Theories of Social Change and Economic Development.* London: Heinemann.

Walby, B. S. 1990. *Theorizing Patriarchy.* London: Blackwell.

Weaver, Mary Anne. 1994. "A Fugitive from Injustice." *New Yorker,* September 12, 48–60.

Weekly Bichitra. 1994. *Weekly Bichitra,* April, 31–38.

Weiner, Eric. 1994. "Muslim Radicals and Police Hunt Feminist Bangladeshi Writer." *Christian Science Monitor,* July 26, 6.

Yasmin, Moumi. 1994. *Taslima Nasriner lajja o ananya.* Dhaka: Pearl.

Zubaida, Sami. 1989. *Islam, the People, the State.* London: Routledge.

Amal Amireh

Framing Nawal El Saadawi:
Arab Feminism in a Transnational World

The reception of a writer's work, as Nawal El Saadawi recognizes, is neither neutral nor arbitrary: "It's not," she says, "a matter of who's good, who's bad. It's a matter of who has the power — who has the power and writes books" (quoted in el-Faizy 1994). This is particularly true of El Saadawi herself, whose reputation as an Egyptian feminist activist and novelist, I argue, has always been an overtly political matter, especially in the West, where her emergence into visibility has been overdetermined by the political-economic circumstances of first-world–third-world relations of production and consumption.[1] In this case study of El Saadawi's reception, I examine both academic and nonacademic writing by and about her, foregrounding the strategies by which the first world reads and understands Arab women's texts and drawing out their implications for issues of cross-cultural inquiry and feminist solidarity. I show that El Saadawi and her Arab feminist work are consumed by a Western audience in a context saturated by stereotypes of Arab culture and that this context of reception, to a large extent, ends up rewriting both the writer and her texts according to scripted first-world narratives about Arab women's oppression. To avoid the pitfalls of such reductionist readings of texts and authors, I argue, it is necessary always to historicize and contextualize El

I would like to thank Lisa Suhair Majaj, Therese Saliba, and the editors of *Signs* for their helpful comments on this article and Lisa Suhair Majaj, Wen-chin Ouyang, and Amalia Saar for their help with research. I am deeply grateful to John Dixon for his insightful criticism of various drafts of this essay.

[1] I choose to use the terms *first world* and *third world* throughout this article although I am well aware of the limitations of such terminology in light of the political-economic changes that make the three-worlds theory problematic. But while this terminology is imperfect, it is still useful in highlighting the asymmetry of power between, in this case, Western and Arab intellectuals and in evoking "structural commonalities of struggles" (Shohat 1992, 111) among diverse people. This asymmetry of power is obscured by terms such as *north/south* and *postcolonial*. For a critique of the latter term and an argument for retaining *third world* as terminology, see Shohat 1992.

[*Signs: Journal of Women in Culture and Society* 2000, vol. 26, no. 1]

Saadawi's work, something I attempt to do in the following pages. Although this article is a somewhat narrowly focused case study, it also raises more general questions about the difficult and often ambivalent role of third-world feminists and Arab dissident intellectuals in a transnational age.

As a reception study, this article emphasizes politics of location. Reception theory takes meaning to be not an attribute immanent in texts but, rather, a product of the larger discursive contexts in which they are read. It considers texts within the circumstances of their production and consumption, that is, within the historical contingencies that make them available for certain readers. From this perspective, what El Saadawi says or writes is less important than the places from which she speaks and writes, the contexts in which her words are received, the audiences who hear and read her, and the uses to which her words are put. This approach recognizes the multiplicity of meanings that a text can have in different contexts. As Linda Alcoff argues, "Not only what is emphasized, noticed, and how it is understood will be affected by the location of both speaker and hearer, but the truth-value or epistemic status will also be affected" (1994, 291). In El Saadawi's case, the relationship between text and context is particularly interesting because El Saadawi does not occupy one fixed location. An Egyptian writer who writes in Arabic for an Arab audience, she is also a "traveling" third-world intellectual who addresses an English-speaking audience through translations of her works and through her lectures and interviews abroad.

Western interest in El Saadawi predates the recent attention to Arabic literature generated by Naguib Mahfouz's receipt of the Nobel Prize in 1988. The first of her books to be translated was the nonfictional *Al-Wajh al-ʿari lil-marʾa al-ʿarabiyyah,* which appeared in Arabic in 1977 and in English in 1980 as *The Hidden Face of Eve: Women in the Arab World* (1980c). Three years later, her novel *Imraʾaʿind nuqtat al-sifr* (1979) was published in English as *Woman at Point Zero* (1983b). For a decade and a half now, a constant stream of El Saadawi's work, mostly fiction, has been appearing in British and American bookstores, making her one of the most translated Arab writers, male or female. At present, fourteen of her books have been translated into English and are in print.

The translation of El Saadawi's books over the past twenty years chronicles her rising star in the English-speaking world. While her books made their imprint on the Arab world in the early to mid-1970s, they were not recognized in the Western literary market until the 1980s. Sometimes a decade or two separates the date of Arabic publication from that of its

English translation.[2] But the gap has been narrowing. Now El Saadawi's books are translated promptly, with the English version appearing shortly after the Arabic, if not simultaneously with it. For instance, *Memoirs from the Women's Prison* (1983a) appeared in Arabic in 1983 and in English in 1986; *The Fall of the Imam* was published in Arabic in 1987 (see 1987c) and in English in 1988; her latest novel, *The Innocence of the Devil* (1994b), appeared in Arabic in 1992 (as *Jannat wa-Iblis* [1992a]) and in English in 1994; and her memoir *A Daughter of Isis* (1999) was published in English almost simultaneously with the Arabic edition. At times, more than one of her books have appeared in English in a single year, an honor of which few writers in any other language can boast.[3]

There is also a noticeable shift in the kind of publishing houses that are bringing her works out. The press that introduced El Saadawi to the English-speaking world was Zed Books of London, which has since published several of her novels, an anthology of her works, and her autobiography. El Saadawi made her American debut through the small, left-leaning Beacon Press in Boston, which published *The Hidden Face of Eve* in 1982. Saqi Books in London and City Lights of San Francisco, both small publishers, brought out *Memoirs of a Woman Doctor* in 1988 and 1989, respectively. However, the new edition of *Memoirs from the Women's Prison*, first published by the Women's Press in London in 1986, was picked up by the University of California Press, a large, prestigious academic publisher, which also brought out *The Innocence of the Devil* in 1994. Obviously, the production of El Saadawi's books for the English-speaking consumer has been shifting from England to the United States and from small, activist-oriented presses to more mainstream academic ones.

The shift to major American presses is consistent with El Saadawi's growing status within the U.S. academy, where she has been inscribed as both a celebrity and a representative Arab writer. The institutionalization of women's studies and, more recently, of postcolonial and multicultural

---

[2] For example, *Imra'atani fi-mra'a* and *Mawt al-rajul al-wahid 'ala al-ard* (1974a) appeared in Arabic in 1968 and 1974, respectively, and in English in 1985 as *Two Women in One* (1985c) and *God Dies by the Nile* (1985b); *Searching* (1991c) appeared in English translation in 1991, more than twenty years after it first appeared in Arabic in 1965 (under the title *Al-Gha'ib* [The absent one]). Similarly, El Saadawi's first novel, *Mudhakkirat tabiba*, was published in Egypt in 1958 and was translated in 1988 (as *Memoirs of a Woman Doctor* [1988b]).

[3] The following pairs of books appeared in English in the same year: *She Has No Place in Paradise* (1987b) and *Death of an Ex-Minister* (1987a); *Memoirs of a Woman Doctor* (1988b) and *The Fall of the Imam* (1988a); and *The Innocence of the Devil* (1994b) and a new edition of *Memoirs from the Women's Prison* (1994c).

studies has helped make a space for El Saadawi's work on the syllabi of a variety of courses. Her books are assigned in both graduate and undergraduate classes on women's writing in general, African and Middle Eastern postcolonial literature, world literature, biography and autobiography, politics, and feminist theory. In the United States, El Saadawi has taught at the University of Washington and at Duke University, and she is currently a visiting professor at Florida State University.[4] Her work also makes a strong appearance in that most canonizing of publications, the anthology; it is ubiquitous in anthologies about Arab and Middle Eastern women.[5] Moreover, she is often the only Arab writer featured in anthologies not specializing in the Middle East: her essays appear in *Sisterhood Is Global: The International Women's Movement Anthology* (1984) and the *Heinemann Book of African Women's Writing* (1993c). She is the only Arab woman writer who has an entry in the bibliographic *Feminist Companion to Literature in English: Women Writers from the Middle Ages to the Present* (Blain, Clements, and Grundy 1990), and she is the only Arab writer, male or female, to be featured in the *Contemporary Authors Autobiography Series* (El Saadawi 1990b) or to have an anthology of her own nonfiction writing published (*The Nawal El Saadawi Reader* [1997]). More than those that address Middle East specialists, these anthologies play a crucial role in establishing El Saadawi in the Western academy as a celebrity and a representative Arab writer.

El Saadawi's inclusion in these anthologies highlights one of her most salient characteristics, her mobility across international borders, which accounts for her high visibility outside the Arab world. In addition to her trips outside Egypt (partially documented in her book *My Travels around the World* [1991a]) and her participation in international conferences, El Saadawi worked for the United Nations for some years. After being dismissed from her job as director of Egypt's Ministry of Health following the publication of her controversial book *Al-Mar'ah wal-jins* (Woman and sex [1971]), she took charge of the U.N. program for African women in Addis Ababa for one year; then she was responsible for the women's program of the U.N. Economic Commission for West Asia in Beirut. The large number of English-language interviews with El Saadawi and her visibil-

---

[4] This information is based on a limited, informal survey I conducted while writing this article. The survey took the form of questions I posted on various on-line lists (women's studies, African-lit, Arabic-lit, postcolonial studies). I asked those who taught El Saadawi to mention the name of the course, which books were assigned, and something about the response of the students. I thank all those who responded to my questions; the information they gave was very helpful.

[5] See, e.g., al-Hibri 1982; Fernea 1985; Badran and Cooke 1990; Bowen and Early 1993.

ity in the mass media in England and North America further attest to her mobility and her accessibility to Westerners.[6] El Saadawi's books are reviewed by mainstream print media, which often recommend them for a general audience; her movements and affairs are consistently reported; and prominent writers review and acknowledge her on the pages of such prestigious newspapers as the *New York Times* and the *Los Angeles Times* (e.g., Mukherjee 1986; Sontag 1994).

All of this makes El Saadawi an interesting subject for a reception study. Much has been written in response to Gayatri Spivak's question, "Can the Subaltern Speak?" (1988), but less attention has been given to figures such as El Saadawi, who is not a subaltern, either in her society or in the West. Not only is she not the stereotypical silent woman of the third world, but she speaks for herself and has direct access to her international audience. However, for El Saadawi, as for other Arab and third-world intellectuals who cross national boundaries and occupy multiple locations, it is a struggle to address the divergent assumptions, expectations, and interests of both Arab and Western audiences. Consequently, these writers, El Saadawi among them, are inevitably caught in the net of power relations that govern interactions between the first and third worlds.

The Hidden Face of Eve in a Western context

Despite her high visibility, her strong presence in the American academy, and her access to a Western audience, El Saadawi is not always in control of either her voice or her image. The history of her reception in the West shows El Saadawi struggling against misappropriation, but it also shows her accommodating the West's reading of her. It is a story of both resistance and complicity, and it begins with the reception of *The Hidden Face of Eve* (1980c), which marked El Saadawi's official crossover to the West. It became one of her most influential books, often hailed as a "classic." In what follows, I will discuss the context in which the book was read in England and the United States, show how it was received by reviewers, and point out the differences between the English and the Arabic editions. The reception history of this book illustrates, I believe, the way an Arab

---

[6] Interviews with El Saadawi include El Saadawi 1980a, 1981, 1990a, 1992b, 1993a, 1993b, 1994a, 1995a. Reviews of her books have appeared in newspapers such as the *New York Times*, the *Washington Post*, the *Christian Science Monitor*, the *Financial Times*, the *Toronto Star*, the *Guardian*, and *Publishers Weekly*. Articles about her have appeared in the *Washington Post*, the *San Francisco Chronicle*, the *Chicago Tribune*, the *Atlanta Journal and Constitution*, the *Sunday Telegraph*, the *Guardian*, *Canadian Dimension*, the *Seattle Times*, and the *Gazette* (Montreal).

woman writer's text is transformed through translation, editing, and reviewing once it crosses cultural and national borders.

El Saadawi's visibility in the West coincided with two major international events: the United Nations' "international decade of women" and the Iranian Revolution and its aftermath. While these contexts facilitated her entrance into the first world, they also defined and framed her for a Western audience.

The United Nations' declaration of the period from 1975 to 1985 as the decade of women signaled official international interest in the lives of third-world women, provided them a forum in which to speak, and gave an impetus to global feminism. One issue of central interest to Western women was clitoridectomy, a topic addressed at the U.N.-sponsored Copenhagen conference of 1980. The coverage of this event in the U.S. media linked clitoridectomy and El Saadawi and gave both a prominent position. Under the headline "Female Circumcision a Topic at UN Parley," a *New York Times* article (Dullea 1980) begins by recounting El Saadawi's own excision, the same story that opens *The Hidden Face of Eve* (1982). Another article credits El Saadawi with bringing clitoridectomy to the attention of the international community and its health organizations. It concludes, "Dr. Saadawi's campaign against this practice was rewarded when the conference recommended adopting national policies and, if necessary, laws against it, and when UNICEF declared itself 'seriously committed' to its eradication" (Slade and Ferrell 1980). Although this article mentions that El Saadawi discussed other issues relating to third-world women, such as education, health, and employment, it is clitoridectomy that it singles out and highlights.

El Saadawi's own accounts of the treatment of excision during the conference and of the role she played are markedly different from this report. In one interview soon after the conference, she criticizes Western feminist attendees for their ignorance of third-world women's concerns and for their focus on issues of sexuality and patriarchy in isolation from issues of class and colonialism. She denounces their treatment of clitoridectomy, making it clear that she resents the "sensationalizing of marginal issues in Copenhagen" and the use of female circumcision to emphasize differences between first-world and third-world women. She insists, rather, that similarity should be underscored, declaring that all women are circumcised, if not physically then "psychologically and educationally" (1980a, 177). El Saadawi had expressed these ideas before Copenhagen, writing in her preface to the British edition of *The Hidden Face of Eve*, "I disagree with those women in America and Europe who concentrate on issues such as female circumcision and depict them as proof of the unusual and barbaric oppression to which women are exposed only in African and Arab countries. I oppose all attempts to deal with such problems in isolation" (1980c, xiv). She argues that Western feminists' concentration on female circumcision diverts attention from "real issues of social and economic change," replacing "effective action" with "a feeling of superior humanity" (xiv). In both the preface and the interview, El Saadawi presents herself as one third-world woman among many, all of whom are breaking with Western feminists' limited agenda and struggling for the advancement of women in the third world on several fronts, and she uses *we* to emphasize this collective identity (1980a, 177; 1980c, xv). In contrast, the American media cast El Saadawi in Copenhagen as an isolated victim of excision fighting a lone campaign against it (Dullea 1980; Slade and Ferrell 1980). This is the image of El Saadawi that eventually prevailed, a one-dimensional simplification both of her far-reaching feminism and of the various issues facing third-world women.

El Saadawi's entrance into the Western public sphere also coincided with an event that rekindled Western fears of Islam, the Iranian Revolution of 1978–79. The deposition of the pro-Western Shah and his replacement by an Islamic government opposed to the United States demonstrated that Islam posed a real threat to Western political and economic interests in the Middle East. In this highly charged political atmosphere, interest in Islam was revived and heightened, and the reception of El Saadawi's *The Hidden Face of Eve*, which appeared in English on the heels of the Iranian revolution, was conditioned by Western interest in and hostility to Islam.

In the preface to the British edition (dated 1979 and absent from the Arabic edition), El Saadawi explicitly connects the aims of her book with those of the Iranian Revolution. Devoting half of her introduction to this momentous event, she celebrates it as a great anti-imperialist blow to the West, especially the United States; defends it against its critics and against Islam's detractors; and exposes the real motives of its enemies, particularly the United States and the Egyptian regime of Anwar Sadat (1980c, vi–vii). She defines the revolution as "in its essence political and economic. It is a popular explosion which seeks to emancipate the people of Iran, both men and women, and not to send women back to the prison of the veil, the kitchen and the bedroom" (iii). Her celebration of the Iranian revolution is also a celebration of Islam and its anti-imperialist impulse (iii–iv). She affirms that her own project is continuous with that of the Islamic revolution since, in her view, the liberation of women is not separate from their political, economic, and national liberation. She emphasizes that "the Iranian Revolution of today . . . is a natural heritage of the historical struggle for freedom and social equality among Arab peoples, who have continued to fight under the banner of Islam and to draw their inspiration from the teachings of the Koran and the Prophet Mahomet" (iv).

El Saadawi's preface to the first English edition is an attempt to exert some control over her feminist critique of her culture, which she locates within an uncompromising critique of imperialism. In doing so, she anticipates the way Western audiences will read her book, realizing that they may try to use her criticism of her culture to further distance the third world from the first and to reaffirm stereotypes of it as underdeveloped and backward. If nothing else, her preface shows El Saadawi's awareness that she is addressing a different audience, with assumptions and expectations different from those of the book's original Arab audience.

But El Saadawi's introduction irked her new readers. Two reviewers writing for feminist journals in England and the United States expressed their disappointment with the introduction, especially its celebration of the Iranian Revolution, Islam, and nationalism. Leila Ahmed admires El Saadawi's feminist critique of her culture and its view of sexuality but dismisses the introduction as mere rhetoric that does not offer a forceful or clear argument. According to her, it is written in anger: "Out of such anger women are driven to support, as El Saadawi does here, revolutionary movements that have nothing to recommend them except that they are indigenous to the third world and are opposed to the West" (1981, 751). She particularly faults El Saadawi for her celebration of the Iranian Revolution. Magida Salman, reviewing the book for the leftist magazine *Khamsin,* was even harsher on El Saadawi's positions on the Iranian Revolution and on Islam and nationalism in general. She sees El Saadawi as "an Arab feminist who has fallen into the deep trap of nationalist justification and defensive reactions designed to prettify reality for the benefit of critical 'foreigners.'" She concludes that El Saadawi "has failed to go an inch beyond the Arab-Muslim nationalism of the Nasserites, B'thists, and their ilk." Particularly troubling for her is El Saadawi's view that "all women's struggles must be subordinated to the battle for national liberation" (Salman 1981, 122). Both Ahmed and Salman indirectly recognize that El Saadawi's problems in that introduction are the result of her attempt to address a Western audience, not the Arab audience originally intended for the book. But neither fully appreciates El Saadawi's difficulties with this new audience, and they perhaps dismiss her too hastily. Not recognizing the complexity of the situation that El Saadawi was struggling to see in its totality, these reviewers implicitly fault her for not being feminist enough, at least in her introduction.

Defending El Saadawi, Irene Gendzier shows a better understanding of the writer's dilemma. In her foreword to the U.S. edition of *The Hidden Face of Eve,* Gendzier makes clear that one of the first encounters between Western and non-Western feminists was over the Iranian Revolution (1982, viii) and locates El Saadawi's position within this charged context. With El Saadawi's preface to the earlier British edition in mind, she justifies El Saadawi's defense of the Iranian Revolution: "In what was sometimes a defensive tone, she argued against Western feminists as well as the reactionary clergy. Saadawi's intention was to undermine the notion of a monolithic Islam while criticizing a policy which she regarded as regressive and a deprivation of women's civil rights" (viii). Gendzier anticipates how the book will be regarded by Westerners, and, like El Saadawi herself, she attempts to control this response by telling her audience how to read it: "For those feminists who have long lamented the deprived status of Middle Eastern Arab women, Saadawi's book will confirm their fears. But it will also require that they reexamine the bases of their strategies vis-à-vis Third World women and women's movements" (viii). While Gendzier was accurate in anticipating Western readers' response to El Saadawi's book, predictably, she could not influence the way it would be read.

The early response to *The Hidden Face of Eve* seems to have caused El Saadawi to rethink how to frame her book for a Western audience. The passionate defense and celebration of the Iranian Revolution disappears from the new introduction she wrote for the U.S. edition in 1982, an omission that probably arose from her experience with the British edition and one that seems tacitly to concede that American audiences would be even less tolerant of open denunciation of U.S. foreign policy. The anti-imperialist rhetoric is also gone.[7] Instead, the new introduction focuses more on the way religion is used as an instrument of oppression by political institutions in the third world (1982, 3–4). She still rejects the Western paradigm, inspired by hostility to Islam, that sees religion as the primary reason for the inferior status of Arab women, and she insists that "any serious study of comparative religion will show clearly that in the very

---

[7] One could also argue that, at this point, El Saadawi was disappointed in the Iranian Revolution and so changed her rhetoric. While this may be partially the case, the absence of all anti-imperialist rhetoric from this introduction indicates that other factors were at work. Moreover, when asked in a 1992 interview if she still saw the Iranian Revolution in the same positive terms as an anticolonialist movement for change, El Saadawi responded that the original Iranian Revolution had totally failed because it was aborted by colonial powers that "played a role to shift it from a political and economic revolution to a religious revolution" (1992b, 35). Speaking to the leftist readers of the *Progressive,* El Saadawi still defended the original anti-imperialist and socialist nature of the revolution. In another interview given during the Gulf War, she mentions again the anti-imperialist nature of the Khomeini regime (1991d, 24).

essence of Islam, as such, the status of women is no worse than it is in Judaism or in Christianity. In fact the oppression of women is much more glaring in the ideology of Christianity and Judaism. The veil was a product of Judaism long before Islam came into being" (4). El Saadawi continues to defend Islam against Western misrepresentations, but the tone here is more subdued and less militant than in the earlier version. Although she is still trying to exert some control over how her book will be received, she has adjusted her rhetoric to accommodate the expectations of her new audience. This accommodation takes the form of appeasement when she discusses the issue of clitoridectomy. In the introduction to the British edition, El Saadawi had denounced those who exploit female circumcision for its sensational value and dwell on this so-called barbaric practice to the exclusion of other serious issues. In the U.S. introduction, however, not only does she neglect to provide such a caution, but she herself calls the practice "barbaric" (5). The reception of the earlier British edition clearly influenced her decisions about how to present her project here. In order to be heard, El Saadawi seems to have felt that she had to compromise, yielding at least partly to her audience's expectations.

But these differences between the British and the U.S. introductions are only part of the story. In crossing from Egypt to Europe and then to the United States, the book itself underwent major alterations in both content and form. *Al-Wajh al-'ari lil-mar'a al-'arabiyyah* (literally, "the naked face of the Arab woman") becomes *The Hidden Face of Eve*. Entire chapters in the Arabic edition disappear from the English translation. Two chapters in particular, "Woman's Work at Home" and "Arab Woman and Socialism," in which El Saadawi critiques capitalism's exploitation of women and argues for a socialist economic and political system, are not in *The Hidden Face of Eve*. These are significant omissions since the critique of capitalism in favor of socialism was central to El Saadawi's project, written at the height of the implementation of Sadat's procapitalist "open door" policy, to which she was vehemently opposed.[8] Also absent are passages that assert Arab women to be ahead of American and European women in demanding equality for their sex, that celebrate the progress Arab women have made, and that exhort them to see wars of liberation as empowering to them. One missing passage reads: "It is important that Arab women should not feel inferior to Western women, or think that the Arabic tradi-

[8] The open-door policy adopted by Anwar Sadat's regime in the mid-1970s opened the Egyptian economy for foreign investments and multinational corporations. The policy was opposed by several political groups and many intellectuals.

tion and culture are more oppressive of women than Western culture" (1977, 166, my translation).[9]

Even more significant than the translation's omissions are its additions. *The Hidden Face of Eve* has sections that do not exist in *Al-Wajh al-ʿari lil-marʾa al-ʿarabiyyah* (1977), including the chapter suggestively titled "The Grandfather with Bad Manners." While both the Arabic and the English editions open with the story of El Saadawi's excision as a six-year-old, only the translation has a chapter called "Circumcision of Girls." The only time El Saadawi mentions circumcision in the original edition is in the flashback to her childhood in the opening paragraphs. No complete chapter devoted to circumcision appears in any of her other theoretical books either, not even in the most controversial one, *Al-Marʾah wal-jins* (Woman and sex [1971]). Although the chapter "Circumcision of Girls" in the English-language editions is adapted from her book *Al-Marʾah wal-Siraʿ al-nafsi* (Woman and psychological conflict [1976a]), even there it does not exist as an independent chapter; rather, it is part of a larger section that discusses several aspects of women's lives, such as early or loveless marriages and the hardships faced by peasant and factory women. This much-quoted chapter, the one usually assigned in courses in U.S. universities, has been added to the English translation, and, to emphasize this chapter and the theme of circumcision even more, the whole first section of *The Hidden Face of Eve* is given the dramatic title "The Mutilated Half," which, again, is not in the Arabic edition.

In addition to these differences at the level of content, the English

[9] In the Arabic edition of *The Hidden Face of Eve,* the chapter "Positive Origins of the Arab Woman" begins with the following paragraph, which is absent from the same chapter in the British and U.S. editions: "The Arab woman was ahead of the European and American woman in resisting the patriarchal class system. The American woman did not realize till the last years of the twentieth century that the dominant language is that of Man, and that the word 'man' means human or all humanity, and that the masculine case includes both men and women. Some women's liberation movements in America and Europe try now to change the language. But the Arab woman did this fourteen centuries ago." Then El Saadawi mentions the incident when Muslim women objected to the prophet that the Quran addresses only men, an objection that resulted in new verses mentioning both men and women (1977, 39). A tamer version of this passage appears in the afterword to the British edition: "Arab women preceded the women of the world in resisting the patriarchal system based on male domination" (1980c, 212). In another instance, she informs her readers in a footnote in the Arabic edition that, while attending a conference in the United States, she criticized the stereotypical representation of Arab women in U.S. movies (1977, 53). This footnote is absent from the English editions. In both of these cases, she is trying to distance herself from Western feminists in front of her Arab audience but then removes these passages from the English-language editions so as not to alienate them.

edition reverses the organization of the chapters as they first appeared. Sections dealing with sexuality, which were originally placed in the last third of the Arabic edition, are put first, while the exposition of Arab women's history is relegated to the end of the book. The earlier parts of the Arabic edition explain the processes that subjugated all women in order to show that woman's inferior status is not natural but the result of particular social and historical conditions. Referring to the history of Arab and Muslim women in particular, El Saadawi illustrates that these women used to be stronger than they are now and that their present disempowerment and degradation are not caused by Islam, implying that true Islam empowers women. The reorganization, however, emphasizes issues of sexuality and underplays the historical context of these issues. It is an arrangement more suitable for a Western audience less interested in history than in satisfying an insatiable appetite for an exotic and oppressed "other."

The new title, too, seems to invite the English-speaking reader to experience the book as a glimpse behind the veil. While the literal Arabic title, "the naked face of the Arab woman," emphasizes the baring of the face — a metaphor suited to the political aim of the book, which is to speak the truth about Arab women's lives in the hope of changing them — the English title foregrounds the covered face.[10] Employing one of the main, and most stagnant, metaphors in hegemonic Western discourse about Arab and Muslim women, the new title confirms rather than unsettles its readers' assumptions. Moreover, the "Arab woman" of the Arabic title disappears, giving way to Eve, which further moves the book away from history into the realm of myth.

It is a very different book, then, that appeared in American bookstores in 1982. Predictably, reviewers emphasized some sections and ignored others — influenced, of course, by the changes to the text. For instance, one writer titled her review "About the Mutilated Half" and focused her discussion on the twin issues of circumcision and Islam (Gornick 1982). She declared the book "a curious work . . . written in a country and for a people that require an educated introduction to the idea of equality for women" (3). Her one-paragraph summary stresses only the parts of the book that discuss Arab women as victims. She portrays El Saadawi herself as a victim by dwelling on her circumcision and her imprisonment, which she claims

---

[10] This original aim is made clear in El Saadawi's dedication, which reads: "To my daughters and sons, the youth of the Arab world, including my daughter Mona and son 'Atif, with the hope that the future be more truthful and enlightened than the past or the present" (1977, my translation).

resulted from El Saadawi's speaking out about taboo sexual matters. In fact, El Saadawi was not a lone victim of patriarchal society, persecuted for her feminist views but, rather, a political activist, imprisoned along with fifteen hundred other Egyptians for her opposition to the Camp David Agreement. As for her defense of Islam, the reviewer easily dismisses it by declaring that "no culture as religion-dominated as Arabic culture can ever accomplish social or political equality for women. . . . Western feminists do have reason to think Islamic law will never grant women full recognition. It may be possible to abolish the practice of circumcision, but it will not be so easy to abolish the idea of woman as an instrument of man's honor or dishonor." She condescendingly concludes, "*The Hidden Face of Eve* reminds us of where we have all come from" (3). In this review, El Saadawi's book becomes a testament to the progress that American women have achieved in contrast to their oppressed Arab sisters, supposedly still groaning under the shackles of Islam.[11]

This review is typical of the reception of El Saadawi's other works in the United States. She is almost always mentioned in the context of circumcision and fundamentalist Islam, as simultaneously a victim and authority on both. By 1991, one writer could remember only that "Saadawi's most famous book, *The Hidden Face of Eve*, [is] about her experience of undergoing a clitoridectomy in her native Delta village" (Roth 1991, 10). Articles by and about her appear under charged headings such as "Betrayed by Blind Faith" (Mukherjee 1986), "Egyptian Pens Terrorized by Islam's Sword" (La Guardia 1992), and "Challenging a Taboo: Going to Jail for Politics, Sex and Religion" (El Saadawi 1985a). El Saadawi is almost always figured as a campaigner "stand[ing] alone in the fight for increased justice and democracy for women" (Roth 1991, 10). Since receiving death threats in Egypt, like so many other secular intellectuals, she has been seen in the United States as the ultimate victim of Islam, declared by Susan Sontag (1994) to be an Arab Taslima Nasrin, who, according to another writer, creates "an anthem for all those nameless millions who died the outer or the inner death, sentenced by fundamentalist Islam's cruel and unjustified repression of women" (Roberts 1993). El Saadawi's story of persecution is told and retold every time her name is mentioned — on cover blurbs, in newspapers, and in articles in academic journals.

This representation of El Saadawi erases important aspects of her political identity and distorts others. For example, Western commentators often claim that her feminist views on female sexuality led Sadat to imprison her

[11] For a response to this review, see Basu 1982.

and Hosni Mubarak to close down the Arab Women's Solidarity Association.[12] In fact, it was actually her opposition to the Camp David Agreement in 1981 and to the Gulf War in 1991—not her feminism per se—that brought these reprisals. If mentioned, El Saadawi's political views are usually dismissed as irrelevant and "far left," as some reviewers put it (Jacoby 1994). Moreover, since El Saadawi is seen as writing of "a way of life that in many aspects has not changed for centuries," the specific historical context of her works is systematically erased (*Publishers Weekly* 1994). Thus different accounts merge, and her books, experiences, and arguments become indistinguishable from one another. According to one report (Fullerton 1989), for instance, while El Saadawi was in prison in 1981, she met Firdaus, about whom she then wrote her novel *Imra'a 'ind nuqtat al-sifr* (Woman at point zero [1979]). (However, that work was actually published in Arabic well before El Saadawi's imprisonment.) According, erroneously, to another (Werner 1991), *The Fall of the Imam* (1988a), a novel immediately connected to the assassination of Sadat, is a critique of Ayatollah Khomeini and the Iranian Revolution. El Saadawi's voice and image, then, are framed by the Western discourse about her in a way that fits first-world agendas and assumptions: the socialist feminist is rewritten as a liberal individualist and the anti-imperialist as a native informant. This framing often discredits El Saadawi with her Arab audiences.

Although she makes some efforts to resist the West's misrepresentation of her, El Saadawi, I argue, also invites it in some ways, allowing her works to be used to confirm prevailing prejudices about Arab and Muslim culture. Furthermore, her self-representation to her Western readers encourages and confirms their readings of her. For instance, she does not show herself as part of a feminist movement, as someone learning from the experiences and building on the achievements of other women, but rather as exceptional and a pioneer.[13] She underscores her difference from other intellectuals by emphasizing that, unlike them, she does not belong to any particular political party (1980b, 170).[14] While she admits that her prison experience taught her the value of "collective political work" (1992b, 35), her representation of that experience in *Memoirs from the Women's Prison*

[12] El Saadawi sometimes encourages this understanding (see, e.g., El Saadawi 1991b, 156).

[13] One obvious example of this self-representation is the obituary that El Saadawi wrote for Aminah al-Said in the *Guardian*, in which she dismisses al-Said's feminism by showing that al-Said was conventional in her views of women and compromising in her dealings with the powers-that-be; she hardly mentions any of al-Said's long feminist history (1995b). For readers' angry responses to this obituary and its omissions, see Croucher 1995; Gindi 1995.

[14] See also El Saadawi 1985a; 1992b, 35; 1994a, 25; 1994c, 30, 126, 159.

(1986) confirms the superiority of her political independence. Some of the main objects of satire in that book are Marxist and Muslim fundamentalist women prisoners, whom El Saadawi represents as fanatic and ideologically dogmatic.[15] At the same time, she casts herself as the leader of the women prisoners, the one making decisions and initiating action.[16] Most important, El Saadawi distinguishes her feminism by claiming for it an authenticity lacking in that of her Arab feminist critics, whom she pronounces "Western" and therefore inauthentic (1993b, 175). In addition to being essentialist (describing an Arab or Eastern thought that is untouched by the West and opposed to it), this claim is also inaccurate, for, as we shall see, El Saadawi's feminism synthesizes concepts and frameworks from disparate origins. But by disqualifying other Arab women's feminism, El Saadawi offers herself to the West as the true representative of Arab feminism. To complete this picture, she narrates her life story either as a success story of the rise to prominence of a rural, third-world woman or as a persecution story about a feminist harassed by a patriarchy intent on subduing her. The two narrative lines often merge, and the organizing principle of both is individualism — not coincidentally, one of the most cherished ideological concepts of her middle-class Western audience.

The Arab context of reception

A different view of El Saadawi emerges if we consider her within the original Arab context of her books. In Egypt and the Arab world, El Saadawi is neither a victim nor a lone campaigner for women's rights but rather a product of a specific historical moment that puts her squarely within her culture, not outside it. Although by the early seventies she had published

---

[15] See, e.g., her caricatures of Bodoor, the Muslim woman, and Fawqiyya, the Marxist woman (El Saadawi 1986, esp. 38, 115, 126, 130). Much of the humor in the book is at their expense, even at the level of making puns on their names. ("Bodoor," meaning "the one with the beautiful face," is given to the prisoner who completely covers her face; "Fawqiyya," meaning "the pedantic one," is given to the Marxist prisoner.) It is significant that when El Saadawi decided on an excerpt from the book to publish (1985a), she chose the episode that makes fun of Bodoor, "the Muslim fundamentalist," thus catering to her Western audience's appetite for stereotypes of Islam.

[16] It is interesting to compare El Saadawi's representations with those of Latifah al-Zayyat in her prison memoir *The Search: Personal Papers* (1996). Two things stand out. First, while al-Zayyat mentions El Saadawi, along with other women prisoners, she does not portray either herself or El Saadawi as a leader. Second, at no point does al-Zayyat put down her fellow prisoners, including the Muslim fundamentalists, who stand at the opposite end of the political and ideological spectrum from her. On the contrary, her solidarity with them as women comes through with poignancy.

some fiction, it was her nonfiction—particularly *Al-Mar'ah wal-jins* in 1971—that brought El Saadawi to the attention of Egyptian and Arab readers. This book was followed by *Al-Untha hiya al-asl* (Female is the origin [1974b]), *Al-Rajul wal-jins* (Man and sex [1976b]), and *Al-Mar'ah wal-sira' al-nafsi* (Woman and psychological conflict [1976a]), all published before *Al-Wajh al-'ari lil-mar'a al-'arabiyyah* (1977). These influential books appeared in the specific context of the post-1967 Arab/Egyptian defeat by Israel. This defeat was a turning point for many intellectuals, who, as a result, directed their critical gaze inward toward themselves and their society. They believed that the unexpected and crushing military blow and the ensuing loss of land were caused as much by a corrupt Arab society as by Israel's military might. Not merely directed at leaders and their corrupt regimes, this approach attempted to scrutinize and expose the roots of the problem as these writers saw it, not its outward manifestations. Their critiques were part of a radical project that aimed at questioning and undermining the various structures of power governing both the individual and the group.[17]

El Saadawi's early writing participates in this cultural project, as she herself acknowledges in her introduction to the U.S. edition of *The Hidden Face of Eve:* "During the past years a number of serious studies have been published, and have contributed to the unmasking of many social ills that require a radical cure if Arab society is to attain real freedom in all fields of endeavor whether economic, political, human, or moral" (1982, 2). In looking for a "radical cure" for Arab society's ills, El Saadawi and other Arab radical cultural critics both diagnosed the disease and prescribed the treatment. A full recovery, they believed, would be attained only by rejecting Western paradigms, perspectives, and scholarship, on the one hand, and religious obscurantism and modernizing Arab neopatriarchy, on the other (Sharabi 1990, 21). This is a crucial point if we are to understand El Saadawi's writing, for it explains both her eclecticism and her attitudes toward the West and Islam. Readers of her nonfiction encounter Sigmund Freud, Karl Marx, and the Prophet Muhammad all on the same page, where she also mixes genres and employs various concepts from different philosophies. In being eclectic, El Saadawi is actually asserting her independence. Moreover, while she rejects Islamic obscurantism and the use of religion as a tool of oppression, she also fights against the Western (mis)understanding of Islam. What might appear as inconsistency in her work is in fact an expression of the dual project of the post-1967 Arab cultural critic, whose long-term goal was "to subvert simultaneously the ex-

[17] See, e.g., al-'Azm 1968; Adonis 1974; Sharabi 1975; Zayour 1977.

isting social and political (neo)patriarchal system and the West's cultural hegemony" (Sharabi 1990, 23).[18] In *Al-Wajh al-'ari lil-mar'a al-'arabiyyah* (1977) in particular, El Saadawi carries out this subversive project by confronting head-on issues such as "the place and meaning of the cultural heritage (*turath*); the relation of historicity, the question of religion, identity, tradition, and modernity" (Sharabi 1990, 27).

El Saadawi, then, is not "something of an anomaly in Egyptian cultural life," as one American critic has called her (Hitchcock 1993, 34).[19] That she was writing not in isolation but as part of an emergent, progressive, secular, cultural critique cannot be overemphasized. Her attack on patriarchy, for instance, was echoed by Hisham Sharabi's (1975) study of the patriarchal Arab family and how it socializes its children into submission, conformity, and dependency. Like El Saadawi, the Lebanese psychologist Ali Zayour (1977) approaches Arab society as an analyst, employing psychoanalysis to study the anxiety and disequilibrium produced in the Arab personality by a changing and contradictory society. However, El Saadawi's original contribution to this radical critique is her foregrounding of sexuality and gender. While the Arab critics mentioned above speak for the most part of a nongendered individual, El Saadawi takes the radical step of gendering her Arab subject.[20] Moreover, El Saadawi's feminist critique was instrumental in popularizing discourses about sexuality and about women's rights. Unlike the more academic writings of radical feminists such as Fatima Mernissi and Khalida Said, hers are written in an accessible language that is neither literary nor technical. Her simple diction, crisp sentences, and short paragraphs give her books a journalistic flavor and appeal to a wide reading public. Her nonfiction mixes genres, juxtaposing critical analysis, scientific discourse, polemic, case histories, personal anecdotes, and autobiography. She addresses readers with the confidence of a physician, the passion of an activist, the credibility of an eyewitness, and the pathos of an injured woman.

El Saadawi's nonfictional writing differed from the prevailing Egyptian feminist discourse of the time in that it focused on poor women, emphasizing their oppression and exploitation. While this emphasis fell within the

[18] See Boullata 1990, 129–30, on what he calls El Saadawi's "ambiguity" toward Islam.

[19] Peter Hitchcock justifies this view of El Saadawi as follows: "She is educated but from the countryside; she is a feminist, but one who emphasizes class struggle in relation to questions of women's oppressed position; she questions the proscriptions of religion, but she is a strong proponent of Islam" (1993, 34). But, as I argue in this essay, the attributes enumerated by Hitchcock place El Saadawi squarely within, not outside, post-1967 Egyptian cultural life.

[20] Other women writers who engaged in a similar kind of critique around the same time are Fatima Mernissi (1975) and Khalida Said (1970).

parameters of the general leftist intellectual discourse, it was subversive in the context of Egyptian feminism, which expressed the interests of middle- and upper-class women and was articulated by members of these classes (such as Qasim Amin, Huda Shaarawi, Dorriyya Shafik, Caisa Nabrawi, and Aminah al-Said, among others). In the 1970s, one must not forget, the self-appointed head of the women's movement in Egypt was none other than Jihan el-Sadat, the Egyptian president's wife. While "establish-ment" feminists like Jihan el-Sadat and al-Said advocated women's rights and acknowledged the need to improve women's condition, they adopted a reformist agenda to effect change. El Saadawi rejected their limited liberal agenda and challenged their strategies for liberation, demanding not piece-meal reform but a socialist restructuring of the whole society. In other words, her polemical writing was as much a response to this feminist tradi-tion as it was a critique of patriarchal society generally.[21]

El Saadawi as novelist

Few Arab critics would question the important contribution that El Saadawi's theoretical/polemical writing has made to oppositional Arab thought.[22] More contested, though, is her status as a novelist. Arab critics and readers are generally surprised at the accolades heaped on El Saadawi's fiction in the West, and some have concluded that the popularity of her novels has less to do with their literary merit than with their fulfillment of Western readers' assumptions about Arab men and women (Hafez 1989). This response to El Saadawi's fiction is usually dismissed in the West as the result of Arab male hostility toward her as a feminist writer.[23] To go beyond all of these rather reductionist explanations, we need to consider El Saa-

[21] For an indication of the rift between El Saadawi and this liberal feminism, see her obitu-ary of al-Said (1995b).

[22] For instance, Hisham Sharabi (1988, 32–33) singles out *Woman and Sex* for its radical impact, as do Joseph Zeidan (1995, 125) and Afif Farraj (1985, 346), among others.

[23] See, e.g., Malti-Douglas 1995a, 1995b. Hitchcock also simplifies El Saadawi's relation to her critics when he writes, "She is one of Egypt's foremost writers, and yet most of her works were initially published and indeed were best known outside Egypt. She is unpopular with Egyptian officialdom and with Islamic scholars, including many of her Arab sisters who see their concerns being represented or reduced through the voice of a renegade from Kafr Tahla" (1993, 34). I do not deny, however, that there is some truth to the notion that El Saadawi's popularity in the West does have something to do with her telling the West what it wants to hear about Arabs, or that there are sexist Arab critics who are hostile to El Saa-dawi's feminism. However, these explanations alone do not suffice to explain her critical re-ception in either the West or the Arab world.

dawi's fiction in the context of the modern Arabic literary tradition within which it is read and judged.

As critics of Arabic literature have noted, the Egyptian novel, although mostly written by men, was from its beginning a "woman-centered" genre. Women were main characters or main problems, as is clear from some of the early titles, such as *Zaynab* (Haykal 1914) and *Sarah* (al-'Aqqad 1938). The theme of love and the question of women's position in society were central to these novels and to other early examples of the genre, including Ibrahim Abd al-Qadir al-Mazini's *Ibrahim al-Katib* (1931) (Ibrahim the writer [1931]), Taha Husayn's *Du'a' al-karawan* (The call of the curlew [1934]), and Mahmud Tahir Lashin's *Hawwa bila Adam* (Eve without Adam [1934]). In the works of the popular romantics of the 1950s and 1960s, women continued to be central characters. Some of these writers, such as Ihsan Abdul Quddus, for instance, attempted "to break down the taboos concerning what can be mentioned in literature" by telling in a sensational and titillating way the story of the "struggles of young girls from good families to liberate themselves, chiefly on the emotional and sexual plane" (Kilpatrick 1992, 246). Alongside this literature, and partly in opposition to it, was the "committed literature" of the 1950s and 1960s, influenced by socialist realism. According to the proponents of this school, the real artist is an active agent with a responsibility to give voice to the oppressed of his or her society. Writing soon after the revolution of 1952, at the height of a period of decolonization in the Arab world, the first generation of "committed" writers was optimistic, confident that the struggle for liberation and justice inevitably would be victorious. This generation includes, for example, Abd al-Rahman al-Sharqawi, whose novel *Al-Ard* (1953; translated as *Egyptian Earth* in 1962) depicts peasants' resistance to oppressive landlords, and Latifah al-Zayyat, whose *Al-Bab al-maftuh* (The open door [1960]) tells the story of one woman's successful struggle for emancipation.

The "revolutionary optimism" (Kilpatrick 1992, 252) of writers such as al-Sharqawi and al-Zayyat could not be sustained after 1967, for the defeat by Israel affected novelists the same way it did other Arab intellectuals. Post-1967 writers, "the Gallery 68 generation" in particular, had a more pessimistic view of their society and its future and wrote against an establishment that, they felt, betrayed the promises of the revolution. In *Al-Hidad* (1969), Muhammad Yusuf al-Qa'id condemns oppressive patriarchal authority, and in his later novels he targets Sadat's Egypt. Yahya al-Tahir Abdallah likewise critiques patriarchy in his *Al-Tawq wa'l-iswirah* (The choker and the bracelet [1975]), in which he traces the lives of three generations of women. And Jamal al-Ghitani in his historical novel *Al-Zayni Barakat* (1971) dissects the workings of the authoritarian state. As a novelist, El Saadawi belongs to this generation of leftist writers, sharing their belief in committed literature and their hostility to the establishment in its various oppressive forms.[24] The hopeful tone of her first novel, *Mudhakkirat tabiba* (Memoirs of a woman doctor [1958]), gives way to the pessimism or, at best, the strained optimism of her later novels, written at what she would describe as a time of counterrevolution.

El Saadawi's literary achievement, however, lies not so much in her social criticism as in the forward push she gave to Arabic feminist narrative. While she was not the first to write "feminist novels," she stands out as the one who made the Arabic feminist novel recognizable as a genre.[25] Other writers of what we might call feminist novels chose not to become full-time novelists: Aminah al-Said, who wrote *Al-Jamihah* (The defiant) in 1950 (the first "Arab feminist novel" according to the Egyptian critic Raga' al-Naqqash [1995]), pursued a pioneering and successful career in journalism, and al-Zayyat, after the defeat of 1967, stopped publishing fiction for twenty-five years, devoting herself instead to teaching and literary criticism (see, e.g., al-Zayyat 1994). El Saadawi was also writing at a more opportune moment than the Lebanese Layla Ba'lbakki, who was tried for the explicit sexual passages in her 1963 book *Safinat hanan ila al-qamar* (Spaceship of tenderness to the moon). More important, El Saadawi succeeded in building on the momentum and name recognition that she had acquired through her nonfiction, writing unambiguously radical, angry works that secured for the feminist novel a place on the literary map of modern Arabic literature.

Arab commentators have recognized this achievement. The Syrian literary critic George Tarabishi has devoted a whole book to El Saadawi's fiction because, in his opinion, she is "the principal exponent of the Arabic feminist novel" (1988, 9). And literary historians of the Arabic novel, Arab and non-Arab alike (e.g., Roger Allen [1995], Joseph Zeidan [1995], and

---

[24] Ouyang 1996 places El Saadawi's fiction within the tradition of the novel of ideas in particular. My thanks to Ouyang for allowing me to read her review before it appeared in print.

[25] Both al-Said's *Al-Jamihah* (1950) and al-Zayyat's *Al-Bab al-maftuh* (1960) portray the struggle of one young women for self-actualization. The similarities between al-Zayyat's novel and El Saadawi's *Two Women in One* (1985c) in terms of themes and plot are considerable. Other writers of feminist novels before El Saadawi include Colette al-Khuri, who wrote *Ayyam ma'ahu* (Days with him [1959]) and Layla Ba'lbakki, who in *Ana ahya* (I am alive [1958]) writes of one woman's search for emancipation and in *Al-Alihah al-mamsukhah* (The disfigured gods [1960]) of Arabs' obsession with the hymen. See Zeidan 1995 for a useful survey of Arab women writers.

Trevor LeGassick [1992]), give El Saadawi a place in their histories specifically as a proponent of the radical feminist novel. However, while these
critics appreciate her contributions, they also point out what they see as
the weaknesses of her fiction. Tarabishi, for instance, criticizes her for ab-
stracting her men and women in *Woman at Point Zero* and reducing them
to "one dimensional" characters. Such characterizations, he argues, fail to
illuminate complex human relations and therefore "do not make for good
literature" (1988, 17–18).[26] Afif Farraj, a more conservative critic than Tarabishi, faults El Saadawi for imposing an ideological discourse on the
world of literature, for shifting between the polemical essay and narrative,
and for presenting her opinion through self-evident statements rather than
through layers of events (1985, 331). He concludes that "character in El
Saadawi's novels is almost an empty board except for the ideological statements written in large type. . . . The Saadawian heroine remains a captive
of the rigid ideological text, and this text controls the narrative, plot and
the fate of the characters. Her mechanical plot is built around an idea, like
an Arab musical built around the words of the songs" (320). Zeidan concurs, pointing out that the novels' strength — their "commitment to the
cause of women's liberation" — is also their weakness, for it tends to "over-
shadow many of her stories to such a degree that, at certain points, the
thoughts and statements of her characters seem forced and inappropriate"
(1995, 130). In certain places in *Memoirs of a Woman Doctor,* for instance,
he claims, "the novel functions as a soapbox from which al-Saadawi
preaches her views in a declamatory manner unsuited to a novel" (1995,
131).

Critics have questioned not only the form of El Saadawi's fiction but
also her message. Tarabishi targets what he calls her "individualistic philosophy" and "elitist attitude." In his view, Firdaus's struggle in *Woman at
Point Zero* "is aimed at liberating not her female sisters, but herself" (1988,
32), and her "nihilistic asceticism" is a way to reject reality, not to change
it. He concludes, "Firdaus's story is undoubtedly worth telling. However,
presenting it as an individual, isolated case is one thing; and elevating it to
the level of a theoretical issue is quite another" (33). In an earlier study of
El Saadawi's *Two Women in One,* he contends that the main character's fears

[26] Roger Allen, however, reserves judgment on El Saadawi's literary merit: "Fiction at the
hands of Nawal al-Saadawi becomes an alternative and powerful means of forwarding her
opinions concerning the rights of women in Middle Eastern society. The voice of her narrators is strident, and the message unequivocal. It remains to be seen what position her works
will retain in the history of modern Arabic fiction, but there can be little doubt that she will
be numbered among the most prominent fighters for her cause in the latter half of the twentieth century" (1995, 107–8).

of the herd and her feelings of exceptionalism, or of difference, do not lead to individuation but to elitism (Tarabishi 1978, 23). Along similar lines, Ahmad Jasim al-Hamidi contends that El Saadawi's fiction changes class struggle into gender struggle (1986, 197) and the "alienated condition" into an "elitist condition" (187). He finds the endings of her novels particularly problematic. Farraj concurs, arguing that there is no hope of liberation for the Saadawian heroine, whose consciousness and behavior is dependent on reaction and who moves in every novel from rebellion to submission (1985, 340). The Egyptian critic Sabry Hafez admires El Saadawi's intentions but pronounces her fiction a failure — ideologically, because it "invert[s] the prevalent patriarchal order without a clear understanding of the dangers involved," and artistically, because of the author's "one dimensional approach" to her material (1995, 166, 170). The Egyptian novelist Salwa Bakr criticizes El Saadawi's view that "the problem of women [is] mainly sexual," arguing that priority should be given instead to women's inferior economic situation (quoted in al-Ali 1994, 65).[27] Bakr is not the only woman writer to criticize El Saadawi as a novelist. The Iraqi novelist Alia Mamdouh charges her of "turning creativity, which is imagination and living memory into a lab to show sick, deformed samples which she presents as generalized social types" (quoted in *Al-Hayat* 1996, 12). El Saadawi is also faulted for her repetitive style, weak language, and lack of technical development (Farraj 1985, 346; Hafez 1989), and the Anglo-Egyptian novelist Ahdaf Soueif, who herself writes about female sexuality, speaks for many when she remarks, "El Saadawi writes good scientific research, but she writes bad novels. It is unfair that the West thinks that what she writes represents Arab women's creative writing" (quoted in *Al-Hayat* 1996, 12).

As the above summary shows, El Saadawi's Arab critics are not homogeneous. Similarly, those who write about her in the West bring to her work a variety of perspectives and approaches, at times recognizing the same issues raised by Arab critics.[28] Others have dealt with the problematic of

[27] Bakr says, "This does not mean that I do not view sexuality to be a problem for women, but it is not the most important one. The most important thing is that services such as health care, nurseries, etc., are very poor because of the bad economic situation" (quoted in al-Ali 1994, 65). Similarly, al-Said criticizes El Saadawi's priorities: "Nawal has the right idea. . . . But this talk of sexual revolution and legalized abortion before most women can read is absurd" (quoted in Roth 1991, 10).

[28] See Emberley 1993; Ouyang 1996, 1997. In addition, some reviewers have pointed out other "problems" in El Saadawi's fiction. In her review of *The Innocence of the Devil*, Laura Cumming argues, "Her naive iconography never varies. . . . The rigid binary oppositions within which her novels operate constrict the purpose El Saadawi avows in her non-fiction, which is to campaign against patriarchy as oppressive to men as well as to women. . . . Deter-

reception (e.g., Hitchcock 1993; Mitra 1995). In general, however, Western critics have received El Saadawi's fiction more positively than their Arab counterparts. This difference can be accounted for in part by the very different frameworks in which they situate her fiction, often discussing it in terms of "resistance literature" (Harlow 1987), "Third World women's texts" (Saliba 1995), "testimonial literature" (Hitchcock 1993), or even more general categories such as "the picaresque novel" (Payne 1992) or "feminist writings" (Accad 1987; Salti 1994; Lionnet 1995). However, while these categories and contexts illuminate some aspects of El Saadawi's novels, they overlook others. As several recent postcolonial critics have pointed out, postcolonial and feminist frameworks can be so generalizing as to be misleading (Mohanty 1991; Ahmad 1992; Donnell 1995). Because the Arab context is largely absent from them, these works tend to exaggerate the subversiveness and exceptionalism of El Saadawi's fiction. Thus, while Fedwa Malti-Douglas in her monograph on El Saadawi declares that, "of all living Arabic writers, none more than Nawal El Saadawi has his or her finger so firmly on the pulse of Arab culture and the contemporary Middle East" (1995a, 2), she treats El Saadawi in isolation from other Arab women writers. As I have pointed out elsewhere, her "few passing references to the contemporary scene seek to show not how El Saadawi emerges from and engages with her culture but how she transcends it" (Amireh 1996, 231). Sometimes El Saadawi's fiction is placed within an Arab context at such a distance from the actual moment of production as to make the connection between text and context tenuous at best.

More pertinent for the present discussion than what Western critics say about El Saadawi's fiction is the way they frame their criticism. They seem to assume that they are more reliable, fair, and disinterested and therefore more qualified to judge El Saadawi's fiction than their Arab counterparts. El Saadawi herself encourages this assumption. In a recent interview she praises her Western critics for being "objective" and declares that she is not interested in what her Arab critics have to say because they are not qualified to appreciate her personality, which is different from anything to which they are accustomed (al-'Uwayt 1992). In another interview she makes clear that she no longer writes for an exclusively Arab audience: "Before, I

---

mined to generalise centuries of female suffering, El Saadawi creates an ahistorical fiction in which women are reduced to symbols of sexual oppression and men are their interchangeable torturers" (1994, 8). Another reviewer writes, "The novel is curiously heavy going, often seeming overwrought and oversignificant. Portentous abstractions and paradoxes . . . are too frequent. . . . [It] tends to sink beneath the weight of its extranovelistic implications. One feels claustrophobically imprisoned within the author's lushly written resentments" (M. D. Allen 1995, 638).

didn't have the pleasure or the freedom to experiment. But now I want to go beyond that, to experiment with the language, to experiment with ideas, to have more freedom. Even if the book is not published in the Arab world. At first, I wrote for the Arab people, men and women. And I had to consider my audience. I was not writing for angels in the sky. My audience was the Arab people. So, if I spoke about something they would totally reject, it would not be there at all. But now I don't care" (1990c, 404). Some Arab readers have picked up on the fact that El Saadawi is not speaking to them anymore. One female reader views with suspicion El Saadawi's popularity in the West: "She's not really fighting for a cause. She is fighting for her own cause. . . . I don't feel she's worth following. She's made her name outside of Egypt, rather than inside Egypt" (Gauch 1991, 1). According to the Egyptian novelist Jamal al-Ghitany, El Saadawi "is living in America because she wants a Nobel Prize. She is writing for the West, she cannot feel the true problems of women" (quoted in Lennon 1994, 29). In using El Saadawi's (dis)location to dismiss her writing, these critics assume that "identities are tied to space, and that a pure and authentic standpoint can be developed only if one remains rooted firmly within the territory of one's origin" (Michel 1995, 87). Ironically, El Saadawi herself has used a similar argument to discredit those who disagree with her, claiming that many of the feminists who criticize her live in the West and therefore are Western in their feminism (1993b, 175). Similarly, according to one interviewer, she calls Edward Said "an arrogant intellectual who has a westernized interpretation of the Middle East" (Winokur 1994, 12).

When critics' "authenticity" cannot be called into question, El Saadawi invokes another strategy. In response to Tarabishi's criticism of her in *Woman against Her Sex* (1988; a response that appears as an appendix in the English translation of his book), El Saadawi declares the book "a personal attack." She objects to, among other things, Tarabishi's arguments that there is autobiographical material in her novels and that she seems to identify psychologically with her heroines. She ridicules Tarabishi for using elaborate theory (Freudian psychoanalysis) to read what she calls "a simple novel" (in Tarabishi 1988, 189–211). However, other critics have written about the autobiographical elements in El Saadawi's writing and about her identification with her heroines or have used elaborate theoretical approaches to read her novels, and neither El Saadawi nor anyone else has objected to their readings.[29] But Tarabishi is more critical of El Saadawi. Many critics in the West have adopted El Saadawi's attitude toward Tarabishi and have defended her against his "personal" attack supposedly moti-

[29] See, e.g., Harlow 1987; Badran and Cooke 1990, 203; Hitchcock 1993; Lionnet 1995.

vated by misogyny and opposition to feminism. They express outrage and amazement that such a book has been written at all, and, for them, the mere fact that it has been translated into English proves that there is a conspiracy to defame El Saadawi.[30]

These sorts of responses to Tarabishi and to other Arab critics of El Saadawi illustrate the imbalance in power relations between Western-based intellectuals and their Arab-based counterparts. They seem to say that it is acceptable for the third world to supply primary texts but that criticism of these texts is more ably done in the first world (see Mitchell 1995, 475). These defenders of El Saadawi generally view Arab male critics with suspicion and hostility. Thus, for instance, Edward Said's passing remark that El Saadawi is "overexposed" and "overcited" in the West (1990, 280) is blown out of all proportion and offered as representative of "one of the negative consensus positions on the Egyptian feminist" (Malti-Douglas 1995b, 283). These defenders often conflate El Saadawi's critics: official state censors, conservative critics who reject the feminism of her nonfiction, and literary critics of her fiction are rolled into one persecuting entity called "Arab male critics."[31] This supposed gap between Arab and Western critics is central to the construction of El Saadawi's identity as a persecuted feminist who is not appreciated in the Arab world she criticizes.

However, these defenses of El Saadawi ignore the context of critiques such as Tarabishi's. They never mention, for instance, that he is not really singling out El Saadawi for his Freudian analysis; in fact, this book is the third in a series of psychoanalytic readings of Arabic literature. In the first (1982), Tarabishi studies the works of feminist Aminah al-Said along with male writers, and, in the second (1983), he analyzes the ideology of manhood in Mahmoud Dib's and Hannah Minah's works.[32] Knowledge of

---

[30] Hitchcock, e.g., expresses his "frustration with the fact that the first book-length work on Nawal El Saadawi available in English happens to be an extended antifeminist diatribe by a Freudian" and hopes that the work of another critic more sympathetic to El Saadawi will "displace Tarabishi's efforts" (1993, 207–8). Similarly, although she does not directly engage Tarabishi's argument itself, Malti-Douglas laments that "the book is the only extended work on El Saadawi in a European language. Such a situation is most extraordinary for a Middle Eastern intellectual" (1995a, 10).

[31] See, e.g., Malti-Douglas 1995b, 283–85, where El Saadawi's "detractors" are all lumped together and given the same motive. Thus Edward Said, Islamic fundamentalists, the Sadat and Mubarak governments, and George Tarabishi all become equivalent "detractors" out to "silence" the feminist writer.

[32] The fact that Tarabishi's book on El Saadawi is the only one of his that has been translated into English has to do with the obvious fact that El Saadawi is a known figure in the West, while writers treated in his other books, though prominent in their own countries, are virtually unknown outside the Arab world.

Tarabishi's other criticism would show that he is not an antifeminist. In his criticism of Minah, for instance, he points to the misogyny and sexism in the Syrian writer's novels and underscores the contradictions between Minah's statements in support of women's liberation, to which Tarabishi is sympathetic, and his misogynist representations of women in his fiction (1983, 87). Tarabishi offers intelligent readings of women characters that many feminists, including El Saadawi herself, would find illuminating. Discussing the stereotypes of women in Minah's work (1983, 115, 117), for example, he shows how Minah attaches negative values to "femininity" and then opposes it to "manhood," with all of its positive connotations (1983, 79). But even beyond Tarabishi's individual readings, his critical project as a whole is, in my view, not opposed to El Saadawi's. His writing foregrounds sex and gender as important categories of analysis, and his readings bring to Arabic literary criticism the same vocabulary that El Saadawi uses in her theoretical feminist writings. Rejecting taboos, both believe that sexuality and gender are legitimate subjects for analysis and study. Although Tarabishi is not a feminist critic and does not claim to be one, neither is he an antifeminist, and his work does not deserve the wholesale dismissal it has received in the United States. One does not need to agree with his readings of individual texts or to embrace his Freudian theoretical framework to recognize that his analysis raises worthwhile questions about El Saadawi's fiction and feminist fiction in general.

Teaching El Saadawi: The Western classroom

The reservations of critics like Tarabishi and Sabry Hafez about El Saadawi's fiction are particularly relevant in light of its popularity in college courses in the West. Arguably the most important site of reception, the Western classroom often assumes that "fiction can do the job that history, geography, economics, sociology, etc., are supposed to" (Bahri 1995, 74). Often the only Arab texts that students encounter, El Saadawi's novels "inform" them about Arab women and Arab society. What complicates matters even more is that fiction and fact get confused both in the novels (as in *Woman at Point Zero* [1983b]) and in El Saadawi's biography. It is not surprising that students, like reviewers and critics, tend to see the novels as windows onto a timeless Islam instead of as literary works governed by certain conventions and produced within specific historical contexts.[33]

---

[33] For example, in their written comments on *The Fall of the Imam* (1988a), graduate students taking a seminar on the postcolonial literature of North Africa and the Middle East at the University of Alberta (taught by Lahoucine Ouzgane and Nasrin Rahimieh) did not mention at any point the relationship between the novel and the assassination of Sadat. Would they have read it differently if that immediate context were emphasized? I believe so.

According to one student, *The Fall of the Imam* (1988a) depicts what "time and history must seem like for freedom-seeking women in Islam: an endless repetition of the same event with only slight variations. This kind of narrative structure . . . captures what I imagine to be Islamic women's extremely limited sense of agency. And the huge question Saadawi presents is: what can women, oppressed by the historically justified patriarchy of Islam, do? How to break out of the endless repetition?"

Several instructors who teach *Woman at Point Zero* (1983b), the most popular of El Saadawi's books, indicate that they have to work hard to prevent their students from using it merely to confirm their stereotypes. In the words of one teacher, Aparajita Sagar, "Western students tend to get fixated on clitoridectomy and the veil." Anticipating this problem, some teachers provide background material on colonialism to help establish a historical context (Mitra and Mitra 1991; Saliba 1995, 143), encourage students to break with essentialist and ethnocentric theoretical perspectives, and remind them of similar abuses that women undergo in Western cultures.[34] As Susan Gingell says, however, these efforts and "reminders" are not always sufficient. One typical reaction, especially to defloration and female genital mutilation, is for students to feel "awed into silence."[35] In addition to the above contextualizing methods, I believe it is important to draw the students' attention to the politics of reception itself and to make this issue an object of study as a way to further historicize El Saadawi's work. Students should be encouraged to question their location as readers

---

It is interesting that Malti-Douglas refuses to put the novel in that immediate context (see 1995a, 92). Not so the Egyptian critic Sabry Hafez. My deepest gratitude to Lahoucine Ouzgane for making student responses available to me.

[34] Despite their call to read El Saadawi's novel in context, Indrani Mitra and Madhu Mitra (1991) make the same mistake as the Western critics they criticize: they read El Saadawi's novel as if it were a sociological text, without much attention to its sociopolitical and literary contexts. Information also from e-mails sent to me by Susan Gingell (April 10, 1995) and Aparajita Sagar (March 5, 1995).

[35] Quotes from e-mails from Gingell and Sagar, respectively. Hitchcock writes, "El Saadawi's novelization of the psychic horrors of clitoridectomy is no less significant in translation, nor indeed is Firdaus's brutalizing experience as a prostitute. For the hegemonic 'Western' consciousness conditioned to a phantasm of the Arab woman as veiled, submissive, or secluded, none of El Saadawi's major characters . . . seems to fit. If nothing else, El Saadawi's fiction would bear testimony to a conscious undermining of orientalist preconceptions even if such forms of oppression are still significant factors in the lives of many Arab women" (1993, 51). This, however, does not seem to be the experience of other teachers who responded to my inquiry. In a June 2, 1995, e-mail, Christine Loflin wrote that the novel "stunned" her students — "they were either entranced by it, or didn't know what to say." In a March 6, 1995, e-mail, Loretta Kensinger wrote that she had "to fight [her students'] tendency to do the 'oh those women over there have it worse' imperialistic view when addressing concerns of women in other non-U.S. societies."

and to examine the mediating processes connected with the translation, editing, reviewing, and academic canonization that make El Saadawi's books available to Western students.

I first read El Saadawi in the mid-seventies, when I was a teenager living in a small West Bank town under Israeli military occupation. With a mischievous smile, the librarian in our two-room public library slipped me a copy of *Woman and Sex*. That smile was familiar, for I had seen it before on his face whenever he recommended a book he thought proper young women were not supposed to read (the list was long and included such works as *Anna Karenina, The Communist Manifesto, A Doll's House, Uncle Tom's Cabin,* and the complete annotated works of Lenin). That night I could not put the book down, and the next day I went back for more. By the end of the week, I had read three of El Saadawi's polemical books. The influence these books had on me, and on the friends with whom I shared them, was profound. They literally gave us voice. Imitating El Saadawi's militant tone, we found in them plenty of ammunition to counter the arguments of the reactionaries, whether Islamists or secularists, whom we energetically debated inside and outside the classroom.

My El Saadawi phase lasted for a year or so. I read a couple of her novels, but their effect was by then tame, and I went on to other stimulating books by both Arab and foreign authors, many of which were then banned by the Israeli military authorities. Years later, while attending graduate school in the United States, I encountered El Saadawi again, on the pages of newspapers and journals and in presentations and conversations at academic conferences. But this encounter was very different from the earlier one. Like some American students, I too was awed into silence. For in both the popular and academic whirlwind of discourses about El Saadawi and Arab women, I hardly recognized the author I knew. Even more disturbingly, I hardly recognized myself.

This article, then, is the result of a personal attempt by an Arab feminist who writes for a largely Western audience to relocate El Saadawi. Through my search I have learned that, in order to undo silences, mine and those of others, in order to bridge the gap between the reception of El Saadawi in the West and in the Arab world, and in order to partially redress the asymmetry of power between those of us who are situated in the first world and those who are not,[36] we need to adopt a different way of reading El Saadawi and other Arab women writers. It is imperative that we always historicize not only the writer and her work but also the reader. We must

[36] For the past three years, I have been working in areas under the Palestinian National Authority in the West Bank.

take into account both the original context of production and reception and the current moment of consumption. Our role as critics and teachers and our relationship to the texts and authors we study at a particular historical moment should become objects of inquiry as much as the books themselves.

English Department
An-Najah National University

References

Abdallah, Yahya al-Tahir. 1975. *Al-Tawq wa'l-iswirah.* Cairo: Matabi' Al-Hay'a al-Misriyya al-'Amma li al-Kitab.

Accad, Evelyne. 1987. "Freedom and the Social Context: Arab Women's Special Contribution to Literature." *Feminist Issues* 7(2):33–48.

Adonis. 1974. *Al-Thabit wa al-mutahawwil: Bahth fi al-ittiba' wa-al-ibda' 'ind al-'arab* (The permanent and the changeable: A study of imitation and originality in Arab culture). Beirut: Dar al-'Awdah.

Ahmad, Aijaz. 1992. *In Theory: Classes, Nations, and Literatures.* London: Verso.

Ahmed, Leila. 1981. Review of *The Hidden Face of Eve,* by Nawal El Saadawi. *Signs: Journal of Women in Culture and Society* 6(4):749–51.

Alcoff, Linda. 1994. "The Problem of Speaking for Others." In *Feminist Nightmares: Women at Odds: Feminism and the Problem of Sisterhood,* ed. Susan Ostrov Weisser and Jennifer Fleischner, 285–309. New York: New York University Press.

al-Ali, Nadje Sadig. 1994. *Gender Writing/Writing Gender: The Representation of Women in a Selection of Modern Egyptian Literature.* Cairo: American University of Cairo Press.

Allen, M. D. 1995. Review of *The Innocence of the Devil,* by Nawal El Saadawi. *World Literature Today* 69(3):637–38.

Allen, Roger. 1995. *The Arabic Novel: An Historical and Critical Introduction.* 2d ed. Syracuse, N.Y.: Syracuse University Press.

Amireh, Amal. 1996. Review of *Men, Women, and God(s): Nawal El Saadawi and Arab Feminist Poetics,* by Fedwa Malti-Douglas. *Middle East Studies Association Bulletin* 30(2):230–31.

al-'Aqqad, 'Abbas Mahmud. 1938. *Sarah.* Cairo: n.p. Trans. M. M. Badawi, under the title *Sara.* 1978. Cairo: General Egyptian Book Organization.

al-'Azm, Sadiq Jalal. 1968. *Al-Naqd al-dhati ba'd al-hazimah.* Beirut: Dar al-Tali'ah.

Badran, Margot, and Miriam Cooke, eds. 1990. *Opening the Gates: A Century of Arab Feminist Writing.* Bloomington: Indiana University Press.

Bahri, Deepika. 1995. "Once More with Feeling: What Is Postcolonialism?" *Ariel: A Review of International English Literature* 26(1):51–82.

Ba'lbakki, Layla. 1958. *Ana ahya.* Beirut: al-Maktab al-Tijari li-al-Tiba'ah wa-al-Tawzi' wa-al-Nashr.

———. 1960. *Al-Alihah al-mamsukhah.* Beirut: Dar Majallat Shi'r.

———. 1963. *Safinat hanan ila l-qamar.* Beirut: al-Mu'assasa al-wataniyya l'l-Tiba'a wa al-Nashr.

Basu, Amrita. 1982. Letter. *New York Times,* May 2, late city final edition, sec. 7, 41.

Blain, Virginia, Patricia Clements, and Isobel Grundy, eds. 1990. *The Feminist Companion to Literature in English: Women Writers from the Middle Ages to the Present.* New Haven, Conn.: Yale University Press.

Boullata, Issa J. 1990. *Trends and Issues in Contemporary Arab Thought.* Albany, N.Y.: SUNY Press.

Bowen, Donna Lee, and Evelyn Early, eds. 1993. *Everyday Life in the Muslim Middle East.* Bloomington: Indiana University Press.

Croucher, Michael. 1995. Letter. *Guardian,* August 22, "Guardian Features" sec., 14.

Cumming, Laura. 1994. "Books." Review of *The Innocence of the Devil,* by Nawal El Saadawi. *Guardian,* March 15, "Guardian Features" sec., 8.

Donnell, Alison. 1995. "She Ties Her Tongue: The Problem of Cultural Paralysis in Postcolonial Criticism." *Ariel: A Review of International English Literature* 26(1):101–16.

Dullea, Georgia. 1980. "Female Circumcision a Topic at U.N. Parley." *New York Times,* July 18, late city final edition, B4.

Emberley, Julia V. 1993. *Thresholds of Difference: Feminist Critique, Native Women's Writings, Postcolonial Theory.* Toronto: University of Toronto Press.

el-Faizy, Monique. 1994. "Between the Devil and the Big Black Book." *Guardian,* March 21, "Guardian Features" sec., 15.

Farraj, Afif. 1985. *Al-Hurriyya fee adab al-mar'ah* (Freedom in women's literature). Beirut: Arab Research Institute.

Fernea, Elizabeth Warnock, ed. 1985. *Women and the Family in the Middle East: New Voices of Change.* Austin: University of Texas Press.

Fullerton, John. 1989. "Egypt's Saadawi Champions Woman's Struggle in a Male World." *Reuter Library Report,* August 6, BC cycle.

Gauch, Sarah. 1991. "A Troublemaker in Egypt Stands Up to Her Government." *Chicago Tribune,* October 27, final edition, "Womanews" sec., 1.

Gendzier, Irene. 1982. "Foreword." In El Saadawi 1982, vii–xix.

al-Ghitani, Jamal. 1971. *Al-Zayni Barakat.* Damascus: Wizarat al-Thaqafah. Trans. Farouk Abdel Wahab, under the title *Zayni Barakat.* 1988. London: Penguin; New York: Viking.

Gindi, Hoda. 1995. Letter. *Guardian,* August 22, "Guardian Features" sec., 14.

Gingell, Susan. 1995. "Nawal El Saadawi." E-mail to the author. April 10.

Gornick, Vivian. 1982. "About the Mutilated Half." *New York Times,* March 14, late city final edition, sec. 7, 3.

Hafez, Sabry. 1989. "Intentions and Realization in the Narratives of Nawal El-Saadawi." *Third World Quarterly* 11(3):188–99.

———. 1995. "Women's Narrative in Modern Arabic Literature: A Typology." In *Love and Sexuality in Modern Arabic Literature,* ed. Roger Allen, Hilary Kilpatrick, and Ed de Moor. London: Saqi.

al-Hamidi, Ahmad Jasim. 1986. *Al-Mar'ah fee kitabatiha: Untha bourjwaziyya fee 'alam al-rajul* (Woman in her writing: A bourgeois female in a man's world). Damascus: Dar Ibn Hani.

Harlow, Barbara. 1987. *Resistance Literature*. New York: Methuen.

Al-Hayat. 1996. "Translating the Life of the Arab Woman." *Al-Hayat*, May 20, 12.

Haykal, Muhammad Husayn. 1914. *Zaynab*. Reprint, 1963. Cairo: Maktabat nahdat misr. Trans. John Mohammed Grinsted, under the title *Zainab*. 1989. London: Darf.

al-Hibri, Azizah, ed. 1982. *Women and Islam*. Oxford: Pergamon.

Hitchcock, Peter. 1993. "Firdaus; or, The Politics of Positioning." In his *Dialogics of the Oppressed*, 25–52. Minneapolis: University of Minnesota Press.

Husayn, Taha. 1934. *Du 'a' al-karawan*. Reprint, 1942. Cairo: Matba 'at al-Ma 'arif. Trans. A. B. al-Safi, under the title *The Call of the Curlew*. 1980. Leiden: Brill.

Jacoby, Susan. 1994. "Nawal El Saadawi: A Woman Who Broke the Silence." Review of *Memoirs from the Women's Prison* and *The Innocence of the Devil*, by Nawal El Saadawi. *Washington Post*, November 27, final edition, X3.

al-Khuri, Colette. 1959. *Ayyam ma'ahu*. Beirut: al-Maktab al-Tijari li-al-Tiba'wa-al-Nashr wa-al-Tawzi'.

Kilpatrick, Hilary. 1992. "The Egyptian Novel from *Zaynab* to 1980." In *Modern Arabic Literature*, ed. M. M. Badawi, 223–69. Cambridge: Cambridge University Press.

La Guardia, Anton. 1992. "Egyptian Pens Terrorised by Islam's Sword." *Sunday Telegraph*, August 2, 18.

Lashin, Mahmud Tahir. 1934. *Hawwa bila Adam*. Cairo: al-Hay'a al-Misriyya al-'Amma li al-Kitab. Trans. Saad el-Gabalawy, under the title *Eve without Adam*. 1986. In *Three Pioneering Egyptian Novels*, ed. Saad el-Gabalawy, 49–94. Fredericton, N.B.: York.

LeGassick, Trevor. 1992. "The Arabic Novel in English Translation." In *Mundus Arabicus*. Vol. 5, *The Arabic Novel since 1950: Critical Essays, Interviews, and Bibliography*, ed. Issa J. Boullata, 47–60.

Lennon, Peter. 1994. "Speaking Out in a Volatile Climate." *Guardian*, May 28, 29.

Lionnet, Françoise. 1995. "Dissymmetry Embodies: Nawal El Saadawi's *Woman at Point Zero* and the Practice of Excision." In her *Postcolonial Representations: Women, Literature, and Identity*, 129–53. Ithaca, N.Y.: Cornell University Press.

Malti-Douglas, Fedwa. 1995a. *Men, Women, and God(s): Nawal El Saadawi and Arab Feminist Poetics*. Berkeley: University of California Press.

———. 1995b. "Writing Nawal El Saadawi." In *Feminism Beside Itself*, ed. Diane Elam and Robyn Wiegman, 283–96. New York: Routledge.

al-Mazini, Ibrahim Abd al-Qadir. 1931. *Ibrahim al-katib*. Cairo: Matba'at dar al-Taraqqi. Trans. Magdi Wahba, under the title *Ibrahim the Writer*. 1976. Cairo: General Egyptian Book Organization.

Mernissi, Fatima. 1975. *Beyond the Veil: Male-Female Dynamics in Modern Muslim Society*. New York: Wiley.

Michel, Martina. 1995. "Positioning the Subject: Locating Postcolonial Studies." *Ariel: A Review of International English Literature* 26(1):81–99.

Mitchell, W. J. T. 1995. "Postcolonial Culture, Postimperial Criticism." In *The Post-Colonial Studies Reader,* ed. Bill Ashcroft, Gareth Griffiths, and Helen Tiffen, 475–79. London: Routledge.

Mitra, Indrani, and Madhu Mitra. 1991. "The Discourse of Liberal Feminism and Third World Women's Texts: Some Issues of Pedagogy." *College Literature* 18(3):55–63.

Mitra, Madhuchhanda. 1995. "Angry Eyes and Closed Lips: Forces of Revolution in Nawal el Saadawi's *God Dies by the Nile.*" In *Violence, Silence, and Anger: Women's Writing as Transgression,* ed. Deirdre Lashgari, 147–57. Charlottesville: University Press of Virginia.

Mohanty, Chandra Talpade. 1991. "Under Western Eyes: Feminist Scholarship and Colonial Discourses." In *Third World Women and the Politics of Feminism,* ed. Chandra Talpade Mohanty, Ann Russo, and Lourdes Torres, 51–80. Bloomington: Indiana University Press.

Mukherjee, Bharati. 1986. "Betrayed by Blind Faith." Review of *God Dies by the Nile,* by Nawal El Saadawi. *New York Times,* July 27, late city edition, sec. 7, 14.

al-Naqqash, Raga'. 1995. "Imra'ah li-kul al-'usur" (A woman for all times). *Al-Musawwar* 18 (August): 28, 73.

Ouyang, Wen-chin. 1996. Review of *Woman at Point Zero* and *The Circling Song,* by Nawal El Saadawi. *International Journal of Middle East Studies* 28(3):457–60.

———. 1997. "Feminist Discourse between Art and Ideology: Four Novels by Nawal Al-Sa'ddawi." *Al-'Arabiyya* 30:95–115.

Payne, Kenneth. 1992. "*Woman at Point Zero:* Nawal El Saadawi's Feminist Picaresque." *Southern Humanities Review* 26 (Winter): 11–18.

Publishers Weekly. 1994. "*The Innocence of the Devil:* Book Reviews." Review of *The Innocence of the Devil,* by Nawal El Saadawi. *Publishers Weekly,* October 24, 54.

al-Qa'id, Muhammad Yusuf. 1969. *Al-Hidad.* Cairo: n.p.

Roberts, Paul William. 1993. "Novels of an Arab Feminist." Review of *Well of Life,* by Nawal El Saadawi. *Toronto Star,* May 15, J14.

Roth, Katherine. 1991. "Nawal El Saadawi: An Egyptian Feminist's Fight to Protect Hard-Won Gains." *San Francisco Chronicle,* September 23, A10.

El Saadawi, Nawal. 1958. *Mudhakkirat tabiba.* Cairo: Dar el-Ma'aref.

———. 1965. *Al-Gha'ib.* Cairo: al-Kitab al-Zahabi.

———. 1968. *Imra'atani fi-mra'a.* Cairo: Dar al-Kitab.

———. 1971. *Al-Mar'ah wal-jins.* Cairo: el-Shaab.

———. 1974a. *Mawt al-rajul al-wahid 'ala al-ard.* Beirut: Dar al-Adab.

———. 1974b. *Al-Untha hiya al-asl.* Cairo: Maktabat Madbuli.

———. 1976a. *Al-Mar'ah wal-sira' al-nafsi.* Beirut: al-Mu'assasa al-'Arabiyah lil-Dirasat wal-Nashr.

———. 1976b. *Al-Rajul wal-jins.* Beirut: al-Mu'assasa al-'Arabiyah lil-Dirasat wal-Nashr.

———. 1977. *Al-Wajh al-'ari lil-mar'a al-'arabiyyah.* Beirut: al-Mu'assasa al-'Arabiyah lil-Dirasat wal-Nashr.

———. 1979. *Imra'a 'ind nuqtat al-sifr*. Beirut: Dar al-Adab.

———. 1980a. "Arab Women and Western Feminism: An Interview with Nawal El Saadawi." *Race and Class* 22(2):175–82.

———. 1980b. "Creative Women in Changing Societies: A Personal Reflection." *Race and Class* 22(2):159–73.

———. 1980c. *The Hidden Face of Eve: Women in the Arab World*. London: Zed.

———. 1981. "Feminism in Egypt: A Conversation with Nawal Sadawi." Interviewed by Sarah Graham-Brown. *MERIP Reports: Middle East Research and Information Project*, no. 95 (March–April), 24–27.

———. 1982. *The Hidden Face of Eve: Women in the Arab World*. Ed. and trans. Sherif Hetata, with a foreword by Irene Gendzier. Boston: Beacon.

———. 1983a. *Mudhakkirati fi sijn al-nisa'*. Cairo: Dar al-Mustaqbal al-'Arabi.

———. 1983b. *Woman at Point Zero*. London: Zed.

———. 1984. "When a Woman Rebels. . . . " Trans. Sherif Hetata. In *Sisterhood Is Global: The International Women's Movement Anthology*, ed. Robin Morgan, 199–206. New York: Anchor.

———. 1985a. "Challenging a Taboo: Going to Jail for Politics, Sex and Religion." *Worldpaper*, June, 6.

———. 1985b. *God Dies by the Nile*. Trans. Sherif Hetata. London: Zed.

———. 1985c. *Two Women in One*. Trans. Osman Nusairi and Jana Gough. London: Saqi.

———. 1986. *Memoirs from the Women's Prison*. London: Women's Press.

———. 1987a. *Death of an Ex-Minister*. Trans. Shirley Eber. London: Methuen.

———. 1987b. *She Has No Place in Paradise*. Trans. Shirley Eber. London: Methuen.

———. 1987c. *Suqut al-imam*. Cairo: Dar al-Mustaqbal al-'Arabi.

———. 1988a. *The Fall of the Imam*. Trans. Sherif Hetata. London: Methuen.

———. 1988b. *Memoirs of a Woman Doctor*. Trans. Catherine Cobham. London: Saqi. Reprint, San Francisco: City Lights, 1989.

———. 1990a. "In Conversation with Nawal El Saadawi." Interview by Marcel Farry. *Spare Rib*, no. 217 (October): 22–26.

———. 1990b. "An Overview of My Life." In *Contemporary Authors Autobiography Series*, vol. 11, ed. Mark Zadrozny, 61–72. Detroit: Gale.

———. 1990c. "Reflections of a Feminist." In Badran and Cooke 1990, 395–404.

———. 1991a. *My Travels around the World*. Trans. Shirley Eber. London: Methuen.

———. 1991b. "Nawal El Saadawi." In *Critical Fictions: The Politics of Imaginative Writing*, ed. Philomena Marian, 155–56. Seattle: Bay.

———. 1991c. *Searching*. Trans. Shirley Eber. London: Zed.

———. 1991d. "Time to Come Together: In Conversation with Nawal El Saadawi." Interview by Marcel Farry. *Spare Rib*, no. 221 (March): 12–15.

———. 1992a. *Jannat wa-Iblis*. Beirut: Dar al-Adab.

———. 1992b. "An Interview with Nawal el Saadawi." Interview by George Lerner. *Progressive*, 56, no. 4 (April): 32–35.

———. 1993a. "Feminism and an Arab Humanism: An Interview with Nawal El

Saadawi and Sherif Hetata." Interview by Gaurav Desai and David Chioni Moore. *Sapina-Bulletin* 5(1):28–51.

———. 1993b. "Living the Struggle: Nawal El Saadawi Talks about Writing and Resistance with Sherif Hetata and Peter Hitchcock." *Transitions* 61:170–79.

———. 1993c. "She Was the Weaker." In *The Heinemann Book of African Women's Writing,* ed. Charlotte H. Bruner, 152–56. London: Heinemann.

———. 1994a. "The Bitter Lot of Women: In Conversation with Nawal el Saadawi." Interview by Hanny Lightfoot-Klein. *Freedom Review* 25 (May–June): 22–25.

———. 1994b. *The Innocence of the Devil.* Trans. Sherif Hetata. Berkeley: University of California Press.

———. 1994c. *Memoirs from the Women's Prison.* Berkeley: University of California Press.

———. 1995a. "'But Have Some Art with You': An Interview with Nawal El Saadawi." Interviewed by Jennifer Cohen. *Literature and Medicine* 14 (Spring): 53–71.

———. 1995b. "A Cure for Blushing: An Obituary of Amina El Said." *Guardian,* August 17, 13.

———. 1997. *The Nawal El Saadawi Reader.* London: Zed.

———. 1999. *A Daughter of Isis: The Autobiography of Nawal El Saadawi.* London: Zed.

al-Said, Aminah. 1950. *Al-Jamihah* (The defiant). Reprint, Cairo: Dar al-Ma'arif, 1987.

Said, Edward. 1990. "Embargoed Literature." *Nation* 251, no. 8 (September 17): 278–80.

Said, Khalida. 1970. "Al-Mar'ah al-'arabiyyah: Ka'in bi ghayrihi la bi-dhatihi" (The Arab woman: Being through the other, not through the self). *Mawaqif* 12:90–100.

Saliba, Therese. 1995. "On the Bodies of Third World Women: Cultural Impurity, Prostitution, and Other Nervous Conditions." *College Literature* 22(1):131–46.

Salman, Magida. 1981. Review of *The Hidden Face of Eve,* by Nawal El Saadawi. *Khamsin* 8:121–24.

Salti, Ramzi. 1994. "Paradise, Heaven, and Other Oppressive Spaces: A Critical Examination of the Life and Works of Nawal El-Saadawi." *Journal of Arabic Literature* 25(2):152–74.

Sharabi, Hisham. 1975. *Muqqadimah li-dirasat al-mujtama'al-'arabi* (An introduction to the study of Arab society). Jerusalem: Salah al-Din.

———. 1988. *Neopatriarchy: A Theory of Distorted Change in Arab Society.* New York: Oxford University Press.

———. 1990. "The Scholarly Point of View: Politics, Perspective, Paradigm." In *Theory, Politics, and the Arab World: Critical Responses,* ed. Hisham Sharabi, 1–51. New York: Routledge.

al-Sharqawi, Abd al-Rahman. 1953. *Al-Ard.* Cairo: Naadii al-Qissah. Trans. Desmond Stewart, under the title *Egyptian Earth.* 1962. London: Heinemann.

Shohat, Ella. 1992. "Notes on the Post-Colonial." *Social Text* 10(2–3):99–113.

Slade, Margot, and Tom Ferrell. 1980. "Ideas and Trends." *New York Times,* July 20, late city final edition, sec. 4, 7.

Sontag, Susan. 1994. "Perspective on Persecution." *Los Angeles Times,* August 17, Metro sec., part B, 7.

Spivak, Gayatri Chakravorty. 1988. "Can the Subaltern Speak?" In *Marxism and the Interpretation of Culture,* ed. Cary Nelson and Lawrence Grossberg, 271–313. Urbana: University of Illinois Press.

Tarabishi, George. 1978. "Untha Nawal El Sa'dawi wa usturat al-tafarrud" (The female of Nawal El Saadawi and the myth of individuation). In *Al-Adab min al-dakhil* (Literature from the inside), 10–50. Beirut: Dar al-Talee'a.

———. 1982. *'Ukdat Odeeb fee al-riwaya al-'arabiyah* (The Oedipus complex in the Arabic novel). Beirut: Dar al-Talee'a.

———. 1983. *Al-Rujulah wa aydyoulojyat al-rujulah fee al-riwaya al-'arabiyah* (Manhood and the ideology of manhood in the Arabic novel). Beirut: Dar al-Talee'a.

———. 1988. *Woman against Her Sex: A Critique of Nawal el-Saadawi.* Trans. Basil Hatim and Elisabeth Orsini. London: Saqi.

al-'Uwayt, 'Aql. "La ahtamm bi-maqalat al-nuqqad, al-qurra' hum alladhin Sana'uni." Al-Anwar, July 18. Quoted in Zeidan 1995, 348.

Werner, Louis. 1991. "Arab Feminist Pens Powerful Prose." *Christian Science Monitor* 25 (June): 3.

Winokur, Julie. 1994. "Uncensored: Egypt's Most Outspoken Feminist Sets Up Her Soapbox at the UW." *Seattle Times* April 24, final edition, "Pacific" sec., 12.

Zayour, Ali. 1977. *Al-Tahlil al-nafsi lil-dhat al-'arabiyyah: Anmat al-sulukiyyah al-usturiyyah* (The analysis of the Arab self). Beirut: Dar al-tali'ah.

al-Zayyat, Latifah. 1960. *Al-Bab al-maftuh* (The open door). Cairo: Maktabat al-Anglo al-Misriyyah.

———. 1994. "On Political Commitment and Feminist Writing." In *The View from Within: Writers and Critics on Contemporary Arabic Literature: A Selection from "Alif: Journal of Comparative Poetics,"* ed. Ferial J. Ghazoul and Barbara Harlow, 246–60. Cairo: American University in Cairo Press.

———. 1996. *The Search: Personal Papers.* Trans. Sophie Bennett. London: Quartet.

Zeidan, Joseph T. 1995. *Arab Women Novelists: The Formative Years and Beyond.* Albany: State University of New York Press.

Muslim Women: Negotiations in the Third Space

T**he politics of being** and doing muslim place women in a dilemma.[1] To demand that issues such as lack of education, violence, poverty, and employment opportunities be addressed, muslim women have to enter political space as muslim. Within this space they are confronted by the regulating discourses of Islam and Orientalism (among others). Although they have different sources and agendas, both reduce *muslim* to a religious category. In addition, members of minority communities in Canada negotiate their lives within a context that promotes and legitimizes multicultural policies and practices. At this intersection, muslim women find themselves inserted into predetermined discourses and practices that shape their agency and determine their strategies of resistance, often to the extent that progressive politics do not appear possible within the category muslim.

This work continues my focus on the notion of muslim women's third space with the stories of Karima and Iram—two very different muslim women living in Canada—as examples. To address the issue of generalizability that such a sample raises, I refer to Dorothy Smith's argument that the individual "case" is also a point of entry into larger social and economic processes (1987, 157). Karima's and Iram's[2] testimonies are part of a larger study (Khan 1995a) that explores the notion of the "Muslim Woman" as a construct ideologically overdetermined by social, political, economic, racial, and religious discourses.[3] Karima's and Iram's stories provide access to the larger social organization of which each woman is a part. However, I make no claim to explain their lives. Instead, I draw from my interviews specific examples of how Karima and Iram enact their own relationships within Orientalist, Islamist, and multiculturalist knowledge production.

---

[1] In intentionally using lowercase for muslim, I want to move away from a sensationalized connotation of "the Muslim" as the violent and exoticized other.

[2] The names used in my work are pseudonyms.

[3] Borrowing from psychoanalysis and linguistics, Louis Althusser uses the term *overdetermined* to describe the effects of contradictions in a practice that arise from such concrete determinations as political law; religion; custom; habit; and financial, commercial, and economic relations. None of these contradictions is outside any other, and together they constitute an original (Althusser 1969).

[*Signs: Journal of Women in Culture and Society* 1998, vol. 23, no. 2]

By elaborating what it means to negotiate the discursive determinations of muslim female identity in Canada, this discussion has the potential to destabilize monolithic assumptions about the muslim in the "First World."

Contemporary social theorists Trinh Minh-Ha (1989), Paul Gilroy (1992), Gayatri Spivak (1993), Homi Bhabha (1994), and Stuart Hall (1992, 1996) have argued for understanding and expressions of ethnicity that move away from notions of authentic and original culture and identity. Rather, they claim individuals' daily interactions constitute their cultural expressions. In particular, Bhabha's notion of hybridized subjectivity in the third space helps to explain how individuals negotiate the contradictory demands and polarities of their lives.

By disrupting the concept of original and homogeneous culture, Bhabha's theory of third space unsettles a pattern of meaning constituted in serial time and challenges the articulation of culture as a homogenizing, unifying force authenticated by the originary past and kept alive in the national tradition of the people.[4] Instead, Bhabha points out that individuals construct their culture from national as well as religious texts and often transform them into Western symbols, signifiers of technology, language, or dress. These new forms of articulation transform "the meanings of colonial inheritance into the liberatory signs of a free people of the future" (1994, 38). In Bhabha's terms, the third space becomes a space of contradiction, repetition, ambiguity, and disavowal of colonial authority that does not allow for original signifiers and symbols in oppositional polarities (1990). Instead, these signs are appropriated, translated, rehistoricized, and reread. Such discursive conditions of enunciation allow for possibilities of supplementary sites of resistance and negotiation: "Once it [third space] opens up, we are in a different space, we are making different presumptions and mobilizing emergent, unanticipated forms of historical agency" (Bhabha 1995, 114).

These dynamic and contradictory forms of agency draw on Bhabha's notion of hybridized states, where dialectic polarities demand the subject's allegiance at the same moment. Hybridized individuals, caught in the discontinuous time of translation and negotiation, erasing any claims for inherent cultural purity, inhabit the rim of an "in-between reality" marked by shifting psychic, cultural, and territorial boundaries. Trinh Minh-Ha speaks of this translation in "Grandma's Story" when she says, "Each woman, like each people, has her own way of unrolling the ties that bind" (1989, 148).

---

[4] Benedict Anderson 1983 argues persuasively for the narrative of the Western nation to be understood as written in homogenous serial time.

In this article, I explore how individual muslim women negotiate and translate the Orientalist and Islamic discourses that regulate their lives into a politics of everyday living within an environment that encourages and promotes multicultural policies and practices. Muslim women in North American diasporic communities come from geographical regions as diverse as China, Iran, and Nigeria. Any attempt to capture their various cultural and religious expressions would be reductive. I am aware that my use of the category "muslim" opens me to charges of reinforcing the originary and authentic, the very notions that I want to move away from. My use of this term is similar to Chandra Mohanty's use of the term *third world woman* to describe an analytical and political category useful in counter-hegemonic struggle (1991a). My vision of the muslim woman is part of a strategy to identify and engage with regional as well as global struggles and religious as well as nonreligious resistance. This investigation, then, offers a notion of muslim women's difference not as static or definitive but, rather, as an opportunity for dialogue and conversation.[5] I accept the category muslim as a starting point and (here and in my other writings) problematize it in an attempt to recognize the fluidity of cultural expressions, particularly those within diasporic communities. This investigation is partly fueled by my own desire to identify and engage with this space of displacement so that I can practice feminist politics within the category muslim.

Negotiating third space: Setting the context

Bhabha speaks to the notion of transparencies as codes written over previous signs and signifiers: "Transparency is the action of the distribution and arrangement of differential spaces, positions, knowledges in relation to each other, relative to a discriminatory, not inherent, sense of order" (1994, 109). Bhabha's notion of transparency suggests a colonial inscription that overwrites earlier codes of authority so that the power of the recent colonial voice cannot be read without the other voices that underlie it. These overlapping transparencies, including postcolonial codes of power, are part of the enunciative process that defines the subordinate colonial. The muslim woman is one such subordinate colonial.

The photographic negative image is also part of Bhabha's notion of transparency. Like a reversed image on film, the muslim woman as subject is always being constructed through negativity and disavowal. Disavowal

---

[5] I use the terms *dialogue* and *conversation* fully aware that these terms have strong materialist implications.

intensifies the power of colonial and now-postcolonial interventions in the notion of woman as muslim. Women's negotiations and translations are coded onto discursive transparencies informed by Orientalist and Islamic discourses, and these transparencies are overwritten in multicultural contexts. Multicultural policies and practices, in a sense, become another layer of transparency.

My use of the terms *Orientalism* and *Islam* is not intended to set up a monolithic binary. Instead, my aim is to identify hegemonic discourses that are constantly being set up and displaced by women's narratives. In turning away from the discourse and image of self as the stereotyped "Muslim Woman," individual women turn toward either the West or Islam for affirmation. Instead, however, they find devaluations and apprehension in the former (Orientalism) and mechanisms for their control in the latter (Islamism). Orientalism draws on stereotypes that, as Bhabha reminds us, are "fixed and static construction[s] of other as the subject of colonial discourse." Implying disorder and inferiority, the stereotype contains what is already known and must be constantly repeated to produce the "colonized as a social reality which is at once an 'other' and entirely knowable and visible" (Bhabha 1994, 70–71). This social reality is more than a false image: it includes "projection and interjection, metaphoric and metonymic strategies, displacement, over-determination, guilt, aggressivity; the masking and splitting of 'official' and phantasmatic knowledges to construct the positionalities and oppositionalities of racist discourse" (81–82).

These strategies of colonial power are identified by Edward Said in his classic text *Orientalism* (1978). Said argues that the ideology embedded in Orientalism is shaped by Europe's historical envy, fear, and hatred of the "infidel" and supplemented by its sense of superiority over the Islamic world. Even those who romanticize and value the Orient are often part of this "Othering" and homogenizing.[6] Although not all the work of European scholars and writers on Islam is easily dismissible, it has been the European ethnocentric accounts that captured popular imagination.[7]

As we move toward the twenty-first century, these Orientalist fantasies remain. In particular, societies in which Islam is the religion of the majority continue to be seen as totalizing religious and ideological orders. This framework gives Islamic religious ideology a preeminent position in the Islamic world, while regional, cultural, and neocolonial differences are ig-

[6] See Clancy-Smith 1992.
[7] Notable among Western scholars who have conducted serious inquiry with integrity are Louis Massignon, Maxine Rodinson, and the English scholar H. A. R. Gibb, who left Oxford to become professor of Arabic at Harvard in 1955.

nored (Kandiyoti 1991; Moghadam 1991). Thus religion, which is viewed as just one of many institutions in "normal" societies, is seen as the overriding influence in Islamic societies, feeding Orientalist assumptions about the role of religion in the lives of individual women.

Orientalist perceptions fueled the notion that the European colonizer did not venture forth as an exploiter. Rather, "he" went out to enlighten and, in the case of the Islamic world, to deliver women from religious oppression. While much Orientalist discourse focused on the liberation of muslim women from Islam, there was also an aspect of Orientalist/colonialist discourse that pointed to the availability of muslim women. Rana Kabbani (1986) argues that the Orient was largely an illicit space and its women convenient chattels offering the sexual gratification denied in Victorian homes. Similarly, Malek Alloula's (1986) collection of commentary and postcards from the time of colonial rule exposes French obsession with the body and the unveiling of the colonial Algerian woman. The postcards of nude and semiclad women are symbolic not only of the violence that such unveiling would visit on the culture and dignity of the colonized but also of the unequal power relations between women and men, as well as between colonizer and colonized. Princess Jasmine in the 1994 feature film *Aladdin* provides an example of the eroticized and available muslim woman of Western popular culture. Moreover, since the 1979 revolution in Iran and the taking of American hostages in Tehran, exotic images have been supplemented by the muslim woman as the shrouded "terrorist" supporting Ayatollah Khomeini. The potency of these dichotomous images of eroticism and violence is backed by colonialism in its newer form, a combination of economic, political, and cultural imperialism.

Although dominated by masculinist, patriarchal, and Western codes, Orientalism is not a monolithic discourse. Some Orientalists have been feminists and some are non-Western. As Mohanty (1991b) has pointed out, some Western feminisms construct the third world woman wholly in discourse, depicting the lives of muslim women as entirely determined by Islamic ideology and uninfluenced by global socioeconomic and political relations.[8] Mohanty states that her critique pertains not only to Western feminists but also "to third world scholars writing about their own cultures, which employ identical analytic strategies" (1991b, 52). Margot Badran's (1995) recent work on upper- and middle-class women indicates that their feminist consciousness at the turn of the century emerged with the modern nation of Egypt and connects early feminist organizing in Egypt to nationalism. In another context, Partha Chatterjee (1986) has

[8] See Deardorn 1975; Jeffery 1979; Minces 1980; and Hosken 1981.

linked nationalist and Orientalist discourses.[9] The latter, he claims, is strongly influenced by colonial thought. Similarly, in her analysis of work on Indian women, Julie Stephens (1989) is critical of feminist scholarship that claims to speak for "real women" rather than the mythic and idealized woman of nationalist discourse. Stephens claims that feminism often collides as well as colludes with Orientalist discourse in searches for the sovereign female subject and in attempts to represent her. Feminist writings grant subject status to those women who fulfill criteria consistent with the feminist position of the author and, in so doing, valorize some subjects of feminist research while seeing others as objectified and oppressed.

In addition to Orientalist discourse, muslim women's negotiations of their subjectivities are to a large extent shaped by discourses that draw on the sacred to legitimize their authority. Islam is a religion, but, as Fatima Mernissi points out, it is also "a set of psychological devices about self-empowerment and making oneself at home everywhere around the globe, in unfamiliar as well as familiar surroundings" (1987, x). However, Islam in the postcolonial world is often informed by popular political movements in muslim countries or in muslim communities in the First World.[10] Often referred to as Islamism, these politicized, frequently anticolonial, anti-West movements exert increasing social and sexual control on the symbolic and chaste woman centered at the core of an identity politics (Moghadam 1991; Helie-Lucas 1994). Thus when women "alienated" by Orientalism turn to Islam for identity, they often face Islamist attempts to contain their bodies within rigid sexist structures.

Although male dominated, and frequently antifemale, Islamist movements also count female activists among their members. The political work and writings of Islamist Egyptians Zainab al-Ghazali (1994), founder of the Society of Muslim Sisters, and Safinaz Kazim (1986) challenge the boundaries of feminist activism. The work of both women reveals an unqualified desire to promote and secure women's empowerment but criticizes feminism as a Western influence. By the 1980s, as Badran (1995) points out, feminists, as well as many women within Islamist movements in Egypt, began to articulate similar positions on gender issues, particularly those focused on employment.

Shahrzad Mojab (1995) is not convinced that what has been referred to as "Islamist feminism" is capable of improving women's status in mus-

---

[9] I want to refer to the connections that Chatterjee 1986 has made between nationalist thought in India and the discourse of Orientalism to help explore the desire of Egyptian women and men for feminism at the turn of the century.

[10] See Stowasser 1987.

lim societies. Referring to the Islamic republic of Iran, Mojab points out that Islamic feminists want to improve female and male relations within theocratic/political institutions that do not have a history of egalitarian class or gender relations. "One can argue," Mojab claims, "that this 'feminism,' far from being an alternative, is a compromise with patriarchy" (1995, 25). Yet Sara Suleri, in her autobiographic novel (1987), questions feminist articulations of women that she says are not able to account for the agency of women such as her grandmother. Suleri questions the practice of basing a political movement on the notion of "woman." Instead, she believes that women's subjectivities are constituted through their performance of social roles.

Islam, and especially current politicized Islamist views of identity, present one model for muslim women in diasporic communities in the First World; Orientalism presents another. The two positions, Orientalism and Islamism, are split not only from each other but also within themselves. Orientalism contains racist colonial imagery, but it also affirms the Muslim Woman in the dominant discourse by giving her a presence (although a negative one) where she would be otherwise absent. Orientalist texts not only affect Westerners but also influence how the colonial subject constitutes herself (Said 1978). Following Bhabha's (1991) line of argument, an "Orientalist" turning away from the stereotype can be a source of affirmation for the colonial subject as it allows her to dissociate from a devalued other.

Orientalism and Islamism act as two contradictory poles of desire/affirmation and aversion/disorientation and help reinforce a structured ambivalence within the notion of the ideal Muslim Woman. Both poles essentialize the ideal Muslim Woman and reduce her to the same symbols and icons.[11] Orientalists offer descriptive and devalued essentialist imagery of Islam as articles of faith.[12] Islamists, in contrast, address contemporary women's needs and present Islamically inspired solutions through persuasion and at times coercion (Stowasser 1987; Moghadam 1991). Orientalist and Islamist narratives pose a dialectic that appears irresolvable; their differences cannot be persuaded or educated away. The narratives of Karima and Iram, the subjects of this discussion, do not disavow, resolve, or transcend the contradictions between Orientalism and Islamism. Instead,

[11] Algerian feminist Marnia Lazreg (1990) points to the uncanny similarity between Western feminist discourse on women from the Middle East and North Africa and theologians' own interpretations of women in Islam. Although the two seem similar on the surface, there are complex differences that are beyond the scope of this discussion.

[12] For discussions of Orientalist constructions of muslim women, see Alloula 1986; Kabani 1986; Lazreg 1990; and Mabro 1991.

in their daily negotiations, the women open up a supplementary space where they, as hybridized subjects, translate the polarities of Orientalism and Islamism into the politics of race, ethnicity, migrant communities in the diaspora, and family life.

As I indicate in the following discussion, the image of the Muslim Woman in Canada, which is at once familiar and yet not quite "doable," often produces emotional responses. Karima names, resists, and challenges the contradictions she faces and expresses emotional uncertainty. Iram's narrative shows how she refuses to accept Orientalist and Islamist codes, categorizations, and prescriptions for behavior in her daily life. Both narratives indicate doubt and disorientation, and regardless of whether they express uncertainty, both women are constrained within a structured ambivalence. Even if Karima and Iram disavow Orientalist colonial stereotypes and Islamism, they cannot escape the structural bind within which the construct "Muslim Woman" places them.[13]

Diasporic context

Contemporary global social, political, and economic events have led to displacements and diasporas of many peoples. Many of these diasporic communities are located in Europe and North America, where multicultural policies and practices play a significant part in the everyday negotiations of the lives of migrants. What it means to be a muslim woman in regions where the majority of the people are muslim is related to social, economic, and political conditions as well as to the larger national polity. However, my analysis does not focus on women's negotiations in their "home" countries. Instead, I explore women's translations and negotiations of the third space in minority diasporic communities in the First World, where grounding as a muslim is significantly more fragile than in the women's "home" countries.

In making a distinction between tourists and immigrants, Tahire Kocturk (1992) points out that the latter are more interested in preserving their history. While messages that assimilation is the key to success appeal to the Turkish immigrants in northwestern Europe whom she describes, they are also producing anxiety. Although Kocturk's study in Sweden indicates that the women lead hybridized lives, their perceptions of themselves

---

[13] The colonial stereotype and the structural condition of ambivalence and simultaneous alienation are central to Bhabha's understanding of the colonial subject in discourse. The colonial stereotype is a source of attraction (in that the colonial subject recognizes her/himself) and a source of aversion (in that the colonial subject turns away from her/himself). Alienation thus occurs at the nexus of desire and aversion and at a point when both the colonized and the colonizer turn away from the stereotype (Bhabha 1994).

often center around myths of nationalism. They either distance themselves from those myths or accept utopian versions of the past in attempts to generate stability within marginalized migrant communities.

Yasmin Ali's (1992) work on muslim migrant communities in Britain identifies a collusion between (unequal) partners to maintain a narrow and static definition of community that severely circumscribes the stage on which women are permitted to perform as political and social actors. Although predetermined discourses and relations affect and limit women's agency, Ali points out that the women do resist sexism but are aware that their resistance could strain or damage their relationships with families and communities, leaving them vulnerable in a society where they face not only sexism but racism as well. Ali argues that "modes of identity through religion must be modified" to release progressive energies (121).

Pluralist multicultural policies promoted by many First World countries such as Britain, Canada, and the United States have been a mixed blessing. In affording diverse communities much-needed respect, multicultural policies and practices allow members of communities to anchor their identities. This acceptance of difference is valid and crucial. Yet the multicultural paradigm assumes pregiven, static, and undifferentiated notions of community that leave the myriad cultures within it unconnected to social and political history. These notions promote a view of culture with a collective tradition or a monolithic community—a static system of reference. It is easy to leap to the next step, educating or legislating away difference and the discrimination that accompanies it. This pedagogical aspect of culture, Bhabha argues (1994, 34), focuses on the effect rather than the structure of the problem and denies the internal heterogeneity of communities.

Similarly, "the Muslim community" is often assumed to be a single, monolithic religious community with few class and race differences. There is certainly no understanding of progressive engagement with religion or any appreciation of feminist positions among muslim women. Talal Asad (1991) points out that the British state, while stereotyping the muslim minority community as a collective, appears to encourage minorities to participate in British life as individuals. The cultural diversity of individuals does not threaten British identity. The politicization of religious tradition by muslims does, for it questions loyalty to the nation-state and its totalizing cultural project, the hegemony of ruling-class culture.

Muslim women in Canada

The struggle for control over the representational and social practices through which the Muslim Woman is defined in Canada needs to be located in the colonial relations of the British Empire. Although Canada was a colony of the British Empire, it was also a "settler colony" with a higher status in the British Empire than many of the former colonies from which muslims have emigrated. The imperial hierarchy continues to influence not only the contradictory discourses that create the Muslim Woman but also reinforces her inferior position as a subordinate colonial.

Colonial Orientalist discourse is fashioned in relation to the broader social and political context. Stereotypes of muslims, whether Orientalist or Islamist, are to a large extent influenced by the West and the unequal power relations between Euro-American and muslim societies. Although Orientalism and Islamism are alienating, each contains a force of attraction and the hope that one can resolve the contradictions generated by the other. Neither, however, can fully resolve the contradictions of the other, so that women often turn away from both. Hence, while they are alienated from Orientalism, they cannot embrace Islamism either.

In Canada, individual muslim women are first relegated to communities of the "Other" (Amin 1976) and then devalued because they belong to those communities. Notions of a monolithic community deny their actual heterogeneous nature in pluralist societies. Patriarchal, ahistorical, and romanticized views of the "old country" deny the fluidity of identity negotiations within immigrant communities. However, escape from or rejection of such entrenched notions of these communities, which have a negative presence in the images and popular culture of mainstream Canadian society, leaves women without a sense of belonging. Nahla Abdo (1993) has studied this marginalization of progressive Middle Eastern women in Canada and in feminist circles in particular. She points out that they are "silenced, ignored and oppressed, not only by structures and institutions, but also by the very social movement whose legitimization is largely derived from its opposition to oppression, namely feminism" (1993, 74).

Recent debates on the veil in Canada provide an example of this marginalization. My earlier analysis (Khan 1995b) of the Toronto-based coverage of the debates in Quebec indicates that muslim feminist voices were not solicited. Instead, media coverage of the controversy reinforced the binaries of us and them, oppressed and free, thereby strengthening the distance between the Orientalist view of the veil as oppressive and the Islamist view of it as liberating. Feminist analysis indicates that the energy surrounding the veil is restless and revisionary as it expands the present into a contradictory site of empowerment (Hassan 1990; Hoodfar 1993; Khan 1995a). The debates on the *hejab* (veil) in Canada illustrate how religion, racism, sexism, and multiculturalism intersect to categorize muslim minority communities in primarily religious terms while assuming them to be internally homogeneous and without conflict. Multiculturalism in Canada works to erase ethnic and national difference so that a first-generation immigrant from Iran and a second-generation woman of South Asian/African descent both come to occupy the position "muslim woman."

To understand this homogenization and reductionism, Bhabha (1994) proposes an exploration of the construction of cultural difference. He suggests that both the pedagogical (understanding of signs) and the performative (understanding the process of signification) be used in passage through a third space, which challenges the notion of culture as a unifying force legitimized by an original mythic and utopian past. Bhabha argues that "all cultural statements and systems of enunciation are constructed in this contradictory and ambivalent space of enunciation" (1995, 37). Frantz Fanon (1963) calls this a "zone of occult instability" where everything is called into question. Here, articulations of new cultural demands, meanings, and strategies in the present become practices of collusion and resistance.

The multiple determinations and uneven discourses deployed to signify the Muslim Woman do not define reality for actual muslim women in Canada. Their lives, although affected by colonial/racist stereotyping and religious ideology and prescriptions, are also influenced by the regional and geographical issues of their countries of origin. For Karima and Iram, being a muslim has different meanings both in terms of their understandings of Islam and in the daily practices of their lives. Although discursive determinations of muslim femaleness do not describe their day-to-day reality, individual muslim women inevitably confront predetermined codes and signifiers and the contradictions contained within them. These women must face not only ambivalent forms of knowledge about themselves but also their own ambivalent responses to that knowledge. Of the women I interviewed, I chose Karima and Iram as subjects for this discussion because they differ both racially and in their relationships to myths of "home." Karima, as a first-generation immigrant, has her own myths of home to refer to. However, Iram, a second-generation immigrant, has been handed these myths by her parents. Her identity as a muslim woman is not as dependent as Karima's on the nostalgia that the myths evoke, but she does encounter myths of her home in her community and at the religious school that she attends.

Introducing Karima and Iram

Karima

Karima, forty-four years old, is white-skinned and originally from Iran. Farsi was the language of instruction at the school she attended in her small town, and so she does not speak English very well. During the interview she spoke in Farsi, and another woman interpreted.

As an Arab, Karima was part of a minority in Iran. Her family came to Canada three years ago to escape harassment in Iran during the Iran/Iraq war. She says that she had a good life in Iran but that the war "messed" everything up. The supermarket attached to her family's house was bombed, and they had to leave. They moved farther away from the border, but, she recalls, "the war kept following us." Then her husband lost his job. He is an Arab and was therefore suspected of opposing the Iranian revolution. Although her sisters finished school and went on to become teachers, Karima did not graduate; instead, at seventeen she married her brother-in-law's brother. Karima did not go to college, and she connects lack of education with lack of power and mobility for women.

> *Karima:* If I had studied, I would have become somebody. I don't have that much status. If I had studied, I wouldn't have needed a translator, I would have been able to talk. If I had studied, I would have been able to drive a car.

Karima wants her daughters to become doctors. She expresses concern about the lack of employment opportunities for women in Iran, even for those who have educational qualifications. She cites better education and employment prospects for her daughters in Canada as another reason for leaving Iran.

Because they did not know any English when they first came to Canada, Karima and her husband could not get jobs. They did not leave the house for six months. Her husband was always nervous and angry, and both of them cried a lot.

> *Karima:* We thought, why did we come out to Canada? Now we don't have anything. Back home at least we had the family. . . . Somebody stole our money too, . . . we couldn't go back to Iran either. . . . My husband was angry at me . . . because he had all the problems in life, and the only person who was a punching box was me. He wasn't a person who would beat me up, but like verbally.

Karima worked as a beautician in Iran; in Canada she works as a cook and waitress in a restaurant she and her husband run but do not own.

Iram

Born in Uganda, of East Indian background, Iram is brown-skinned and twenty-four years old. Her few memories of Uganda center around her father's physical and verbal abuse of their male domestic servant. She has been in Canada since she was four, and her identity appears to be shaped greatly by her life in Canada. Once here, she recalls her father treating her mother as he did the servant back "home." She also remembers the racism that her older sister faced as they were growing up in Canada, particularly when Iram was six and her sister was eight. The boys at school would call her sister "Paki" and "Punjab," and Iram would rush to defend her. Iram did not suffer the same racism because, she says, she was more aggressive. "I also remember beating up a kid who was significantly older than me. On the way to school one day when he was trying to pick on my sister. So people knew that I wasn't afraid of these guys." Iram and her sisters did not tell their parents what was going on in school because they were afraid of their father and because their mother had enough to deal with. Iram believes that the racial harassment at school occurred because of her family's name and skin color and because of cultural stereotyping (e.g., it was assumed, she claimed, that they ate curry all the time). Being muslim did not make a difference at school until Iram chose to emphasize it.

Iram believes she was confronted in high school by considerable Western myths about Islam largely because of the 1979 Iranian revolution. She recalls that while other students were either too embarrassed or too afraid to identify themselves as muslims, she began to emphasize her muslim difference. Iram believes this is because she is a rebel.

> *Iram:* Everybody always said Khomeini was a crazy man, an "asshole," a terrorist. Terrorist was the key word. I would point out that he was maybe a terrorist, but you have got terrorists all over the world. Why aren't you calling the IRA terrorist? Why don't you go back in Canadian history and find out who in Canada was a terrorist? Then I particularly talked about American terrorists around the world. I remember very clearly I had a locker across from another girl's, and in her locker she hung an American flag. I was so incensed by that, that in my locker I hung a poster [that] depicted basically an airplane with two wings. On one wing was a Soviet emblem [and] on another wing was an American flag and in the middle was a hand with an Islamic crescent crushing both of them. . . . And in the background were muslim women and men with their hands raised up in the air, with their fists clenched. In the background was Arabic writing, and I can't remember what it said.
>
> The vice-principal was passing by our lockers one day. He saw this [poster] in mine. He said that I had to take it down. I said no, I would not. He said you have to, this is ridiculous, this is propaganda and terrorism, and I asked him to turn around and I pointed to the

American flag in that girl's locker. First of all, I told him how I felt about the very fact that "that" represented the same thing to me, and I told him that until she takes that down I will not take this down. And he said, "I am afraid that your interpretation is very skewed and you know that you are just going to have to take it down." I reiterated to him why I wouldn't, and I said that if he wanted to take it to the school board I would be very happy to show up at the school board and debate this in front of him. He knew that he was not getting across to me so he just left it at that.

Iram's rebellious spirit also caused conflict at a school of Islamic religious instruction that she attended as a child. She was permanently expelled for asking too many questions and insisting on answers. Blind faith was not enough for her. Currently Iram works as a journalist for a mainstream publication, and her work environment provides her with ample opportunities to confront people about their views on Islam. Iram claims that her employers and coworkers actually listen to what she has to say although they do not always agree with her.

> *Iram:* Well, for example, just this past Friday in memory of December 6th, I wrote an article on abuse that women face in Canada. . . . I specifically blasted the paper for running a feature last summer, on "Women behind the Veil: Back to Fundamentalist Islam in a Male Dominated Society," . . . and I pointed out in that article of mine that, sure, abuse goes on in Islamic countries, but keep in mind that it goes on all over the world; let's look at Canada. And I pointed out all the different abuses that happen in Canada. I made it very very clear that I was not denying the pain that women face in Islamic countries. What I am denying is [the notion that] it is worse than it is in Canada.

Karima and Iram enact their identities

Karima

To an extent, Karima's narrative draws on the notion of the muslim collective, or the *Umma,* and her life in Canada appears polarized against her utopically conceptualized past in Iran under Khomeini. Yet the concept of a cohesive muslim collective can be quite fragile, for even the unity of the mythical *Umma* could not prevent the Iran/Iraq war. In this conflict between two muslim countries, she and her husband, as Arab minorities, were considered undesirable and came to Canada as refugees.

Karima: They were saying that he [her husband] helped Saddam. I lost everything, and only got the children out. They didn't have shoes on even. . . . All the family lived in relatives' houses, everybody lost everything, so I can't even go back to stay with somebody else. . . . I was upset because they were Muslim too, and that these two powers, Khomeini and Saddam, are creating everything, not the people.

In this narrative of diasporic displacement, Karima factors in the myth of solidarity of the muslim collective by blaming the leaders of the two countries and pointing out that it was they, not the people, who were responsible for the war. In this way, she is able to integrate war between muslim countries into her utopian vision of her past life in Iran.

Karima's identity in Iran was enacted in her everyday negotiations and involved her family and social networks. This provided her with a stable space and a certain degree of empowerment, which were disrupted when the Iran/Iraq war brought to the fore her minority status as an Arab in Iran. Amrita Chhachhi (1989) argues that romanticized "traditionalism" is often precipitated by the disintegration of familial and kinship structures. Karima's extended family networks either were destroyed by war or were left behind in Iran. Her memories of her life in Iran appear to be crucial in maintaining a continuity with her identity as a Muslim Woman.

As Karima cannot replicate her networks in Canada, her muslim identity becomes more dependent on her day-to-day practices, which provide her a sense of continuity of self as a Muslim Woman. Yet Karima's notions of the authentic Muslim Woman's everyday enactments conflict with the mechanics of her actual life in Canada. For instance, she does not believe that muslims should drink, yet in Canada she is placed in the position of selling alcohol in her restaurant.

Karima: In the restaurant, we are full of sins. At the beginning when I was working here, [if] somebody wanted something from the bar, I would tell them that I don't work for the bar, I work for the restaurant, I am in this section, not that section. Somebody else would get it. Back home [in Iran] my husband would drink sometimes, and [if] anything bad happens [*sic*] in the house, I would tell him that it was because of the drinking.

Karima regards nonconsumption of alcohol as central for the Muslim Woman. In selling it, she compromises herself. However, in her case, the compromise is borne not out of a need to create cultural meaning and pleasure but out of material necessity. The ambivalence she expresses is muted and arises from her need for a muslim identity and her difficulty fully enacting it in Canada.

Karima also faces contradictions because she believes that *Shari'a* (Islamic religious law) is "Islam's law" and that the Muslim Woman must adhere to it. At the same time, she does not think Islamic inheritance laws are fair. Her father did not leave a will, and she got only half as much as her brothers when he died. Moreover, Karima believes that if *Shari'a* is used to oppress a woman, she should reject it and even Islam itself:

> *Karima:* She should say, "I am not a muslim" . . . so the law would not apply to her.
>
> *Shahnaz Khan:* What do you think will happen to that woman in terms of heaven and hell?
>
> *Karima:* She will go to hell.
>
> *Shahnaz:* If the woman has to say that she is not a Muslim in order to survive in this society, wouldn't God understand and accept the problem as it is and not send her to hell?
>
> *Karima:* Maybe God understands because I don't know what God does. Maybe God understands and she wouldn't go to hell. If the woman says that she is not a muslim, and she has to say that, God may forgive her because of the good things that she does.

Karima says that she would sympathize with a woman put in the position of disavowing Islam in order to survive: "I will not judge; God will judge." Even though she is not ready to submit to the oppressive nature of Islamic law, her narrative locates being and doing muslim in God, community action, and belief.

Karima recognizes that in Canada she often engages in practices that demarcate an Islamic identity with which she is familiar. Yet she never denies the validity of those practices. She hopes that God will decide in her favor, and she wrestles with the notion of being more observant than she is. While she expresses ambivalence about some of her practices, which are not in keeping with the familiar muslim requirements for women, she is clear about her identity as a muslim. But she can succeed in Canada materially, socially, and psychologically only to the degree that she fails as a muslim. This is a painful paradox for Karima.

The mothering of the next generation of muslims, particularly girls, is crucial for the Muslim Woman. Karima tries to extend the everyday practices of her muslim identity to her daughters, but she faces opposition.

> *Karima:* They [the girls] don't know what is good for them.
>
> *Shahnaz:* What is good for them?

Karima: A girl is supposed to be a girl to all the points in Islam, and God and the Prophet has said they have to go along with that; they have to listen to the parents.

Shahnaz: But in every muslim household there are different points that the parents stress. What points do you stress?

Karima: I want my daughters to be the girlish type. When they are living under my roof, I want them to cover themselves, not the head, but the body. They can't wear short skirts, always long. . . . I don't mind if they don't pray and they don't fast. It is the dress code, the going out, no boyfriends, no sex before marriage. They have to stay a virgin till the day they get married. . . . They can't go around like a man.

Karima's story suggests cultural affirmations through prescriptions of morality for women, an attempt to keep women chaste and pure and firmly within the collective. For Karima, more than for any of the women interviewed for my earlier study (Khan 1995a), the role of the Muslim Woman as mother appears to be reduced to control of the bodies of girl children without accompanying spiritual or ritual requirements.

Karima endorses this control of her daughters, which is enforced primarily by her sons and also by her husband.

Karima: Like ten minutes late, if they come back, they are going to get into trouble, because you know, they [the girls' brothers] want an account for every minute. The elder brother he is twenty-three; he is more strict even than the father. He comes home and tells the fourteen-year-old that he does not like the "false nails you have on." The girl doesn't say anything because he is standing there and he is mad, but [later] she tells me "what does he want from me; he has a girl friend himself,". . . and I say, "Men have needs. . . . The girls have to get married. They can't go around like a man."

Shahnaz: Do your daughters listen to you?

Karima: They get upset, but I don't listen to them.

Shahnaz: What do they say?

Karima: They are kids, they don't listen. I tell them we are muslim. They get upset; they say, "Oh, well, I don't want to be muslim, if you are going to control me so much." They don't understand.

The category of muslim that is mobilized by Karima's family focuses on the social and sexual control of the girl child and on the role of the muslim mother in maintaining it. However, control of the Muslim Woman (which prescriptions of Islamist authenticity demand) comes in conflict with economics. As more and more women find themselves working outside the home for money, conventional methods of controlling women, such as seclusion, are no longer an option. Although Karima herself worked outside the home in Iran, she was in an environment where familial and societal pressures ensured control of the girl child. In Canada these controls are challenged not only by society but by her daughters as well.

Karima claims that her own life would have been different if she had had more education, and she maintains that her daughters will need education to find employment.

> *Karima:* In Iran I had everything economically, but because I did not study, my education was very limited. I want my daughters to have more education. I want her [*sic*] to become a doctor or somebody so that she has status.

Karima had status in Iran even with little education, so she may be referring to a lack of status in Canada. In sending them to school, Karima may be hoping that her daughters will become physicians and, as such, valued members of Canadian society. However, she has grave concerns about the freedoms that her daughters will be exposed to in school and that she will not be able to control.

> *Karima:* In the class, the girls are sitting here, the boys are sitting here, they are watching sex education classes, and anatomy, and that is not right, . . . and my son sees the condom commercial and he says "What is that?" I say, "It is not for you." If the children go and ask the teacher, she says, "That is [a] condom." If they ask in Iran, the teacher would say, "When you grow up you will know," rather than explain it to him.

Condoms are perceived as useless for children because Karima does not believe that the children from Iran and other muslim countries engage in sexual relations. As Ali (1992) points out, the discourse of "the community" presents an ahistorical and romanticized view of the "old country" and the transplanted community in the First World. This view includes edited versions of "home" that are more in harmony with the ideal than with the complexity of current practices and that date back to the period when members of diasporic communities left their home countries. Life has changed in their countries of origin, but their nostalgic views remain frozen in time. Such edited and nostalgic views deny the sexuality of Karima's teenage daughters.

While Karima voices concern about her ability to exercise control over her daughters in Canada, she is aware of the opportunities they have.

Shahnaz: How is it for you as a muslim mother in Canada?

Karima: I am afraid of the effect of things here on the children. The drinking and dancing . . . the sleeveless dress. I am afraid of too much freedom for the girls. [Otherwise] education is good and everything is good. The children can study without having much money, and if we were in Iran, we would have to send them out here and we would have paid a lot of money for them to study here. It is great [in Canada], but all the prostitution, and all the openness, all the sexual freedom, I don't like.

Karima's life in Canada is such that she is not always able to enact her vision of herself as a Muslim Woman or the Muslim Mother anymore than she can enforce her ideals for her daughters.

Karima: Everybody goes to hell anyway [laughs] because we don't cover up, because we don't do fasting, so what the heck, you know, we sell alcohol here, we have done it our self [*sic*] in our restaurant.

Shahnaz: So you don't believe in drinking alcohol but you sell it anyway?

Karima: I have to sell it because our life depends on selling things. And I can't cover up because I am serving in a restaurant.

As a woman who believes that particular practices delineate a muslim identity, being able to enact those practices in Canada matters to Karima. The ways of serving God are prescribed, and if one does not follow the prescriptions in this world, one will not be rewarded in the next. Her statement "what the heck" suggests that she feels trapped by circumstances she cannot control. Thus it does not matter if she sells alcohol because of all the other sins that she has committed. When she says "what the heck," she comes close to disavowing something that is fundamental to her notion of muslim identity.

Karima's past life in Iran is central to her sense of identity and culture in Canada. This past is part of the myth of the beyond within which, Bhabha argues, individuals often locate culture. Yet, "the 'beyond' is neither a new horizon, nor a leaving behind of the past . . . [instead] we find ourselves in the moment of transit where space and time cross to produce complex figures of difference and identity, past and present, inside and outside, inclusion and exclusion" (1994, 1). In Bhabha's notion of culture there is no past or future, culture is always constructed in the present moment. Although Karima's erasure of her difficulties in her homeland polarizes her view of her world into Iran versus Canada, her story conveys how she constructs her culture in the present by negotiating in the third space, even as that negotiation draws on her life in Iran and purist notions of female identity. It could be that she reconciles herself to Canada not just out of material necessity but also out of a recognition that the homeland society and her life in it were already riddled with tension and contradictions. Her comment "what the heck" suggests that her notion of self as a muslim woman and muslim mother is unworkable in Canada. Karima comes close to questioning the overall structure of the Muslim Woman and to regarding the everyday practices central to her notion of identity as an impossibility in her current life. And yet, her logic, because of a notion of identity that focuses on the past she cannot have, leads her to conclude that she is damned to hell.

Iram

Iram has lived in Canada since age four and learned to defend herself early in life. As a child she suffered emotional and physical abuse and racial harassment. Her childhood memories include those of her father physically and verbally abusing her, her sisters, and their mother, as well as the racism which she and her sisters faced at school. Iram was subjected to stereotyping and racism not because she was identified as muslim but because people responded to her as South Asian, or East Indian.[14]

> *Iram:* In the early seventies most people didn't know the difference between being muslim and being just plain brown. All they could see was your name and your skin color, and they immediately assumed that you were some sort of Indian who ate curry all the time.

Being East Indian in Canada, as I have argued elsewhere (Khan 1991), often means being seen as inferior and belonging to a decadent culture and civilization. Being a muslim became an issue both to Iram and to those around her at school because, as the political climate surrounding muslims and Islam changed, Iram emphasized it.

> *Shahnaz:* When did being muslim start making a difference, if it ever did?
> *Iram:* Let me make one thing clear, that if it ever made a difference it was because I emphasized the difference.
> *Shahnaz:* Why did you feel the need to emphasize it?
> *Iram:* It probably started making a difference for me in high school . . . there was enough Western-promoted mythology about

---

[14] Conventional wisdom holds that all muslims are Arabs. Therefore, as a South Asian, Iram would not be considered muslim.

Islam thanks to the [Irani] revolution. If I did bring it up, there would be a whole new series of attacks on me.

Shahnaz: Why would you bring it up?

Iram: Because I was very proud to be muslim.

Shahnaz: What made you proud of something that people thought was negative?

Iram: Keep in mind that I was always a rebel. Remember that ever since I was five years old [if] somebody said dark, I would say light. So the fact that people had negative images of Islam just drove into me the need to raise it and to educate people.

Unlike Karima, who is white-skinned, Iram is brown and can be phenotypically othered. Her visibly racial location as South Asian compounds with her defense of Islam as a "religion of terrorists" in a political climate in which the "Islamic threat" horrifies popular imagination.

Shahnaz: Were you called a . . . terrorist in high school?

Iram: Even though racism was clear, I never was the overt target of it. A lot of people respected me, because I did speak out. I was very involved in the school, so personally I never was called a terrorist, but my religion was called terrorism.

Shahnaz: And that made you angry?

Iram: It made me angry, not because I denied it. I never denied that there was terrorism. What I denied was that this [Islam] was the only bastion of terrorism.

Angered by what she encounters, Iram turns away from an Orientalist/racist construction of her identity. Yet she finds that she cannot restructure herself in what Islam appears to offer. Her experiences with the fundamentalist-influenced and -organized Islamic/Shi'a community in Vancouver provide an example.

Iram: I remember when I was twelve or thirteen being kicked out, permanently, from Saturday school.

Shahnaz: Why?

Iram: Because I asked too many questions.

Shahnaz: About what?

Iram: About everything. When the teacher was teaching, let's say about Islamic history, I would say, why this? Why that? Why didn't Khadija do this? . . . And at one point he told me, "Look, either you believe what I say or you get out."

Shahnaz: So pure faith on the basis of "what I say" was not enough?

Iram: Well, I shut up for a while, then I started to ask questions again because things didn't make sense to me, and I wanted to know. And I got so angry with the fact that he became so angry with me that I said this is it. "If you are not going to answer my questions, and if you are going to invalidate my questions, then I don't think that I have a place here." And I walked out.

Shahnaz: For you, did he symbolize Islam, or did he symbolize the organized aspect of it?

Iram: He symbolized the organized aspect of it. Always, always, always, I have always had a very deep respect for Islam in its purest form.

Shahnaz: So what do you respect?

Iram: I respect the fact that to me it is almost like a utopia, like communism, which I respect in theory. Islam in its purest form will never be attained, can never be attained.

Iram appears to rebel against the loaded categorization of "muslim" and what that might entail. Instead, her very insistence that she is a rebel suggests that she at once accepts what conventional definitions of muslim might mean and refuses to acquiesce to those definitions. To a large extent, Iram is living her life according to what makes sense to her outside of the accepted codes of "muslim." Yet she is not able to speak to the space she creates in her life. Instead, by placing Islam into the realm of utopia and unlivable, she appears to be suggesting that she can only practice progressive politics outside the category "muslim."

Iram's disenchantment with members of the organized Islamic/Shi'a community in Vancouver was reinforced by the way in which they reacted to her parents' divorce. Iram realized that despite the abuse her mother was suffering, the men at the mosque were more interested in keeping the family unit together. She claims they "tried to scuttle the divorce proceedings on more than one occasion." Patriarchal leaders appeared, in Iram's view, to be more interested in maintaining an image of an ideal Islamic community where divorce does not occur and where the systemic nature of abuse in the patriarchal family is disavowed. Such views ignore the abuse individuals suffer and attribute it to the pathology of the people involved.

Influenced by family trauma and feminism, Iram claims she became "an activist and very defiant." It dawned on her that the religion she was defending was very sexist.

Iram: I didn't drop it, mind you, but I became far more critical of religion, far more critical.

Although Iram continues to react to prejudice against Islam, because of the sexism that she experienced she became very selective of what aspects of religion she would enact in her own life.

> *Iram:* I have a real aversion to organized anything. So I pick and choose from Islam what I want to do and what I want to practice . . . what I agree with and understand.

In an attempt to anchor her identity, Iram turns away from Orientalism and goes back to the only option she believes is available to her, Islamism. But she contains it in theory and cannot bring it to her everyday life. She separates herself from the "practicing Muslim Woman," who for Iram wears the *hejab,* prays five times a day, and lives her life within the traditional tenets of Islam. Her comments affirm the notion of the authentic muslim presented in religious terms, which she affirms in principle but does not practice. Iram does not raise this contradiction, she just lives it. Because she cannot accept the sexism in Islam, she cannot be a practicing Muslim. Yet she will not let go of Islam because she finds no other space in which to restructure her identity in Canadian society. She will defend Islam, she says, the way she defends her brown skin.

> *Shahnaz:* When you say, "Islam to me is a theoretical thing, it is not something which is lived in my day-to-day life," how would you consider lived Islam in a day-to-day life?
> *Iram:* If I were to call myself a practicing muslim?
> *Shahnaz:* I am not saying that. That is a particular category.
> *Iram:* But I would have to say this in order to answer the question. I would pray five times a day, I would wear the *hejab,* I would do this and I would do that.
> *Shahnaz:* So you are defining being muslim within the traditional tenets.
> *Iram:* That is right.
> *Shahnaz:* But nothing else that you do has been defined within the traditional tenets. Why are you defining this?
> *Iram:* Because that is all I know. I have had this debate before. And even though I am not willing to exclude my muslim upbringing from my identity, I am also not willing to call myself a muslim.
> *Shahnaz:* If you define [being a muslim] in a very narrow sense, then obviously you will have to exclude your day-to-day life.
> *Iram:* Yes, yes.

Iram appears to have accepted the Orientalist and Islamist notions of the Muslim Woman as defined by religion. She appears to be caught between the two polarities; she cannot accept one or the other. She feels the need to defend Islam in view of the racialization of muslims in Canada. She defends Islam with nonmuslims and criticizes Islam only among muslims.

> *Iram:* When a white person raises objections towards Islam, I immediately jump to Islam's defense. I always point out that in theory this is what I agree with; . . . [however] when one of my uncles or one of my relatives, or somebody I know who is a muslim jumps to Islam's defense in terms of sexism, I immediately start criticizing Islam.

She believes in Islam at the ideological level, but because of the sexism and inequality it reproduces, she herself does not want to have anything to do with it in her life. Such a contradiction expresses the complexity of her relationship to Islamic identity. Racism and antimuslim sentiment appear to make Iram support Islam defensively and aggressively and raise the question, How much would she need to fight for Islam if Canada had not been such an antimuslim society? Perhaps she may not have severed her connection to Islam if she were living in a muslim society. She may have just lived it differently.[15] In Canada, the space for struggle is restricted by an antimuslim society and within beleaguered muslim communities. The restrictions no doubt reinforce Iram's options for living the identity but cannot be definitively stated to be the cause of her retaining her muslim identity.

Leila Ahmed notes that after having lived in the United States, she realizes that Arabs and muslims feel almost compelled to take the defensive stance even though they are aware of the gender inequalities rampant in Islamic societies. This is because "despite America's heavy embroilment in the area, and despite the fact that Muslims constitute something like one-quarter of the world's population: it is, rather that Americans 'know,' and know without even having to think about it, that the Islamic peoples — Arabs, Iranians, whatever they call themselves — are backward, uncivilized peoples totally incapable of rational conduct. This is overwhelmingly the attitude of the media and of the society at large and also, unfortunately, often that of the smaller groups supposedly representing American informed opinion" (1982, 522).

Miseducation is responsible for the stereotypes of Muslims, Iram states. She has tried to correct and educate people since she was at school and

---

[15] Many feminists in muslim contexts refuse to abandon muslim identity and are struggling over what it means.

claims that she "would try to debunk some of the images they had of Islam."

As Iram educates people about Islam, she also positions herself as a lesbian. She has "come out" to her family and in her community of friends. She does not see any contradiction between being a muslim and being a lesbian. She states that there are no *suras* (verses) in the Koran (1983) that forbid homosexuality, although she admits that the focus and tone of the Koran is clearly heterosexual.[16] Initially, Iram's mother had mixed feelings about her sexual orientation and had tried to impose some degree of sexual control on Iram according to perceived notions of Islamic mothering. Iram claims, however, that because her mother was never happy in her own marital relationship, she particularly wanted her children to be happy in theirs. She has told Iram that if being a lesbian makes her happy then she is willing to accept it. As for the religious aspect, Iram states:

> *Iram:* I don't think Allah has it out for me.
> *Shahnaz:* So you feel you can have a relationship with God and have a relationship with a woman at the same time?
> *Iram:* Absolutely.
> *Shahnaz:* And you think there is no contradiction?
> *Iram:* And I believe that Allah believes that too, I really do.

Iram is not ambivalent about the contradictions she lives. She knows what she wants out of Islam, and it is not what Islamists advocate for the Muslim Woman. Her ambivalence is more of a response to the structural contradictions, for she does not express any emotional ambivalence. She is comfortable with her position as she self-identifies with feminism and Western values.

Iram claims that although her mother is an important influence in her life, there is a spiritual difference between them. Her mother is a muslim, while Iram is a woman who happened to be raised in a muslim home. If she had a choice, she would not have chosen to be raised in Islam or any other religion. She was raised a muslim, and since she has never walked away from what she considers a relevant battle, and because she has grown up in Canada fighting, she will fight for Islam.

> *Iram:* The fact that I didn't think that there was anything wrong with having been brought up muslim, that I was so angry towards racism itself, you know, and that I was so proud of who I am and

---

[16] Homosexuality is condemned in the Qur'an in reference to the story of Lot and his followers. While directing that offenders be punished, the Qur'an does not specify the punishment. As well, forgiveness is offered to those who repent (Greenberg 1984).

what I am, and for that matter if this country is really going to stop being so hypocritical . . . lauding multiculturalism when it is convenient and blasting it when it is not . . . I have to be allowed to be who and whatever the hell I want to be.

In the context of racism and Islamphobia, Iram's desire to maintain some kind of muslim identity inevitably leads her to confront how the muslim woman is constructed. Iram disavows Islam as a day-to-day practice, but her narrative makes an argument for the way in which the structure of racism produces an investment in the identity of Muslim Woman.

> *Iram:* You know I am caught right in the middle when it comes to racism, and sexism, and for that matter homophobia, . . . when any of this stuff comes up, I feel the urge to come to the battle and fight for it.

Iram's response indicates mutually alienating positions. The positions seem contradictory, and yet Iram does not experience confusion or uncertainty about asserting those contradictions. Thus, there is a structure of ambivalence (in Bhabha's terms) within that response, an ambivalence that is necessarily an inherent response to the contradictions within the space for Muslim Woman itself.

Iram grew up in Canada, and unlike Karima, does not have what Bhabha (1994) would call sustaining myths of a past muslim identity she once performed and then imported to Canada. Her relationship to home has been transmitted to her by her family and her family's social and cultural community. Much of what "home" constitutes she rejects because of the sexism and because of the leap of faith she feels is required of her. Reference to home cannot ease the pain of racism and religious fundamentalism. Instead, she appears very aware that home is in Canada and that she must carve her space out here.

In primary school, Iram was made aware that she was "brown" and different, and since high school she has chosen to emphasize her muslim difference. It is significant that these are the two points of her identity that she articulates and defends. I realize that because of the way ethnicity is linked according to geographical, cultural, and political space, Iram may find it difficult to be accepted as a Ugandan in Canada or indeed in Uganda itself as a Ugandan. However, her narrative could have emphasized a South Asian identity. Instead, she chooses to identify herself as part of a religious collective. Although she resists the pressures of what she believes it entails, Iram appears to have accepted the "Islam equals religion" equation and has been negotiating a muslim identity in the third space. She has been defending Islam. As she defends, she articulates, performs, and contests a notion of muslim female identity in Canada.

Conclusion

Ethnicity has often been associated with an exotic otherness, or with a sense of authenticity that might be attributed to minority cultures, "alien" religions, or "mother tongues." The recent emerging cultural politics, however, has emphasized hybridity and diaspora rather than roots as central themes. In particular, these trends have been articulated in the work of cultural theorists such as Homi Bhabha, Gayatri Spivak, Paul Gilroy, Stuart Hall, and Ali Rattansi. Whether their work suggests linguistically or materially based dynamic notions of identity, their analysis shifts away from narrow identity politics determined by static or essentialized notions of race, gender, and class and toward a rearticulated politics of difference. In particular, Rattansi argues for a definition of culture that is no longer limited to religious beliefs, communal rituals, and shared traditions but instead understands culture as a process and knowledge "through which particular communities are defined" (1992, 4). This politics recognizes structures of inequality and discrimination but contests them through a mobile and shifting strategy of representation and association, encompassing diverse perspectives and experiences.

Within this view, Bhabha's notions of hybridity and third space (1990) identify the mixing that occurs in urban space in contemporary diasporic communities. I want to reinforce this process of social imaginary as a muslim woman's third space. This third space emerges from the dynamic notion of culture and also gives rise to it. It is a process of intellectual and political intervention to resolve the ambivalence that muslim women face. Karima's and Iram's stories are testimony of these women's attempts to constitute a third space in which they are recognized as muslim and also to contest the regulatory pressures of the fundamentalist-influenced myth of the *Umma*.

In her analysis of the process of claiming and speaking to Latina identity, Lourdes Torres (1991) points out that women in the United States must work through cultural and gender socializations and misinformation. These discourses and practices have left women with contradictory and fragmented identities. The radical and progressive negotiation of this fragmented self, Torres believes, is the refusal to accept one position. Similarly, Karima's and Iram's marginalization by racist, sexist, and religious discourses leads them to reject prescriptions of authenticity. Although neither Iram or Karima is connected to a fundamentalist or Islamist context, their narratives to some extent promote an Orientalist conflation of Islam and Islamism. Yet they also negotiate dynamic identities of collusion, resistance, and contestation. In their daily lives, they forge new possibilities by defying prescriptions and expectations.

Although Karima's account conveys depression and hopelessness, these emotions arise out of a sense of not living up to predetermined notions of muslim identity. In her daily negotiations, she does not passively receive and accept Islamic or dominant cultural practices but actively engages with her circumstances in pragmatic, insightful, and dynamic ways. Her notion of female identity, while conceptualized through her life in Iran, is nevertheless contested by and performed within her Canadian circumstances. Her daily negotiations help reinforce and substantiate the notion of a muslim women's third space in Canada.

Iram's story, in contrast, is secondhand, for she has been in Canada since she was a small child. Her daily negotiations with being brown and being muslim are clearly influenced by her life in Canada. Also, she is aware of and identifies politically with a struggle for affirmation, identity, and space in Canada as brown, as a lesbian, and as a muslim.

To facilitate and reinforce the notion of the third space, feminist scholarship and practice must continue to reinforce a splitting that is happening within Orientalism as well as Islamic fundamentalism. Continued devaluation of muslim women in the popular imagination and in academic scholarship will no doubt generate disorientation in those women who are coded as muslim or who self-identify as muslim. The Orientalist notion of the Muslim Woman as synonymous with passivity must be challenged continually by notions of muslim women as active agents in the third space. Deconstructing racist discourses, particularly those that emphasize the need to modernize traditional cultures and religions, will generate a view of cultures as interconnected. Such a framework helps diffuse the rigid boundaries between Islam and the West and gives women individual freedom of choice at the intersection of the two, without being labeled anti-Islamic by their families and communities or as "fanatics" by those outside.

The deconstruction of Islamism as a means of encouraging a splitting needs to acknowledge two interconnected visions. The first vision draws on the strength of women who want to and/or have to incorporate religion into a strategy of women's empowerment. Progressive interpretations of the sacred, which are consciously more egalitarian but still acknowledge God's authority are not legitimized within either muslim societies or muslim communities. Work that feminist scholars such as Fatima Mernissi, Leila Ahmed, and Riffat Hassan are doing to undermine the androcentric foundations of patriarchal interpretation of religious texts is crucial in this regard. Muslim women's use of their work to establish legal precedents in Pakistan is one example of praxis of the theoretical with the political.[17]

The second vision acknowledges women who do not want and/or are unable to work outside religious frameworks. There is little historical precedent for a clear separation of religion and the state in Islam. Thus, for the second group of visionaries, in view of the sexist nature of the interpretations that are legitimized, the conflation of "Islamic" and "muslim" position women so that any move toward equality becomes a questioning of divine authority. Under current conditions, where the influence of Islamism is increasing globally in conjunction with racist stereotypes about muslims in the West, a splitting of "Islamic" into Islam (the religion) and muslim (the person) reinforces women's empowerment. For those women who wish to and are able to work outside the religious frameworks, a separation of the sacred from the cultural will allow them to claim their social and political histories without being confined to religious prescriptions.

The separation of Orientalism and Islamism is difficult to sustain in everyday life in the Western metropole, where muslim women are racialized and have to face increasing social and sexual control within their own communities and families, with no established alternative they can turn to for affirmation. Expressions of ambivalence occur because women are pulled in different directions by Islamism, Orientalism, and the splitting that is happening within the two. The struggle for agency and identity as a muslim woman thus becomes a site of both affirmation and disorientation.

Feminist work on the concept of agency in women's lives would enliven that possibility by reinforcing the notion of third space for the contradictory lives of muslim women. In North America, the contested notion of the Muslim Woman is a marginalized unsettling diasporic experience of what Bhabha (1994) calls hybridization,[18] which begins with the location of the women in a context where culture and religion play an important but not defining part. For muslim women in North America, culture and religion are the facets of identity through which their experiences of gender, class, race, social and political location, and sexuality are mediated. In this way, there is no return to an "original" past that is not mediated by present circumstances and experience.

Karima's and Iram's daily negotiations suggest a hybrid and dynamic

[17] For a broader discussion of how women-centered interpretations of Islamic religious texts have informed and empowered women's struggles in Pakistan, see Mumtaz and Shaheed 1987.

[18] The complex concept of hybridization arises from the contradictory diasporic experience. For a broader discussion of hybridization, see Bhabha 1994.

notion of muslim identity, a reality of the postmodern, postcolonial world. It challenges scholars and activists to recognize a muslim identity that is not monolithic and homogeneous and to engage a more open notion of muslim culture as a multiple, shifting, and contradictory site. Perhaps feminist scholars ought to reconsider Julie Stephens's (1989) proposal that feminism engage with all of the tensions that converge in women's struggles. For those women who identify with muslims or are coded by others as muslim, the sites of struggle are never singular but always plural, shifting, and dynamic.

Women's Studies Program
University of Guelph

References

Abdo, Nahla. 1993. "Race, Gender, and Politics: The Struggle of Arab Women." In *And Still We Rise: Feminist Political Mobilizing in Contemporary Canada,* ed. Linda Carty, 73–98. Toronto: Women's Press.

Ahmed, Leila. 1982. "Western Ethnocentrism and Perceptions of the Harem." *Feminist Studies* 8(3):521–34.

Ali, Yasmin. 1992. "Muslim Women and the Politics of Culture and Ethnicity in Northern England." In *Refusing Holy Orders,* ed. Gita Sahgal and Nira Yuval-Davis, 101–23. London: Virago.

Alloula, Malek. 1986. *The Colonial Harem.* Minneapolis: University of Minnesota Press.

Althusser, Louis. 1969. *For Marx,* trans. Ben Brewester. London: Allen Lane.

Amin, Samir. 1976. *Unequal Development.* New York: Monthly Review.

———. 1989. *Eurocentrism.* New York: Monthly Review.

Anderson, Benedict. 1983. *Imagined Communities: Reflections on the Origin and Spread of Nationalism.* New York: Verso.

Asad, Talal. 1991. *Genealogies of Religion.* London: Johns Hopkins University Press.

Badran, Margot. 1995. *Feminism, Islam and Nation.* Princeton, N.J.: Princeton University Press.

Bhabha, Homi. 1990. "The Third Space." In *Identity: Community, Culture, Difference,* ed. Jonathan Rutherford, 207–21. London: Lawrence & Wishart.

———. 1991. "The Other Question: Difference Discrimination and the Discourse of Colonialism." In *Out There: Marginalization and Contemporary Cultures,* ed. Russell Ferguson, 71–88. Cambridge, Mass.: MIT Press.

———. 1994. *The Location of Culture.* London and New York: Routledge.

———. 1995. "Interview." *Artforum,* March, 80–119.

Chatterjee, Partha. 1986. *Nationalist Thought and the Colonial World: A Derivative Discourse.* Delhi: Oxford University Press.

Chhachhi, Amrita. 1989. "The State Religious Fundamentalism and Women: Trends in South Asia." *Economic and Political Weekly,* March 18, 567–78.

Clancy-Smith, Julia. 1992. "The 'Passionate Nomad' Reconsidered: A European Woman in *L'Algerie francaise* (Isabelle Eberhardt, 1877–1904)." In *Western Women and Imperialism,* ed. Nupur Chaudhuri and Margaret Strobel, 61–78. Bloomington: Indiana University Press.

Deardorn, Ann. 1975. *Arab Women.* Report no. 27. London: Minority Rights Group.

Fanon, Frantz. 1963. *The Wretched of the Earth.* New York: Grove Weidenfeld.

Al-Ghazali, Zainab. 1994. *Return of the Pharaoh: Memoir in Nasir's Prison,* trans. Mokrane Guezzou. Leicester: Islamic Foundation.

Gilroy, Paul. 1992. "The End of Antiracism." In *Race, Culture, and Difference,* ed. James Donald and Ali Rattansi, 49–61. London and Newbury Park, Calif.: Sage, in association with Open University.

Greenberg, M. F. 1984. *Marriage and Sexuality in Islam: A Translation of al-Ghazali's Book on the Etiquette of Marriage.* Salt Lake City: University of Utah Press.

Hall, Stuart. 1992. "New Ethnicities." In *Race, Culture, and Difference,* ed. James Donald and Ali Rattansi, 252–59. London and Newbury Park, Calif.: Sage, in association with Open University.

———. 1996. *Stuart Hall: Critical Dialogues in Cultural Studies,* ed. David Morley and Kuan-Hsing Chen. London and New York: Routledge.

Hassan, Riffat. 1990. "Is the Shariah Divine?" In Shirkat Gah, *Newsheet* (Women Living under Muslim Laws), 1–4.

Helie-Lucas, Marie-Aimee. 1994. "The Preferential Symbol for Islamic Identity: Women in Muslim Personal Laws." In *Identity Politics and Women: Cultural Reassertions and Feminisms in International Perspective,* ed. Valentine Moghadam, 391–407. Boulder, Colo.: Westview.

Hoodfar, Homa. 1993. "The Veil in Their Minds and on Our Heads: The Persistence of Colonial Images of Muslim Women." *Resources for Feminist Research* 22(3–4):5–18.

Hosken, Fran. 1981. "Female Genital Mutilation and Human Rights." *Feminist Issues* 1(3):3–23.

Jeffery, Patricia. 1979. *Frogs in a Well: Indian Women in Purdah.* London: Zed.

Kabbani, Rana. 1986. *Europe's Myths of Orient.* Bloomington: Indiana University Press.

Kandiyoti, Deniz. 1991. "Introduction." In her *Women, Islam and the State,* 1–21. Philadelphia: Temple University Press.

Kazim, Safinaz. 1986. *An al sijn wa al hurriyya* (On prison and freedom). Cairo: Al Zahra' lil A'lam Al'Arabi.

Khan, Shahnaz. 1991. "Influences Shaping Relations between the East Indians and the Anglo-Canadians in Canada: 1903–1947." *Journal of Ethnic Studies* 19(1): 101–15.

———. 1995a. "Muslim Woman: Interrogating the Construct in Canada." Ph.D. dissertation, University of Toronto.

———. 1995b. "The Veil as a Site of Struggle: The *Hejab* in Quebec." *Canadian Women Studies* 15(2–3):146–52.

Kocturk, Tahire. 1992. *A Matter of Honour: Experiences of Turkish Women Immigrants*. London and Atlantic Highlands, N.J.: Zed.

Koran. 1983. Trans. N. J. Dawood. London and New York: Penguin.

Lazreg, Marnia. 1990. "Feminism and Difference: The Perils of Writing as a Woman on Women in Algeria." In *Conflicts in Feminism,* ed. Marianne Hirsch and Evelyn Fox Keller, 326–48. New York: Routledge.

Mabro, Judy. 1991. *Veiled Half-Truths: Western Travelers Perceptions of Middle Eastern Women*. London: I. B. Tauris.

Mernissi, Fatima. 1987. *Beyond the Veil*. Bloomington: Indiana University Press.

Minces, Juliette. 1980. *The House of Obedience: Women in Arab Society*. London and Atlantic Highlands, N.J.: Zed.

Moghadam, Valentine. 1991. "Islamist Movements and Women's Responses in the Middle East." *Gender and History* 3(3):268–84.

Mohanty, Chandra. 1991a. "Introduction." In *Third World Women and the Politics of Feminism,* ed. Chandra Talpade Mohanty, Ann Russo, and Lourdes Torres, 1–50. Bloomington: Indiana University Press.

———. 1991b. "Under Western Eyes: Feminist Scholarship and Colonial Discourses." In *Third World Women and the Politics of Feminism,* ed. Chandra Talpade Mohanty, Ann Russo, and Lourdes Torres, 51–80. Bloomington: Indiana University Press.

Mojab, Shahrazad. 1995. "Islamic Feminism: Alternative or Contradiction." *Fireweed* 47:18–25.

Mumtaz, Khawar, and Farida Shaheed. 1987. *Women in Pakistan: Two Steps Forward One Step Back*. London and Atlantic Highlands, N.J.: Zed.

Rattansi, Ali. 1992. "Changing the Subject: Racism, Culture, and Education." In *Race, Culture, and Difference,* ed. James Donald and Ali Rattansi, 11–48. London and Newbury Park, Calif.: Sage, in association with Open University.

Said, Edward. 1978. *Orientalism*. London: Routledge & Kegan Paul.

Smith, Dorothy. 1987. *The Everyday World as Problematic*. Toronto: University of Toronto Press.

Spivak, Gayatri. 1993. *Outside in the Teaching Machine*. London and New York: Routledge.

Stephens, Julie. 1989. "Feminist Fictions: A Critique of the Category 'Non-Western Women' in Feminist Writings on Indian Women." In *Subaltern Studies 6,* ed. Ranajit Guha, 92–131. Delhi: Oxford University Press.

Stowasser, Barbara. 1987. "Religious Ideology, Women and the Family: The Islamic Paradigm." In *The Islamic Impulse,* ed. Barbara Stowasser, 262–96. London: Croom Helm, in association with Center for Contemporary Arab Studies, Georgetown University.

Suleri, Sara. 1987. *Meatless Days*. Chicago: University of Chicago Press.

Torres, Lourdes. 1991. "The Construction of the Self in U.S. Latina Autobiographies." In *Third World Women and the Politics of Feminism,* ed. Chandra Talpade Mohanty, Ann Russo, and Lourdes Torres, 271–87. Bloomington: Indiana University Press.

Trinh T. Minh-Ha. 1989. *Woman, Native, Other.* Bloomington: Indiana University Press.

About the Contributors

S.M. Shamsul Alam is associate professor of sociology at the Southern Oregon University, Ashland, OR. During 2000–01 and 2001–02, he taught sociology at University of Nairobi, Nairobi, Kenya as a Fulbright fellow. He is the author of *The State, Class Formation and Development in Bangladesh* (Lanham: University Press of America, 1995) and currently working on a manuscript titled "For Land and Freedom: Rethinking Mau Mau in Colonial Kenya."

Carolyn Allen is professor of English adjunct professor of women's studies at the University of Washington. She is author of *Following Djuna: Women Lovers and the Erotics of Loss* (Indianapolis: Indiana University Press, 1996) and articles on a variety of topics in twentieth-century studies and in feminist theory. Her most recent project is on cultural power and theories of emotion. She is also a former coeditor of *Signs: Journal of Women in Culture and Society.*

Amal Amireh is an assistant professor of English and world literature at George Mason University. She has received a B.A. in English literature from Birzeit University in the West Bank and an M.A. and a Ph.D. in English and American literature from Boston University. She is author of *The Factory Girl and the Seamstress: Imagining Gender and Class in Nineteenth-Century American Fiction* (New York: Garland, 2000), and is co-editor, with Lisa Suhair Majaj of *Going Global: The Transnational Reception of Third World Women Writers* (New York: Garland, 2000) and *Etel Adnan: Critical Essays on the Arab-American Writer and Artist* (North Carolina: McFarland, 2002). Her writings on Arab women and Arabic literature have appeared in *Signs: Journal of Women in Culture and Society, Against the Current, The Women's Review of Books, World Literature Today,* and *Edebiyat: The Journal of Middle Eastern Literatures.* Before joining George Mason University, Amireh taught at An-Najah National University and Birzeit University (both in West Bank/Palestine). Her current research focuses on gender, nationalism, and Islam in postcolonial literature.

Mary Elaine Hegland studies the connections between gender, politics, and religion, focusing on Shi'a Islam. Her main geographical concentration is Iran, where she conducted her dissertation research about religion and politics in the Iranian Revolution, from the perspective of a village near Shiraz. She has also done anthropological field work in Peshawar, Pakistan and among Iranians and Pakistanis in California's Bay Area. Hegland teaches social cultural anthropology, with an emphasis on gender and the Middle East, at Santa Clara University.

Judith A. Howard is chair of the department of women studies and professor of sociology at the University of Washington. She studies gender dynamics and their intersections with race, class, and sexuality, emphasizing micro-level cognitions and interpersonal interactions. She is co-author with Jocelyn Hollander of *Gendered Situations, Gendered Selves: A Gender Lens on Social Psychology* (Newbury Park, CA: Sage 1997), and co-editor with Jodi O'Brien of *Everyday Inequalities: Critical Inquiries* (Blackwell, 1998), and with Carolyn Allen of *Provoking Feminisms* (Chicago: University of Chicago Press, 2000) and *Feminisms at a Millennium* (Chicago: University of Chicago Press, 2000). She is also a former co-editor of *Signs: Journal of Women in Culture and Society.*

Shahnaz Khan is assistant professor in the women's studies program and the department of sociology and anthropology at St. Francis Xavier University, Nova Scotia, Canada. Her publications include *Aversion and Desire: Negotiating Muslim Female Identity in the Diaspora* (Toronto: Women's Press 2002), and articles in the on-line journal *Genders, Canadian Woman Studies,* and *Canadian Journal of Women and the Law.*

Anouar Majid is currently professor and chair of English at the University of New England in Maine. He is the author of *Unveiling Traditions: Postcolonial Islam in a Polycentric World* (Durham, NC: Duke University Press, 2000) and the novel *Si Yussef* (London: Quartet, 1992). He is working on a book that examines the meaning of Islam in the post-Andalusian age and the promise of cultures for human civilization.

Valentine M. Moghadam is director of women's studies and associate professor of sociology at Illinois State University. She is the author of *Modernizing Women: Gender and Social Change in the Middle East* (Boulder, Colo: Lynne Rienner,1993; second and updated edition to appear in 2003), *Women, Work, and Economic Reform in the Middle East* (Boulder, Colo.: Lynne Rienner, 1998), and numerous articles and book chapters. She has edited five books, including *Identity Politics and Women: Cultural Reassertions and Feminisms in International Perspective* (Boulder, Colo.: Westview, 1993). While a fellow of the Woodrow Wilson International Center for Scholars (2001–2002), she is finalizing a book on globalization and transnational feminist networks.

Julie Peteet is associate professor and chair of the department of anthropology at the University of Louisville. Her publications include *Gender in Crisis: Women and the Palestinian Resistance Movement* (New York: Columbia University Press, 1991) and articles in various journals such as *American Ethnologist, Cultural Anthropology, Cultural Survival,* and *Social Analysis.* She has just completed a book manuscript, "Landscape of Hope and Despair: Place and Identity in Palestinian Refugee Camps."

Therese Saliba is faculty of third world feminist studies at The Evergreen State College and former associate editor of *Signs*. She is coeditor, with Lisa Suhair Majaj and Paula Sunderman, of *Intersections: Gender, Nation, and Community in Arab Women's Novels* (Syracuse: Syracuse University Press, 2002), and the author of numerous essays on postcolonial literature, media representations, and Arab American and Arab feminist issues.

Elora Shehabuddin is assistant professor of humanities and political science at Rice University. Prior to coming to Rice, she was assistant professor of women's studies and political science at the University of California, Irvine. She received her Ph.D. in politics from Princeton University and her B.A. in social studies from Harvard University. She has published a book, *Empowering Rural Women: The Impact of Grameen Bank in Bangladesh* (Grameen Bank, 1995), and articles in *Signs* and *Asian Survey*. She teaches classes on the political economy of gender, development, religion and politics in South Asia, Islam and politics, and feminist methodologies.

Gabriele Vom Bruck received her Ph.D. in social anthropology from the London School of Economics, and is lecturer in the department of anthropology, University of Edinburgh. She has carried out extended field research in Yemen. Her recent publications include *A House Turned Inside Out: Inhabiting Space in a Yemeni City*, in D. Robbins (ed.) *Pierre Bourdieu: Masters of Social Theory*, ed. D. Robbins (London: Sage, 2000); and "Le nom commesigne corporel," *Annales: Histoire, Sciences Sociales* 2001, No.2, pp. 283–311. She has completed a book which examines the impact of revolutionary change on a Yemeni hereditary elite that had been exercising political authority over a millenium. She is at present co-editing (with Barbara Bodenhorn) a book on names and naming.

Index